Leniency Regimes

Jurisdictional comparisons **Third Edition 2010**

General Editors: Kevin J. Arquit & Jacques Buhart

General Editors
Kevin J. Arquit & Jacques Buhart

Publisher
Mark Wyatt

International Director
Michele O'Sullivan

Publishing Services Director
Ben Martin

Publishing and Production Manager
Emily Kyriacou

Production Editor
Caroline Pearce

Design and Production
Dawn McGovern

Sub editor
Lisa Naylor

Published by
The European Lawyer
Futurelex Limited
23-24 Smithfield Street
London EC1A 9LF
T: +44 (0) 20 7332 2582
F: +44 (0) 20 7332 2599
www.europeanlawyer.co.uk

Printed in Great Britain
Printed in the UK by CPI William Clowes Beccles NR34 7TL
ISBN: 978-0-9565440-3-2
© *Futurelex Limited 2010*

While all reasonable care has been taken to ensure the accuracy of the publication, the publishers cannot accept responsibility for any errors or omissions.
This publication is protected by international copyright law:
All rights reserved. No paragraph or other part of this document may be reproduced or transmitted in any form by any means, including photocopying and recording, without the written permission of Futurelex Limited or in accordance with the provisions of the Copyright Act 1988 (as amended).
Such written permission must also be obtained before any paragraph or other part of this publication is stored in a retrieval system of any kind.

Contents

Foreword Kevin J. Arquit, Simpson Thacher & Bartlett LLP & Jacques Buhart, Herbert Smith LLP — v

Foreword Paul Malric-Smith, Acting Director, Cartels, DG Competition of the European Commission — vii

Australia David Poddar, Lisa Huett & Morag Bond, Mallesons Stephen Jaques — 1

Austria Franz Urlesberger, Stefanie Stegbauer, Schönherr — 15

Belgium Thomas De Meese, Crowell & Moring — 27

Brazil Leonor Cordovil, Grinberg Cordovil e Barros Advogados — 37

Bulgaria Peter Petrov, Borislav Boyanov & Co — 45

Canada Graham Reynolds QC and Janet Bolton, Osler Hoskin & Harcourt LLP — 55

Cyprus Eleana Spyris, Andreas Neocleous & Co LLC — 81

Denmark Jens Munk Plum, Erik Bertelsen & Morten Kofmann Kromann Reumert — 93

Estonia Tanel Kalaus & Heleri Tammiste, Raidla Lejins & Norcous — 105

European Union Adrian Brown and Hanna Anttilainen, Herbert Smith LLP — 115

Finland Johan Åkermarck & Hanna Laurila, Dittmar & Indrenius — 131

France Sergio Sorinas & Estelle Jégou, Herbert Smith LLP — 145

Germany Dr Matthias Karl & Dr Martin Beutelmann, Gleiss Lutz — 161

Hungary Dr Chrysta Bán, Bán S.Szabó & Partners in cooperation with Gleiss Lutz — 175

India Farhad Sorabjee & Reeti Choudhary, J. Sagar Associates — 187

Italy Massimo Merola & Luciano di Via, Bonelli Erede Pappalardo — 199

Japan Hideto Ishida, Shigeyoshi Ezaki, Yusuke Nakano & Koya Uemura, Anderson Mori & Tomotsune	211
Luxembourg Léon Gloden & Stéphanie Damien, Elvinger Hoss & Prussen	221
Mexico Ricardo Ríos Ferrer & Alejandro González Muñoz, Ríos-Ferrer Guillén-Llarena Treviño y Rivera SC	229
The Netherlands Maurice Essers, Gert Wim van de Meent, Robin A. Struijlaart & Marc Wiggers, Loyens & Loeff N.V.	245
South Korea Kyung Taek Jung, Han Woo Park, Michael H. Yu, Kim & Chang	255
Spain Pedro Suárez, Herbert Smith LLP	267
Sweden Tommy Pettersson, Dr Johan Carle & Elin Gilmark, Mannheimer Swartling	283
Switzerland Dr Franz Hoffet, Dr Marcel Dietrich & Dr Gerald Brei, Homburger	293
Turkey Kayra Üçer & Derya Genç, Hergüner Bilgen Özeke Attorney Partnership	309
UK Stephen Wisking & Kim Dietzel, Herbert Smith LLP	317
USA Kevin J. Arquit & Andrew M. Lacy, Simpson Thacher & Bartlett LLP	343
Contact details	361

Foreword

Kevin J. Arquit Simpson Thacher & Bartlett LLP
Jacques Buhart Herbert Smith LLP

Detection and punishment of secret cartels remain a top priority of antitrust agencies in a globalised world. The economic crisis has not had a noticeable impact on the level of enforcement activity of most agencies. Moreover, notwithstanding the fact that in the fight against cartels *ex officio* action by regulatory agencies remains an important policy tool to signal to companies the risks of detection, a vast number of cartel cases are now initiated on the basis of leniency applications. For example, in 2009 five out of the six cartel decisions taken by the European Commission were based on leniency applications. Leniency programmes are thus important for competition authorities and companies alike.

In light of the gigantic amounts of fines that are now being levied for cartel infringements in many jurisdictions, sometimes reinforced by civil and/or criminal sanctions imposed on executives, companies involved in a cartel must carefully weigh their options. Leniency regimes create important incentives in this regard, typically by providing for full immunity from financial sanctions and immunity from prosecution for individuals for the undertaking being first in to co-operate. Accordingly, leniency regimes make it likely that sooner or later one of the cartel members will come forward and denounce the cartel to the competent authorities.

Like the previous editions, this book is designed to give companies and their legal advisers critical insight into the increasingly complex and important questions they face when considering whether to apply for leniency.

Since the last edition was published in 2007 the multiplication of leniency regimes around the globe has continued, programmes having been introduced for the first time recently in India, Spain, Estonia and Turkey. This third edition covers Australia, Austria, Belgium, Brazil, Bulgaria, Canada, Cyprus, Denmark, Estonia, the European Union, Finland, France, Germany, Hungary, India, Italy, Japan, South Korea, Luxembourg, Mexico, the Netherlands, Spain, Sweden, Switzerland, Turkey, the United Kingdom and the United States.

While the basic tenets of most programmes are likely to be similar, there are also important differences, for example in relation to the types of infringements covered by the leniency regime, the amount of evidence required to support an immunity application and the extent of on-going co-operation with the authorities. Moreover, considerations in relation to applications for leniency are becoming more complex due to the tension between leniency regimes and increased private enforcement activity, and

Foreword

the introduction of settlement procedures. We have added some questions to this edition to take stock of these developments.

We would like to thank all the authors, special contributors and Christine Jorns and Romain Maulin, as well as the team of *the European Lawyer* for their efforts in bringing this Third Edition to fruition.

Kevin J. Arquit, New York
Jacques Buhart, Paris
August 2010

Foreword

Paul Malric-Smith
Acting Director, Cartels, DG Competition of the European Commission

Along with globalisation and the explosion in international trade come large scale uncompetitive practices. Cartels spanning several continents have become an important target on the agenda of competition authorities. Cartels affecting multiple jurisdictions, or cartel networks involving similar types of conduct and some of the same companies acting in different jurisdictions, form an important part of the European Commission's docket. Large numbers of these cases are based on an application for leniency.

Anti-cartel enforcement has become a priority in a growing number of jurisdictions. As a result, many of them have also adopted leniency policies. Today many countries have in place leniency programmes that display a number of similarities, in particular with respect to their fundamental elements. However, there are also many differences, notably as regards the approach to applicants who have lost the race for immunity and the specific requirements that are placed on applicants as a condition for obtaining beneficial treatment.

International cartels and cartel networks expose their members to potential liability in many jurisdictions. Hence a decision whether to break ranks and report the existence of the cartel to the authorities is a complex one with global reach. Companies weigh numerous factors when deciding whether to report, and if so in which jurisdictions to apply. The parameters of the relevant leniency programmes and their application in practice by the relevant competition authorities are of paramount significance in the company's decision-making process. Any competing or conflicting requirements in the leniency programmes of different jurisdictions are likely to influence the decision to report and put the potential applicant in a position where it may be forced to act strategically and prioritise between the different jurisdictions in which it could apply.

In view of these considerations and the effects that one jurisdiction's leniency programme and its actions may have on other jurisdictions' ability to prosecute and punish a cartel, convergence and international co-operation assume great importance. International anti-cartel enforcement is neither a zero sum nor a one-shot game. Co-operation, and the appropriate consideration for the interests of other affected jurisdictions, can render greater payoffs for all the competition authorities involved. Therefore, it has to be emphasised that inconsistencies or outright conflicts between leniency programmes should be avoided to the greatest extent possible. This applies both to the actual black letter of a leniency programme and its application in practice by the competition authority.

It is clear that leniency policies do not exist in a vacuum. Many of the differences between leniency policies in various jurisdictions stem from the differences in legal cultures and the set-up of enforcement systems. Nevertheless, insofar as these result in possible reduced effectiveness of the leniency programmes involved, competition authorities should use the room for manoeuvre they may have in such situations to temper these negative effects. Indeed, to maximise the benefits and effectiveness of their leniency policies, competition authorities from different jurisdictions should consider active co-operation in order to reinforce their actions against the deleterious effects of cartels. However, such is practically possible only as long as it does not threaten the co-operating jurisdiction's own leniency policies. In this respect convergence in leniency policies may help to reduce such a threat and hence should be seen as highly commendable.

Leniency programmes are the most important and effective tools in combating cartels and great attention should be paid to avoiding unnecessary disincentives for leniency applicants which may arise from their application in different jurisdictions. Further convergence of leniency policies may reduce complications in reporting global cartels in several jurisdictions and reinforce the effectiveness of the leniency policies of all the jurisdictions involved. But convergence is a time consuming process and has its limits that stem from the differences in legal cultures. Competition authorities should consider applying the flexibilities that may exist in their own programmes and policies to minimise any possible conflicts with the requirements of other jurisdictions that may arise, so as to maximise the incentives for cartel participants to report cartel behaviour and thereby optimise the costs and benefits of leniency policies for both business and enforcement authorities.

With its comprehensive review of leniency policies in jurisdictions across the globe, the third edition of this tome will be an invaluable resource both to enforcement agencies and to businesses and their advisers.

Paul Malric-Smith
August 2010

Australia

Mallesons Stephen Jaques David Poddar, Lisa Huett & Morag Bond

BACKGROUND
1. What is the relevant legislation concerning the leniency policy and what is the enforcing body?
Australia's competition laws, including the prohibition on cartel conduct, are contained in the Trade Practices Act 1974 (Cth) (TPA). The Australian Competition and Consumer Commission (the ACCC), the independent government body responsible for administering and enforcing the TPA, has had an immunity policy for cartel conduct in place since July 2002.

The immunity policy was recently revised following the introduction of parallel civil and criminal offences for cartel conduct. The ACCC will grant immunity from civil proceedings for cartel conduct in accordance with the ACCC Immunity Policy 2009 (the Immunity Policy) while the Commonwealth Director of Public Prosecutions (CDPP), who is responsible for bringing criminal prosecutions for cartel conduct, will have the power to grant immunity from criminal prosecutions for cartel conduct. The policy applying to criminal immunity is contained in Annexure B to the prosecution policy of the Commonwealth (the Criminal Prosecution Cartel Immunity Policy).

The Immunity Policy, the Criminal Prosecution Cartel Immunity Policy, the ACCC immunity policy interpretations guidelines (the Interpretation Guidelines) and the Memorandum of Understanding between the CDPP and the ACCC regarding serious cartel conduct are available on the ACCC's website (*www.accc.gov.au*).

All immunity applications – including applications for immunity from both civil and criminal proceedings – should be made to the ACCC and in accordance with the procedures set out in these documents.

2. What are the basic tenets of a leniency/immunity programme? Is leniency available also for other types of competition law violations than cartels?
The Immunity Policy provides the first successful corporate or individual applicant with immunity (full amnesty) from ACCC initiated civil proceedings for cartel conduct and, if the CDPP is satisfied the requirements for immunity from criminal prosecution are met, with immunity from criminal prosecution for cartel conduct. The CDPP's decision will be in accordance with the CDPP's prosecution policy including the Criminal Prosecution Cartel Immunity Policy and upon the recommendation of the ACCC.

Cartel conduct covers the making or giving effect to a contract, arrangement or understanding between competitors containing a cartel provision. A cartel provision is a provision relating to price fixing, output restriction, bid rigging or market sharing. Immunity is not available for any other violations of the TPA, including resale price maintenance.

Only serious cartel conduct will be referred by the ACCC to the CDPP for criminal prosecution. Referral of possible serious cartel conduct will concentrate upon conduct of the type that can cause large scale or serious economic harm.

The Immunity Policy operates a marker system, allowing a corporate or individual applicant to hold its place in the 'immunity queue' for a limited period of time in order to allow the applicant time to investigate the extent of their individual participation and to gather information in support of an application.

After gathering the necessary information, the applicant can make a written or oral immunity application to the ACCC (seeking immunity from civil proceedings brought by the ACCC and immunity from criminal prosecution). Provided the applicant meets the specified conditions, the ACCC will grant the applicant 'conditional immunity' from ACCC initiated civil proceedings and the CDPP will grant the applicant immunity from criminal prosecution. Where a corporation qualifies for immunity, all current and former directors, officers and employees of the corporation who admit their involvement in the cartel conduct and who provide full disclosure and co-operation to the ACCC will be eligible for immunity in the same form as the corporate applicant.

The applicant will generally only be granted final immunity from ACCC initiated civil proceedings after the resolution of the ACCC court proceedings against cartel conduct.

Subsequent applicants (ie, the cartel member who is second or third in the queue) are not eligible for any reduction in penalty under the Immunity Policy. However, the ACCC operates a co-operation policy which provides that where a party assists the ACCC in an investigation, the party will receive more lenient treatment than if the party did not co-operate. The co-operation policy, which is also available on the ACCC website, sets out a series of general principles which are applied on a case-by-case basis.

3. How many cartels have been unveiled and punished since the adoption of the leniency programme?

The first ACCC policy providing upfront immunity was published in June 2003. Since that date, the ACCC has instituted 33 first instance proceedings in relation to alleged cartel matters. The majority of these have arisen from cartel immunity applications including 10 arising from the air cargo immunity application. Another proceeding is listed for hearing in March 2010.

4. What is needed to be a successful leniency applicant? Is documentary evidence required or is testimonial evidence sufficient?

A corporation party to a cartel will be eligible for 'conditional immunity' if:
- the corporation is the first person to apply for immunity from the ACCC (ie, the ACCC has not received a request for a marker from either an

individual or a corporation);
- the corporation admits that its conduct in respect of the cartel may constitute a contravention of the TPA;
- the corporation has not coerced others to participate in the cartel and was not the clear leader in the cartel;
- the corporation has either ceased its involvement in the cartel or indicates to the ACCC that it will cease its involvement in the cartel;
- the corporation's admissions are a truly corporate act (as opposed to isolated confessions of individual representatives); and
- the corporation undertakes to provide full disclosure to and co-operation with the ACCC.

Further, immunity will only be available if, at the time the ACCC receives the application, it has not received written legal advice that it has sufficient evidence to commence proceedings in relation to at least one contravention of the TPA arising from the cartel conduct.

In order to be eligible for final immunity, the applicant must provide ongoing full disclosure and co-operation.

Individuals participating in cartel conduct are exposed to penalties following ACCC initiated civil proceedings and criminal prosecution by the CDPP, and are also eligible for immunity. The requirements for individual 'conditional' immunity are broadly the same as for corporate 'conditional' immunity:
- the individual is the first person to apply for immunity in respect of the cartel and at the time the ACCC receives the application, it has not received written legal advice that it has sufficient evidence to commence proceedings in relation to at least one contravention of the TPA arising from the conduct in respect of the cartel;
- the individual has not coerced persons in other corporations to participate in the cartel and was not the clear individual leader in the cartel;
- the individual admits that they have participated, or are participating in conduct in respect of the cartel that may constitute a contravention or contraventions in breach of the TPA;
- the individual has either ceased their involvement in the cartel or indicates to the ACCC that they will cease their involvement in the cartel;
- the individual undertakes to provide full disclosure to and co-operation with the ACCC.

Where immunity from criminal prosecution is sought, the ACCC will assess the application prior to submitting it to the CDPP. The ACCC will make a recommendation to the CDPP based on whether the applicant meets the criteria set out in the ACCC Immunity Policy. The CDPP will exercise an independent discretion when considering a recommendation by the ACCC.

Where the CDPP is satisfied that the criteria in the ACCC Immunity Policy are met, the CDPP will grant immunity. There are no additional upfront criteria that need to be met to obtain immunity from criminal prosecution.

Where the CDPP decides to grant immunity, a written undertaking will be provided to the applicant, which will be subject to on-going obligations and conditions. The conditions for immunity will include that the applicant provide on-going full co-operation during the ACCC investigation and in respect of an individual:
- that they will appear as a witness for the prosecution and where requested, any proceedings against other cartel participants; and
- that any evidence that they are called upon to give will be given truthfully, accurately and withholding nothing of relevance.

The decision of the CDPP as to whether to grant immunity from criminal prosecution will be communicated to the applicant at the same time as the ACCC's decision.

The ACCC allows oral (paperless) applications for immunity. This option enables the applicant to make an application without generating any new documents which may involve admissions and which may assist a third party bringing a private enforcement action. The ACCC, however, makes it clear in its Interpretation Guidelines that it will create its own records in respect of all marker requests and applications received. The ACCC will also record the applicant's response to the ACCC information requests in writing.

Provisions were introduced to protect confidential cartel information provided to the ACCC (including as part of an immunity application) as part of the Trade Practices Amendment (Cartel Conduct and Other Measures) Act 2009. These protections are outlined in the response to question 18.

TIMING
5. What are the benefits of being 'first in' to co-operate?
An applicant may only be granted conditional immunity, and ultimately final immunity, if it is the first to approach the ACCC. Second or subsequent applicants will only be granted conditional immunity if the earlier applicant has withdrawn its application, is ineligible for conditional immunity, or has had conditional immunity revoked by the ACCC.

It is also important to note that immunity will not be available to any applicant if the ACCC has already received written legal advice that it has sufficient evidence to commence proceedings in relation to at least one TPA contravention arising from the conduct in respect of the cartel.

6. What are the consequences of being 'second'? Is there an 'immunity plus' or 'amnesty plus' option?
There are no reductions available under the Immunity Policy for the second or third cartel member to come forward to the ACCC. However, if the first cartel member to secure a marker is not found to meet the conditions of immunity (for example, if it was found to have coerced the other cartel participants or full and frank disclosure and co-operation is not provided to the ACCC), the second applicant may then be eligible for immunity.

The ACCC does operate an 'amnesty plus' policy. Where a person is:

ineligible for immunity in respect of a cartel (the first cartel) because another person has been granted conditional immunity, but nevertheless co-operates with the ACCC; and reports a second cartel to the ACCC and obtains conditional immunity in respect of the second cartel, the ACCC will recommend to the court that the person receives a reduced penalty in civil proceedings for the first cartel and will also recommend to the CDPP that a reduced fine or sentence be sought for the first cartel.

This will be in addition to any reduced penalty that the ACCC may recommend to the court as a result of the co-operation provided by the party under the ACCC co-operation policy.

7. Are subsequent firms given any beneficial treatment if they make a useful contribution? How are 'useful contributions' defined?
The second or third cartel member to come forward to the ACCC will not receive any benefit under the ACCC Immunity Policy (unless they meet the requirements of the amnesty plus policy).

However, cartel members who make a useful contribution to the ACCC's investigation may receive the benefit of lenient treatment under the ACCC's co-operation policy. While the ACCC will assess applications for lenient treatment under the co-operation policy on a case-by-case basis, the policy provides that lenient treatment is more likely where the applicant:
- gives important evidence to the ACCC;
- takes prompt action to cease its anti-competitive conduct;
- was not the ringleader of the conduct;
- has not encouraged other firms to engage in unlawful conduct;
- is prepared to make restitution where appropriate; and
- does not have a prior record of contraventions of the TPA.

SCOPE/FULL LENIENCY
8. Is it possible to receive full leniency? If so, what are the conditions required to receive full leniency? Does the regulatory authority require the applicant to cease participation in the cartel conduct after its application?
It is possible to receive full immunity from ACCC initiated civil proceedings for cartel conduct and from criminal prosecution for cartel conduct provided the applicant meets the requirements for immunity set out in response to question 4. The applicant will, however, remain vulnerable to actions initiated by third parties in relation to the cartel conduct.

8.1 Can ringleaders/coercers receive full leniency?
One of the conditions to immunity is that the applicant has not coerced others to participate in the cartel and was not the clear leader in the cartel (or in the case of an individual applicant, that the individual has not coerced persons in other corporations to participate in the cartel and was not the clear individual leader in the cartel).

The ACCC recognises in its Interpretation Guidelines that in many cartels there may not be any coercion or a clear leader. The mere fact that one cartel participant has arranged a meeting (including the first meeting of the cartel) or maintained records will not necessarily exclude the application of the Immunity Policy to that participant, particularly when the other participants took part in the cartel willingly. However, the ACCC indicates that where the immunity applicant pressured one or more persons into joining or maintaining the cartel, that this may amount to coercion.

Full and final immunity from any civil penalties imposed by a court will be granted by the ACCC after the resolution of the court proceedings against cartel participants and is conditional on the applicant having continued to provide full, frank, expeditious and continuous co-operation and disclosure to the ACCC.

8.2 If there is a requirement to 'co-operate fully and on an on-going basis' what does it entail?

The ACCC has provided extensive guidance on what full disclosure and co-operation will involve in its Interpretation Guidelines. At a minimum, this would include:
- providing full details of all known facts relating to the cartel, including who was involved, who had knowledge of the cartel and how the cartel was implemented;
- not disclosing to third parties any dealing with the ACCC without its consent except where required by law (where disclosure is required the ACCC must be notified prior to the applicant releasing any information);
- providing to the ACCC promptly and at the applicant's expense, all evidence and information available to the applicant regarding the cartel;
- using its best endeavours to comply with any timetables set down by the ACCC; and
- making available all directors, officers and employees for interviews with the ACCC and using their best efforts to secure and promote their ongoing, full and truthful co-operation for the duration of the investigation and any subsequent court proceedings.

Immunity from criminal prosecution by the CDPP will be conditional on the applicant providing on-going full co-operation during the ACCC investigation and, in respect of an individual that:
- they will appear as a witness for the prosecution and where requested, in any proceedings against other cartel participants; and
- any evidence that they are called upon to give will be given truthfully, accurately and withholding nothing of relevance.

9. How many companies have received full immunity from fines to date?

Since June 2003 the ACCC has granted conditional immunity to 36 applicants. As set out above, there is only one level of immunity (full immunity) available in Australia. This figure includes both corporations and individuals and will include cases where the ACCC has ultimately not commenced proceedings.

PROCEDURE

10. What are the practical steps required to apply for leniency?
The ACCC operates a marker system and also allows hypothetical inquiries about the availability of a marker.

10.1 Hypothetical inquiries
A prospective immunity applicant or its legal representative may make a hypothetical inquiry to the ACCC as to whether a 'first in' marker is available. The ACCC will not confirm or deny the existence of any investigation into cartel conduct, but will advise prospective applicants if a first in marker is available in respect of the potential cartel.

10.2 Requesting and obtaining a marker
The purpose of obtaining a marker is to enable the immunity applicant a limited amount of time to gather the information necessary to demonstrate that they satisfy the requirements for conditional immunity. As long as the applicant holds the marker for particular cartel conduct, no other participant in the cartel will be allowed to take the applicant's place in the immunity queue.

To obtain a marker, the applicant must provide a description of the cartel conduct in sufficient detail to allow the ACCC to confirm that no other person has already applied for immunity (or obtained a marker from the ACCC) and that the ACCC has not received legal advice that it already has sufficient evidence to commence proceedings in respect of the conduct.

The applicant will be informed if a marker is available and if it is, the ACCC and the applicant will discuss the time required for the applicant to complete its internal investigation and provide the ACCC with the information required to satisfy the requirements for conditional immunity. The ACCC has indicated that a marker will generally be available for 28 days, but this period may only be a few days if the ACCC's pre-existing investigation is advanced – it may also be longer if the applicant can satisfy the ACCC that its internal investigation will be complex. If the applicant is an individual rather than a corporate, they will have a much shorter period in which to provide the information.

Where the applicant is a corporation and derivative immunity is sought for directors, employees and officers, the applicant will need to name all current and former directors, officers and employees for whom individual immunity is sought.

Once the applicant has perfected the marker – through the provision of information and submission of the immunity application (which can be made orally or in writing) – the ACCC will advise the applicant whether its application for conditional immunity is successful.

At the same time as the applicant is informed of the ACCC's decision to grant immunity, the applicant will be informed of the CDPP's decision whether to grant immunity from criminal prosecution.

The conferral of conditional immunity from civil proceedings by the ACCC will only be made final following the conclusion of court proceedings against the other cartel members. An undertaking given by the CDPP that they will not bring a criminal prosecution will remain in place unless revoked and a final undertaking granting full immunity from criminal prosecution is therefore not required.

11. Is there an optimal time to approach the regulatory authority?
As immunity is only available to the first successful applicant and only where the ACCC has not already received written legal advice that it has sufficient evidence to commence proceedings, there is a significant incentive for a party to apply for a marker for conditional immunity (or make a hypothetical enquiry as to whether a marker is available) as soon as it is realised that they are implicated in a cartel.

12. What guarantees of leniency exist if a party co-operates?
The ACCC makes it clear that if an applicant meets the conditions set out in the response to question 4, the applicant is guaranteed immunity from ACCC initiated civil proceedings. While the CDPP will exercise its independent discretion when deciding whether to grant immunity from criminal prosecution, immunity from criminal prosecution will be granted if the CDPP is satisfied that the ACCC conditions for immunity are satisfied.

The applicant will however, have ongoing co-operation obligations to meet.

CONSEQUENCES
13. What effects does leniency granted to a corporate defendant have on the defendant's employees? Does it protect them from criminal and/or civil liability?
Under the Immunity Policy, if a corporation qualifies for conditional immunity, all current and former directors, officers and employees of the corporation who admit involvement in the cartel conduct and provide full disclosure and co-operation to the ACCC will be eligible for conditional immunity in the same form as the corporation. The corporation seeking immunity must list all current and former directors, officers and employees on whose behalf derivative immunity is sought at the time of submitting the Immunity Policy. Subject to continuing to provide full disclosure and co-operation to the ACCC, the ACCC will grant the directors, officers and employees final immunity when immunity is granted to the corporation.

Similarly, if the CDPP grants a corporate applicant immunity from criminal prosecution, all past and present directors, officers and employees who request immunity, admit their involvement in the cartel conduct (via their corporation) and undertake to provide full disclosure and co-operation to the ACCC will be eligible for immunity from criminal prosecution in the same form as the corporation.

In some circumstances, the ACCC may specifically exclude certain current or former directors, officers and employees from immunity. For example, the ACCC would be unlikely to grant immunity to an executive who has left the immunity applicant corporation's employment and has continued to participate in the cartel while in the employment of another participant.

In the event that some of the corporation's directors, officers or employees do not wish to co-operate, the ACCC will ascertain whether the application is a 'truly corporate act' before deciding whether to grant immunity to the corporation. In doing this, the ACCC will consider whether the corporation has taken all reasonable and legal steps to secure the co-operation of all directors, officers and employees. They will also look at the number and importance of the individuals who choose not to co-operate and the explanation for non-co-operation.

The ACCC has also made it clear in its Interpretation Guidelines that an application for immunity made on behalf of a corporate group will cover each member of that corporate group where they are wholly owned by the applicant. Where a member of a corporate group is only partly owned, the ACCC will take into account the applicant's degree of control and ownership over the company.

Corporate immunity applicants must advise the ACCC of the corporate entities it seeks to be covered by derivative immunity. When requested to do so, the applicant must demonstrate to the ACCC the relationship between the applicant company and the entity.

14. Does leniency bar further private enforcement?
No, the immunity granted by the ACCC is only in respect of ACCC initiated civil proceedings. Private civil proceedings can still be brought by third parties.

A recent example is Cadbury Schweppes' claim for more than A$200 million in damages from Amcor Ltd for losses allegedly suffered as a result of a cartel in the packaging markets in Australia. Amcor Ltd was one of two participants in the cartel and had received full immunity from the ACCC. The other participant was Visy Industries Holdings Pty Ltd and its related entities (Visy) who were the subject of highly-publicised enforcement proceedings by the ACCC. This case and the Cadbury Schweppes follow-on claim for damages are discussed in more detail in the response to question 18.

Class actions against cartel members are also a very real possibility. The Australian participants in the vitamins cartel paid A$30.5 million to settle a class action brought by purchasers following successful civil proceedings brought by the ACCC. There is also a class action proceeding against both Amcor and Visy in relation to the packaging cartel.

These cases demonstrate the availability of private enforcement claims and this risk is an increasingly important factor for those weighing up the pros and cons of seeking immunity.

PROTECTION AGAINST DISCLOSURE/CONFIDENTIALITY
15. Is confidentiality afforded to the leniency applicant and other co-operating parties? If so, to what extent? Is the identity of the leniency applicant/other co-operating parties disclosed during the investigation or in the final decision? Is information provided by the leniency applicant/other co-operating parties passed on to other undertakings under investigation? Can a leniency applicant/other co-operating party request anonymity or confidentiality of information provided?
The ACCC affords confidentiality to all parties during the course of its

investigation, subject to the ACCC's practice of fully publicising the cartel from the time the ACCC commences proceedings. Once proceedings are commenced, the ACCC will often initiate substantial publicity. The ACCC will not settle an investigation on a confidential basis where breaches of the TPA are established.

The ACCC will use its best endeavours to protect confidential information provided by immunity applicants. Information received in support of an immunity application (including a request for a marker) is received on the basis that the ACCC will not use the information as evidence in proceedings against the applicant in respect of which immunity is sought If a conditional grant of immunity is later revoked because the applicant failed to satisfy the requirements for immunity, the ACCC will be entitled to use such information against the immunity applicants (and any directors, officers or employees of the applicant).

The information provided by the immunity applicant will be used by the ACCC in bringing civil proceedings against the other members of the cartel and may be used by the CDPP in bringing a criminal prosecution against other parties.

16. Is the evidence submitted by the leniency applicant protected from transmission to other competition authorities with whom the authority in question co-operates? If so, how?

The ACCC will not share confidential information provided by the immunity applicant, or the identity of the applicant, with competition authorities in other jurisdictions without the consent of the applicant, but the ACCC will seek consent as a matter of course, particularly for international cartels.

Information obtained from sources other than the immunity applicant, including information obtained as a result of inquiries arising from the information provided by the applicant, will not be subject to this limitation and will, in appropriate circumstances, be shared where permitted by law.

The Interpretation Guidelines have, however, made it clear that disclosure obligations may require the CDPP to disclose such information although it does not make it clear who this information may be disclosed to.

17. To what extent can evidence submitted by the leniency applicant (transcripts of oral statements or written evidence) become discoverable in subsequent private enforcement claims? Can leniency information be subjected to discovery orders in domestic or foreign courts? Can leniency information submitted in a foreign jurisdiction be subjected to discovery orders in the domestic courts?

As a result of recent amendments to the TPA, the ACCC has the ability to effectively prevent private litigants in subsequent enforcement actions from accessing documents it holds which have been provided by an immunity applicant. However, evidence provided by an immunity applicant to the ACCC will be discoverable from a third party, including the immunity applicant and other parties to the cartel to the extent they hold that information.

The Trade Practices Amendment (Cartel Conduct and Other Measures) Act 2009, which introduced the criminal cartel offence, also introduced protections preventing the ACCC from being required to disclose protected cartel information to a court or tribunal. Protected cartel information is broadly defined to capture any information given to the ACCC in confidence concerning a breach of the prohibitions on cartel conduct.

Under the new provisions, the ACCC will not be required to produce or disclose protected cartel information to a party to court proceedings to which the ACCC is not a party, or to a court or tribunal without the leave of the court or tribunal.

In deciding whether to grant leave the court or tribunal is required to have regard to the matters set out in section 157B(2) of the TPA. These matters are clearly weighted towards the non-disclosure of evidence provided by an immunity applicant. They include the need to avoid disruption to national and international efforts relating to law enforcement and the fact that the disclosure of protected cartel information may discourage informants from giving protected cartel information in the future. The court must not have regard to any matters other than those listed. A Commission official in deciding whether to disclose protected cartel information to a party to court proceedings must have regard to the same list of factors.

Despite the new provisions in the TPA, the ACCC may choose to disclose evidence provided by an immunity applicant. The ACCC's current approach, however, is not to provide this information to private litigants unless compelled to by order of a court.

However, a private litigant seeking damages for cartel conduct may seek discovery of documents submitted by the immunity applicant from it directly and from the other parties to the cartel. The cartel participants will normally be required to produce these documents to a private litigant, unless it can be shown that legal professional privilege attaches to the document. This may present private litigants, as it did in the Cadbury litigation, with an opportunity to indirectly access the evidence held by the ACCC. Many of the most important documents associated with an immunity application are provided to the cartel participants by the ACCC during its enforcement action against the cartel participants, and can therefore be accessed through discovery in proceedings brought by a private litigant against a cartel participant.

An order of a foreign court requiring the discovery of documents submitted to the ACCC by the immunity applicant will not normally be enforceable in Australia. Evidence submitted as part of an immunity application to the ACCC may, however, be discoverable in foreign proceedings if the information is transferred to that jurisdiction via email or other means.

Similarly, an Australian court will not make an order requiring a foreign-based regulator or other party to discover documents held outside of Australia. However, if these documents are provided to the ACCC or an Australian subsidiary of one of the cartel participants, these documents may be discoverable.

18. Are there any precedents in which evidence from a leniency application has been discovered in a private enforcement claim?

Yes, the trend in Australia in recent years has been for private litigants to seek evidence provided by an immunity applicant for the purposes of proving damages claims against cartel participants. These documents are sought from not only the ACCC, but also the immunity applicant and the other parties to the cartel. The documents sought by private litigants include not only the immunity application itself, but also:
- meeting notes, board papers and other internal documents created by the ACCC;
- transcripts of the ACCC's interviews with employees of the immunity applicant; and
- witness statements provided by the immunity applicant's employees who participated in the cartel.

The ability of private litigants to access evidence submitted by the immunity applicant will be hindered by the recent changes to the TPA. However, the frequency of private litigants accessing documents associated with the immunity application held by cartel participants – rather than the ACCC – is likely to increase following the developments in the law arising out of the Cadbury litigation.

RELATIONSHIP WITH THE EUROPEAN COMMISSION'S LENIENCY NOTICE AND LENIENCY POLICY IN OTHER EU MEMBER STATES

19. Does the policy address the interaction with applications under the Commission Leniency Notice? If so, how?

Not applicable.

20. Does the policy address the interaction with applications for leniency in other EU member states? If so, how? Does the authority accept summary applications in line with the ECN Model Leniency Programme?

Not applicable.

RELATIONSHIP WITH SETTLEMENT PROCEDURES

21. What is the relationship between leniency and applicable settlement procedures? Are they mutually exclusive?

As a successful immunity applicant will obtain full amnesty, it will not be necessary for the applicant to enter into separate settlement discussions to reduce its penalty with the ACCC (the grant of conditional immunity will, however, typically be documented in an agreement between the applicant and the ACCC and this agreement is known as a settlement agreement).

Subsequent applicants who may seek a reduction from the penalty that would otherwise by imposed under the terms of the ACCC co-operation policy may be able to agree a penalty with the ACCC. However, ultimately the pecuniary penalty to be paid by a cartel member is determined by the Federal Court which has a broad discretion within the statutory limits.

Where the ACCC has agreed a penalty to be paid with the contravening party, the Federal Court's practice is generally to accept the agreed penalty if, after examining the circumstances, it is appropriate and within the range of what the court would otherwise impose.

REFORM/LATEST DEVELOPMENTS
22. Is there a reform underway to revisit the leniency policy? What are the latest developments?

The Immunity Policy was revised following the introduction of the parallel civil and criminal cartel offences in July 2009. There is no indication that the policy will be the subject of reform in the immediate future.

It is worth noting, however, that there may be significant developments to the New Zealand leniency policy, which is operated by the New Zealand Commerce Commission. The New Zealand Ministry of Economic Development issued an extensive discussion document on cartel criminalisation in January 2010 and should a criminal cartel offence be introduced in New Zealand, changes to the New Zealand leniency policy, which was recently updated in March 2010, are likely to be required. This may be relevant given the degree of trade between Australia and New Zealand.

Austria

Schönherr Franz Urlesberger & Stefanie Stegbauer

BACKGROUND
1. What is the relevant legislation concerning the leniency policy and what is the enforcing body?
The Austrian leniency programme (which entered into force on 1 January 2006) is based on section 11(3) to (6) of the Competition Act (*Wettbewerbsgesetz*) and section 36(3) of the Cartel Act (*Kartellgesetz*). Details on the leniency practice are set out in the leniency handbook of the Austrian Federal Competition Authority (*Bundeswettbewerbsbehörde* or FCA), which may be retrieved (in German and English) from the FCA's website *www.bwb.gv.at*.

In terms of public enforcement, the Austrian antitrust rules are enforced by the Official Parties (*Amtsparteien*), ie, the FCA and the Federal Cartel Prosecutor (*Bundeskartellanwalt* or FCP), and the Cartel Court (*Kartellgericht*). However, the Official Parties have no decision making power; they may only submit applications to the Cartel Court (notably request the imposition of a fine on an undertaking in breach of the Austrian antitrust provisions). The exclusive decision making body therefore is the Cartel Court.

While both FCA and FCP have the power to apply to the Cartel Court, the application of the leniency programme is in the sole discretion of the FCA; the FCP is not empowered to enforce the leniency policy. If the FCA intends to grant to an undertaking immunity from fines or a reduction of fines respectively according to section 11(3) Competition Act, it has to inform the FCP accordingly. As a result, the latter loses its power to apply for fines.

In the court proceeding initiated by the application of the FCA, the Cartel Court must not impose a higher fine than requested by the FCA.

2. What are the basic tenets of a leniency/immunity programme? Is leniency available also for other types of competition law violations than cartels?
In line with the Commission notice on the co-operation with the Network of Competition Authorities, the aim of the Austrian leniency programme is to: '*either grant full immunity from fines or a substantial reduction of fines which would otherwise have been imposed on a participant in a cartel in exchange for fully and voluntarily disclosing information on a cartel which meets specific criteria prior to or during the investigation of the case*'.

In contrast to the leniency programme of the EU Commission, the Austrian provisions may not only apply to horizontal, but also to vertical agreements and concerted practices.

Section 11(3) Competition Act, the provision on which the Austrian leniency handbook is based, explicitly outlines the scope of the programme regarding infringements against section 1 Cartel Act and Article 81 EC Treaty (now Article 101 Treaty on the Functioning of the European Union), ie, infringements of the cartel prohibition (be it horizontal or vertical). However, the Official Parties could, in theory, also refrain from applying for the imposition of a fine in cases where the requirements of section 11(3) Competition Act are not met, such as abuse of a market dominant position or early implementation of a merger.

3. How many cartels have been unveiled and punished since the adoption of the leniency programme?

As of 1 July 2009, 18 leniency requests have been submitted to the FCA. However, in one-third of these cases, proceedings are conducted by the EU Commission, another third of the initiated proceedings have been terminated by the FCA by a no action letter and one case has already been time-barred. Upon completion of this chapter, in only two proceedings involving leniency applicants have legally binding decisions been rendered (the Austrian elevator cartel case and a cartel concerning the wholesale of industrial chemicals); a third proceeding (concerning printing chemicals) has been decided by the Cartel Court in April 2010 (but may be appealed to the Cartel Court of Appeals).

4. What is needed to be a successful leniency applicant? Is documentary evidence required or is testimonial evidence sufficient?

Probably the most essential factor for a successful leniency application is timing. The earlier an application is submitted, the bigger the chances for immunity or a high reduction of a potential fine.

However, an undertaking taking into consideration an application for leniency should nevertheless conduct a thorough antitrust due diligence in order to have a complete and detailed picture of all possible infringements and to collect as much evidence as possible for a submission to the authority. Ideally, the first applicant already provides so much information that subsequent undertakings cannot provide any more added value to the investigation and, as a result, will therefore not be granted a reduction (for details on the prerequisites for a successful leniency application, see question 8 below).

There is no general rule on what evidence is required in order to successfully apply for leniency. The burden of proof on the first applicant is lower than what is required from subsequent applicants, who have to provide 'added value'.

In practice, the FCA will request undertakings to submit a statement summarising all the facts of the case and affidavits from their employees in order to substantiate the corporate statement. Nevertheless, the FCA often subpoenas these employees before the initiation of the court proceedings in order to get a clear picture about what the witnesses will testify during the subsequent trial.

TIMING
5. What are the benefits of being 'first in' to co-operate?
Only the first undertaking to inform the FCA of an infringement previously unknown to the authority qualifies for a reduction of 100 per cent of a possible later fine (for further details on the prerequisites for full immunity see question 8 below).

If the authority already knows about the infringement at the time of a leniency application, the undertaking applying for leniency will not get full immunity but may still qualify for a reduction of fines (see question 6 below).

In the first Austrian leniency proceedings, the first leniency applicant was not even made a party to the proceeding before the Cartel Court, which had the additional benefit of cost savings and not even a declaratory judgment was issued against it. However, in all subsequent leniency cases the FCA has involved the leniency applicant in the court proceedings and applied for a declaratory judgment with regard to it thereby making it a party to the court proceeding and obliging it to co-operate further.

Another benefit of being 'first in' relates to the scope and depth of the information to be provided to the FCA. In contrast to the EU regime, where the information has to enable the Commission to carry out a targeted inspection or to find an infringement, there is no such substantive threshold in Austria. Therefore, the mere indication of the existence of a (previously unknown) cartel would already suffice for the first applicant to receive full immunity. However, it has to be borne in mind that another prerequisite of the leniency programme is that the applicant discloses all evidence in its possession; therefore available information must not be withheld. Otherwise the leniency applicant will lose its status of full immunity, and this was the case in the most recent decision of the Cartel Court concerning the printing chemicals cartel, where the first leniency applicant was, in the end, sentenced to the highest fine, because it didn't fully co-operate with the authority during the proceedings.

6. What are the consequences of being 'second'? Is there an 'immunity plus' or 'amnesty plus' option?
The second undertaking to apply for leniency or an undertaking which informs the FCA of an infringement about which the authority has already been aware may be granted a reduction of between 30 and 50 per cent. In order to be granted such a reduction, all criteria laid down in section 11(3) Competition Act (except for being the first to inform the authority) have to be fulfilled (for details see question 8 below).

In order to qualify for leniency, the second (and any subsequent) applicant has to provide added value to the investigation of the FCA by helping the authority to more conclusively and completely substantiate the infringement. This may in particular be achieved by providing evidence which makes the case 'court-proof'. In this context, the handbook sets out that original written evidence stemming from the time of the infringement (such as protocols of cartel meetings) are of higher value than indirect or only subsequently created proof (such as a corporate statement).

In the Austrian elevator cartel case, the FCA granted the full reduction of 50 per cent to the second undertaking to inform the authority in order to encourage undertakings to make use of the leniency programme.

7. Are subsequent firms given any beneficial treatment if they make a useful contribution? How are 'useful contributions' defined?

The second undertaking to meet the requirements laid down in section 11(3) sentence 2 Competition Act (ie, the third undertaking applying for leniency or, if the authority learned of the infringement on their own, the second undertaking providing information with added value) may be granted a reduction of between 20 and 30 per cent (with regard to the definition of 'added value' see question 6 above).

For any subsequent undertaking to meet the requirements set out in section 11(3) sentence 2 Competition Act, the reduction may amount to up to 20 per cent.

However, the FCA reserves its right to grant a bigger or smaller reduction than specified above, if – depending on the case – the added value submitted by the applicant is extraordinarily big or extraordinarily small.

SCOPE/FULL LENIENCY

8. Is it possible to receive full leniency? If so, what are the conditions required to receive full leniency?

The first undertaking to inform the FCA may receive full immunity from fines. According to section 11(3) Competition Act the FCA may refrain from applying to impose a fine, if an undertaking:

- has ceased its participation in an infringement of section 1 of the Cartel Act or Article 81 EC (now Article 101 paragraph 1 TFEU);
- informs the FCA about this infringement before the authority has learned about the facts of the case itself;
- subsequently co-operates with the FCA promptly and without restrictions in order to fully clarify the matter; and
- has not coerced any other undertaking/association of undertakings to participate in the infringement.

8.1 Can ringleaders/coercers receive full leniency?

An undertaking which has coerced another undertaking to participate in the infringement, does not qualify for leniency. However, there is no definition of what is meant by coercing. It can therefore not be ruled out that not only someone who coerced another party to participate but also someone who hindered other undertakings from leaving the cartel could be excluded from the benefits of the leniency programme. In academic literature, it has been argued that only undertakings with a certain degree of market power should be regarded as coercers.

As the leniency programme encourages undertakings involved in an illicit behaviour to disclose the infringement and is therefore, in principle, available to all undertakings, it may be assumed that the exclusion from the leniency programme (by being a coercer) will be applied narrowly. So far, there is no case known in Austria where leniency has been refused to an undertaking because of having been a coercer.

8.2 If there is a requirement to 'co-operate fully and on an ongoing basis' what does it entail?

The obligation for a leniency applicant to co-operate 'promptly and without restrictions in order to fully clarify the matter' means that the undertaking concerned has to submit all evidence in its possession or otherwise available and that it has to explain the content and context of the evidence submitted. Furthermore, the leniency applicant has to promptly, truthfully and completely reply to all requests of the FCA.

The undertaking must, in particular, not disclose the fact of its co-operation to any other participant in the alleged infringement.

It is unclear whether the obligation to co-operate extends to the subsequently initiated court proceedings. The court will take into account any co-operation during the court proceedings as a mitigating factor when determining the final amount of fine.

8.3 Does the regulatory authority require the applicant to cease participation in the cartel conduct after its application?

Although section 11(3) Competition Act provides that the leniency applicant 'must have ceased' its involvement in the infringement, the FCA's handbook specifies this insofar as it states that the undertaking 'ceases its participation in accordance with the FCA'. Therefore the FCA determines the exact timing and modalities of the exit from the cartel in order to safeguard the success of the investigation. In practice, the FCA has not yet asked an undertaking to continue its participation. If it were to do so, it would most likely only ask the undertaking to act passively in line with previous cartel conduct by, for instance, accepting phone calls or receiving messages from other cartel members.

It needs to be emphasised that the case law applies very strict standards to the question as to when the infringement was terminated. In the printing chemicals cartel case, the Cartel Court found that it did not suffice that an undertaking ceased to attend the cartel meetings, but requested the undertaking which wished to terminate its anticompetitive conduct to announce openly to the other cartel participants that it left the cartel (*contrarius actus*). In consequence, the court found that for one party it was not the last contact with the other cartel members which was relevant for the termination of the infringement, but only the later date of the exit from the relevant market.

In one decision of the Cartel Court of Appeals concerning an abuse of a market dominant position of the former Austrian telecommunications monopolist (*Kombipaket* case) it was even found that the infringement lasts as long as it has an impact on the affected market. More specifically, as long as long-term contracts with customers stemming from an infringement are not terminated, the infringement was considered to be ongoing.

9. How many companies have received full immunity from fines to date?

In both cases where legally binding decisions have been rendered, the first leniency applicant has received full immunity from fines. However, in the printing chemicals cartel case (see question 5 above), the Cartel Court imposed substantial fines on the first leniency applicant since the latter in its application allegedly failed to set out the full scope of the infringement (which was only unveiled by the second leniency applicant).

PROCEDURE
10. What are the practical steps required to apply for leniency?
10.1 Full disclosure

The leniency applicant has to submit to the FCA all evidence on the alleged infringement in its possession or otherwise available.

10.2 Initial contact is there a 'marker' system?

For the initial contact with the authority, the undertaking concerned has to submit the application form (by fax or email) which forms an integral part of the handbook available on the website of the FCA. Upon the applicant's request and in case of well founded reasons the undertaking may also submit its application orally at the FCA, where it will be recorded by completing the application form.

The following has to be provided in the leniency application form:
(i) information on the undertaking applying for leniency;
(ii) the type of the relevant infringement;
(iii) the affected markets;
(iv) the duration of the infringement;
(v) the other undertakings involved in the infringement; and possibly
(vi) other competition authorities to which the leniency applicant has applied for leniency.

Although there is no marker system as such in Austria, for the first undertaking to inform the authority of an infringement previously unknown to the FCA, the leniency request serves as a kind of marker, as the date of receipt of the duly and fully completed form determines the position of the undertaking as being 'first in'. This rank is indeed subject to full subsequent co-operation (see question 8 above), but the undertaking only has to provide all evidence in its possession within a certain time limit set by the authority.

However, for all subsequent undertakings or in case of an infringement already known to the FCA, the position of the leniency applicant depends on the provision of added value (see question 6 above). This means, that in such case the mere submission of the form is not enough in order to reserve a certain rank, but rather the undertaking which is the first to provide added value will be ranked second, third etc.

10.3 Conditional reduction of fine

Upon the request of the leniency applicant and after having examined the facts of the case, the FCA has to notify the undertaking of whether or not it considers granting immunity or a reduction of fines. As for the amount of the reduction, the authority will only state a bandwidth, not yet an exact percentage.

Such notification by the FCA is non-binding, as the granting of immunity/a reduction of fines is always subject to the subsequent full and unrestricted co-operation of the undertaking; the FCA may always withdraw the benefit granted if it is of the opinion that this prerequisite is not fulfilled.

10.4 Final reduction
Only shortly before the FCA applies to the Cartel Court for the imposition of a fine, will it inform the leniency applicant of the final reduction by stating a certain percentage. This (second) notification is unconditional.

The exact amount of the fine (in euros) applied for will only be determined by the FCA at the end of the court proceedings in a supplement to its initial fine application. The fine applied for by the FCA may not be exceeded by the Cartel Court which renders the (fining) decision.

11. Is there an optimal time to approach the regulatory authority?
There is no optimal time to approach the authority. However, the earlier the undertaking informs the FCA of illicit conduct, the higher the chances of receiving full immunity/a higher reduction of fines. In any case, undertakings should conduct due diligence in case the FCA directs an information request to them, as in the past, such request was often based on the information previously provided by the first leniency applicant. In such case it is of major importance to find evidence which would be regarded as added value in order to possibly achieve a reduction up to 50 per cent for being second.

12. What guarantees of leniency exist if a party co-operates?
The first, though still conditional, notification of the FCA provides a certain guarantee of leniency, since the FCA cannot abstain from granting leniency without a special reason. For details on the second notification and the final amount of reduction, see question 10 above.

Even if the FCA decides not to further investigate a case of which it has been informed by a leniency applicant, there is a guarantee of leniency as the authority will issue a no action letter, which ensures that the undertaking keeps its first rank if the FCA decides to pick up the case again at a later point in time.

CONSEQUENCES
13. What effects does leniency granted to a corporate defendant have on the defendant's employees? Does it protect them from criminal and/or civil liability?
Employees of an undertaking are neither protected from criminal liability nor from civil liability. Beyond that, the FCA is even obliged to report any suspected infringement of criminal law to the Public Prosecution Service.

The most relevant provision of the Austrian Criminal Code

(*Strafgesetzbuch*) in relation to anti-competitive conduct is the provision on bid-rigging which constitutes a criminal offence. As regards the scope of this offence, it is disputed whether it only relates to public tender procedures or whether private tender procedures are also caught. The FCA previously informally stated that it will only report bid-rigging in public procurement procedures to the Public Prosecution Service.

However, someone is not to be punished for bid-rigging if they have deliberately prevented the awarding party from accepting the tender offer or rendering its service or, if the offer had been rejected/the service not rendered for other reasons, if they had deliberately and honestly tried to prevent it.

Furthermore, an infringement of competition law may qualify as fraudulent behaviour within the meaning of the Austrian Criminal Code. As with rigging bids, the law provides for an exemption from punishment in the case of active repentance.

Further, there also exists criminal responsibility for undertakings according to the Corporate Responsibility Act (*Verbandsverantwortlichkeitsgesetz*). Although there is no case law yet, it can be assumed that if an undertaking has already been fined based on the Cartel Act, it may not be fined because of a criminal offence due to the principle of double jeopardy.

Additionally, there may also be consequences under labour law. Employees could be expelled for being involved in a cartel or not co-operating in the internal due diligence because of their failure to comply with instructions and rules. Employees could even be subject to damages claims caused by their illicit behaviour.

Finally, it has to be mentioned that under public procurement law, undertakings involved in a cartel could be deemed excluded from subsequent bids because of their involvement in illicit behaviour.

14. Does leniency bar further private enforcement?
A leniency application does not provide immunity from private damages claims. On the contrary, in line with the approach of the European Commission, the FCA in its press releases encourages third parties who may have suffered damages from a cartel to initiate private damages claims against the undertakings involved in the infringement.

PROTECTION AGAINST DISCLOSURE/CONFIDENTIALITY
15. Is confidentiality afforded to the leniency applicant and other co-operating parties? If so, to what extent?
Formally there are some provisions which are designed to safeguard the confidentiality of leniency applicants and other co-operating parties. However, as the Austrian leniency regime is new, no reliable practice on the application of these rules exists (for details see the questions below). However, the sensitivity of the courts and authorities with regard to confidentiality increases steadily.

15.1 Is the identity of the leniency applicant/other co-operating parties disclosed during the investigation or in the final decision?

In the past, the FCA posted a press release on its website at the latest when it applied for a fine to the Cartel Court. At this point in time the FCA will usually not unveil the names of the companies involved. Typically only once the decision of the Cartel Court becomes legally binding, which will most likely be only after the decision of the Supreme Court sitting as Cartel Court of Appeals, will the FCA disclose the names of the companies in a press release, even though the decision of the Cartel Court of Appeals will only be available in a redacted version.

15.2 Is information provided by the leniency applicant/other co-operating parties passed on to other undertakings under investigation?

The information provided by the first leniency applicant is frequently the basis for an information request by the FCA to the other alleged cartel participants. Other than that, no information or documents are disclosed to the other undertakings involved during the preliminary investigation phase of the FCA.

However, when applying to the Cartel Court for the initiation of a fine proceeding, the FCA submits all useful evidence provided by the leniency applicants to make its case. The application of the FCA (including all annexes) will subsequently be passed on to the other undertakings involved in the proceeding.

15.3 Can a leniency applicant/other co-operating party request anonymity or confidentiality of information provided?

Unrestricted access to the court's file will be granted to all parties of the court proceeding. Therefore, any information which has been made part of the court's file (by the FCA or any other undertaking) will be accessible to every party of the court proceedings. In the past, undertakings helped themselves by agreeing on confidentiality of business secrets and sharing sensitive information only on a counsel-to-counsel basis by providing redacted versions of the respective documents/pleadings to the other parties.

16. Is the evidence submitted by the leniency applicant protected from transmission to other competition authorities with whom the authority in question co-operates? If so, how?

In principle, the European Competition Authorities inform each other of the existence of a cartel and its substantive and geographic scope via a form circulated in their network.

However, the FCA must not base an application to the Cartel Court on information received via the European network which stems from a leniency application in another country.

17. To what extent can evidence submitted by the leniency applicant (transcripts of oral statements or written evidence) become discoverable in subsequent private enforcement claims?

Section 39 paragraph 2 of the Cartel Act provides that the file of the Cartel Court is only accessible by third parties if all parties to the proceeding agree.

However, it has not been clarified in the past whether this provision may be circumvented by initiating a private damages claim and asking the Civil Court to produce the Cartel Court's file. In such case, some are of the opinion that the Cartel Court would have to follow such request for administrative assistance and forward its file to the Civil Court (where all parties to the civil proceeding could then access the content of the file). In the only completed private damages claim to date following a cartel law infringement (the case concerned a regional cartel of driving schools), the private claimant managed to get hold of the file of the Cartel Court by way of such request (this proceeding, however, did not involve leniency applicants).

The same result could also be achieved by joining a criminal proceeding as private party and to ask the Criminal Court to request disclosure of the Cartel Court's file. In the first leniency proceeding, the file of the Cartel Court has indeed been provided to the Criminal Court by way of such request.

Although in principle nobody may access the file of the FCA it cannot be ruled out that the FCA would forward its file if asked by a court for administrative assistance. Until now, the FCA seems to consider disclosing its file only to Criminal Courts, but not to Civil Courts (because in civil proceedings the private claimant has to prove its case, whereas in a criminal proceeding the case is investigated *ex officio*).

17.1 Can leniency information be subjected to discovery orders in the domestic courts?

The Austrian legal system does not provide for discovery orders as such, meaning that the claimant in principle has no possibility of getting access to information which is in the possession of the defendant. However, with regard to information/evidence which is already part of the file of the FCA/Cartel Court, see question 17 above.

As for civil proceedings, the Civil Procedure Code (*Zivilprozessordung*) provides that upon application of a party, the court may assign the other party to produce a document in its sole possession. There are certain documents which have to be produced but the law also provides for reasons why the production may be denied, such as an obligation to secrecy, business secrets, the private content of the document, or if the party would incriminate itself or certain other persons. However, even if no such reasons for a denial exist, the production of the document may not be enforced. It is, however, in the discretion of the judge how to assess such denial.

17.2 Can leniency information be subjected to discovery orders in foreign or domestic courts?

As described above, there is no clear practice yet with regard to requests for administrative assistance/discovery orders even in purely domestic cases. Therefore, it is not possible to make a clear statement as to how an Austrian court would react to a request of a foreign court or as to whether and how it would request disclosure from foreign courts for the purposes of a domestic proceeding.

18. Are there any precedents in which evidence from a leniency application has been discovered in a private enforcement claim?
There are no such precedents. However, private claimants might gain access to leniency applications via criminal proceedings which were initiated against certain individuals involved in anti-competitive conduct. It is to be expected that such documents will (sooner or later) be used also in private damage claim proceedings.

RELATIONSHIP WITH THE EUROPEAN COMMISSION'S LENIENCY NOTICE AND LENIENCY POLICY IN OTHER EU MEMBER STATES
19. Does the policy address the interaction with applications under the Commission Leniency Notice? If so, how?
The handbook does not explicitly address the interaction with the Commission Leniency Notice. An application for leniency on the European level or in any other jurisdiction has no effect on the competence of the Austrian Official Parties to investigate an infringement and to apply for the imposition of fines. Therefore, an undertaking applying for leniency should in any case do so before all competition authorities that may possibly be competent to investigate the relevant infringement.

20. Does the policy address the interaction with applications for leniency in other EU member states? If so, how? Does the authority accept summary applications in line with the ECN Model Leniency Programme?
With regard to the interaction with competition authorities of other member states, the same principles apply as with regard to the co-operation with the EU Commission (see question 18 above). Although the leniency handbook does not explicitly provide for the possibility of a summary application, the regular leniency form serves the same purpose for the first undertaking to inform the authority. An undertaking applying for leniency in another country or at European level may and should fill in the Austrian form and submit it to the FCA and thereby secure the first rank. If the EU Commission then takes over the case, the FCA would refrain from investigating the case.

RELATIONSHIP WITH SETTLEMENT PROCEDURES
21. What is the relationship between leniency and applicable settlement procedures? Are they mutually exclusive?
Other than on the European level, there is no formalised settlement procedure in Austria, although Austrian procedural law provides for the possibility of a settlement.

According to the Austrian bipartite system, the investigating authority (FCA) has no power to decide on the case, but may only apply to the Cartel Court for the imposition of a fine. If, in such a system, a settlement were to be agreed before court between the undertakings concerned and the FCA, no legally binding decision would be rendered (in contrast with proceedings before the European Commission). This may be considered detrimental for private enforcement. Furthermore, there is no benefit for the FCA in settling the case, when the court proceeding has already been initiated because at this point in time, the case is – in the view of the FCA – already court-proof. Finally, a settlement would only be sensible if all parties were to submit to it. Therefore, it may not be expected that the FCA would agree to settle a case if hardcore cartel infringements in multi-party proceedings are at stake.

REFORM/LATEST DEVELOPMENTS
22. Is there a reform underway to revisit the leniency policy? What are the latest developments?
Currently, a working group has been set up within the Federal Ministry of Justice to analyse whether leniency applicants in cartel cases shall be exempt from criminal liability. However, it is doubtful that in the foreseeable future such benefits for cartel cases will be introduced into the criminal legislature because for other offences no leniency programme (except for one provision concerning criminal organisations) exists.

Further developments are to be expected with regard to the case law on private enforcement since various damages claims following a major cartel case were submitted to the civil courts at the beginning of 2010.

Belgium

Crowell & Moring Thomas De Meese

BACKGROUND
1. What is the relevant legislation concerning the leniency policy and what is the enforcing body?

The Belgian Competition Authority consists of: (i) the Competition Service (*Service de la Concurrence/Dienst voor de Mededinging*) which is part of the Ministry for Economic Affairs; and (ii) the Competition Council (*Conseil de la Concurrence/Raad voor de Mededinging*), which is composed of: (a) the Council (*Conseil/Raad*); (b) the Auditorat; and (c) the Registry (*greffe/griffie*). The Auditorat leads the investigations with the assistance of the Competition Service. The Council is the decision making body.

The Belgian leniency programme was initially introduced following the adoption by the Competition Council and the Corps of Examiners (ie, the predecessor of the Auditorat) of a joint notice which was published in the Belgian Official Journal on 30 April 2004 (the 2004 Leniency Notice).

The reform of the Belgian Competition Act in 2006 (Act on the Protection of Competition coordinated on 15 September 2006, Belgian Official Journal, 29 September 2006 – the CCA) gave a more formal legal basis to the leniency programme. Article 49 of the CCA sets out the basic principle of the leniency programme and the basic procedural rules governing leniency applications.

The Competition Council subsequently adopted a new Leniency Notice which was published in the Belgian Official Journal on 22 October 2007 (the Leniency Notice). It entered into force on the same day.

The Leniency Notice is inspired by the European Competition Network's model leniency programme.

2. What are the basic tenets of a leniency/immunity programme? Is leniency available also for other types of competition law violations than cartels?

Article 49 of the CCA provides that the Competition Council can grant full or partial immunity for fines to undertakings or associations of undertakings which were involved in infringements of Article 2 of the CCA (the Belgian equivalent of Article 101 of the Treaty on the Functioning of the European Union).

The reference to Article 2 of the CCA in its entirety suggests that leniency should be available in respect of all types of infringements of Article 2 of the CCA, including vertical practices and horizontal agreements other than cartels.

However, the Leniency Notice explicitly states that it only applies to cartels ie, price fixing, market sharing, bid rigging, etc. The fact that one or more non competitors are also involved in the cartel will not preclude the application of the Leniency Notice. Vertical agreements and horizontal practices that are not cartels are explicitly excluded from its scope.

Leniency applications in respect of such other infringements of Article 2 of the CCA should nevertheless remain possible given the clear the wording of Article 49 of the CCA. Such applications will however not be covered by the Leniency Notice.

Article 49 of the CCA provides that full or partial immunity can be granted by the Council on the condition that the leniency applicant contributes to the demonstration of the existence of an infringement and to the identification of the participants to it, *inter alia* by:
- providing new information to the competition authority ie, information previously unknown to the authority;
- providing evidence of an infringement of Article 2 of the CCA the existence of which had not been established before; and
- admitting the existence of an infringement.

3. How many cartels have been unveiled and punished since the adoption of the leniency programme?

Two cartel decisions have been made public since the adoption of the leniency programme. One decision taken on 4 April 2008 with respect to a cartel in the chemical industry concerns the application of the 2004 Leniency Notice (Decision n° 2008-I/O-13 of 4 April 2008, Case CONC-I/O-04/0051, *Bayer AG – Ferro (Belgium) SPRL – Lonza S.p.A and Solutia Europe S.A.*). One cartel participant received full immunity. Three other participants benefited from reductions ranging from 35 to 12 per cent. The other decision was adopted on 20 May 2010 and relates to a cartel in the sector of radiators. It constitutes the first decision in which the new Leniency Notice was applied. According to the press release, one cartel participant received full immunity while another participant benefited from a reduction.

As far as we are aware, several other matters in which leniency applications were made are currently pending with the Belgian Competition Authority.

4. What is needed to be a successful leniency applicant? Is documentary evidence required or is testimonial evidence sufficient?

Neither the CCA nor the Leniency Notice rule out the possibility of submitting testimonial evidence. On the contrary, Article 49 of the CCA provides that full or partial immunity can be granted to applicants providing information (*inlichtingen/éléments d'information*) unknown to the Competition Authority. This wording seems to confirm that testimonial evidence must also be considered by the Competition Authority when assessing a leniency application.

The Leniency Notice explicitly refers to statements (*verklaringen/ declarations*) as a form of evidence that can be taken into consideration. Statements may, however, need to be made in writing.

However, the definition of 'significant added value' in the Leniency

Notice indicates a clear preference for documentary evidence over testimonial evidence.

TIMING
5. What are the benefits of being 'first in' to co-operate?
Article 49 of the CCA does not explicitly specify what the benefits of being 'first in' to co-operate are. However, the leniency criteria it lists refer to 'information not known to the competition authority' and 'evidence establishing the existence of an infringement that had not been proven before'. They confirm the practical importance of being 'first in'.

The Leniency Notice provides that the company that is first to provide evidence allowing the Competition Authority to conduct targeted dawn raids and/or to establish the existence of an infringement of Article 2 of the CCA or 101 of the TFEU can obtain full immunity.

The applicant who does not meet the conditions for full leniency but is first to provide evidence of an infringement representing significant added value compared with the evidence the Competition Authority already had at its disposal at the time of the application, can benefit from a 30 to 50 per cent reduction of the fine.

6. What are the consequences of being 'second'? Is there an 'immunity plus' or 'amnesty plus' option?
Article 49 of the CCA does not explicitly specify what the consequences are of being 'second'. However, as discussed in the answer to question 5, the criteria listed in this provision confirm the practical importance of being first and the increased difficulty in qualifying for leniency for any subsequent applicants.

Under the Leniency Notice, being second deprives the leniency applicant of the possibility of obtaining full immunity. However the 'second in' can still benefit from a 30 to 50 per cent reduction of the fine if it is the first to provide evidence that offers significant added value to the investigation. The reduction of the fine will be of 10 to 30 per cent if the 'first in' was unsuccessful in obtaining full immunity but did obtain a 30 to 50 per cent partial immunity.

There is no leniency plus or amnesty plus option.

7. Are subsequent firms given any beneficial treatment if they make a useful contribution? How are 'useful contributions' defined?
Article 49 of the CCA does not explicitly specify what the consequences are for subsequent applicants. However, as discussed in the answers to questions 5 and 6, the criteria listed in this provision confirm the practical importance of being first and the increased difficulty of qualifying for leniency for any subsequent applicants.

Under the Leniency Notice, any subsequent applicant offering significant added value may still qualify for a 10 to 30 per cent reduction of the fine.

Added value is defined in paragraph 15 of the Leniency Notice as the extent to which the evidence submitted increases, because of its nature and accuracy, the possibility for the Competition Authority to prove the facts.

Written evidence that is contemporaneous to the cartel shall have greater value than subsequent evidence. Direct evidence shall have greater value than circumstantial evidence. Similarly, evidence that is in itself sufficient to establish the facts will receive precedence over evidence which needs to be confirmed by other sources.

SCOPE/FULL LENIENCY
8. Is it possible to receive full leniency? If so, what are the conditions required to receive full leniency?

Article 49 of the CCA confirms the possibility for the Competition Council to grant full immunity to a leniency applicant. However, it does not specify what conditions have to be met for a leniency applicant to be granted such immunity. The actual conditions will be determined in a leniency declaration (*clementieverklaring/avis de clémence*) adopted by the Council following receipt of the leniency application (see the answer to question 10 below).

Under the Leniency Notice, full immunity can only be granted to an undertaking which:
- is the first to provide evidence allowing the Competition Authority to conduct targeted dawn raids (Type I.A. Immunity). This implies that the Competition Authority does not, at the time of the submission of this evidence, have sufficient elements to justify a dawn raid in respect of that infringement ; or
- is first to submit evidence allowing the Competition Authority to establish the existence of an infringement of Article101 TFEU or Article 2 of the CCA in Belgium (Type I.B. Immunity). This implies that the Competition Authority does not, at the time of the submission of this evidence, have sufficient evidence to establish the existence of that infringement.

8.1 Can ringleaders/coercers receive full leniency?
Full immunity is not available for undertakings or associations of undertakings who forced other undertakings or associations to participate in the cartel or continue to participate in it.

8.2 If there is a requirement to 'co-operate fully and on an ongoing basis' what does it entail?
Leniency applicants are required to co-operate fully and on an ongoing basis. This entails that they :
- do not destroy, tamper with or remove evidence;
- keep their (intention to file a) leniency application confidential until the *Auditorat* has filed the statement of objections with the Competition Council, unless agreed otherwise with the *Auditorat*;
- co-operates fully, swiftly, in good faith and on an ongoing basis with the Competition Authority during the investigation and supplies all the evidence with respect to the suspected infringement it has in its possession or can have access to, remains at the disposal of the

authorities to respond quickly to all questions which can help to establish the facts and uses its best endeavours to ensure that its current and former employees, executives and/or directors are available to appear before the Competition Authority.

8.3 Does the regulatory authority require the applicant to cease participation in the cartel conduct after its application?

The Leniency Notice requires applicants to cease their involvement in the suspected infringement no later than at the time they file their leniency application, except if requested otherwise by the Competition Authority in order not to jeopardise the chances of success of a dawn raid.

9. How many companies have received full immunity from fines to date?

To date, two companies have received full immunity from fines in Belgium – one under the 2004 Leniency Notice and one under the new Leniency Notice. As far as we are aware, several matters in which an application for full immunity was made are currently pending with the Belgian Competition Authority.

PROCEDURE

10. What are the practical steps required to apply for leniency?

Leniency applications should be filed in writing. They should be addressed to the *Auditeur-Général*, but sent to the Registry (*greffe*) of the Competition Authority.

Filing is possible by fax, email or registered letter (Postal address: North Gate, Koning Albert II-laan 16, 1210 Brussels, Tel: 02 277 52 72, Fax: 02 277 53 23, E-mail: *raco@economie.fgov.be*) on condition that eight copies of the application are hand delivered to the registry before close of business (4pm) on the next working day.

The applicant can request the Registry to acknowledge receipt of the application in writing. The acknowledgement mentions the date and time of receipt of the application.

The leniency application consists of a corporate statement and the substantiating evidence. The corporate statement can be submitted in Dutch, French, German or English. If it is submitted in English, a full translation into either Dutch, French or German must be submitted within two weeks. At the request of the applicant, the corporate statement can be made orally.

10.1 Full disclosure

The application needs to disclose:
- the name and address of the applicant and the name and position of any individuals that are or have been involved in the cartel;
- the name and address of the other undertakings that are or have been involved in the cartel and the name and position of the people who have been involved in it;
- a detailed description of the cartel (aim, activities, *modus operandi*,

Belgium

affected products and services, geographic scope, duration, estimated market volume, place, time, content and participants to cartel meetings and the nature of the cartel).
- information regarding existing or future leniency applications with respect to the cartel within and outside the EU; and
- all relevant evidence available to the applicant.

10.2 Initial contact/is there a 'marker' system?
An undertaking wishing to make an application for immunity may make initial contact with the Competition Authority. The Leniency Notice does not provide anything with respect to such initial contacts. Hence, no information can be provided as to the place in the queue nor can any assurance be given that the information communicated in this context will not be used to start an investigation.

The potential applicant for full immunity can, however, initially apply for a 'marker'. The marker application can be made orally or in writing. The marker protects the applicant's place in the queue for a given period of time and allows it to gather the necessary information and evidence in order to meet the relevant evidential threshold for full immunity. The application for a marker must indicate the reasons why a marker is needed and provide the name and address of the applicant, the parties to the cartel, the products and territories affected, the estimated duration of the cartel, the nature of the cartel and the existence of other leniency applications within or outside of the EU.

The *Auditeur* decides whether to grant a marker based on the seriousness and credibility of the reasons invoked by the applicant. If requested, the decision of the *Auditeur* is confirmed in writing.

If a marker is granted, the *Auditeur* will determine within which time period the applicant will need to complete its application. If the applicant does complete its application within this time period, its leniency application will be deemed to have been made at the time of the grant of the marker.

10.3 Conditional reduction of fine
Article 49 of the CCA states that, following receipt of the leniency application, the Council will, at the request of the *Auditeur-Général* and after receipt of the observations of the applicant, issue a leniency declaration laying out the conditions to be complied with for the applicant to benefit from full or partial immunity. This leniency declaration will be notified to the applicant. It will not be made public.

10.4 Final reduction
At the end of the investigation, the Council can, provided the conditions of the leniency declaration have been complied with, grant a reduction of the fine in its final decision, in proportion to the applicant's contribution to the establishment of the infringement.

11. Is there an optimal time to approach the regulatory authority?
Given the importance of being 'first in' or at least second or third in, time

is clearly of the essence. At the same time, it is obvious that 'going in' only makes sense if the applicant has gathered sufficient evidence to have a fair chance of offering convincing evidence and/or significant added value to the Competition Authority.

12. What guarantees of leniency exist if a party co-operates?
As described under question 10, following receipt of a leniency application, the Council will adopt a leniency declaration determining the conditions to be complied with for the applicant to obtain full or partial immunity. If the applicant was 'first in', the leniency declaration may specify that full immunity may be granted provided the conditions specified in the declaration are complied with. For subsequent applicants however, the declaration will give no assurances as to the percentage of the reduction they will be entitled to.

CONSEQUENCES
13. What effects does leniency granted to a corporate defendant have on the defendant's employees? Does it protect them from criminal and/or civil liability?
Belgian competition law does not provide for personal liability of employees for anti-competitive practices. There are no criminal sanctions for anti-competitive behaviour either. Hence, there is no need for the leniency programme to address the issue of liability of the defendant's employees. Paragraph 8 of the Leniency Notice explicitly states that it does not apply to physical persons who are not undertakings within the meaning of the CCA.

14. Does leniency bar further private enforcement?
Leniency does not bar criminal or private enforcement. However, it has to be kept in mind that Belgian law does not provide for criminal sanctions for anti-competitive behaviour.

As to private enforcement, Article 49 of the CCA only grants immunity for the administrative fines imposed by the Council. Hence, it does not affect civil liability or the rights of victims of anti-competitive practices to claim compensation. Paragraph 9 of the Leniency Notice explicitly confirms that the leniency applicant is not protected against the civil consequences of his participation in the infringement of Article 2 of the CCA.

PROTECTION AGAINST DISCLOSURE/CONFIDENTIALITY
15. Is confidentiality afforded to the leniency applicant and other co-operating parties? If so, to what extent? Is the identity of the leniency applicant/other co-operating parties disclosed during the investigation or in the final decision? Is information provided by the leniency applicant/other co-operating parties passed on to other undertakings under investigation? Can a leniency applicant/other co-operating party request anonymity or confidentiality of information provided?
Article 49 of the CCA explicitly provides that the leniency declaration is notified only to the leniency applicant concerned and that it is not made public.

However, the fact that a company applied for leniency will be mentioned in the final decision of the Competition Council, in particular in the section discussing the amount of the fine, if any.

Addressees of the statement of objections will have access to the corporate statement filed by the leniency applicant provided they undertake not to use it for any purposes other than the cartel investigation. Third parties will not be given access to the corporate statement.

Finally, it goes without saying that leniency applicants benefit from the ordinary procedural rules protecting their business secrets.

16. Is the evidence submitted by the leniency applicant protected from transmission to other competition authorities with whom the authority in question co-operates? If so, how?

Only corporate statements can be communicated to other competition authorities within the EU and only if the conditions for co-operation within the European Competition Network's Notice are complied with and the receiving authority offers guarantees in terms of confidentiality that are at least equivalent to those under Belgian law.

17. To what extent can evidence submitted by the leniency applicant (transcripts of oral statements or written evidence) become discoverable in subsequent private enforcement claims? Can leniency information be subjected to discovery orders in the domestic or foreign courts? Can leniency information submitted in a foreign jurisdiction be subjected to discovery orders in the domestic courts?

The rule is that leniency information cannot be used for any other purpose but the cartel investigation.

There is no discovery under Belgian law, but courts can order parties to submit relevant documentary evidence to them. In theory, the corporate statement and related evidence could be the subject of such a court order. We are currently not aware of any case regarding the question whether such measure could be ordered in respect of a leniency application filed with the Competition Authority.

The possibility of filing oral leniency applications is provided for in order to address the risk of discovery in countries such as the UK and the US.

18. Are there any precedents in which evidence from a leniency application has been discovered in a private enforcement claim?

No.

RELATIONSHIP WITH THE EUROPEAN COMMISSION'S LENIENCY NOTICE AND LENIENCY POLICY IN OTHER EU MEMBER STATES

19. Does the policy address the interaction with applications under the Commission Leniency Notice? If so, how?

The Leniency Notice provides for the possibility of a summary application for immunity applicants who have or intend to file a leniency application with the European Commission. The summary application is only available for immunity applicants of type I.A. It must contain the name and address of the applicant, the identification of the other parties to the cartel, the nature of the cartel, the member state where most of the evidence is likely to be found and the identification of the leniency applications that were or will be filed with other competition authorities within and outside the EU.

The applicant needs to provide swiftly any additional information requested by the *Auditeur*. If the *Auditeur* decides to proceed with the case, it will determine the time period within which the applicant will need to complete its application in order to qualify for a type I.A immunity. If the applicant does complete its application within this time period, this additional information and evidence provided will be deemed to have been submitted at the time of the summary application.

20. Does the policy address the interaction with applications for leniency in other EU member states? If so, how? Does the authority accept summary applications in line with the ECN Model Leniency Programme?
Leniency applicants need to inform the Competition Authority of other leniency applications filed within or outside the EU. However, the Leniency Notice does not in any other manner address the interaction with leniency applications in other EU member states nor does it provide for summary applications in this context.

RELATIONSHIP WITH SETTLEMENT PROCEDURES
21. What is the relationship between leniency and applicable settlement procedures? Are they mutually exclusive?
There is no fast track settlement procedure provided for in the CCA. The Leniency Notice does not contain any guidance regarding a possible interaction between leniency and settlements.

REFORM/LATEST DEVELOPMENTS
22. Is there a reform underway to revisit the leniency policy? What are the latest developments?
Some discussions are currently ongoing regarding the opportunity to introduce criminal sanctions for hardcore cartel activity in Belgium. In the context of these discussions, an extension of the scope of the Leniency Notice is being contemplated so as to encompass a potential immunity for criminal sanctions for individuals who contribute to the leniency application filed by their company/employer.

Brazil

Grinberg Cordovil e Barros Advogados Leonor Cordovil

BACKGROUND
1. What is the relevant legislation concerning the leniency policy and what is the enforcing body?
The main Brazilian law concerning leniency is Law n° 8884/94, as amended by Law n° 10149/00 (Articles 35-B and 35-C). A rule that has recently been enacted by the Ministry of Justice is also relevant (SDE Rule n° 456/10.).

Before 2000, leniency was not provided for the Brazilian legal system. In 2003, leniency eventually became an important tool for investigating cartels, which came to be the preferred targets among violators of economic order. The Brazilian authorities that cover cartel investigations are the Secretariat of Economic Law (SDE) and the Administrative Council for Economic Defence (CADE). The SDE is the investigating authority in charge of the execution of leniency agreements – an instrument which ensures benefit to the cartel's informant. The public prosecutor's office, whether federal or state, may also be a party to the execution of the leniency agreement, since cartel activity is a crime in Brazil.

CADE is in charge of the trial, and it may order gathering of new evidence if it deems it convenient. CADE does not have the power to approve or dismiss a leniency agreement but it can check if an applicant actually performed under the agreement and acknowledge the granted benefit.

At present, there is a serious trend towards taking antitrust disputes to court. This means that leniency cases, as well as all administrative proceedings, usually turn into litigation tried by the courts. No final decisions on leniency have been rendered by the courts as yet. However, starting with the early decisions, the Brazilian courts will be considered an important body in antitrust enforcement.

2. What are the basic tenets of a leniency/immunity programme? Is leniency available also for other types of competition law violations than cartels?
The basic tenet is co-operation, in exchange for either complete immunity from a penalty or the reduction of between one- to two-thirds of the penalty applicable to individuals or corporations which violate the economic order. The law also establishes that, in cases of crimes against the economic order, the execution of the leniency agreement interrupts the statute of limitation and prevents the public prosecutor's office from filing information with the courts.

In the administrative investigation, the applicants must plead guilty (after which a leniency agreement is executed) and must fully co-operate until the proceeding is completed (at trial).

In Brazil, the leniency agreement may be executed in the event of any violation of the economic order, but, up to now, leniency agreements have been executed only in cartel cases. The fight against cartels has been the top priority of the SDE since 2003.

3. How many cartels have been unveiled and punished since the adoption of the leniency programme?

Until now, there has been only one conviction by CADE resulting from a leniency agreement executed by the SDE (the private security firms cartel). There are no official statistics on the number of leniency agreements, but, pursuant to SDE's rough estimate, about 15 agreements have already been executed in Brazil, and 14 applications are under negotiation.

4. What is needed to be a successful leniency applicant? Is documentary evidence required or is testimonial evidence sufficient?

The applicant must be the first to identify itself and must promptly cease the practice. At the moment of application, the SDE should not be in possession of documents and information which allow proceedings to commence with a good chance of conviction (in this event, leniency will not be necessary). The applicant must be ready to admit to their participation and fully co-operate with the investigation.

It is important that the applicant supplies useful documents and holds data such as when the activity took place, how it operated and who took part in it, to supply to SDE. If there is more than one applicant for leniency, nothing will prevent, in theory, the authority from discarding a candidate – even if they made the application first – in favour of a second one who holds more information and evidence.

TIMING
5. What are the benefits of being 'first in' to co-operate?

Brazilian law only allows full leniency to the first individual and/or corporation who identifies itself as an informant. The benefits – full leniency or a reduction in the fine and protection from prosecution – will only be granted to the first informant. Penalties in Brazil may reach 30 per cent of gross turnover in the next preceding year for corporations, and up to 50 per cent of the amounts to be paid by the corporation, for individuals.

6. What are the consequences of being 'second'? Is there an 'immunity plus' or 'amnesty plus' option?

If the first in line executes the leniency agreement, the second in line will not be granted any benefit. However, if it identifies a second (unknown to the authorities) cartel and meets the requirements for leniency (for instance, not being the ringleader of the second cartel), it may get full administrative and criminal immunity for the second cartel and a one-third reduction in fine with respect to the first violation. The second cartel must be identified before the first one is taken to trial.

7. Are subsequent firms given any beneficial treatment if they make a useful contribution? How are 'useful contributions' defined?

Companies wishing to co-operate may execute the cease and desist commitment (TCC), set forth in Article 53 of Law n° 8884/94. To execute it, in the event of a cartel, the applicant must admit to its participation and offer full co-operation with the investigation and pay a pecuniary contribution to the Fund for the Defence of Diffuse Interests (a minimum of 1 per cent of gross turnover). The amount is negotiated by CADE. If it is executed, the investigation will be interrupted in relation to the informant and, at the end, if it has co-operated and paid the contribution, the investigation will be shelved without the conviction of the informant.

SCOPE/FULL LENIENCY
8. Is it possible to receive full leniency? If so, what are the conditions required to receive full leniency?

Yes, it is possible to receive full leniency. Corporations or individuals who committed the violation must co-operate with the authorities by identifying the other co-conspirators and helping to procure documents and information which serve as evidence of the violation.

8.1 Can ringleaders/coercers receive full leniency?

No, they cannot. Brazilian law is clear that the ringleader cannot receive the benefit of leniency. However, it may receive the benefit of 'leniency plus' if it informs against another cartel.

8.2 If there is a requirement to 'co-operate fully and on an ongoing basis' what does it entail?

Co-operation in Brazil includes supplying documents and data which help to identify the infringement and the participants therein at an initial stage. After the agreement is executed and the investigation begins, co-operation implies answering defendants' allegations, participating in the depositions by preparing questions for witnesses, formally making a deposition before the antitrust authorities, etc.

8.3 Does the regulatory authority require the applicant to cease participation in the cartel conduct after its application?

Brazilian law requires the individual or undertaking to completely cease its engagement in the cartel from the date the leniency agreement is offered.

9. How many companies have received full immunity from fines to date?

Until now, only one cartel case involving the execution of a leniency agreement has been tried. The cartel was formed by security firms which rigged public bids in the relevant state. The informant (a small enterprise) submitted documents and even wiretap recordings. CADE judged that it fully co-operated with the investigation and no penalties were imposed against it.

PROCEDURE
10. What are the practical steps required to apply for leniency?
The law does not set forth all the requirements. Rather, the SDE has been establishing them in practice:
- The applicant must call, schedule a meeting, or send an email to the Secretary of Economic Law or to its head of office, with basic information on the market, the relevant players and the date of the conduct. It may make a hypothetical inquiry to SDE about the availability of a specific market for a cartel informant.
- If the SDE's answer is affirmative, it will mean that it has no information on the practice. The applicant should provide SDE with the documents and information it collected. If it does not have all the information or documents to propose a leniency agreement, it may give only its name, the affected market, the geographic scope, the parties involved and, if possible, the duration of the violation.
- The applicant has 30 days to submit its proposal for a leniency agreement and may negotiate this leniency agreement for between six to 12 months.
- If an agreement is executed, the Secretary will forward the case to the Director of the Department of Economic Protection and Defence (the Director), in order to proceed with the investigation.

If the Secretary judges that the applicant is not fit to co-operate and execute the leniency agreement, or if the applicant decides not to sign the agreement, it may pass on to the next in line, if any. In this case, no information will be sent to the Director, who will not be aware of the existence of negotiations with the Secretary.

11. Is there an optimal time to approach the regulatory authority?
The applicant must approach as soon as it knows the violation, the affected market, the geographic markets affected and, if possible, the duration of the violation. The applicant must act quickly, since only the first one will receive the benefit. The important thing is to gather the initial data and 'ring the bell'. Later, the authority will give it, within three days, a letter attesting that the applicant was the first to approach the authority. The applicant will be granted a 30-day period to submit its leniency agreement proposal.

12. What guarantees of leniency exist if a party co-operates?
After the initial contact with the authorities, the marker will be executed by the Secretary, who will ensure that the party negotiates with the authority on an exclusive basis. However, there is no guarantee that the leniency agreement will be executed. This will depend on the information and documents that the applicant is able to give, on the possible contact which the authorities make with other jurisdictions and the applicant's

qualifications (not being the ringleader; if its participation led it to hold relevant information, etc).

Even after the execution of the leniency agreement, granting the actual benefits will depend on the co-operation of the interested parties. At the end, CADE will have the power to decide if they co-operated properly and if they deserve the benefits set forth in the law.

As already mentioned, there is only one precedent in Brazil and there are no judicial disputes on the subject. As the number of cases increases, there will be more certainty regarding the parameters for granting the benefits.

CONSEQUENCES
13. What effects does leniency granted to a corporate defendant have on the defendant's employees? Does it protect them from criminal and/or civil liability?
If a company wishes to extend the benefits to the employees who participated in the conduct, they must execute the leniency agreement and also plead guilty. If its employees do not wish to plead guilty and execute the agreement, they may be convicted at the end of the investigation. This is a strange situation, but it is possible: that a corporate defendant provides information which helps to convict one of its own employees. It may happen, for example, in cases where the employee's confession may harm investigations in other jurisdictions.

14. Does leniency bar further private enforcement?
No. The execution of a leniency agreement only ensures benefits regarding administrative penalties and criminal conviction. There is no provision in law ensuring that the successful applicant is protected against private enforcement. Were this so, the constitutionality of this provision would probably be an object of dispute. According to the Brazilian legal system, one cannot prevent those harmed by a cartel from claiming damages for their losses. This is a fundamental right, according to Article 5 of the Brazilian Federal Constitution. Actually, it would be unfair. There would be flagrant discrimination between those who bought from the applicant in relation to those who bought from the non-applicant defendant. Therefore, all those who sustained losses may file for indemnifications and damages pursuant to Article 29 of Law n° 8884/94, and the action may be filed even before the final administrative conviction.

PROTECTION AGAINST DISCLOSURE/CONFIDENTIALITY
15. Is confidentiality afforded to the leniency applicant and other co-operating parties? If so, to what extent? Is the identity of the leniency applicant/other co-operating parties disclosed during the investigation or in the final decision? Is information provided by the leniency applicant/other co-operating parties passed on to other undertakings under investigation? Can a leniency applicant/other co-operating party request anonymity or confidentiality of information provided?
According to the new rule, Portaria 456/2010, confidentiality is afforded to

Brazil

the leniency applicant until the final analysis by CADE.

During the time that the negotiations for executing the agreement are taking place, only the Secretary and its head of office have information on the case and on the terms provided by the applicant. After the execution of an agreement, the Director and its assistants will be aware of the case.

After execution of the agreement, if searches and seizures are required, the investigation will continue to be confidential until those procedures have been conducted at the defendants' premises. If they are not required, the investigation is usually disclosed to the public and the defendants are served process. The SDE publishes it on its website and in newspapers.

However, since leniency is a new concept in Brazil, it is not possible to ensure that confidentiality will be confirmed by the courts. In a recent decision, a judge ordered SDE to disclose the name of the applicants and the leniency agreements, based on the full right of defence argument.

Applicants may request confidentiality of their own information and documents before foreign authorities. Therefore, if the Brazilian authorities get in touch with foreign authorities, they may not transmit data and documents which may have been supplied by applicants, without the latter's authorisation.

16. Is the evidence submitted by the leniency applicant protected from transmission to other competition authorities with whom the authority in question co-operates? If so, how?

According to the procedure adopted by the Brazilian authorities (chiefly by the SDE), the co-operation with foreign authorities regarding a practice under investigation and concerning data and information supplied by applicants, may only be established with the express agreement of the applicant. The supplied documents and information will only be shared with the foreign authorities if this is agreed to either orally or in writing. The Brazilian authorities call this agreement a waiver.

17. To what extent can evidence submitted by the leniency applicant (transcripts of oral statements or written evidence) become discoverable in subsequent private enforcement claims? Can leniency information be subjected to discovery orders in domestic or foreign courts? Can leniency information submitted in a foreign jurisdiction be subjected to discovery orders in the domestic courts?

In Brazil, there are no precedents on this subject. However, from analysis of the Brazilian law and judicial precedents in cartel cases, it is fair to conclude that all evidence submitted by an applicant may be used in subsequent private enforcement claims. The evidence may be taken to the judicial proceeding by the administrative authority, if it is called to be a party to the proceeding and accepts it (this is not mandatory), or it may be taken by the plaintiffs to the action (since the administrative proceeding is available to the public and may be fully examined).

In recent cases, Brazilian judges have decided that they may analyse all the evidence submitted in the administrative proceeding. This judgment stems from the interpretation of Article 5 of the Federal Constitution, which establishes that no threat to a right may be excluded by examination of evidence by the courts.

In Brazil, however, the discovery mechanism does not exist as in other countries. There is no provision allowing the judge to require the parties to submit to the courts everything which was submitted in Brazil and other jurisdictions. Likewise, there is no legal provision ordering Brazilian judges, or the administrative authorities, to send information to foreign courts.

18. Are there any precedents in which evidence from a leniency application has been discovered in a private enforcement claim?
No, there are not. As already mentioned, leniency is a new subject in Brazil, and there has been only one conviction by the administrative authority involving leniency. There is news of private enforcement claims regarding this conviction but they are not far advanced. In this case, however, all the documents submitted at the administrative stage were submitted to the courts. It remains unknown whether the information will be taken into account by the judge when establishing damages.

RELATIONSHIP WITH SETTLEMENT PROCEDURES
19. What is the relationship between leniency and applicable settlement procedures? Are they mutually exclusive?
In order to receive the benefits of leniency, applicants have to execute an agreement in which they agree to co-operate and plead guilty to the practice. The SDE will start the investigation and the defendants will be served process. The defendants, if they wish to avoid the investigation, may execute a cease and desist commitment, in which they:
i) undertake to promptly cease the practice;
ii) plead guilty to the violation; and
iii) pay a financial contribution of no less than 1 per cent of their turnover, to be negotiated with CADE.

Several defendants may execute such commitments. However, the greater the number of parties that make commitments and plead guilty, the higher the amount to be paid in terms of the financial contribution will rise.

The investigation of those parties who execute a cease and desist commitment is suspended. If they comply with their obligations, the investigation is against them will be discontinued, with no application of penalties.

RELATIONSHIP WITH THE EUROPEAN COMMISSION'S LENIENCY NOTICE AND LENIENCY POLICY IN OTHER EU MEMBER STATES
20. Does the policy address the interaction with applications under the Commission Leniency Notice? If so, how?
Not applicable.

21. Does the policy address the interaction with applications for leniency in other EU member states? If so, how?
Not applicable.

REFORM/LATEST DEVELOPMENTS
22. Is there a reform underway to revisit the leniency policy? What are the latest developments?
The information provided above is already updated according to the new Rule no 456 of 15 March 2010. There is also a bill currently underway which will amend Law n° 8884/94. The bill makes slight amendments to Article 35, which provides for leniency. The chief two amendments are: i) the jurisdiction to execute leniency agreements will pass from the SDE to CADE; and ii) if the applicant fails to comply with the leniency agreement, it will be prevented from executing a new leniency agreement for the term of three years, counting from the trial date.

Bulgaria

Borislav Boyanov & Co Peter Petrov

BACKGROUND
1. What is the relevant legislation concerning the leniency policy and what is the enforcing body?
The principal piece of legislation setting out the basic rules on leniency is the Bulgarian Protection of Competition Act. The local antitrust enforcing body is the Commission for the Protection of Competition (the Commission), an independent body, elected by Parliament, consisting of seven members, which is supported by an administration of slightly more than 100 civil servants and other staff.

On the basis of the Protection of Competition Act, the Commission adopted a programme on immunity from fines or reduction of fines in case of participation of an undertaking in a secret cartel (leniency programme) on 10 February 2009, repealing an earlier leniency programme which had been in effect since 2004.

2. What are the basic tenets of a leniency/immunity programme? Is leniency available also for other types of competition law violations than cartels?
Under the Commission's programme and the Protection of Competition Act, leniency is available only in cases of a secret cartel. A 'cartel' is defined as an agreement or concerted practice among two or more undertakings – competitors in the relevant market, aimed at restricting competition by fixing prices or pricing conditions for purchase or sale, sharing of production quotas or sales or sharing of markets, including rigging of public bids or public procurement procedures.

Neither the Protection of Competition Act, nor the Commission's leniency programme provide information on when a cartel would be considered clandestine. This distinction may ultimately be irrelevant, since the law and the Commission's programme does allow cartels to apply for leniency even where the cartel is already known to the Commission, but the applicant provides decisive evidence in support of the authority's cartel investigation.

Leniency is not available for other antitrust violations, different from cartels.

3. How many cartels have been unveiled and punished since the adoption of the leniency programme?
For the first year following the adoption of its current leniency programme the Commission has issued one decision sanctioning a cartel discovered by it.

4. What is needed to be a successful leniency applicant? Is documentary evidence required or is testimonial evidence sufficient?

Normally the leniency application should be in writing. As an exception to that rule, the Commission will accept an oral application, subject to the applicant giving sufficient reasons for its request not to submit an application in writing. An oral application will still need to be accompanied by a full set of information, unless a marker is given during which the application should be supplemented with information and evidence. The Commission's rules on the application of the programme do not provide for the form of evidence – written or oral, for most of the facts that need to be disclosed. They do require, however, declarations to certify that: the applicant has stopped its participation in the cartel at the time of the application; it has not coerced other undertakings into participating in the cartel; it has not destroyed or forged evidence related to the application of the leniency programme; it has not disclosed the fact that it is considering or preparing for a leniency application or any part of its leniency application; it commits not to destroy or forge evidence; and not to disclose details of its application or the fact of its participation in the programme except to other authorities of the European Competition Network (ECN).

Even in the case of an oral application, a written document will be prepared in the form of a protocol of the oral submission. The rules on the application of the leniency programme require the protocol to be signed both by the Commission officers making the record and also by a person duly authorised to represent the applicant.

TIMING
5. What are the benefits of being 'first in' to co-operate?

The Protection of Competition Act provides two hypotheses of the 'first in' principle, which are alternative.

Firstly, full immunity from sanctions is offered to an undertaking which has provided first evidence, on the basis of which the Commission is able to obtain a court order for a dawn raid, provided that at the time of the application it has not been in possession of sufficient evidence and data to make an application for such court order.

Secondly, full immunity from sanctions is offered to an undertaking which was the first to provide evidence allowing the Commission to prove the clandestine cartel, provided the Commission has not granted conditional immunity to another undertaking in the first hypothesis above, or has not been in possession of sufficient evidence and data to make an application for a court order authorising a dawn raid and at the time of the application the Commission has not been in possession of sufficient evidence to issue a decision establishing the cartel infringement.

The 'first in' leniency applicant can receive full immunity from sanctions in the definitive decision of the Commission following its investigation, subject to complying with the conditions of the leniency programme. If the input of the applicant is not sufficient to allow full immunity, it can apply for partial immunity on the basis of the content and evidence attached to its original application.

6. What are the consequences of being 'second'? Is there an 'immunity plus' or 'amnesty plus' option?

The undertaking that is second can benefit from a reduction of sanctions of between 30 and 50 per cent provided that it has submitted, at its own initiative and before the conclusion of the proceedings before the Commission, evidence that has material significance in proving the cartel infringement. Partial immunity will be granted with the final decision, provided the undertaking has also complied with the other conditions of the leniency programme.

The Bulgarian leniency programme does not have specific 'immunity plus' provisions.

7. Are subsequent firms given any beneficial treatment if they make a useful contribution? How are 'useful contributions' defined?

Subsequent undertakings who have submitted at their own initiative and before the conclusion of the proceedings before the Commission, evidence that has material significance in proving the cartel infringement have a chance of receiving a reduction of fines (subject to complying with the requirements of the programme) of 20 to 30 per cent for the third (or second if no undertaking is receiving full immunity) and of 10 to 20 per cent for each subsequent undertaking.

SCOPE/FULL LENIENCY

8. Is it possible to receive full leniency? If so, what are the conditions required to receive full leniency? Can ringleaders/coercers receive full leniency? If there is a requirement to 'co-operate fully and on an ongoing basis' what does it entail? Does the regulatory authority require the applicant to cease participation in the cartel conduct after its application?

To receive full leniency, the applicant must:
- either be the first to submit evidence, on the basis of which the Commission is able to obtain a court order for a dawn raid, provided, that at the time of the application it had not been in possession of sufficient evidence and data to make an application for such court order; or
- be the first to provide evidence allowing the Commission to prove the clandestine cartel, provided the Commission has not granted conditional immunity to another undertaking, or has not been in possession of sufficient evidence and data to make an application for a court order authorising a dawn raid and at the time of the application the Commission had not been in possession of sufficient evidence to issue a decision establishing the cartel infringement.

In addition, to receive full immunity the applicant:
- must have discontinued its participation in the cartel at the time of the

Bulgaria

application and not continue it, unless specifically instructed otherwise by an express resolution of the Chairman of the Commission;
- must not have been a ringleader, who has coerced other participants to join or to continue their participation in the cartel;
- must not have destroyed or forged evidence relating to the application of the leniency programme;
- must not have disclosed in any way the fact that it is considering or preparing the submission of a leniency application; and
- must continue to co-operate with the Commission in accordance with the leniency programme.

To comply with its obligation for co-operation, the relevant undertaking must:
- provide to the Commission immediately the entire information and any evidence in connection with the claimed cartel that the undertaking receives in its possession or control;
- provide to the Commission timely answers to any information request related to the case;
- allow the Commission to take oral statements from all existing and former members of the staff of the relevant undertaking as well current and former managers;
- not destroy, conceal, or forge information or evidence relevant to the case; and
- not disclose in any way the fact of its participation in the leniency programme, any part of its leniency application, except to other authorities within the ECN.

9. How many companies have received full immunity from fines to date?

To date, the Commission has not issued decisions granting full immunity from fines, based on a leniency application.

PROCEDURE

10. What are the practical steps required to apply for leniency?

A leniency application must contain full disclosure of the details of the cartel. This includes:

a) an express admission to participation in the alleged cartel by the applicant;
b) full details about the corporate and contact details of the applicant;
c) names and position (current or former) of the individuals that have been involved on behalf of the applicant in the alleged cartel;
d) names, address and details, if known, of the other undertakings which have taken part in the alleged cartel;
e) names and position (current or former) of the individuals that have been involved on behalf of the other participants in the alleged cartel;
f) a detailed description of the alleged cartel, including: its objectives, activities, manner of functioning, participants; the type of the alleged cartel behaviour; the affected products and/or services; the affected

territories; an estimate of the value of the goods and services marketed which have been affected by the alleged cartel; the duration of the cartel; the dates, places and methods of contact, the content of the contacts, and the participants in the contacts among the members of the alleged cartel; and detailed explanations in connection with the evidence presented in support of the application;

g) evidence about the organisation and activities of the alleged cartel, held or under the control of the applicant (especially evidence dating from the period in which the cartel was active); and

h) information about any prior or future leniency applications to another competition authority, within or outside the EU, concerning the alleged cartel.

In cases where a leniency application has already been made or is in the process of being made before the European Commission, and the Commission is also well placed to investigate the case, the leniency applicant can submit a short-form leniency application to the Commission. A short-form application must contain the data under b), d), f) (only as regards the affected products or services, the affected territories, the duration and the nature of the cartel) and h) above, as well as information about the member states where evidence is likely to be located.

Initial contact should be made with the officers of the Commission, listed on its website. The rules on the application of the programme allow for first contact on a no-names basis, as well as the giving of informal guidance by the Commission in that respect. Upon filing a leniency application the undertaking is entitled to receive evidence of the date and exact time of submission.

The rules on the application of the programme allow for the setting of the so-called 'marker', where notwithstanding the requirements for completeness of the application, the undertaking will be allowed a time period to supplement its submission with evidence and data, while still retaining priority in the order of submission of the applications, provided the information and evidence is submitted within the deadline set by the Commission. In its request to receive a 'marker' the applicant, as a minimum, must provide the data under b), d), f) (only as regards the affected products or services, the affected territories, the duration and the nature of the cartel) and h) above, as well as state the reasons that have lead to the leniency application, and the reasons preventing it from submitting a complete application.

Following submission of the application and evidence, and based on its content and its priority, the Chairman of the Commission will grant or refuse to grant full or partial conditional immunity from sanctions. The applicant should be notified in writing.

If the Chairman refuses to grant conditional full immunity, the applicant is entitled to request that its application is being reviewed and considered as an application for partial immunity, ie, a reduction of the sanctions. Alternatively the applicant is entitled to withdraw its admission and the evidence attached to its application, but the Commission can request this evidence again through its normal information and document request procedure.

Final immunity will be granted with the decision of the Commission at the end of the proceedings. The final decision should set out the amount of the sanction from which immunity or reduction is granted. A final immunity/reduction may not be granted, even if conditional immunity were granted, if it is established that the undertaking has coerced other participants into taking part in the cartel or has not fulfilled the other conditions for immunity. The conditional immunity can also be withdrawn before the final decision, on these grounds.

11. Is there an optimal time to approach the regulatory authority?

Given the conditionality of the immunity or reduction of sanctions, applicants should be advised to make the application as early as possible in the proceedings or before proceedings have been initiated. Later applications should be made only where the applicant is reasonably certain that the evidence it presents would constitute a significant contribution to the Commission's case.

12. What guarantees of leniency exist if a party co-operates?

The Protection of Competition Act, as well as the Commission's leniency programme and the rules on its application, provide for a possibility, but not an obligation on the Commission, to grant immunity or a reduction of sanctions. In this respect, while the basic rules are set out in regulatory documents, from a legal perspective the authority has significant discretion in the assessment of how they are applied. Nonetheless, any failure to abide by these rules should be subject to judicial review within the framework of the appeals process against the Commission's final decision.

CONSEQUENCES

13. What effects does leniency granted to a corporate defendant have on the defendant's employees? Does it protect them from criminal and/or civil liability?

Bulgarian law does not provide for specific criminal liability of individuals participating in a cartel on behalf of undertakings or of undertakings themselves. The leniency programme does not lead to release of individual defendant's employees or managers from the administrative fines that are provided under the Protection of Competition Act for their participation in the infringement.

It shall also be noted that under Bulgarian law, undertakings have full recourse against employees and managers for damages caused by their wilful acts, eg the participation in a cartel. Accordingly, employees found to have engaged in cartel infringements will be fully responsible for any damages caused to the company as a result of their involvement. By limiting the damage caused to the undertaking by the imposition of a reduced fine or even no fine at all (full immunity), the leniency programme therefore permits the employee to reduce their own liability towards the undertaking.

14. Does leniency bar further private enforcement?
Leniency does not affect the possibility for injured parties to bring a private action for damages.

PROTECTION AGAINST DISCLOSURE/CONFIDENTIALITY
15. Is confidentiality afforded to the leniency applicant and other co-operating parties? If so, to what extent? Is the identity of the leniency applicant/other co-operating parties disclosed during the investigation or in the final decision? Is information provided by the leniency applicant/other co-operating parties passed on to other undertakings under investigation? Can a leniency applicant/other co-operating party request anonymity or confidentiality of information provided?
All information and evidence related to the application of the leniency programme, as well as the contents of any interviews held in this regard with the applicant/s are covered by the professional secrecy obligations of the officers of the Commission.

The information about the applicant's identity and its application, where it is to be used to request a court order authorising a dawn raid, are to be submitted separately as a legally protected secret to the court.

During the investigation, information provided by the leniency applicant should not be passed on to other undertakings under investigation. A leniency applicant can request confidentiality of the information provided.

In the final decision, information and evidence provided by the applicant should be disclosed, unless confidentiality has specifically been requested and granted by the Commission. It is questionable whether, if full or partial immunity is granted, this in itself would be considered confidential and not be revealed in the final decision.

16. Is the evidence submitted by the leniency applicant protected from transmission to other competition authorities with whom the authority in question co-operates? If so, how?
The leniency programme expressly provides that the data and evidence provided to it by leniency applicants can be shared within the ECN, subject to compliance with the guarantees laid down in paragraphs 40 and 41 of the European Commission Notice on co-operation within the Network of Competition Authorities (ECN notice).

17. To what extent can evidence submitted by the leniency applicant (transcripts of oral statements or written evidence) become discoverable in subsequent private enforcement claims? Can leniency information be subjected to discovery orders in domestic or foreign courts? Can leniency information submitted in a foreign jurisdiction be subjected to discovery orders in the domestic courts?
The intersection of the obligation of the Commission to protect confidentiality and the power of the courts to demand information from any person or authority is yet to be tested in respect of leniency. No specific provisions regulate the protection of the evidence and information provided

in the framework of a leniency application from discovery by the courts. To date the practice of the Commission, upon judicial review, has been to submit its entire file to the court, with the confidential information and evidence being submitted in separate folders to which the parties do not have access. However, nothing prevents the court from forming its judgment on the basis of such confidential information.

Another aspect of the intersection of public and private enforcement of antitrust violations is the binding nature of the Commission's decision upon the courts, once the decision has entered into effect. The grant of immunity from sanctions presupposes the finding of a cartel infringement. Therefore, in a possible civil damages litigation both the *corpus* and the *animus delicti* would have been established in a binding manner for the court, where the Commission's decision has come into effect. It would then be for the claimants in the private enforcement action to prove the causal link between the infringement and any damages they may have suffered, as well as the amount of such damages, in order to obtain a favourable award.

Any information to be obtained in respect of discovery before foreign courts would be subject to a letter rogatory request, subject either to a bilateral legal assistance treaty (Bulgaria has an extensive network of such bilateral treaties both in respect of civil and criminal cases), or of the provisions of Council Regulations (EC) 1348/2000 and 1206/2001 within the European Union. Where bilateral legal assistance treaties are applied, the primacy of local public interest in enforcing and terminating a cartel with the help of leniency, may be a valid ground for refusing compliance with the discovery request by the foreign jurisdiction.

The same applies for the requests of local courts to obtain evidence in respect of a leniency application made outside Bulgaria.

18. Are there any precedents in which evidence from a leniency application has been discovered in a private enforcement claim?
Based on publicly available information, no attempt has been made to discover a leniency application in a private enforcement claim in Bulgaria.

RELATIONSHIP WITH THE EUROPEAN COMMISSION'S LENIENCY NOTICE AND LENIENCY POLICY IN OTHER EU MEMBER STATES
19. Does the policy address the interaction with applications under the Commission Leniency Notice? If so, how?
The Bulgarian leniency programme provides specific rules in respect of applications submitted before the European Commission. The submission of such applications is not considered to allow full or partial immunity to be granted by the Commission, unless a short-form or a full application is submitted. The rules are ambiguous as to when the Commission would expect such an application to be submitted, noting that an applicant would be encouraged to submit such an application where it considers that the Commission is also well placed to investigate the case, within the meaning of paragraph 14 of the ECN notice.

A short-form application (whose content is akin to a marker application) would entitle the applicant to receive a confirmation about whether it has been the first undertaking to request leniency before the Commission, but cannot serve as grounds to initiate proceedings by the Commission in itself. If, however, based on the short-form application, the Commission decides that is also well placed to investigate the case, and considers the evidence sufficiently convincing, it will open a full investigation and request from the applicant the full scope of information that would be required under the normal leniency process. In that case the short-form application will serve as a marker, and allow the undertaking immunity, provided it submits the requested additional information within the deadlines set by the Commission.

The submission of a short-form application will be considered by the Commission as authorising it to share information received from the applicant with other authorities of the ECN, subject to paragraphs 40 and 41 of the ECN notice.

20. Does the policy address the interaction with applications for leniency in other EU member states? If so, how? Does the authority accept summary applications in line with the ECN Model Leniency Programme?
The submission of a leniency application before another competition authority of an EU member state will not be considered a leniency application before the Commission and therefore would not afford the applicant the possibility to obtain immunity from sanctions if the Commission starts its own investigation.

By contrast to the cases where a leniency application was submitted first to the European Commission, the Commission's leniency programme and rules do not allow specifically for the submission of a short-form application. Nonetheless the submission of a marker application could have a similar effect. The alternative would be the submission of a full scope leniency application to the Commission.

RELATIONSHIP WITH SETTLEMENT PROCEDURES
21. What is the relationship between leniency and applicable settlement procedures? Are they mutually exclusive?
The Bulgarian leniency programme does not deal with the issue of a possible correlation between leniency and a settlement in the framework of cartel proceedings. However, since the Protection of Competition Act excludes the possibility for a settlement in case of grave violations of the law, one can assume that a settlement is unlikely to be entered into in a cartel case.

REFORM/LATEST DEVELOPMENTS
22. Is there a reform underway to revisit the leniency policy? What are the latest developments?
The current Bulgarian leniency programme is the result of the local competition law reform that started at the end of 2008 with the adoption

of the new Protection of Competition Act. It is yet to be seen whether the new programme will be more effective when compared with the previous one. In that respect, the Commission will likely have to respond more categorically to potential applicants' concerns with stronger guarantees for objectiveness of the leniency process, the confidentiality of information and evidence submitted, and the prevention of the risk of a leniency application to facilitate private enforcement against them, particularly given Bulgaria's liberal system of class actions.

Cyprus

Andreas Neocleous & Co LLC Eleana Spyris

BACKGROUND
1. What is the relevant legislation concerning the leniency policy and what is the enforcing body?
The relevant legislation is the Protection of Competition Law 13(I)/2008 (the Law) and the enforcing body is the Commission for the Protection of Competition (the CPC).

2. What are the basic tenets of a leniency/immunity programme? Is leniency available also for other types of competition law violations than cartels?
The leniency/immunity programme is based on section 24 of the Law which states that the CPC is entitled to impose sanctions in the form of fines on any undertaking or group of undertakings found to be in violation of section 3 (restriction of competition) and section 6 (abuse of dominant position) of the Law. The same section gives the CPC the power to exempt and/or reduce the fine according to certain criteria and conditions to be determined by regulation issued at a later stage, where the undertaking or group of undertakings co-operates and/or provides a contribution or evidence which assists the CPC in proving the violation.

Accordingly, in theory leniency is available not only for cartels (which fall under section 3) but also for abuse of a dominant position under section 6. However, the draft leniency programme currently available only refers to, and is applicable to, infringements relating to section 3 of the Law and/or Article 101 TFUE.

3. How many cartels have been unveiled and punished since the adoption of the leniency programme?
No leniency programme is yet in force in Cyprus. Prior to the enactment of the Law in 2008 the CPC's website contained details of a programme, but this was never formally adopted or applied. The new programme is currently expected to be approved by the Minister of Commerce, Industry and Tourism (the Minister) and passed into secondary law in the form of a Ministerial Regulation as specified under the Law in the next few months. The following information is based on the draft leniency programme and is therefore subject to change. Nevertheless, it should give an indication of the upcoming legal framework.

4. What is needed to be a successful leniency applicant? Is documentary evidence required or is testimonial evidence sufficient?

Section 24 of the Law specifies that an exemption and/or reduction of the fine is available to an undertaking or group of undertakings which co-operates and/or provides such contribution or evidentiary material that assists the CPC in proving a violation of section 3 or section 6 of the Law. Thus, a successful leniency applicant must have co-operated or provided information that has significantly assisted the CPC in its investigations of an infringement of the Law.

The draft leniency programme provides that the leniency programme is applicable to cartels and/or concerted practices and/or agreements between two or more undertakings or groups of undertakings, that have as their object or effect the coordination of competitive behaviour in the market and/or a practical influence on competition through the fixing of purchase or sale prices, or other transaction terms, production or sales quotas, market sharing, including bid rigging, or the limitation of imports or exports and/or other anti-competitive behaviour to the detriment of other competitors.

Under the draft leniency programme, to be a successful leniency applicant (for full immunity) the undertaking must be the first to submit information and evidence either sufficient for the initiation of an investigation into an infringement of section 3 of the Law, or sufficient for the purposes of successfully proving the infringement.

A successful leniency applicant must co-operate fully, actively and on an ongoing basis from the date of the application for leniency, to the end of the procedure, and must provide without delay any information or evidence in its possession, or which may come into its possession at a later date with regard to the infringement. The leniency applicant must cease its participation in the cartel at the latest when it submits the evidence in accordance with the programme. It must not have encouraged or prompted other undertakings to take part in the infringement, and it must not disclose the fact that it has submitted a leniency application until the CPC has concluded the case. Moreover, the undertaking must not have participated in the past in a forbidden cartel and/or concerted practice and/or agreement for which a decision was rendered by a national competition authority or the European Commission.

The application provided by a successful leniency applicant should be in written form (as per rule 6 set out below in question 10) and should contain certain information with regard to the suspected infringement. Testimonial evidence will most likely be accepted; however it should be pointed out that written irrefutable evidence has greater value and is considered a much more useful contribution than evidence of a testimonial nature that requires confirmation. Thus the type of evidence provided (documentary/testimonial) plays a role in the CPC's assessment of how useful the applicant's contribution is.

TIMING
5. What are the benefits of being 'first in' to co-operate?
Complete immunity is available only to the first undertaking that submits information and evidence which is sufficient to commence an investigation with regard to a serious violation of section 3 of the Law and/or Article 101 TFUE, or to prove a serious violation of section 3 of the Law and/or Article 101 TFUE. The benefits of being 'first in' to co-operate are considerable, as long as the applicant fulfils the remaining criteria for full immunity as set out in the leniency programme.

When an undertaking despite not fulfilling the above criteria for full immunity, (i) is the first to comply with rule 18 of the programme, ie providing evidence of significant added value which fulfils the criteria of parts 1-4 of rule 5 (see below), and (ii) ceased its involvement in any infringement no later than the date of submission of the evidence, the CPC may reduce its fine from 30 to 50 per cent. The level of reduction within the range specified is determined on the basis of the point in time when the evidence was submitted and the added value such evidence represented. In addition, the CPC can also take into account the extent and consequences of the undertaking's co-operation after the date of submission of evidence.

6. What are the consequences of being 'second'? Is there an 'immunity plus' or 'amnesty plus' option?
An undertaking that is second to provide evidence of a violation of section 3 of the Law is not eligible to receive full immunity, but may benefit from a reduction of fines. The draft leniency programme provides that the second undertaking that complies with rule 18 of the programme as set out above is entitled to a reduction ranging up to 30 per cent of the fine. The level of reduction is determined on the basis of the point in time when the evidence was submitted, the added value provided and the extent and consequences of the undertaking's subsequent co-operation.

There is no 'immunity plus' or 'amnesty plus' option under the draft leniency programme.

7. Are subsequent firms given any beneficial treatment if they make a useful contribution? How are 'useful contributions' defined?
Beneficial treatment is given to subsequent firms in the event that they provide evidence of significant added value in accordance with rule 18 as set out above, in the form of a reduction of fines of up to 20 per cent.

The term 'evidence of significant added value' (useful contributions) is defined according to the extent to which it enhances, due to its nature and/or level of detail, the ability of the CPC to prove the possible infringement. Written evidence that is contemporaneous with the facts and that is directly related to them generally has greater value than evidence that relates to a later period or that is only indirectly related. In addition, the extent to which evidence requires verification from other sources in order to be considered credible against the other undertakings involved also affects its value, in that irrefutable evidence has greater value than evidence such as statements that require confirmation once contested.

SCOPE/FULL LENIENCY
8. Is it possible to receive full leniency? If so, what are the conditions required to receive full leniency?
Yes, it is possible to receive full leniency. The conditions required to receive full leniency are detailed below.

The applicant must be the first undertaking to submit information and evidence which is sufficient to enable the CPC to either instigate an investigation with regard to a serious violation of section 3 of the Law and/or Article 101 TFUE, or prove such a violation. Immunity is granted only if, at the time of submission of the application, the CPC did not have sufficient evidence to establish an infringement of section 3 of the Law and/or Article 101 TFUE, and if no other undertaking has been granted full immunity in relation to the infringement. In order to qualify for full leniency, the undertaking must be the first one to submit incriminating evidence relating to the possible cartel and/or concerted practice and/or agreement in the same time frame as the infringement that will allow the CPC to determine an infringement of section 3 and/or Article 101 TFUE.

In addition, the undertaking must comply with rule 5, ie it must co-operate fully, actively and continuously from the date of the application for leniency, to the end of the procedure, and must provide without delay any information or evidence in its possession, or which may come into its possession at a later date with regard to the infringement. It must completely cease its participation in the possible infringement at the latest when it submits the evidence in accordance with the programme. It must not have encouraged or prompted other undertakings to take part in the infringement, and it must not disclose the fact that it has submitted a leniency application until the CPC has concluded the case. Moreover, the undertaking must not have participated in the past in a forbidden cartel and/or concerted practice and/or agreement for which a decision was rendered by a national competition authority or the European Commission.

8.1 Can ringleaders/coercers receive full leniency?
No, in accordance with rule 5(3) an undertaking that has coerced other undertakings to take part in the infringement cannot be a candidate for full leniency, although it can request a reduction of its fine, if it fulfils the relevant criteria and conditions as set out in the programme.

8.2 If there is a requirement to 'co-operate fully and on an ongoing basis' what does it entail?
There is a requirement to 'co-operate fully and on an ongoing basis' which entails that the undertaking provide without delay all information and evidence with regard to the possible infringement, that it has or that may come into its possession at a later stage, in particular to:
- provide willingly and directly to the CPC all the relevant information and evidence that it has in its possession with regard to the possible

cartel and/or concerted practice and/or agreement;
- remain at the disposal of the CPC to answer willingly and directly any request of the CPC that will contribute to the verification of the relevant facts;
- place at the disposal of the CPC any current (and if possible, former) employees and executive staff for interviews with the CPC or by an authorised member of the CPC;
- not to destroy, counterfeit or conceal any relevant information or evidence with regard to the possible cartel and/or concerted practice and/or agreement; and
- not to reveal the existence or the contents of its application prior to the CPC having proceeded to a reasoned decision with regard to the case, unless agreed otherwise.

8.3 Does the regulatory authority require the applicant to cease participation in the cartel conduct after its application?
The regulatory authority requires that the applicant ceases participation in the cartel conduct at the latest upon its submission of the evidence mentioned in paragraphs (a) or (b) of rule 6 (set out below in question 10).

9. How many companies have received full immunity from fines to date?
To date there has been no undertaking that has received full immunity from fines.

PROCEDURE
10. What are the practical steps required to apply for leniency?

10.1 Full immunity
Prior to the official application for immunity, an undertaking may anonymously approach the chairman of the CPC to obtain guidance in relation to its application.

An undertaking that wishes to apply for leniency contacts the CPC and requests an initial priority number (marker system), until all the necessary information or evidence is collected so that it may then submit an official application for immunity from fines. The CPC will then issue the priority number provided the undertaking has submitted the following information:
- name and address of the applicant, the parties that are taking part in the alleged cartel and/or concerted practice and/or agreement;
- information with regard to the participation of the applicant in the alleged cartel and/or concerted practice and/or agreement;
- the affected product(s) and geographical area(s);
- the estimated time frame of the alleged cartel and/or concerted practice and/or agreement;
- the nature of the contentious issue; and
- relevant details with regard to other past or possible future applications for leniency to other competition authorities with regard to an alleged

cartel and/or concerted practice and/or agreement and a justification of the application for a priority number.

Once the application is submitted, the CPC issues a timetable by which the applicant must submit the required information and evidence deemed to have significant evidential value sufficient for the undertaking to be granted leniency. If the undertaking submits the information and evidence within the time frame set by the CPC it will be considered as having done so from the date on which it was given a priority number.

An undertaking which submits an application for immunity must provide the CPC with all the available evidence listed in rule 6 at the time when it submits its application. Alternatively it may initially provide the information and evidence on a hypothetical basis, by giving a list containing a detailed description of the evidence that the undertaking intends to provide to the CPC at a date to be stipulated by the CPC. The list must mention the specific nature and content of the evidence while maintaining the hypothetical nature of the application. Copies of documents from which confidential sections have been omitted can be used to illustrate the nature and content of the evidence.

The evidence that must be provided as set out in rule 6 is as follows:
a) written statement by the applicant undertaking that consists of (provided such information is known to the applicant at the time of submission of the application):
   (i) a detailed description of the possible cartel and/or concerted practice and/or agreement and specifically its aim, its activities and operations, the product or service it concerns, the geographical area it covers, its duration, and the extent to which the market is estimated to be affected, the specific dates, places, content and participants of the meetings with regard to the alleged cartel and/or concerted practice and/or agreement as well as the relevant explanation of the evidence submitted in support of the application;
   (ii) the name and address of the legal entity that submits the leniency application, as well as the names and addresses of all the other undertakings that participated (or that had participated) in the alleged cartel and/or concerted practice and/or agreement;
   (iii) the name, position, office address, and where necessary, home address of all the individuals, (to the extent that the applicant is aware of such individuals) that are or were involved in the possible cartel and/or concerted practice and/or agreement, including those that are involved on behalf of the applicant; and
   (iii) reference to other national competition authorities, within and outside the European Union, which the applicant has approached, or intends to approach with regard to the alleged cartel and/or concerted practice and/or agreement.
b) any other information regarding the alleged cartel and/or concerted practice and/or agreement that the applicant has in its possession or at its disposal at the time of the submission of the application, especially if that evidence dates from the time of the suspected infringement.

The Service of the CPC (the Service) provides the applicant with a proof of receipt of the application for leniency confirming the date and time of submission of the application. The CPC then directs the Service to examine the application within five business days to determine whether the requisite conditions are met, and provide a report to the CPC. If the undertaking has provided information and evidence on a hypothetical basis, the CPC then gives directions to the Service to examine the relevant list within seven business days and to certify that the nature of the evidence stipulated in the list fulfils the requirements of the programme.

If the undertaking fulfils the conditions for leniency, the CPC will grant full immunity from fines in its decision in relation to the suspected violation and will directly inform the applicant. Where the conditions are not fulfilled, the CPC will not grant full immunity and will immediately inform the undertaking concerned that its application for full immunity was not accepted.

The CPC does not examine other applications for full immunity until it has first decided on the application that precedes the others that have been submitted for the same possible infringement.

10.2 Reduction of fines

An undertaking that wishes to benefit from a reduction of fines must submit the relevant application to the CPC accompanied by sufficient evidence with regard to the purported cartel and/or concerted practice and/or agreement. The application must formally confirm that the evidence is provided voluntarily by the undertaking in order to support its application for preferential treatment in the form of reduction of a fine.

The Service of the CPC provides the applicant with proof of receipt of the application and for every document subsequently submitted, confirming the date and time when such documents were submitted.

The CPC does not determine an application for reduction of a fine until it has decided on any possible application for full immunity with regard to the same suspected infringement.

With the receipt of an official application for the reduction of a fine, the CPC directs the Service to examine and determine whether the evidence submitted by the applicant constitutes evidence of significant added value and complies with rules 5 and 18, and to submit a reasoned recommendation with regard to the application to the CPC within seven days.

11. Is there an optimal time to approach the regulatory authority?

In view of the fact that total immunity is only available to the first undertaking to provide evidence of an infringement it is advisable to approach the CPC as soon as possible to carry out all necessary actions as set out above to be the first to obtain a marker. The importance of being first in is also emphasised by the fact that the CPC will not examine other applications for full immunity until it has determined any preceding application in respect of the same possible infringement.

Even where the undertaking does not fulfil the criteria for full immunity, the sooner an application for reduction of a fine is made the better, as the CPC takes into account the time of submission of evidence in assessing the level of the reduction of the fine (first undertaking to fulfil the criteria for reduction of a fine: 30-50 per cent reduction, second undertaking obtains 20-30 per cent and any other undertaking fulfilling the criteria is eligible for a reduction of up to 20 per cent).

12. What guarantees of leniency exist if a party co-operates?

If a party co-operates and fulfils the criteria and conditions set out by the programme, the CPC is obliged to grant either full immunity or reduction of a fine depending on the criteria which the undertaking fulfils. It may only refuse immunity or the reduction of a fine if the applicant fails to meet all the conditions set out in the programme. Any false, inaccurate or misleading statements made by the applicant, or failure to fulfil a condition required at any stage of the procedure may result in a loss of the benefits of the programme.

If failure to co-operate fully with the CPC is used to justify a full or partial refusal of leniency, the applicant may apply to the Supreme Court of Cyprus for judicial review. Otherwise the CPC's decision is final.

CONSEQUENCES

13. What effects does leniency granted to a corporate defendant have on the defendant's employees? Does it protect them from criminal and/or civil liability?

There is no mention in the programme of the defendant's employees, other than that the undertaking applying for leniency is required to make its current (and if possible, past) employees available to the CPC for questioning.

14. Does leniency bar further private enforcement?

No. Immunity from a fine or a reduction of a fine does not protect the undertaking from any civil liability due to its taking part in an infringement.

PROTECTION AGAINST DISCLOSURE/CONFIDENTIALITY

15. Is confidentiality afforded to the leniency applicant and other co-operating parties? If so, to what extent?

If the CPC rejects an application for leniency it will not use the evidence or information submitted by the applicant without the applicant's consent, unless the evidence or information came to the knowledge of the CPC in another way.

The CPC protects the identity of the undertaking requesting immunity, as well as the contents of the undertaking's application for immunity and the undertaking's co-operation, until the CPC's reasoned decision is prepared, unless it is bound to reveal such identity by another legal obligation, or with the consent of the applicant.

The chairman, members and supplementary staff of the CPC and employees of the Service are all obliged to keep confidential information (such as business secrets, etc) which comes into their possession either due to the position they hold or in the course of execution of their duties. They must not disclose or publish such information unless and to the extent necessary for establishing an infringement of sections 3 and/or 6 of the Law and/or Article 101 TFUE and/or Article 102 TFUE, and for the purposes of applying the provisions of the Law.

It should also be noted that in order to receive full immunity the applicant may not reveal the fact that an application for leniency has been made, or any of the evidence or information submitted to the CPC, until the CPC has made its final decision on the suspected infringement.

15.1 Is the identity of the leniency applicant/other co-operating parties disclosed during the investigation or in the final decision?

The applicant's identity will be revealed in the final decision, unless agreed otherwise by the applicant and the CPC. The applicant is also under an obligation not to disclose details of its application or information provided to the CPC prior to its reasoned decision on the investigation.

15.2 Is information provided by the leniency applicant/other co-operating parties passed on to other undertakings under investigation?

The CPC is not required to notify all the administrative case file contents to the undertaking or group of undertakings against which the charges are made or the investigation is conducted. However, it must disclose documents on the file on which it will rely in its decision, apart from documents that constitute confidential business information, or provide a written list of such documents, so that the undertaking or group of undertakings is duly informed of all the documents that will be used by the CPC as evidence. The CPC may not base its decision on a document that has not been disclosed to the undertakings under investigation, and if it intends to rely on a document that it has not previously disclosed, the CPC must disclose the document and allow the other parties reasonable time to examine it and consider its contents.

Bearing in mind the above provisions, the CPC has the discretionary power to withhold access by interested third parties (physical or legal persons) to applications for leniency or reduction of a fine, as well to the accompanying evidence and information.

15.3 Can a leniency applicant/other co-operating party request anonymity or confidentiality of information provided?

Yes, please see above.

16. Is the evidence submitted by the leniency applicant protected from transmission to other competition authorities with whom the authority in question co-operates? If so, how?

The draft programme does not specifically address this issue. However, it appears that information will be made available to other EU competition authorities, since section 30 of the Law gives the CPC power to collect information necessary for the implementation of the Law, for and on behalf of other competition authorities of other EU member states, and since the draft programme requires the CPC to co-operate with other national competition authorities of the EU on matters relating to leniency programmes.

17. To what extent can evidence submitted by the leniency applicant (transcripts of oral statements or written evidence) become discoverable in subsequent private enforcement claims? Can leniency information be subjected to discovery orders in domestic or foreign courts?

The Law specifically states that in the case of a private enforcement claim for damages due to an infringement of the Law and/or Article 101 and 102 TFUE, the final decision of the CPC, the competition authority of another EU member state or the European Commission represents refutable evidence of the truth of its contents. The decision of the CPC, which will most likely make mention of the information given by the leniency applicant, is therefore discoverable in a subsequent private enforcement claim.

Although the programme does not stipulate in detail what is meant by a legal obligation, it should be noted that the CPC could be bound to reveal the identity of the leniency applicant, as well as the contents of the undertaking's application for immunity and its co-operation, where the CPC is bound to reveal such identity by another legal obligation. Such legal obligation could be in the form of a court order in a private enforcement claim.

17.1 Can leniency information submitted in a foreign jurisdiction be subjected to discovery orders in the domestic courts?
The CPC has not yet formulated a detailed approach to this issue.

18. Are there any precedents in which evidence from a leniency application has been discovered in a private enforcement claim?
No.

RELATIONSHIP WITH THE EUROPEAN COMMISSION'S LENIENCY NOTICE AND LENIENCY POLICY IN OTHER EU MEMBER STATES

19. Does the policy address the interaction with applications under the Commission Leniency Notice? If so, how?
The draft policy states that the CPC co-operates with the European Commission and the national competition authorities of other member states on matters with regard to the leniency programme. An undertaking's compliance with the leniency programme does not entail the granting of immunity or the reduction of a fine from the European Commission or from

the national competition authorities of other member states, on the basis of the information provided by the undertaking to the CPC. The undertaking may have to submit applications for leniency to the European Commission or to the national competition authorities of other member states which are affected by the restriction of competition under investigation.

In addition, where a full and complete leniency application has been submitted to the European Commission on the basis of the Commission Leniency Notice, the CPC accepts a *pro forma* application for immunity from the imposition of a fine (please see below).

20. Does the policy address the interaction with applications for leniency in other EU member states? If so, how? Does the authority accept summary applications in line with the ECN Model Leniency Programme?

Yes. As stated above, the CPC is required to co-operate with national competition authorities of other member states on matters with regard to the leniency programme. In addition, any application for leniency must state whether any similar application has been made or is intended to be made in another EU member state for the same infringement.

In the case where an undertaking has submitted a full leniency application to the European Commission or to another national competition authority which is *prima facie* the appropriate forum to handle the case, the CPC accepts a summary application which includes as a minimum, information on the following: relevant product/service; relevant geographical market; duration; parties involved; nature and type of infringement; the type of existing evidence; and the other competition authorities to which the applicant has applied, particularly the competition authority to which it has submitted a full application for leniency.

In such a case, the CPC issues a written confirmation to the applicant that it has received the application for immunity, and that it is the first to apply to the CPC for immunity for the specific infringement. The CPC may request further information from the undertaking in order to grant full immunity or a reduction of the fine, and such information must be provided within the time limit set by the CPC. The CPC may also decide to initiate an investigation of any possible infringement of the Law, setting a timetable for the applicant to submit its full application.

RELATIONSHIP WITH SETTLEMENT PROCEDURES
21. What is the relationship between leniency and applicable settlement procedures? Are they mutually exclusive?
The CPC has not yet formulated a detailed approach on this issue.

REFORM/LATEST DEVELOPMENTS
22. Is there a reform underway to revisit the leniency policy? What are the latest developments?
As mentioned above, the leniency programme has not yet been formally

Cyprus

adopted. An earlier leniency programme, which had been formulated in 2003 and published on the CPC website, was never implemented and became obsolete when the law was revised in 2008. It is expected that the current draft leniency programme will be approved and passed sometime in 2010.

Denmark

Kromann Reumert Jens Munk Plum, Erik Bertelsen & Morten Kofmann

BACKGROUND
1. What is the relevant legislation containing the leniency policy and what is the enforcing body?
It has now been almost three years since the bill introducing a leniency programme into the Denmark Competition Act took effect.

The leniency programme is based on the European Commission's Notice on immunity from fines and reduction of fines in cartel cases (OJ 2002 c45/3) and the ECN Model Leniency Programme. The key principles behind the leniency provisions are similar, although the unique division of competences between the competition authorities, public prosecution office and the Danish courts are also taken into account.

Under the current legislation, the Danish Competition Authority (DCA) will conduct most of the preliminary investigations. After these preliminary investigations the DCA decides on one of three possible main steps to take. Firstly, the DCA can simply close the case if it finds that there has been no infringement. Secondly, the DCA can pursue the case itself and issue a decision. If the DCA finds that an infringement has occurred which should result in a fine, the case will be handed over to a public prosecutor. The public prosecutor will then decide whether to bring the case before the Danish courts as a criminal proceeding. Thirdly, the DCA can hand the case over to the public prosecutor without investigating it themselves.

In 2007, along with the introduction of the Danish leniency programme, the DCA was given a new, limited power to impose fines for competition law infringements. Usually, fines can only be imposed by the criminal courts and the public prosecutor. With the leniency programme, the DCA is able to issue fines only where: (i) the undertaking has admitted an infringement; (ii) there exists an established court practice for the calculation of fines for similar infringements; and (iii) the public prosecutor has consented to the case being settled in this way and has approved the level of fines. The DCA cannot enter into discussions with an undertaking in this regard until the second and third requirements are fulfilled. Generally, cases that involve the imposition of fines will be handed over to the public prosecutor and the competence to impose fines for cartel infringements will lie with the criminal courts. It is rare that the DCA uses its powers – so far there have been no instances where the DCA has imposed fines.

In relation to fines, the amendments state that fine reductions may be granted by the 'investigating body', which suggests that both a public prosecutor and the DCA have power to grant fine reductions. A qualification on that power is that the investigating body – either the public prosecutor or the DCA – must first consult the other body.

The authorities do not have the same discretion as the European Commission in deciding the level of fine reduction for the second and third applicants. The Danish authorities only have discretion in any fine reduction for the fourth and following applicants.

Notably, the DCA does not have power to grant immunity to an undertaking. Since only the public prosecutor has the power to bring cartel cases before the courts, they hold the power to grant immunity, but only after consulting with the DCA.

Apart from the above exception, the competence to impose fines for cartel infringements lies with the criminal courts. If an infringement has been established, the court will decide on the amount of the fine. However, the court's discretion is limited by leniency granted by either the DCA or the public prosecutor during the administrative procedure.

The Danish leniency programme is based on well-established principles from the EU and its member states. However, the unique characteristics of the Danish legal system provide for some interesting challenges. The unique structure of the Danish authorities offers a certain degree of legal protection in the sense that two or more authorities must assess and agree on the case before any fine can be imposed. The two-authority structure can potentially result in extra administration and prolonged case-handling, but this has been addressed by strict internal deadlines between the authorities.

2. What are the basic tenets of a leniency/immunity programme? Is leniency available also for other types of competition law violations than cartels?

The leniency programme only applies to cartel infringements. However, the general provisions in the Danish criminal code may in principle apply to other types of competition law infringements. The practical scope of these provisions is limited.

Only the first undertaking to submit information about the cartel can obtain immunity from fines. Immunity from fines requires that the undertaking provides the DCA with information that the DCA did not have at the time of the application and this information enables the DCA to carry out a targeted inspection. If a targeted inspection has already been carried out, the information must enable the DCA to find an infringement.

The second and third applicants are eligible for a 50 per cent and 30 per cent fine reduction, respectively, that would otherwise have been claimed before the criminal courts by the public prosecutor. Subsequent applicants are eligible for a fine reduction of up to 20 per cent depending on the applicant's contribution to the cartel investigation. This is subject to the discretion of the authorities. It should be noted that in relation to the second and third applicants the authorities do not have the same discretion as the European Commission in deciding the level of reduction.

All applicants applying for a fine reduction must submit information which represents significant added value compared with the evidence already in the possession of the authorities at the time of the application. The term 'significant added value' will be interpreted in accordance with the practice of the European Commission.

In addition to the conditions mentioned above, the following conditions must always be satisfied in order for an undertaking to qualify for immunity or a reduction of the fine:
- the undertaking must co-operate with the authorities on a continuous basis throughout the procedure;
- the undertaking must end its involvement in the cartel immediately following its application; and
- the undertaking did not coerce other undertakings to participate in the cartel.

If an undertaking does not satisfy the requirements for leniency, the undertaking will not benefit from any favourable treatment. It should be noted that contrary to the European Commission's leniency programme an undertaking cannot, under the Danish rules, be eligible for fine reductions if it has coerced other undertakings to participate in the cartel. Ringleaders are, however, eligible for leniency.

There is no 'right of advancement' for subsequent applicants if a preceding applicant, as a result of non-compliance with the requirements, loses its place in the 'leniency order'.

Secondly, the leniency programme does not recognise the use of a marker system similar to that of the European Commission. Therefore, all information must be submitted at the time of the application. In particular, an applicant must provide the competition authorities with information and details of the applicant's participation in the cartel, the nature of the infringement, other participants, the relevant product and geographical markets and the duration of the cartel.

3. How many cartels have been unveiled and punished since the adoption of the leniency policy?

As at 2010, three years after the introduction of the leniency programme, there have been seven applications of which none has led to complete or partial leniency.

4. What is needed to be a successful leniency applicant? Is documentary evidence required or is testimonial evidence sufficient?

The applicant must submit 'all information' about the cartel infringement to which the applicant has access, comes into possession of, or which the undertaking can reasonably obtain. This includes both documentary evidence and testimonial evidence.

In particular, an applicant must provide the competition authorities with information and details of the applicant's participation in the cartel, the nature of the infringement, other participants, the relevant product and geographical markets and the duration of the cartel.

The applicant may not submit any false or misleading information, and the applicant may not conceal any facts about the cartel.

An applicant is also obliged not to inform any other members of the alleged cartel of the leniency application or disclose any information in connection with the ongoing investigation.

The DCA will accept summary leniency applications as provided for by the ECN model leniency programme.

Normally, an undertaking must admit participation in the cartel and the infringement in order to apply for leniency. It is unlikely that an undertaking would be required to admit an infringement of the Danish Competition Act in order to apply for leniency if this cannot be established with certainty at the time of application. However, it is also not possible to submit a hypothetical leniency application. In these cases, the undertaking may instead seek guidance from the authorities.

TIMING
5. What are the benefits of being 'first in' to co-operate?
There may be substantial benefits to being 'first in' to co-operate when considering the object of avoiding or reducing the exposure to fines. Other considerations regarding reputational damages, exposure to damage claims etc are of course also relevant. Immunity from fines is only granted to the undertaking if that undertaking is the first to submit the required information. If multiple applications for immunity are made in the same cartel case, the decisive factor in determining the order of priority is the point in time when the authorities received the information. Likewise, the possibility of a fine reduction is determined by the timing of the application.

It is the general principle that sentencing is based on the severity and duration of the infringements. Infringements are divided into three groups based on their severity. In Danish law, the basic fine for a less serious infringement, such as restrictive vertical agreements with limited effect on the market, lies between DKK 10,000 and 400,000 as a basic amount. A serious infringement, like resale price maintenance, can result in a fine ranging from DKK 400,000 and up to 15 million as a basic amount. Fines above DKK 15 million can be imposed for a very serious infringement, such as cartel activities or very serious abusive conduct. The basic amount will be adjusted according to the gravity and duration of the infringement. To date, the maximum fine imposed has been DKK 5 million for abuse of a dominant position.

All decisions rendered by the DCA are made public under the Danish Competition Act section 13(2). Similarly, all cases in which an undertaking has been fined are made public. Apart from this, neither the DCA nor the public prosecutor makes administrative procedures public. The question arises whether an undertaking that receives full immunity and thereby a withdrawal of charges can avoid the publication of the infringement.

The question is not addressed in the preparatory works. The purpose of the introduction of a leniency policy is not to give infringing undertakings a chance to avoid publicity or to limit the scope of civilian lawsuits. On this basis, it is in our opinion likely that an undertaking eligible for immunity cannot avoid the infringement being made public.

6. What are the consequences of being 'second'? Is there an 'immunity plus' or 'amnesty plus' option?

The second undertaking to apply for leniency does not qualify for immunity. Instead, the second undertaking is eligible for a 50 per cent fine reduction if the requirements mentioned above under questions 2 and 4 are fulfilled.

The principle of 'leniency plus' is not recognised by Danish competition law, and it is in our view unlikely that the Danish courts will take 'leniency plus' into consideration.

7. Are subsequent firms given any beneficial treatment if they make a useful contribution? How are 'useful contributions' defined?

As described above under question 2, the third undertaking to apply for leniency will be eligible for a fine reduction of 30 per cent while subsequent undertakings will be eligible for a fine reduction of up to 20 per cent if the requirements described under questions 2 and 4 are met.

The information submitted by a subsequent undertaking must meet the threshold of having significant added value to the DCA compared with the information already in the DCA's possession.

The European Commission has stated that 'the concept of 'added value' refers to the extent to which the evidence provided strengthens, by its very nature and/or its level of detail, the Commission's ability to prove the alleged cartel'. The threshold under the Danish rules is interpreted in accordance with this definition and in accordance with the practice of the European Commission.

SCOPE/FULL LENIENCY

8. Is it possible to receive full leniency? And, if so, what are the conditions required to receive full leniency? Does the regulatory authority require the applicant to cease participation in the cartel conduct after its application? Can ringleaders/coercers receive full leniency? If there is a requirement to 'co-operate fully and on an ongoing basis' what does it entail?

It is possible to receive full leniency, see questions 2, 4 and 5 above.

It is a requirement that the undertaking ends its involvement in the cartel immediately following its application for leniency. However, in certain cases, ongoing participation is needed during investigation of the cartel in order to avoid suspicion from other undertakings. The DCA cannot instruct the applicant to continue in the cartel – this would be contrary to the law regarding *agent provocateurs*.

Immunity or fine reduction is not available to applicants that took steps to coerce other undertakings into participating in the cartel. The term 'coerce' is to be interpreted in accordance with the Danish criminal code. Ringleaders are included in the leniency programme.

The requirement to co-operate fully and on ongoing basis entails that an applicant is required to co-operate fully with the authorities on a continuous basis and must therefore supply the authorities with all relevant information concerning the cartel infringement that it has or comes across under the investigation. Furthermore, the applicant must provide prompt answers to any questions the authorities may have during the investigation.

It is not possible at this point in time to fully assess the extent of the ongoing co-operation obligation since the leniency programme has not yet been applied in any specific decisions. However, the obligation to co-operate is likely to be similar to the obligations that follow from the European Commission's leniency programme.

9. How many companies have received full immunity from fines to date?
As at 2010, two years after the introduction of the leniency programme, no companies have received full immunity from fines.

PROCEDURE/CONFIDENTIALITY
10. What are the practical steps required to apply for leniency?
As a main rule, applications should be submitted to the DCA which will conduct the preliminary investigation. In cases where the public prosecutor is already investigating the cartel in question, the application can be submitted to the prosecutor's office. The DCA recommends that the application is submitted in person. This way the DCA can ask any questions they might have and thereby ensure that the applicant fulfils the information threshold. The DCA has established a special cartel hotline where undertakings can ask questions or apply for leniency.

The Leniency programme does not recognise the use of a marker system similar to that of the European Commission. All information must therefore be submitted at the time of application.

After submitting the application, the procedure is divided into three steps. First, the authority which receives the application issues a receipt which includes the identity of the applicant, the information given, and date and time of the application. The receipt will not contain any information on the leniency status.

Second, the competent authority informs the applicant of its leniency status. There is no time limit within which the DCA must inform the applicant of this. If the DCA, based on the information submitted, considers that leniency may be granted, the applicant must be informed in writing of its preliminary status in terms of being granted immunity or if the conditions for a fine reduction are likely to be satisfied.

The leniency status is subject to the undertaking's fulfilment of the requirements outlined under question 2 (above) and the applicant's status may therefore change during the investigation if the applicant fails to co-operate on a continuous basis or has failed to submit all information about the cartel, etc.

Third, the applicant is informed of its final leniency status with binding effect on the authorities and the courts upon completion of the investigation.

If an application for immunity is dismissed, it will automatically be treated as an application for a reduction of fine. There is no 'right of advancement' for subsequent applicants if a preceding applicant, as a result of non-compliance with the requirements, loses its place in the 'leniency order'.

11. Is there an optimal time to approach the regulatory authority?

The optimal time to approach the authorities depends on the circumstances. Among other things, it depends on whether immunity is still available or whether the cartel is already under investigation.

A preliminary but sufficiently detailed analysis must first be conducted in order to determine whether there has been an infringement under the Danish Competition Act. If this is the case, there must be an assessment of what the impact on the business will be if the infringement is made public. Depending on the circumstances it can be better to simply quietly end the infringement and make sure that future business complies with the competition rules. This way, no attention is drawn to the undertaking and the risk of subsequent claims for damages from competitors and/or customers is reduced. In this case no application should be submitted.

If it appears that a leniency application is the best way to proceed, the application should be submitted as soon as possible. The time of application is the only criterion for determining the leniency status. The leniency programme does not recognise the use of a marker system similar to that of the European Commission. It is the information submitted with the application which determines the leniency status. It is therefore necessary to gather enough information to ascertain that the undertaking satisfies the requirements for leniency.

Before an application is submitted it should be assessed whether the infringement has effects in other jurisdictions and if applications should be submitted to these accordingly.

12. What guarantees of leniency exist if a party co-operates?

When submitting an application for leniency, there are no guarantees as to whether leniency will be granted. It is for the DCA to decide whether the information submitted is sufficient to meet the threshold of the Danish leniency rules.

If the DCA informs the undertaking that the information submitted is sufficient for it to be granted leniency, the DCA is bound by this statement. If the undertaking fulfils the subsequent requirements as described under questions 2 and 4 the undertaking is guaranteed leniency.

It is the authority which handles the leniency application that decides if the subsequent requirements are fulfilled. If the authority decides that these requirements are not fulfilled the undertaking will be charged with the infringements. During the criminal proceedings the undertaking will then be able to have this decision tried before the courts.

CONSEQUENCES
13. What effects does leniency granted to a corporate defendant have on the defendant's employees?
In principle, persons can be prosecuted for cartel infringements under the Danish Competition Act. While the prime subject for prosecution for cartel infringements is generally the undertaking, it has become customary that management will also be charged with the offence if they personally participated in the infringement. Infringements of the competition rules are only sanctioned by fines.

The leniency programme applies equally to persons and undertakings. An undertaking's application for leniency automatically includes all current and former employees and members of the board of directors and/or the management. The application shall be made in writing and be signed by authorised representatives of the undertaking.

Applications made by former employees or persons currently employed by the undertaking but without authority to represent the undertaking will not include the undertaking. Applications from current employees with authority to represent the undertaking will only include the undertaking if this is explicitly mentioned in the application.

Even though an undertaking is given full immunity, a leniency application does not come without a price. A leniency application exposes the cartel to the public, potentially resulting in serious consequences for the undertaking and in some cases, its employees. Before submitting a leniency application, the undertaking will have to consider whether a leniency application is the right measure to take in the particular situation.

14. Does leniency bar further private enforcement?
No, as it is not the intention that civil lawsuits should be limited with the introduction of leniency.

PROTECTION AGAINST DISCLOSURE/CONFIDENTIALITY
15. Is confidentiality afforded to the leniency applicant and other co-operating parties? If so, to what extent? Is the identity of the leniency applicant/other co-operating parties disclosed during the investigation or in the final decision? Is information provided by the leniency applicant/other co-operating parties passed on to other undertakings under investigation? Can a leniency applicant/other co-operating party request anonymity or confidentiality of information provided?
There are no special provisions regarding confidentiality for undertakings seeking leniency. However, it is stated in the legislative history that it is important that leniency applications are treated with the highest possible level of confidentiality. This applies only during the investigation of the cartel.

As mentioned under question 5 above, all decisions made by the DCA are made public under the Danish Competition Act, section 13(2). It is not the intention that civil lawsuits should be limited with the introduction of leniency. Undertakings and other co-operating parties should therefore not expect to be able to keep the infringements confidential.

Additionally, the Danish Competition Act sets out specific rules regarding public access to documents. As a general rule only parties to a case can have access to the documents relating to it. A person is party to a case if it has significant, direct and individual legal interest. As a curiosity, it can be mentioned that an undertaking which has been subject to a dawn raid is not under current DCA practice considered a party to the case until the DCA has decided if the case should result in a decision or should be handed over to the public prosecutor.

The question arises whether competitors and/or customers who have a possible claim for damages pending the outcome of the investigation of the infringement can be regarded as parties. It must be considered doubtful that such 'parties' can be seen as having a sufficient significant, direct and individual legal interest to qualify as parties to the case. Not even a competitor/customer filing a complaint with the DCA will automatically be considered a party in the processing of the complaint.

Certain types of information submitted to the DCA will be held confidential at all times. The undertaking should at the time of submitting information highlight which information it regards as confidential.

16. Is the evidence submitted by the leniency applicant protected from transmission to other competition authorities with whom the authority in question co-operates? If so, how?

According to Danish law, under certain circumstances it is possible for the DCA to transmit evidence submitted by the leniency applicant to other competition authorities (under section 18 of the Danish Competition Act).

The DCA must ensure that the foreign competition authority is bound by similar professional secrecy. There must be reciprocity between the authorities – the DCA can only pass on confidential communication to another country's authority if the authority in question passes confidential information back where needed in the enforcement of the Danish competition rules. Further, the passing of the evidence must be 'necessary' – meaning that a passing is possible if it is done either to enable the foreign authority to enforce its national law or to make sure that Denmark fulfils its obligations under bilateral or multilateral accords with other countries.

17. To what extent can evidence submitted by the leniency applicant (transcripts of oral statements or written evidence) become discoverable in subsequent private enforcement claims? Can leniency information be subjected to discovery orders in domestic or foreign courts? Can leniency information submitted in a foreign jurisdiction be subjected to discovery orders in the domestic courts?

Evidence submitted by the leniency applicant is not covered by The Danish Act on Public Access to Documents on Public Files, which generally does not apply to competition law cases (except for minor exceptions). One of the main reasons is that companies would be more reluctant to share information with the DCA. Requests for access to files for persons which are not parties to proceedings are therefore refused. On the other hand, parties to proceedings can access the file and leniency information.

Legislation governing discovery orders is found in the Danish Administration of Justice Act. There are no special rules concerning leniency so the general rules about discovery orders apply. As part of the investigation of a public offence, a person who is not a suspect can be asked to submit documents if there is reason to believe that they will serve as evidence in the trial. Discovery orders can not be granted, if there is a disproportion between the measure and the significance of the case or the loss or burden, which it might cause. This reflects the general Danish principle of proportionality, which applies in all coercive measures in criminal proceedings.

18. Are there any precedents in which evidence from a leniency application has been discovered in a private enforcement claim?
No, we are still yet to see our first sanctioned leniency application in Denmark.

RELATIONSHIP WITH THE EUROPEAN COMMISSION'S LENIENCY NOTICE AND LENIENCY POLICY IN OTHER EU MEMBER STATES

19. Does the policy address the interaction with applications under the Commission Leniency Notice? If so, how?
The interaction with applications under the European Commission's leniency notice is not addressed thoroughly by the Danish leniency policy. However, the DCA will accept summary leniency applications if a full application is submitted to either the European Commission or competition authorities in other EU member states as provided for by the ECN model leniency programme.

Furthermore, the DCA will be able to submit data in accordance with the European Commission's notice on co-operation within the Network of Competition Authorities.

20. Does the policy address the interaction with applications for leniency in other EU member states? If so, how? Does the authority accept summary applications in line with the ECN Model Leniency programme?
See question 19 above. Further, it seems likely that the DCA will be able to release data submitted in the context of a leniency application to the competition authorities in Sweden, Norway and Iceland under the Nordic agreement on co-operation in competition matters on a confidential basis.

RELATIONSHIP WITH SETTLEMENT PROCEDURES
21. What is the relationship between leniency and applicable settlement procedures? Are they mutually exclusive?
Unlike the EC rules, there are no applicable settlement procedures in Danish competition law.

Denmark

REFORM/LATEST DEVELOPMENTS
22. Is there a reform underway to revisit the leniency policy? What are the latest developments?
The leniency policy entered into force on 1 July 2007.

Three years after the introduction of the leniency programme, we have yet to see the first leniency case decided under the Danish rules. Only time will tell if the Danish leniency programme will have the same effect as in other jurisdictions. In this respect, the very limited number of fines imposed for cartel activities so far under Danish competition law makes it difficult to assess the advantages involved in 'going lenient'.

The level of fines in the most recent cartel case (concerning price recommendations made by the Danish Christmas tree-growers association) was DKK 400,000, together with a personal fine of DKK 15,000 imposed on the director of the association.

The authors wish to thank associate Michael Byrup for his diligent assistance in preparing this text.

Estonia

Raidla Lejins & Norcous Tanel Kalaus & Heleri Tammiste

BACKGROUND
1. What is the relevant legislation concerning the leniency policy and what is the enforcing body?

The leniency policy is set out in the Estonian Competition Act (CA) and the Estonian Criminal Procedure Code (CPC).

The Estonian Competition Act (CA) prohibits agreements between undertakings, concerted practices and decisions by associations of undertakings, which have as their object or effect the restriction of competition, provided that they are not exempted under Articles 4(2), 5, 6 or 7 of the CA (Article 4 CA). The provisions of the CA should be interpreted in line with the relevant EC law.

The above prohibited activities qualify as criminal offences (Article 400 of the Penal Code) for which a natural person may be subject to a pecuniary punishment of 30-500 daily rates (calculated on the basis of their income) or up to three years' imprisonment. The same activities by a legal person (a legal person is deemed to act through its bodies and senior officials) may be subject to a pecuniary punishment of up to 10 per cent of the person's turnover in the financial year immediately preceding the year when the criminal proceedings were initiated (or – if the person has been acting for less than a year – in the year when the criminal proceedings were initiated). The pecuniary punishment of legal person shall not exceed EEK 250 million (approximately €16 million).

The main bodies enforcing the leniency policy in the pre-trial phase are the Estonian Competition Authority and the Prosecutor's Office. Certain orders (such as termination of the criminal proceedings in respect of the leniency applicant) can only be issued by the Office of the Prosecutor General. The punishments are determined (and diminished on grounds of leniency) only by the court.

2. What are the basic tenets of a leniency/immunity programme? Is leniency available also for other types of competition law violations than cartels?

The conditions for application of leniency are the following (Article 78 (5) CA):
- the leniency application has been submitted on the applicant's own initiative;
- the leniency application contains thorough information, including identities of the cartel participants, description of the cartel (affected goods, geographical extent, etc), all evidence available and known to the

applicant, etc;
- the applicant terminates its participation in the cartel as coordinated with the Prosecutor's Office, except when the applicant is asked to participate in surveillance activities;
- the applicant fully reveals and enables access to all evidence about the cartel that is known to the applicant;
- full co-operation by the applicant at its own cost;
- the applicant has not induced others to participate in the cartel and has not led the preparation or execution of cartel activities; and
- the applicant has not destroyed or hidden relevant evidence in bad faith nor revealed (without the permission of the Prosecutor's Office) the circumstances of leniency application or criminal proceedings.

In Estonia, full leniency is applied in the form of termination of the criminal proceedings by the Office of the Prosecutor General, ie the successful applicant will not be convicted. However, the Office of the Prosecutor General is free to decide the exact time when to terminate the criminal proceedings regarding the successful applicant.

The qualifying applicant is entitled to full leniency if (Articles 205 (1) and 205 (2) CPC):
- the applicant is the first to submit a leniency application which contains information that enables the initiation of criminal proceedings, provided that criminal proceedings have not been started prior to submission of the application; or
- the criminal proceedings have already been initiated by the time of submission of the leniency application, but the applicant is the first to submit a leniency application which includes evidence that, in the opinion of the Prosecutor's Office, significantly assists in bringing the charges, provided that no-one else is entitled to full leniency under the first ground.

Leniency may also be applied to applicants not qualifying for full leniency, if they otherwise meet the leniency conditions and have provided assistance in criminal proceedings. Their punishments will be diminished proportionally to the assistance they have provided in the criminal proceedings (Article 205 (3) CPC).

The leniency programme as such is only available for cartel violations and other anti-competitive agreements, practices or decisions. For other competition violations, criminal proceedings can be terminated or the punishment diminished on general grounds stipulated in the CPC and the Penal Code (e.g. termination of proceedings upon lack of public interest for criminal proceedings, provided that the suspect's or defendant's guilt is not severe; termination of proceedings upon significant assistance by the suspect or defendant in discovery and proving of a crime subject to high public interest for criminal proceedings; confession on one's own initiative, sincere remorse and active assistance in discovery of the crime as mitigating circumstances). Such general options are also applicable in cartel cases in addition to the leniency programme.

Estonia

3. How many cartels have been unveiled and punished since the adoption of the leniency programme?

Amendments to the Penal Code, CPC and CA establishing the leniency programme only entered into force on 27 February 2010. No information has been made public about any leniency applications.

Therefore, at the time of writing (middle of March 2010), it is not yet possible to estimate the effect of the leniency programme in Estonia.

4. What is needed to be a successful leniency applicant? Is documentary evidence required or is testimonial evidence sufficient?

For the conditions required to fulfil a leniency application, please see answer to question 2.

The leniency application must be submitted in a form that can be reproduced in writing. Apart from that, the leniency clauses do not stipulate specific requirements as to the form of evidence.

TIMING

5. What are the benefits of being 'first in' to co-operate?

Being the 'first in' is one of the prerequisites for qualifying for full leniency. However, if the applicant who is 'first in' does not satisfy all the conditions for full leniency (eg the application does not include enough evidence) then such opportunity shall pass on to the next applicant.

6. What are the consequences of being 'second'? Is there an 'immunity plus' or 'amnesty plus' option?

Punishments applicable to persons who do not qualify for full leniency due to not being the 'first in', but who otherwise meet the leniency conditions shall be diminished proportionally to the assistance provided by these persons in the criminal proceedings (Article 205 (3) CPC). This is not limited to those being 'second'.

Moreover, as indicated above, if the applicant who is 'first in' does not provide enough evidence then the applicant who is 'second' may still be granted full leniency.

There is no formal 'immunity plus' or 'amnesty plus' option. However, the general options described in the last paragraph of the answer to question 2 could still be applicable.

7. Are subsequent firms given any beneficial treatment if they make a useful contribution? How are 'useful contributions' defined?

Diminishing of the punishment proportionally to the assistance provided by the defendant is not limited to the defendant who was 'second', but is applicable to all defendants who otherwise meet the leniency conditions and who have provided assistance in the criminal proceedings.

SCOPE/FULL LENIENCY
8. Is it possible to receive full leniency? If so, what are the conditions required to receive full leniency?
Yes. For a description of the conditions required for full leniency, please see answer to question 2. All such conditions must be met. Only one applicant can benefit from full leniency.

8.1 Can ringleaders/coercers receive full leniency?
No.

8.2 If there is a requirement to 'co-operate fully and on an ongoing basis' what does it entail?
The applicant must co-operate fully and in good faith at its own cost.

The applicant may be asked to participate in surveillance proceedings. The applicant must reveal as well as enable full, open and undistorted access to all evidence known to it regarding the cartel.

8.3 Does the regulatory authority require the applicant to cease participation in the cartel conduct after its application?
Generally, yes. However, the applicant may be asked to participate in surveillance proceedings (Article 78 (5)2) CA).

9. How many companies have received full immunity from fines to date?
The leniency programme entered into force on 27 February 2010. To the best of our knowledge, it has not yet been applied to anyone in Estonia. There has been one case where the criminal proceedings were terminated with respect to one cartel member and its manager on grounds similar to those required for full leniency under the previous leniency regime (general grounds for termination of criminal proceedings stipulated in the CPC). However, the company and the manager were still made to pay certain amounts to the state revenues.

PROCEDURE
10. What are the practical steps required to apply for leniency?
Before approaching the Competition Authority, the relevant person needs to carry out a thorough analysis of the pros and cons of the application (including the degree of probability that criminal proceedings will be commenced and the possible severity of the punishment) and how certain it is that it will satisfy all the conditions required to qualify for leniency. Among others, this involves predicting the information that is already at the disposal of the investigators. Therefore the potential applicant may never be absolutely sure that it will qualify for and benefit from the leniency programme.

When foreign jurisdictions are involved, the potential applicant also needs to analyse and plan the order and timing of the submission of the applications to different authorities in order to benefit from leniency in all relevant jurisdictions (if possible).

Estonia

Once a decision has been made to apply for leniency, the applicant must file the application with the Competition Authority in a form that can be reproduced in writing and in a way that enables determination of the date and time when the application was received by the Competition Authority.

10.1 Full disclosure
Full disclosure of information and evidence known and available to the applicant is one of the preconditions for the application of leniency.

When submission of evidence together with the application is not technically possible, the evidence may be submitted in another way. When instant submission of evidence is not possible, then submission of a description of the evidence with a statement of its location is regarded as sufficient (Article 78 (2)4) CA).

After receipt of notification from the Competition Authority about the leniency application, the Prosecutor's Office may give the applicant additional time of up to one month for submission of evidence. If the investigator and the Prosecutor's Office review the evidence received and find no grounds for the application of leniency under Articles 205 (1) – 205 (3) CPC, the Prosecutor's Office shall notify the applicant about its rejection of the application (Article 205 (4) CPC).

10.2 Initial contact/is there a 'marker' system?
The Estonian leniency programme does not include a 'marker' system. In order to be considered for leniency (ie to determine the order of the applications), the applicant's name must be disclosed.

10.3 Conditional reduction of fine
When criminal proceedings have been terminated under the leniency programme and it later becomes evident that leniency should not have been applied, then the Office of the Prosecutor General may issue an order to renew the proceedings with respect to the successful applicant (Article 205 (5) CPC).

10.4 Final reduction
In Estonia, full leniency is applied in the form of termination of the criminal proceedings.

11. Is there an optimal time to approach the regulatory authority?
In order to be able to benefit from full leniency, an applicant needs to be 'first in' with the list of participants in the cartel as well as thorough information and evidence about the cartel. Moreover, by that time criminal proceedings should not have been initiated. Otherwise the applicant (even though 'first in') could qualify for full leniency only upon provision of evidence that, in the opinion of the Prosecutor's Office, significantly assists in bringing the charges.

Therefore, for the applicant to be as certain as possible that it will benefit from the leniency programme, then full information about the cartel should be provided as soon as possible.

12. What guarantees of leniency exist if a party co-operates?
The conditions for granting leniency (including full leniency) have been described in the answer to question 2.

Full co-operation is one of the prerequisites of applying for leniency in all cases. When the conditions for full leniency have been met, then the Office of the Prosecutor General must apply full leniency. However, when proceedings have been initiated prior to submission of the application, the prosecutors have more discretion to determine whether conditions for full leniency have been met.

All other applicants are entitled to have their punishment diminished proportionally to the assistance they provided in the criminal proceedings. However, the determination of this proportion as well as the initial punishment is at the discretion of the court, and the co-operating parties do not have any guarantees about punishment caps other than the general maximum of three years' imprisonment or EEK 250 million (approximately €16 million).

CONSEQUENCES
13. What effects does leniency granted to a corporate defendant have on the defendant's employees? Does it protect them from criminal and/or civil liability?
If a leniency application has been submitted on behalf of a legal person, then the legal person together with natural persons affiliated to it are considered to be the applicants. The group of affiliated natural persons includes the representatives, members, shareholders, members of management or supervisory bodies as well as employees (including those whose affiliation has terminated). However, leniency will not be applied to those affiliated natural persons who do not comply with the preconditions for application of leniency (including *inter alia*, termination of participation in the cartel, disclosure and enabling of access to evidence, and full co-operation) or who have been specifically excluded by the legal person in its leniency application (Article 78 (3) CA).

Full leniency granted to the legal person also protects the relevant affiliated natural persons from criminal liability.

Unlike the natural persons, other companies belonging to the same group or otherwise connected with the legal person who applied for leniency are not entitled to leniency alongside the applicant.

The Estonian leniency provisions do not address civil liability.

14. Does leniency bar further private enforcement?
Estonian leniency provisions do not address civil liability. Under Estonian law, even acquittal of the defendant does not bar civil law claims (Article 310 CPC).

At the same time, it is important to mention that punitive damages are not available under Estonian law. Also, to the best of our knowledge, there have been no cases of private damages claims submitted against cartel participants in Estonia.

Estonia

PROTECTION AGAINST DISCLOSURE/CONFIDENTIALITY

15. Is confidentiality afforded to the leniency applicant and other co-operating parties? If so, to what extent?

The only clause regulating confidentiality in leniency cases is Article 226(4)(1) CPC which states that a copy of the crime notice or other document serving as a basis for the initiation of criminal proceedings shall not be added to the statement of charges sent to the court if such document contains information about the leniency application.

Otherwise, information regarding and received from the applicant and other co-operating parties is treated pursuant to the standard rules of criminal procedure.

When talking about disclosure of information to the general public, data regarding pre-trial criminal proceedings may be disclosed only with the permission of the Prosecutor's Office to the extent determined by the Prosecutor's Office, provided that the data disclosed is in the interests of the criminal proceedings, the general public or the data subject and disclosure does not excessively (Article 214 CPC):

- further criminal activities or hinder the discovery of crimes;
- damage the interests of the Republic of Estonia or criminal proceedings;
- put a business secret at risk or damage the activities of a legal person; and
- damage the rights of the data subject or third persons, especially upon disclosure of delicate personal data.

Also, the data possessor must treat information gathered in the course of criminal proceedings as internal, except for data to be disclosed on the terms and conditions stipulated in the CPC (Article 35(1)1) of the Public Information Act).

However, parties to the criminal proceedings, including the other defendants, their defence attorneys and the victims, have access to the court file after conclusion of the pre-trial proceedings. Court hearings are generally open to the public, except for closed hearings in exceptional cases.

One should always keep in mind the fact that if a cartel is unveiled and all but one of its members are subject to criminal proceedings then the identity of the person who received full leniency is easily deduced. This is especially relevant considering the small size of the Estonian market.

15.1 Is the identity of the leniency applicant/other co-operating parties disclosed during the investigation or in the final decision?

The leniency programme entered into force on 27 February 2010. Therefore, at the time of writing (middle of March 2010) there had been no precedents establishing practice in this matter.

15.2 Is information provided by the leniency applicant/other co-operating parties passed on to other undertakings under investigation?

Although there is yet no practice in this matter, our best estimation is that such information will become accessible to the remaining defendants and their defence attorneys at the latest after conclusion of the pre-trial proceedings. Access to the file of the criminal proceedings is one of the most important rights of defence.

15.3 Can a leniency applicant/other co-operating party request anonymity or confidentiality of information provided?
Estonian leniency provisions do not give this specific right. There are general procedures in place to protect the anonymity of witnesses in exceptional cases.

16. Is the evidence submitted by the leniency applicant protected from transmission to other competition authorities with whom the authority in question co-operates? If so, how?
Estonian leniency provisions do not prevent transmission of such evidence.

17. To what extent can evidence submitted by the leniency applicant (transcripts of oral statements or written evidence) become discoverable in subsequent private enforcement claims? Can leniency information be subjected to discovery orders in domestic courts?
It is important to bear in mind that there is no institution of discovery in Estonian law comparable to discovery procedures in, for example, the United States. Civil courts can order a party or third persons to present documentary evidence upon the request of the other party. However, in such an application the other party must describe the document and its contents (Article 278 of the Estonian Code of Civil Court Procedure). Therefore, document request applications can only be submitted for documents that the other party is already aware of. There are no 'fishing expeditions' allowed.

There are no specific rules about requesting evidence submitted by the leniency applicant. Therefore, such evidence can be requested by a civil judge pursuant to the same order as other evidence gathered in criminal proceedings.

17.1 Can leniency information be subjected to discovery orders in foreign courts?
Estonian leniency provisions do not directly address this issue. Upon accession to the Convention on the taking of evidence abroad in civil or commercial matters (dated 18 March 1970), Estonia made an Article 23 declaration that a letter of request will be executed provided that: the corresponding proceedings have been initiated; the requested documents are identified by date, content or other information; and the letter of request presents reasons to believe that the documents are in the person's ownership, possession, or known to the person.

17.2 Can leniency information submitted in a foreign jurisdiction be subjected to discovery orders in domestic courts?
There is no institution of discovery in Estonian law – please see above. Whether foreign authorities will provide the requested documents will

depend on the rules applicable in the specific jurisdiction.

18. Are there any precedents in which evidence from a leniency application has been discovered in a private enforcement claim?
The leniency programme entered into force on 27 February 2010 and at the time of writing, to the best of our knowledge, no leniency applications as such have been submitted in Estonia.

As outlined in question 9 above, so far it has been possible to terminate criminal proceedings on grounds similar to leniency under the general rules of criminal procedure. However, we are not aware of any precedents in which evidence from corresponding applications (comparable to a leniency application) has been discovered in a private enforcement claim.

RELATIONSHIP WITH THE EUROPEAN COMMISSION'S LENIENCY NOTICE AND LENIENCY POLICY IN OTHER EU MEMBER STATES
19. Does the policy address the interaction with applications under the Commission Leniency Notice? If so, how?
In the spirit of international co-operation against cartels, especially within the EU, the leniency application must contain information about other competition authorities or other institutions to whom the applicant has submitted or intends to submit a leniency application (Article 78 (2)(5) CA). However, the Estonian leniency programme does not stipulate anything further about international co-operation.

20. Does the policy address the interaction with applications for leniency in other EU member states? If so, how? Does the authority accept summary applications in line with the ECN Model Leniency Programme?
The policy does not address the interaction with applications for leniency in other EU member states. The requirements for a leniency application stipulated in the CA and CPC are described in answer to question 2. The leniency programme does not foresee submission of summary applications.

RELATIONSHIP WITH SETTLEMENT PROCEDURES
21. What is the relationship between leniency and applicable settlement procedures? Are they mutually exclusive?
In the case of full leniency, criminal proceedings will be terminated without a conviction by an order of the Office of the Prosecutor General. Therefore, the optional settlement procedure will be relevant only to persons not qualifying for full leniency.

Among others, the settlement procedure will not be available (Article 239 (2) CPC):
- if not agreed to by the defendant, defence attorney or the prosecutor;
- in a criminal case with multiple defendants when at least one of the defendants does not agree to the application of a settlement procedure; or

- if not agreed to by the victim or civil law defendant.

However, the settlement is not binding on the court. If the court does not agree with the qualification of the crime, the amount of the civil claim, or the type or level of the punishment agreed in the settlement, then it will send the case back to the prosecutor's office (which will allow the parties to reach a new settlement) (Article 248 (1)(2) CPC).

REFORM/LATEST DEVELOPMENTS
22. Is there a reform underway to revisit the leniency policy? What are the latest developments?
No. The latest development is the establishment of a leniency programme in Estonia.

European Union

Herbert Smith LLP Adrian Brown & Hanna Anttilainen

BACKGROUND
1. What is the relevant legislation containing the leniency policy and what is the enforcing body?

The European Commission (the Commission) operates a leniency policy in respect of cartel conduct which infringes Article 101 of the TFUE.

The policy was first set out in the Commission's 1996 Notice on the non-imposition or reduction of fines in cartel cases. This notice was replaced by a revised version in 2002, which was replaced by a further version in December 2006, the Commission Notice on immunity from fines and reduction of fines in cartel cases (the Leniency Notice). The 2006 Leniency Notice was published in the EU Official Journal on 8 December 2006 (OJ C298/17) and came into force on that date.

The Commission's leniency policy operates in parallel with the leniency policies of the EU member states, which enforce their own national competition laws and also share competence with the Commission to apply Article 101 in their respective territories. The Commission's notice on co-operation within the network of competition authorities (OJ C101, 27/4/04) (the EC Network Notice) indicates that the Commission is likely to be considered the best placed [European] authority to carry out an investigation (and hence the most appropriate recipient of a leniency application) where the effects of the cartel activity are felt in more than three EU member states. However, as a leniency application to the Commission will not be considered an application for leniency to an EU member state, and an applicant may be exposed under a member state's national competition law, prospective applicants are advised to seek leniency from all competition authorities competent to apply Article 101 in the territory affected by the infringement which may be considered 'well placed' to act against the infringement.

The European Competition Network (the network of the national competition authorities of the member states and the Commission – ECN) has sought to alleviate the burden of multiple leniency applications by introducing the ECN Model Leniency Programme which includes, among other things, a model for a uniform summary application to be submitted to national competition authorities when the applicant intends to seek immunity/leniency from the Commission. The uniform summary application model which was introduced in September 2006 requires adoption into the leniency policies of EU member states in order to take effect. According to the ECN's report on the state of convergence of the member states' leniency programmes, published in October 2009, 23 member states have to date adopted a summary application model (those that have not are Cyprus, Estonia, Slovenia and Malta).

Quite separate from the Commission's leniency policy is the availability of a reduction in fine for mitigating factors, including effective co-operation by an undertaking beyond its legal obligation to do so. However, the Commission's Guidelines on the method of setting fines imposed pursuant to Article 23(2)(a) of Regulation No 1/2003 (the Fining Guidelines) make it clear that such co-operation will only be considered a mitigating factor if it takes place outside the scope of the Leniency Notice.

2. What are the basic tenets of the leniency/immunity programme? Is leniency available also for other types of competition law violations than cartels?

The Commission's leniency policy covers undertakings which have participated in secret cartels that may infringe Article 101 TFUE who wish to terminate their involvement and inform the Commission of the existence of the cartel.

The Commission's definition of a cartel is limited to agreements and/or concerted practices between competitors aimed at restricting competition (such as agreements to fix prices, allocate production or sales quotas, share markets or engage in bid rigging). Unlike the position in the UK, the Leniency Notice does not cover vertical price fixing (resale price maintenance).

As the Commission currently has no powers to impose penalties on individuals other than undertakings, there is no leniency policy for individuals.

The leniency policy offers immunity (full leniency) for the first undertaking to come forward with information, and a sliding scale of lenient treatment (partial leniency) for those undertakings that come forward subsequent to the first applicant.

In order to qualify for immunity, the applicant will need to provide information that meets the relevant immunity threshold. The immunity threshold applicable will depend on whether immunity is sought before or after a Commission inspection (dawn raid). If immunity is sought prior to an inspection, the applicant will need to provide information which is sufficient to enable the Commission to carry out a targeted inspection. If immunity is sought after an inspection, the applicant will need to provide information which is sufficient for the Commission to find a breach of Article 101 of TFUE.

The applicant will also need to meet the conditions for obtaining immunity which require the applicant to, among other things, provide the Commission with all evidence relating to the cartel and make employees and directors available for interview by the Commission. The applicant will also be ineligible for immunity if it coerced other participants to join or remain in the cartel. The full list of conditions for immunity is set out in the response to question 8.

Leniency applicants that come forward subsequent to the first immunity applicant may be eligible for lenient treatment in the form of a reduction in fine (partial leniency) if they provide evidence that represents 'significant added value' as compared with the evidence already on the file. The Leniency Notice makes it clear that evidence which requires little or no corroboration provides greater value than evidence which requires corroboration. The first undertaking to submit evidence that provides significant added value (after the initial immunity applicant) will receive a reduction of 30–50 per cent; the second undertaking to submit significant added value will receive a reduction of 20–30 per cent and the third undertaking to submit significant added value will receive a reduction of 20 per cent. The exact level of leniency will be determined at the end of the administrative procedure and will depend on the time at which the evidence was submitted and the extent to which it represents added value.

Applicants wishing to apply for immunity or lenient treatment need to make a formal application to the European Commission. This will usually take the form of a corporate statement and the submission of evidence which meets the relevant immunity threshold, or in the case of an applicant for partial leniency, the submission of evidence which provides significant added value.

Applicants for immunity (full leniency) may also make use of either the marker system or a hypothetical application. The marker system will enable an undertaking to protect its place in the leniency queue while it gathers the evidence required to make a formal application, while a hypothetical application allows an undertaking to check whether the Commission considers the information it holds meets the immunity threshold, without disclosing the identity of the undertaking or the infringement.

Neither the marker system nor the hypothetical application procedure are available to cartel members that are not the first undertaking to come forward, ie those seeking a reduction in fine (partial leniency).

3. How many cartels have been unveiled and punished since the adoption of the leniency programme?

The EU first adopted a leniency policy in 1996 (Commission Notice on the non-imposition or reduction of fines in cartel cases [1996] OJ C207/4). This was replaced by a new policy in 2002 (Commission Notice on immunity from fines and reduction of fines in cartel cases [2002] OJ C45/2, 'the 2002 Leniency Notice') which was subsequently replaced by the current policy in December 2006 (Commission Notice on immunity from fines and reduction of fines in cartel cases [1996] OJ C298/17).

There have been 73 cartel infringement decisions by the Commission since 1996.

4. What is needed to be a successful leniency applicant? Is documentary evidence required or is testimonial evidence sufficient?

An undertaking will be eligible for total immunity (ie full leniency) if it is the first cartel member to provide the Commission with information and evidence which will enable the Commission to either: carry out a 'targeted' inspection in connection with the alleged cartel; or find an infringement of Article 101 TFUE in connection with the alleged cartel.

The first case covers the scenario where an applicant comes forward prior to a Commission inspection (dawn raid), while the second case covers the scenario when a Commission inspection has already taken place. In both cases, the applicant must be the first cartel member to come forward to the Commission.

Immunity will only be granted under the first scenario above, if the Commission does not already possess sufficient information to carry out an inspection or find an infringement, and the applicant provides information which will enable the Commission to carry out a 'targeted inspection'.

The Commission has explained that this immunity threshold reflects its expectation that cartel members should be able to provide it with 'insider' information on the cartel that would enable the Commission to better target its inspection with more precise information as to, for instance, what to look for, and where, in terms of evidence. The assessment as to whether the information is sufficient to enable a targeted inspection will be carried out on the basis of type and quality of the information submitted by the applicant and will not take into account whether a given inspection is successful or whether it has been carried out.

Immunity is only available under the second scenario, if the Commission did not have sufficient evidence to find an infringement of Article 101 TFUE, and the applicant provides incriminating evidence that originates from the time of the infringement, which would enable the Commission to find an infringement of Article 101 TFUE.

In both cases, the Leniency Notice requires applicants to submit a corporate statement which contains detailed information and evidence regarding the alleged cartel arrangement, including (*inter alia*) the specific dates, locations, content of and participants in alleged cartel contacts.

An immunity applicant is also required to meet the cumulative conditions for the grant of immunity (set out in response to question 8 below). One of these conditions requires the applicant to co-operate genuinely, fully, on a continuous basis and expeditiously with the Commission. The Commission has prescribed that, as part of this condition of co-operation, an applicant must provide the Commission with all information and evidence available to the applicant regarding the cartel and make its employees and directors available for interview by the Commission.

Importantly, the Leniency Notice expressly contemplates that the Commission may, on the applicant's request, accept an oral corporate statement (provided the applicant has not already disclosed the content of the corporate statement to third parties). An oral corporate statement may be preferred in order to limit the possibility that it could be discoverable in civil proceedings, both in Europe and in the US.

Applicants, who are not the first to request immunity may be eligible for a reduction in fine that would otherwise be imposed upon them (partial leniency). In order to qualify for partial leniency, an undertaking must provide the Commission with evidence of the alleged infringement which represents 'significant added value' with respect to the evidence already in the Commission's possession.

The concept of 'added value' refers to the extent to which the evidence provided strengthens, by its very nature or its level of detail, the Commission's ability to prove the alleged cartel. In this respect, the Commission will generally consider written, contemporaneous evidence to have a greater value than evidence subsequently established, and incriminating evidence directly relevant to the facts in question will generally be considered to have a greater value than evidence which is only indirectly relevant. Similarly, the degree of corroboration required from other sources before the evidence can be relied upon will also impact on the value of the evidence – compelling evidence will be attributed a greater value than evidence such as witness statements which require corroboration if contested.

An undertaking requesting partial leniency is required to meet the same conditions as that of an immunity applicant with one exception: partial leniency, unlike immunity, is available to a cartel member which coerced another undertaking to join or remain in the cartel.

Further detail on the procedure for applying for either immunity or a reduction in fines is set out in the response to question 10 below.

TIMING
5. What are the benefits of being 'first in' to co-operate?
Total immunity is only available to the first undertaking to come forward and provide the Commission with requisite information relating to the cartel. Undertakings which are not the first to come forward are not eligible for total immunity.

6. What are the consequences of being 'second'? Is there an 'immunity plus' or 'amnesty plus' option?
Undertakings which are not the first to come forward are ineligible for immunity (full leniency). An undertaking which comes forward subsequent to another leniency applicant will, however, be eligible for a partial reduction in fine if they provide the Commission with evidence of the alleged infringement which represents 'significant added value' and they meet the relevant conditions.

The Leniency Notice does not provide for an amnesty plus option. However, if an applicant for lenient treatment is the first undertaking to submit compelling evidence and that evidence is used by the Commission to establish additional facts increasing the gravity or duration of the infringement, the Commission will not take such additional facts into account when setting a fine to be imposed on the applicant that provided that evidence.

7. Are subsequent firms given any beneficial treatment if they make a useful contribution? How are 'useful contributions' defined?
Yes, a cartel member that comes forward subsequent to another leniency applicant may receive a reduction in the fine that would otherwise be imposed, provided the cartel member supplies evidence which represents

'significant added value' with respect to the evidence already in the Commission's possession, and meets the first four (cumulative) conditions set out in response to question 8 below. An applicant for partial leniency does not need to meet the fifth condition that an immunity applicant must meet, remaining eligible for partial leniency even if it did take steps to coerce another cartel member to join or remain in the cartel.

As explained under question 4 above, the concept of 'added value' refers to the extent to which the evidence provided strengthens the Commission's ability to prove the cartel – either by the level of detail of the evidence or its very nature. In making this assessment, the Commission will consider written evidence from the time of the cartel to have greater value than evidence subsequently established. Likewise, incriminating evidence directly relevant to the facts in question will have greater value than evidence which is only indirectly relevant and compelling evidence, which does not require corroboration, will be attributed a greater value than evidence – such as statements – which will require corroboration if tested.

The level of reduction (which will be decided by the Commission at the end of the administrative procedure) will be determined according to the following bands:

- the first undertaking to provide significant added value is eligible for a reduction of 30-50 per cent;
- the second undertaking to provide significant added value is eligible for a reduction of 20-30 per cent; and
- subsequent undertakings that provide significant added value are eligible for a reduction of up to 20 per cent.

In order to determine the level of reduction within each of these bands, the Commission will take into account the time at which the relevant evidence was submitted and the extent to which it represents added value.

Applications for partial leniency may be disregarded by the Commission if they are submitted after the statement of objections has been issued.

SCOPE/FULL LENIENCY

8. Is it possible to receive full leniency? And, if so, what are the conditions required to receive full leniency? Can ringleaders/coercers receive full leniency? If there is a requirement to 'co-operate fully and on an ongoing basis' what does it entail? Does the regulatory authority require the applicant to cease participation in the cartel conduct after its application?

Yes, full leniency (total immunity from fines) is available if the undertaking is the first cartel member to come forward and provide the Commission with either (a) information and evidence which will enable the Commission to carry out a targeted inspection in connection with the alleged cartel; or (b) if an inspection has already been carried out, information and evidence which will enable the Commission to find an infringement of Article 101 TFUE in connection with the alleged cartel.

In addition to being the first cartel member to come forward, the

applicant must meet the following cumulative conditions to qualify for total immunity:
1. the undertaking must provide the Commission with:
   (a) a corporate statement which describes the cartel arrangements and includes: the names and addresses of cartel participants; the names, position, work addresses, and if necessary home addresses, of all individuals involved in the cartel, and information on approaches made by the undertaking to other competition authorities; and
   (b) all other evidence relating to the alleged cartel in its possession.
2. the undertaking must co-operate genuinely, fully, on a continuous basis and expeditiously from the time it submits its application throughout the Commission's administrative procedure. As part of this obligation, the applicant must:
   (a) provide the Commission promptly with all information and evidence regarding the cartel;
   (b) respond promptly to any Commission request which may contribute to establishing the facts;
   (c) make current (and if possible, former) employees and directors available for interviews with the Commission;
   (d) not destroy, falsify or conceal information relating to the cartel; and
   (e) not disclose the fact or content of its application before the Commission issues a statement of objections, unless otherwise agreed.
3. the undertaking must refrain from further participation in the alleged cartel immediately following its application except for what would, in the Commission's view, be reasonably necessary to preserve the integrity of the inspections;
4. the undertaking must not have destroyed, falsified or concealed evidence of the alleged cartel at any time when the undertaking was contemplating making the application to the Commission, nor disclosed the fact or content of its contemplated application to any party (other than other competition authorities); and
5. the undertaking must not have taken steps to coerce other undertakings to join or remain in the cartel.

In respect of 1(a), an applicant will only need to provide the home addresses of individuals involved in the cartel, if this information is necessary to the Commission investigation and it is available to the undertaking. The Commission may carry out inspections of other premises, including the homes of directors, managers or other members of staff, if a reasonable suspicion exists that relevant books or other records related to the business or the cartel are being kept in these premises.

The obligation in 1(b) is subject to the important qualification that an applicant should not take any measure in preparing its application that would jeopardise the inspection. An applicant should therefore inform the Commission if there is a risk that internal inquiries carried out for the purposes of completing an application may alert other cartel members prior to an inspection.

European Union

The exception contemplated in 2(e) is intended to address the conflict that may arise between the obligation on an immunity applicant under the Leniency Notice not to disclose the fact of an actual or intended leniency application with its legal obligations (eg, as a listed company) which may require the undertaking to make such an application public.

It is also worth noting that the obligation not to destroy, falsify or conceal evidence of the alleged cartel in point 4 covers the period when the applicant was contemplating making an application, as well as the period after the application was made.

Immunity will only be granted if the information provided by the applicant meets the relevant threshold for immunity: ie if the information and evidence is submitted prior to an inspection, it must enable the Commission to carry out a targeted inspection or, if the information is submitted after an inspection, it must enable the Commission to find an infringement of Article 101 TFUE.

The conditions for lenient treatment (partial leniency) are identical to those for immunity (full leniency) except that a cartel member found to have coerced other cartel members to join or remain in the cartel remains eligible for partial leniency, but not for immunity.

9. How many companies have received full immunity from fines to date?

Between 2002 and 2009, 27 decisions were taken on the basis of the 2002 or 2006 Leniency Notice. Those cases contained 28 immunity applications and 74 applications for a reduction in fines (where several immunity applications were received for the same alleged infringement, the first application was counted as an immunity application and the subsequent ones as applications for a reduction of fines unless the first application for immunity was rejected). Of the 28 immunity applicants, 20 were granted full immunity. Up to the end of 2009, the Commission had granted immunity under the 2006 Leniency Notice in one decided case. We understand, however, that a large number (well over 50) of immunity applications have been received by the Commission on the basis of the 2006 Leniency Notice.

PROCEDURE/CONFIDENTIALITY

10. What are the practical steps required to apply for leniency?

Initial contact

An undertaking wishing to apply for immunity or lenient treatment should contact one of the Commission officials involved in operating the leniency policy. The Commission has a dedicated fax line for leniency applications but recommends that an applicant first make telephone contact with a member of the Commission's leniency team by calling one of the dedicated telephone numbers (+32 2 298 41 90 or +32 2 298 41 91). Contact can be made directly by the undertaking or via its legal adviser.

10.1 Applying for immunity (full leniency)

An undertaking seeking immunity may either initially apply for a marker or immediately proceed to making a formal immunity application, which can also initially be made on hypothetical terms.

The marker system is a key new feature of the 2006 notice. A marker can be sought by an applicant from the Commission and if granted, will protect the applicant's place in the 'leniency queue' for a specified period, allowing the undertaking time to gather the information and evidence necessary to make a formal application. In order to obtain a marker, the applicant must identify itself and supply information on the alleged cartel including its duration, the other participants and the affected product(s) and territories. If a marker is granted, the Commission will set a period within which the applicant has to perfect the marker by submitting a formal application (a corporate statement) and all information and evidence available to it. If the applicant perfects the marker within the period set by the Commission, the information and evidence provided will be deemed to have been submitted on the date on which the marker was granted.

An undertaking (via its legal adviser) is also able to make an initial approach to the Commission on hypothetical terms in order to ascertain whether the evidence in its possession would meet the immunity threshold, without disclosing the identity of the applicant or the infringement. Under this procedure the applicant is required to provide a detailed descriptive list of the evidence that it proposes to disclose at a later agreed date and the Commission has recommended that copies of documents redacted to remove information which would identify the applicant should also be provided. Once the Commission has reviewed the list of information to be provided, it will verify whether the evidence described meets the relevant threshold and conditions. Following disclosure of the information described (no later than the date agreed with the Commission), and verification by the Commission that the evidence corresponds to the description, the applicant will be granted conditional immunity.

The Commission has emphasised in its Revised Leniency Notice Q&A that a marker and a hypothetical application serve different purposes and are appropriate in different circumstances: a hypothetical application enables companies to ascertain whether evidence in their possession would meet the immunity threshold and involves disclosure of the evidence (albeit by means of description or edited copies) while a marker is granted to protect an applicant's place in the queue while evidence is collected. The Commission has made it clear that a hypothetical application cannot be combined with a marker request. Once a marker has been obtained or guidance received following a hypothetical application, the applicant then needs to provide the Commission with all relevant evidence and information and a corporate statement (in effect, submitting the full formal application).

The Commission will inform the applicant if immunity is not available or if the conditions for obtaining immunity are not met (eg it appears that the applicant has coerced other participants to take part in the cartel). The applicant may then either withdraw its application or request the Commission to consider its application as a request for partial leniency.

The grant of immunity will be conditional until the end of the administrative procedure. If at the end of the administrative procedure the Commission finds that the applicant has not fulfilled the conditions for immunity, the undertaking will not benefit from full leniency/immunity. This will mean that immunity will be withheld if an applicant is found to have coerced other participants to join or remain in the cartel, or has failed to co-operate fully, on a continuous basis and expeditiously with the Commission.

10.2 Applying for lenient treatment (partial leniency)
There is no marker system for applicants seeking partial leniency. It is also not possible for such applicants to submit a hypothetical application.

An applicant for partial leniency must submit a corporate statement to the Commission and provide information and evidence which meets the threshold for obtaining leniency – 'significant added value'. If an applicant makes any voluntary submissions of evidence separately from the formal application, the applicant should identify, at the time the submission is made, whether it wishes that evidence to be treated as part of its application.

The Commission will not make a decision on an application for partial leniency before it has taken a position on any existing applications for immunity (full leniency).

The Commission will inform the applicant of its preliminary conclusion as to whether the evidence submitted by the applicant constitutes significant added value no later than the date on which the statement of objections is issued.

The final position, and the degree of lenient treatment, will not however be evaluated until the end of the administrative procedure. The Commission will determine in any such final decision:
- whether the evidence provided by the undertaking represented significant added value with respect to the evidence already in the Commission's possession at that time;
- whether the conditions for obtaining lenient treatment had been met; and
- the exact level of reduction from which an undertaking will benefit within the specified bands.

An undertaking will not receive any reduction in fines under the Leniency Notice if it fails to meet the conditions for partial leniency.

11. Is there an optimal time to approach the regulatory authority?
Total immunity is only available to the first cartel member to provide information to the Commission in relation to the cartel activities and apply for immunity.

In order to ensure that an undertaking secures a marker as the first in the queue, the undertaking should make contact with Commission officials and request a marker as soon as possible after identifying the basis for the suspected infringement. Alternatively, if the undertaking is not sure whether the evidence it holds meets the relevant immunity threshold, the undertaking could, via its legal adviser, submit a hypothetical application seeking guidance from the Commission as to whether the evidence held meets the relevant threshold.

A hypothetical application will not, however, secure the applicant a place in the leniency queue and if an undertaking is concerned that other cartel members may approach the Commission and seek immunity, a request for a marker should be made without delay.

12. What guarantees of leniency exist if a party co-operates?
Immunity (full leniency) is only available if the undertaking is the first cartel member to come forward with evidence on the cartel, the evidence provided meets the relevant immunity threshold and the undertaking meets the necessary conditions for obtaining immunity, including the condition that the undertaking 'co-operates genuinely, fully, on a continuous basis and expeditiously throughout the Commission's administrative procedure'.

Partial leniency is only available if the applicant submits evidence that provides significant added value to the Commission's investigation and the conditions for obtaining partial leniency are met. The conditions for partial leniency include an identical co-operation requirement.

The Commission has elaborated on the content of the co-operation condition in the Leniency Notice and has prescribed the following requirements that must be met in order for the co-operation condition to be fulfilled:
- the applicant must provide the Commission promptly with all information and evidence regarding the cartel;
- the applicant must respond promptly to any Commission request which may contribute to establishing the facts;
- the applicant must make current (and if possible, former) employees and directors available for interviews with the Commission;
- the applicant must not destroy, falsify or conceal information relating to the cartel; and
- the applicant must not disclose the fact or content of its application before the Commission issues a statement of objections.

This list is not exhaustive and an applicant should be careful to ensure that it co-operates with the Commission throughout the administrative process.

Provided all of the relevant conditions are met, then the immunity or reduction in fines are in principle guaranteed, ie, the Commission is bound to grant them. However, in practice the Commission has significant discretion in deciding whether the conditions are met, particularly given the subjective nature of terms such as 'significant added value' and 'full' co-operation.

CONSEQUENCES
13. What effects does leniency granted to a corporate defendant have on a defendant's employees? Does it protect them from criminal and/or civil liability?
There is no civil or criminal liability under European law for the employees

and directors of an undertaking that has engaged in cartel conduct.

However, the national competition laws of certain EU member states (principally the UK and Ireland) do contain a criminal cartel offence and there have been concerns that an undertaking seeking immunity/leniency from the European Commission could inadvertently expose its employees and directors to prosecution under a national criminal cartel offence, following an exchange of information between the European Commission and national competition authorities.

The Office of Fair Trading (the principal UK authority responsible for administering the cartel offence) has sought to allay these concerns and has made clear in its guidance note on the handling of leniency and no-action applications, that it will not use, either as intelligence or evidence, any leniency-derived information obtained from the Commission, to further its criminal cartel enforcement function. The situation may, however, be different in other EU member states.

14. Does leniency bar further criminal or private enforcement?

No, the Commission is unable to prevent private enforcement claims against leniency applicants in the national courts of EU or non-EU states.

While the Commission is unable to bar criminal enforcement by national bodies against a leniency applicant, the restrictions on access to the corporate statement (see question 17 below) are likely to apply equally to attempts to use corporate statements in a criminal prosecution. More importantly, at least one jurisdiction (the UK) has indicated that it will not use any leniency-derived information obtained from the Commission to further its criminal cartel enforcement functions.

PROTECTION AGAINST DISCLOSURE/CONFIDENTIALITY

15. Is confidentiality afforded to the leniency applicant and other co-operating parties? If so, to what extent? Is the identity of the leniency applicant/other co-operating parties disclosed during the investigation or in the final decision? Is information provided by the leniency applicant/other co-operating parties passed on to other undertakings under investigation? Can a leniency applicant/other co-operating party request anonymity or confidentiality of information provided?

The Leniency Notice does not contain any specific provisions regarding the confidentiality of immunity and leniency applications. It will, however, clearly be in the interests of the Commission to keep the identity of the immunity applicant confidential until the Commission has at least conducted an investigation, and possibly until the issue of the statement of objections. In any event, the identity of the leniency applicant and/or other co-operating parties will generally become public at the very latest at the time of the final decision (usually in a Commission press release).

The addressees of the Commission's statement of objections (the undertakings which have participated in the cartel) will receive access to the Commission file following the Commission's notification of the statement of objections (the statement of objections will identify all parties concerned).

European Union

This is a procedural guarantee intended to apply the principle of equality of arms and to protect the rights of the defence. The statement of objections will contain information provided by the leniency applicant and/or other co-operating parties.

Access to business secrets (eg production secrets, customer lists or pricing and cost data) may however be restricted. The rules governing access to files are set out in the Commission Notice on the rules for access to the Commission file (2005/C325/07).

Quite separate from the rights of access contained in Commission Notice on the rules for access to the Commission file, are the rights contained in Regulation (EC) No 1049/2001 of the European Parliament and of the Council regarding public access to European Parliament, Council and Commission documents (OJ L145, 31.5.2001). The general right contained in this notice is subject to different criteria and has specific exceptions. The Commission is anxious to protect corporate statements submitted by leniency applicants and has put in place steps to restrict access to corporate statements and to prevent them being used against leniency applicants in a civil action for damages.

16. Is the evidence submitted by the leniency applicant protected from transmission to other competition authorities with whom the authority in question co-operates? If so, how?

The Commission treats leniency applications and subsequent evidence on a confidential basis. However, leniency applications may be transmitted to members of the ECN under strict conditions without the permission of the leniency applicant (the ECN members in turn are bound by confidentiality).

As for competition authorities outside the scope of the ECN, the Commission will only share the leniency application and further evidence submitted if the submitting party has granted the Commission a waiver. In practice, it is expected that an undertaking waives confidentiality in respect of those competition authorities to whom it has also submitted a leniency application. This allows the Commission to co-ordinate its actions with other competition authorities.

17. To what extent can evidence submitted by the leniency applicant (transcripts of oral statements or written evidence) become discoverable in subsequent private enforcement claims? Can leniency information be subjected to discovery in domestic or foreign courts? Can leniency information submitted in a foreign jurisdiction be subjected to discovery orders in domestic courts?

The Commission is anxious to ensure that the risk of discovery of corporate statements in civil damage proceedings does not dissuade potential leniency applicants. It has therefore put in place a procedure to restrict access to corporate statements in order to limit this risk. The aim of the Commission's procedure is to ensure that, in the event of a private enforcement claim, leniency applicants are not in any worse position than their fellow cartel members.

The first limb of this procedure is the ability of immunity applicants to provide a corporate statement orally to the Commission. Oral corporate statements will be recorded and transcribed by the Commission and then checked for accuracy by the applicant. The transcript will form part of the Commission's file and will be used as evidence.

The second limb of this procedure is the restrictions on access to corporate statements. The Commission will only grant access to corporate statements to the addressees of the statement of objections, and then only on the condition that the addressee will not make a copy of the information contained in the corporate statement and will only use the information contained in the corporate statement for the purposes of judicial or administrative proceedings applying the competition rules at issue. The Commission has indicated that the corporate statements will be accessible only at the Commission premises and normally on a single occasion following formal notification of the objections.

Use of the information contained in the corporate statement for a different purpose may be regarded as a lack of co-operation (and hence failure to fulfil the conditions of immunity) and if the information is used after the Commission's decision has been adopted, the Commission may, in any legal proceeding before the European Community Courts, ask the court to increase the relevant undertaking's fine. The Commission may also report an external counsel's involvement to the bar of that counsel with a view to disciplinary action.

The Commission Notice on the co-operation between the Commission and the courts of the EU member states in the application of Articles 101 and 102 TFUE (OJ C101/54 27.4.2004) clearly states that the Commission will not transmit voluntary information supplied by a leniency applicant to national courts without the consent of that applicant. Similarly, to date, the Commission has been able to resist discovery requests from the US.

18. Are there any precedents in which evidence from a leniency application has been discovered in a private enforcement claim?

No. There have been numerous attempts to gain access to leniency statements but so far the Commission has been successful in refusing such access.

There are a number of cases pending before the European Courts whereby private damage claimants are challenging the Commission's refusal to grant access to documents in cartel files (eg Cases T-344/08, T-380/08 and T-437/08). A German court has also referred questions to the ECJ seeking clarification on whether disclosing information related to leniency applications made under national rules could harm co-operation between different competition authorities belonging to the ECN (Case C-360/09).

RELATIONSHIP WITH THE EUROPEAN COMMISSION'S LENIENCY NOTICE AND LENIENCY POLICY IN OTHER EU MEMBER STATES

19. Does the leniency policy address the interaction with an application under the Commission Leniency Notice? If so, how?
Not applicable.

20. Does the policy address the interaction with applications for leniency in other EU member states? If so, how? Does the authority accept summary applications in line with the ECN Model Leniency Programme?
The Leniency Notice does not expressly address the interaction with applications for leniency in EU member states. However, the principles contained in the EC Network Notice will govern case allocation and information-sharing arrangements between the Commission and the member state's national competition authorities in the context of a leniency application.

As set out in the EC Network Notice, the European Commission will be considered the best placed authority to act where the cartel has an effect on competition in more than three member states. However, as a leniency application to the Commission will not be considered an application for leniency to an EU member state, and an applicant may be exposed under a member state's national competition law, prospective applicants are advised to seek leniency from all competition authorities competent to apply Article 81 in the territory affected by the infringement which may be considered 'well placed' to act against the infringement.

The burden associated with multiple filings has been recognised by the ECN, and the Model Leniency Programme (introduced by the ECN in September 2006) provides for a 'summary application' system to be used when immunity is sought from the European Commission.

The Model Leniency Programme, a soft law instrument, is aimed as a first step towards harmonising leniency policy throughout the EU. In addition to setting out the main procedural and substantive rules that the ECN members believe should be common to all leniency programmes, the Model Leniency Programme also sets out a model for a uniform summary application system.

The model summary application system provides that, where the Commission is 'particularly well placed to act' (ie, where the cartel has an effect in more than three EU member states) and the applicant has or is in the process of filing an application for immunity with the Commission, the applicant may file a summary leniency application with the national competition authorities which the applicant considers might be 'well placed to act'. The proposed requirements of the summary application are set out in the Model Leniency Programme and are significantly abridged from the requirements of a standard leniency application. However, as set out above, the Model Leniency Programme will need to be incorporated into the national leniency policies of the EU member states before it can take effect. According to the ECN's report on the state of convergence of the member states' leniency programmes, published in October 2009, 23 member states have adopted a summary application model (those that have not are Cyprus, Estonia, Slovenia and Malta), although the information required in the summary application may vary slightly. In the majority of member states the summary application is only available when immunity is sought prior to any dawn raids having taken place. It is not possible to make a summary application to the European Commission.

RELATIONSHIP WITH SETTLEMENT PROCEDURES
21. What is the relationship between leniency and applicable settlement procedures? Are they mutually exclusive?

In July 2008, the Commission introduced a new policy of 'direct settlements' under which a 10 per cent fine reduction can be granted in exchange for recognition of the infringement and a commitment to pay the fine. The Commission amended Regulation (EC) No 773/2004 to include settlement procedures in cartel cases and published a notice on the conduct of settlement procedures ('Settlement Notice', OJ C167/1, 2/7/2008).

Leniency and settlement are not mutually exclusive. A company can first apply for leniency and at a later stage engage in settlement discussions. However, it is important to note that once a company engages in settlement discussions, it can no longer apply for leniency. The Settlement Notice makes clear that if the Commission asks the parties to a cartel whether they have an interest in engaging in settlement discussions, it may disregard any applications for leniency that are submitted by these parties after the expiry of the time-limit by which the parties had to respond to the Commission's query as to settlement interest.

If the parties settling have also applied for leniency, the reduction of the fine received from settlement is added to any reduction received as a result of leniency.

REFORM/LATEST DEVELOPMENTS
22. Is there a reform underway to revisit the leniency policy? What are the latest developments?

As the new Leniency Notice was introduced in December 2006, there are no immediate plans for reform. However, it can be expected that the Commission will keep the system under constant review and may adjust its procedural practices in the light of its experience in applying the (new) Leniency Notice.

The Commission's leniency policy should also be considered in light of the ECN Model Leniency Programme and the developments in convergence of the national programmes.

Finland

Dittmar & Indrenius Johan Åkermarck & Hanna Laurila

BACKGROUND
1. What is the relevant legislation concerning the leniency policy and what is the enforcing body?

A leniency programme was introduced into the Finnish Act on Competition Restrictions (480/1992, the Competition Act) by amendments which took effect on 1 May 2004. The rules on the reduction and non-imposition of an administrative fine are contained in Articles 8 and 9 of the Competition Act. The application of Articles 8 and 9 of the Competition Act has been further clarified in guidelines issued by the Finnish Competition Authority (the FCA).

The regulatory authority responsible solely for competition matters is the FCA (*Kilpailuvirasto*). The relevant court is called the Market Court (*Markkinaoikeus*). The competences between these two institutions are divided in the following manner. The FCA investigates and renders decisions on competition restrictions at the first instance. The FCA also makes a proposal to the Market Court for the imposition of a fine. The FCA lacks, however, the power to impose fines on undertakings found to have infringed either the Competition Act or Articles 101 or 102 of the Treaty on the Functioning of the European Union (TFEU).

The power to impose pecuniary sanctions on infringing undertakings lies in the exclusive competence of the Market Court. However, in imposing a fine, the Market Court must always act upon a proposal from the FCA. It cannot *ex officio* impose a fine. The FCA's proposal is, however, not binding upon the Market Court. In addition to its power to impose fines, the Market Court also reviews the FCA's decisions on appeal at first instance. The ultimate appellate body in competition matters is the Supreme Administrative Court, which functions as the second appellate instance for the FCA's decisions and as first instance for the Market Court's decisions to impose fines.

It follows from this division of competences between the FCA and the Market Court that in respect of the non-imposition of a fine, the decision rests solely with the FCA. The Market Court recently affirmed that the FCA's decision to award leniency cannot be appealed. Conversely, as for the reduction of a fine, it is ultimately the Market Court that decides, on a proposal from the FCA, the actual amount of the fine and the reduction of it. While the FCA's proposal will include an appropriate reduction in the final amount of a fine reflecting the infringing undertaking's voluntary co-operation with the FCA, this proposal is not binding upon the Market Court, which may depart from it either downwards or upwards.

2. What are the basic tenets of a leniency/immunity programme? Is leniency available also for other types of competition law violations than cartels?

According to Article 9 of the Competition Act, the following five cumulative criteria must be satisfied by an undertaking applying for immunity:
- the applicant undertaking must provide the FCA with information on a competition restriction, which allows the FCA to intervene in the suspected restriction;
- this information must be submitted to the FCA before it has been obtained from other sources;
- the applicant must provide the FCA with all information and documents in its possession;
- the applicant must co-operate with the FCA during the whole investigation into the suspected competition restriction; and
- the undertaking must immediately cease its participation in the illegal activity.

The FCA's guidelines on the application of Articles 8 and 9 of the Competition Act provide further details, for instance, on issues such as the qualitative criteria applicable for the information to be submitted to the FCA, the order of priority in cases of multiple applications and the submission of anonymous applications. It should be noted that under Article 9 of the Competition Act, only one applicant can benefit from immunity, and immunity is available only in respect of so-called hardcore cartels (ie, price fixing, output limitation or market, customer or supplier-sharing). In practice the FCA may request that the applicant not immediately cease its cartel activity in order not to reveal the matter to the other members of the cartel.

Article 8 of the Competition Act provides that the Market Court may reduce a fine imposed on an undertaking pursuant to a violation of the Competition Act where the undertaking has 'considerably assisted' the FCA in the investigation of a competition restriction. In contrast to immunity, a reduction of a fine is possible in respect of several undertakings and can be sought in respect of any competition restriction, including vertical restrictions and abuses of a dominant position.

The FCA's guidelines specify that in order to benefit, for instance, from immunity, the applicant is not required to submit conclusive evidence on the existence of a cartel or the complicity of the other undertakings involved where it does not have such information in its possession at the time of the application. Further, should the information submitted subsequently turn out to be incorrect or incomplete, it does not result in the disqualification of the immunity applicant, provided that the information has been given in good faith.

3. How many cartels have been unveiled and punished since the adoption of the leniency programme?

The FCA has adopted a policy according to which it does not publish any statistics or other information on leniency applications submitted to it. The

FCA has, however, on a couple of occasions published press releases stating that a particular investigation has been based on information supplied by a leniency applicant.

Based on information collected mainly from public sources, it seems that 10-15 applications for immunity or leniency have been made to the FCA since the introduction of the national leniency programme in 2004. In at least two cases the FCA did not find sufficient evidence of competition infringement and closed the investigation. So far the most significant leniency case involved competition restrictions in the raw wood procurement market.

The first leniency-based cartel case was brought before the Market Court in 2006. The case concerned the collective boycott/exchange of sensitive information in the market for car spare parts. The FCA raided the companies suspected of the cartel in July 2004 after one of the companies involved, Oy Arwidson Ab, confessed its participation in the cartel. The aggregate amount of fines proposed by the FCA on four of the alleged participants was €3.76 million while the leniency applicant was granted full immunity. In February 2009 the Market Court lowered the aggregate amount of fines to approximately €1 million. The case is currently pending in the Supreme Administrative Court.

In a case relating to a wood procurement cartel, UPM-Kymmene Plc informed the FCA of its participation in forbidden price co-operation and exchange of information in the purchase of timber. The investigations into the timber trade began in May 2004 after UPM-Kymmene's submission to the FCA after which the FCA raided the companies suspected of the cartel. In December 2009 the Market Court imposed fines totalling €51 million: €30 million to Stora Enso Plc and €21 million to Metsäliitto Cooperative. UPM-Kymmene was exempted from the fine and Metsäliitto's fine was reduced by 30 per cent due to its assistance during the FCA investigation.

4. What is needed to be a successful leniency applicant? Is documentary evidence required or is testimonial evidence sufficient?

The FCA has specified in its guidelines on the application of Articles 8 and 9 of the Competition Act that for an undertaking to be eligible for immunity, it must provide the following information, either at the time of submitting the application or, where the application is anonymous, at a date agreed upon by the FCA and the applicant:
- the applicant's identity;
- details of the applicant's participation in anti-competitive conduct;
- the nature of the anti-competitive conduct (whether price fixing, output limitation, market, customer or supplier sharing);
- the identity of the other participants in the anti-competitive conduct;
- the relevant product and geographical markets;
- the implementation of the anti-competitive conduct (how, where and when an agreement has been reached on the cartel);
- the manner in which the cartel has been implemented and adherence monitored; and

- the persons who have agreed on the cartel or otherwise participated in its implementation.

The guidelines further state that although the information given is to be extensive and accurate, the applicant is not required to provide conclusive evidence of the existence of an anti-competitive agreement or the complicity of the participating undertakings, should the applicant not be in possession of such detailed facts at the time of its application. There is no explicit requirement to provide documentary evidence, however if the applicant possesses important documents, they should be submitted. Also, provided that the information is given in good faith, the fact that some of the information provided subsequently proves to be incorrect or incomplete does not result in the applicant being disqualified from immunity. The evidentiary threshold is currently under review.

TIMING
5. What are the benefits of being 'first in' to co-operate?
Immunity from fines can only be granted to one applicant and only in respect of hardcore cartels, ie, agreements or other arrangements under which undertakings have agreed to fix price, limit output, or share markets, customers or sources of supply. An applicant receives a separate decision from the FCA on whether or not it has satisfied the conditions for the grant of immunity. Where the conditions for the application of Article 9 of the Competition Act are met, the FCA refrains from making a proposal to the Market Court for the imposition of a fine.

Under Article 9 of the Competition Act, immunity can only be granted to one applicant, ie the first undertaking to satisfy the conditions stipulated in that provision. Where multiple applications for immunity have been made in respect of one cartel, the decisive factor in determining the order of priority is the point in time at which the FCA has at its disposal the relevant information.

Conversely, a reduction of a fine under Article 8 of the Competition Act is possible in respect of several undertakings in any one cartel or other competition-restricting case. However, the amount of the reduction is likely to decrease progressively where several applications under Article 8 of the Competition Act have been made. Further, it may be increasingly difficult to satisfy the criteria that the applicant has 'considerably assisted' the FCA in the detection of a competition restriction where the FCA has already obtained information from several prior applicants.

The possibility of obtaining immunity from fines is determined by the timing of an application. The application must contain information which allows the FCA to initiate an investigation. In particular, an applicant undertaking must always provide the FCA with details of its identity (unless the application is initially made anonymously) and participation in a cartel. In addition, the applicant must describe in the application the nature of the restriction, the other cartel participants, the relevant product and geographical markets and the duration of the cartel. The position in the queue is determined exclusively by the timing of a proper application (ie, an application which contains all the required information) and not for instance by the amplitude and preciseness of the information provided.

6. What are the consequences of being 'second'? Is there an 'immunity plus' or 'amnesty plus' option?

While according to Article 9 of the Competition Act immunity can only be granted to one applicant, ie, the first undertaking to satisfy the conditions contained in the said provision, Article 8 provides that the Market Court may reduce a fine imposed on an undertaking where it has 'considerably assisted' the FCA in the investigation of a competition restriction. According to the guidelines of the FCA, considerable assistance means active participation in the investigation of the infringement. This entails, for instance, providing the FCA on the applicant's own initiative with information which the FCA does not have or which would be difficult for the FCA to obtain. Merely responding to the inquiries of the FCA is, as such, not considered sufficient.

In contrast to immunity, a fine reduction is possible in respect of several undertakings and can be sought in respect of any competition restriction, including vertical restrictions and abuses of a dominant position. Further, an application under Article 8 of the Competition Act can be made even after the FCA has initiated its own investigation, but where it lacks sufficient evidence to make a finding of infringement.

Neither Article 8 of the Competition Act nor the FCA's guidelines provide for a percentage scaling for the reduction to be given to a successful leniency applicant. The appropriate percentage of reduction is determined solely by reference to the criterion of considerable assistance. Under Article 8 of the Competition Act, the reduction could theoretically vary between zero and 100 per cent. Accordingly, and should it be considered appropriate, the Market Court could in theory refrain from imposing a fine under Article 8 of the Competition Act.

The Finnish leniency programme does not provide for an 'immunity plus' or 'amnesty plus' option.

7. Are subsequent firms given any beneficial treatment if they make a useful contribution? How are 'useful contributions' defined?

Please see answer to question 6. Rules concerning reduction of fines are currently under review.

SCOPE/FULL LENIENCY
8. Is it possible to receive full leniency? If so, what are the conditions required to receive full leniency?

Please see answer to question 4.

8.1 Can ringleaders/coercers receive full leniency?

Under the current rules full leniency is not excluded for coercers. There is a legislative proposal regarding this policy, please see below question 22.

8.2 If there is a requirement to 'co-operate fully and on an ongoing basis' what does it entail?

The obligation to co-operate with the FCA during the whole of its investigation is one of the key criteria to receiving full leniency. In practice, this obligation is interpreted broadly by the FCA. The applicant is expected, for instance, to actively provide all information and documents in its possession relating to the infringement, to respond quickly to any queries of the FCA and allow the FCA to interview its employees. The applicant must not mislead the FCA with regard to its own role and actions during the cartel, nor hamper the investigation of the FCA, for instance, by destroying evidence or by informing the other cartel members of the leniency application. The co-operation obligation is not fulfilled if a large number of employees or the key employees connected to the infringement do not co-operate with the FCA. Further clarifications to this policy have been proposed. Please see the answer to question 22.

8.3 Does the regulatory authority require the applicant to cease participation in the cartel conduct after its application?

Under current rules, the applicant must immediately cease participation in the cartel in order to receive full leniency. In practice, the FCA may, however, request that the applicant not immediately cease its cartel activity in order not to reveal the matter to the other members of the cartel. Lastly, please note that there is a legislative proposal regarding this policy.

9. How many companies have received full immunity from fines to date?

It is clear that the national leniency policy has proved useful and undertakings have taken advantage of it. By a rough estimate, since the beginning of May 2004, at least 10 leniency or immunity applications have been submitted to the FCA. On the basis of public information, final immunity decisions have been issued in two cases which have been handled by the Market Court (see above question 3).

PROCEDURE
10. What are the practical steps required to apply for leniency?

As for applications for immunity under Article 9 of the Competition Act, one of the most important elements is the timing of the application, as only one (usually the first) undertaking can benefit from immunity. The FCA should be contacted as soon as the undertaking has gathered sufficient evidence which allows the FCA to intervene in a competition restriction.

Where immunity is not available and an application is consequently made under Article 8 of the Competition Act for the reduction of a fine, both the timing of the application and the quality of evidence are of great significance.

Please see answer to question 2 for a brief description of the basic tenets of the Finnish leniency/immunity programme.

10.1 Initial contact/is there a 'marker' system?
The Competition Act does not include such a system. The FCA has shown its willingness to operate something essentially similar to a marker system in respect of anonymous leniency applications. In such cases an undertaking can approach the FCA anonymously through its legal counsel to ascertain whether immunity is available. The undertaking does not initially have to disclose its identity or provide any information on the cartel, although it must identify the affected industry along with the nature of the cartel. Where the FCA is not in possession of information allowing it to take action against such a cartel, it informs the anonymous applicant that immunity is available. A date is then agreed on which the undertaking must, at the latest, provide the FCA with the information in its possession. The FCA has specified in its guidelines that disclosure of identity and the provision of the necessary information must occur promptly after the anonymous inquiry. The timing of the application is then considered to be the point in time of the anonymous contact with the FCA. However, should the anonymous applicant fail to provide the required information by the agreed deadline, it will lose its position of priority. This practice of the FCA is however not included in the Competition Act.

10.2 Conditional reduction of fine
Once the FCA has verified that the information submitted is comprehensive and precise enough, it will inform the applicant in writing that the first conditions for full leniency are fulfilled. If the applicant fulfils the additional co-operation obligations, it will be granted full leniency at the end of the investigation.

10.3 Final reduction
In connection with submitting a proposal for a fine to the Market Court, the FCA issues a separate decision on whether or not the applicant fulfils all the conditions for full leniency. This decision cannot be appealed separately. Although the FCA has the authority to grant immunity, it can only propose to the Market Court a reduction of a fine for any other co-operating company and the Court will make the final decision.

11. Is there an optimal time to approach the regulatory authority?
The best time to approach the authorities when applying for immunity or leniency will vary depending on whether immunity under Article 9 is still available, or whether an undertaking can only benefit from a reduction of a fine under Article 8 of the Competition Act. A preliminary, but sufficiently detailed analysis must first be undertaken in order to identify whether there has been an infringement within the meaning of either Article 4 of the Competition Act or Article 101(1) of the TFEU. After this, it must be assessed and a decision made on whether immunity is still available (usually by contacting the FCA on an anonymous basis) and whether the conditions of Article 9 can be satisfied.

Please see also answer to question 4.

12. What guarantees of leniency exist if a party co-operates?
Where an undertaking seeks immunity under Article 9 of the Competition Act, the grant of immunity is automatic upon fulfilling the criteria contained in that provision. Conversely, where immunity is no longer available, either by reason of a prior application or the conditions of Article 9 having not otherwise been fulfilled, and instead a reduction of fine under Article 8 of the Competition Act is sought, there are no guarantees during the investigative stage that a reduction will actually be granted as a result of voluntary co-operation. This is because it is ultimately for the Market Court to decide, on a proposal from the FCA, the actual amount of the fine including any reduction to it. While the FCA's proposal will include an appropriate reduction to the final amount of a fine, reflecting the infringing undertaking's voluntary co-operation with it, this proposal is not binding upon the Market Court, which may depart from it either downwards or upwards.

CONSEQUENCES
13. What effects does leniency granted to a corporate defendant have on the defendant's employees? Does it protect them from criminal and/or civil liability?
The provisions of the Competition Act are only applicable to 'business undertakings', which are defined in Article 3 as a 'natural person, or a private or public person, who professionally offers for sale, buys, sells, or otherwise obtains or delivers goods or services in return for compensation'. Thus, issues such as director's personal liability for anti-competitive behaviour do not arise under the Competition Act. A criminal sanction is possible under the Criminal Code if a person provides an authority with false documents. Leniency has no affect on the imposition of such sanctions.

14. Does leniency bar further private enforcement?
The Finnish Competition Act relates only to administrative law, and thus provides only for the imposition of administrative fines in addition to possible civil law liability for damages. An infringement of the Competition Act by an undertaking does not expose its management or personnel, to criminal law penalties.

PROTECTION AGAINST DISCLOSURE/CONFIDENTIALITY
15. Is confidentiality afforded to the leniency applicant and other co-operating parties? If so, to what extent?
Neither the Competition Act nor the FCA's interpretative guidelines address the issue of confidentiality of immunity/leniency applications. According to Finnish Act on the Openness of Government Activities (621/1999, the Openness Act), all documents written by public authorities or submitted to them are public unless there is a legitimate reason to classify the document as confidential. Business secrets will in general remain confidential.

In addition, the FCA has indicated that information supplied by the leniency applicant can be kept confidential from the public and the parties as long as publication would jeopardise its own investigation. Such documents would only be accessible after the FCA has rendered its final decision and/or made a proposal to the Market Court.

In its guidelines, the FCA notes that it is under an obligation to inform the Commission of an application for immunity or reduction of fines. The FCA may also inform the competition authorities of other member states. In releasing information to the Commission and other national competition authorities, the FCA must ensure that an undertaking's business secrets are duly protected.

15.1 Is the identity of the leniency applicant/other co-operating parties disclosed during the investigation or in the final decision?

The identity of a leniency applicant is not disclosed before the FCA has conducted an unannounced inspection. The FCA does not automatically disclose the identity of the leniency applicant even after an inspection but such information will, in practice, often become public at this stage. The companies alleged to have committed competition law violations may have to make the inspections public due to stock exchange rules. In such a case the FCA will also issue its own statement confirming the inspection and this statement will typically reveal that the inspections were based on a leniency application. The identity of the leniency applicant and the other parties for which the FCA proposes a reduction of fines will become public at the latest in the proposal for the imposition of fines submitted by the FCA to the Market Court.

The identity of the leniency applicant is disclosed to the parties concerned during the FCA investigation at the latest when the FCA sends a draft of its proposal to the Market Court to the parties for their comments.

15.2 Is information provided by the leniency applicant/other co-operating parties passed on to other undertakings under investigation?

There are no specific rules or case law regarding the treatment of the leniency application. In practice, the FCA has given other parties access to the leniency application at the latest when the FCA makes its proposal for the imposition of fines to the Market Court. In the case of an oral application, the other parties may not be given the actual recording but a transcript made by the FCA instead.

15.3 Can a leniency applicant/other co-operating party request anonymity or confidentiality of information provided?

Please see responses above. There is a legislative proposal relating to the confidentiality of leniency applications. Please see the answer to question 22.

16. Is the evidence submitted by the leniency applicant protected from transmission to other competition authorities with whom the authority in question co-operates? If so, how?

The Competition Act does not include specific provisions on this issue.

Finland

Transfer of information between competition authorities in the EU is governed by Regulation 1/2003 and the Commission's notice on co-operation within the Network of Competition Authorities.

17. To what extent can evidence submitted by the leniency applicant (transcripts of oral statements or written evidence) become discoverable in subsequent private enforcement claims? Can leniency information be subjected to discovery orders in domestic or foreign courts? Can leniency information submitted in a foreign jurisdiction be subjected to discovery orders in domestic courts?

17.1 Availability of public documents

On the basis of the Openness Act, anyone has a right to request copies of public documents from public authorities. As a general rule, documents submitted to or obtained by the FCA are regarded as official documents which are public unless otherwise provided in the Openness Act.

Based on a decision by the Supreme Administrative Court (12 April 2006 T 883), the documents submitted to the FCA by the leniency applicant can be considered secret under the Openness Act during the FCA's cartel investigation as long as publication of the information could jeopardise the investigation. After the FCA has given its decision (typically to take or not to take the case to the Market Court), the documents submitted by the leniency applicant, including its corporate statement, will be regarded as official documents which are public unless otherwise provided in the Openness Act. The FCA can refuse to disclose business secrets but a claimant can request the FCA to disclose versions of the relevant documents from which business secrets have been removed.

17.2 Rules of evidence

The Finnish legal system does not recognise discovery as understood and applied in the common law system. However, according to the Code of Judicial Procedure, a court may, upon request by a party to the proceedings, order the opposing party or even a third party to disclose specific documents which may be relevant as evidence in the proceedings. The Code of Judicial Procedure also includes rules on documents and information which do not have to be disclosed, including business secrets.

The leniency applicant will be able to refer to confidentiality of business secrets but it is unlikely that, for instance, a statement of confession in its entirety would be regarded as a business secret. The treatment of leniency applications is still developing in Finland and there is a legislative proposal which aims to increase the confidentiality of leniency documents. Please see question 22.

In relation to the cross-border provision of evidence, Finland is a party to the 1970 Hague Convention on the taking of evidence abroad. Finland is also a member state of the European Union within which Regulation (EC) No 1206/2001 on co-operation between the courts of the member states in the taking of evidence in civil or commercial matters applies to cross-border cases. Under these provisions, the rules on the right of a party to refuse to give evidence, and the rules on documents and information which do not have to be disclosed in both the requesting and the requested court, come into play. In addition, evidence may under certain limited circumstances not be provided because it is contrary to the fundamental principles or *ordre public*. In addition, Finland has made a declaration under Article 23 of the Hague Convention. Accordingly Finland will not execute letters of request issued for the purpose of obtaining pre-trial discovery, which require a person: i) to state what documents relevant to the proceedings are, or have been, in its possession, custody or power; or ii) to produce any documents other than particular documents specified in the letter of request, which are likely to be in its possession, custody or power.

18. Are there any precedents in which evidence from a leniency application has been discovered in a private enforcement claim?
So far there has been very little private litigation in Finland and no precedents relating to the handling of leniency applications exist.

RELATIONSHIP WITH THE EUROPEAN COMMISSION'S LENIENCY NOTICE AND LENIENCY POLICY IN OTHER EU MEMBER STATES

19. Does the policy address the interaction with applications under the Commission Leniency Notice? If so, how?
The Competition Act does not address the interaction with applications under the Commission Leniency Notice. The FCA's guidelines on the application of Articles 8 and 9 of the Competition Act provide clarification on the interaction with applications under the Commission Leniency Notice and information exchange with the Commission. According to chapter 2.8 of the FCA's guidelines, even if a business undertaking exposes an alleged cartel to the FCA, this does not imply that the undertaking will be awarded immunity in other member states on the basis of information supplied to the FCA. The FCA shall inform the Commission of the proceedings in a case involving a leniency application. As a general rule, the FCA may also inform other member states. The business undertaking is advised to apply for leniency from the Commission or from all competition authorities whose territories may have been affected by the competition restraint.

20. Does the policy address the interaction with applications for leniency in other EU member states? If so, how? Does the authority accept summary applications in line with the ECN Model Leniency Programme?
Please see answer to question 19. The Competition Act does not currently recognise summary applications, but similar information may fulfil the requirements for national initial information and thus enable summary applications. There is a legislative proposal with regard to this matter.

RELATIONSHIP WITH SETTLEMENT PROCEDURES
21. What is the relationship between leniency and applicable settlement procedures? Are they mutually exclusive?
The Competition Act does not include a settlement procedure. Under the EU rules it is in the interests of a leniency applicant to also ask the Commission for a settlement procedure, as the reductions of fine are cumulative.

REFORM/LATEST DEVELOPMENTS
22. Is there a reform underway to revisit the leniency policy? What are the latest developments?
A Government Bill for a new Competition Act was submitted to the Parliament in June 2010. The Bill is based on the Competition Law 2010 working group report published in January 2009. A number of amendments are proposed. One of the aims is further alignment with the Commission's Leniency Notice and the Model Leniency Programme of the European Competition Network, which is expected to make the national leniency system more predictable and to increase incentives for companies to blow the whistle.

The main proposals relating to the leniency system can be summarised as follows:
- Full leniency would be available for secret cartels including purchase cartels. Full leniency could be granted even after the FCA has carried out an inspection if no other party has been granted conditional immunity and the applicant is the first company to submit evidence which allows the FCA to find an infringement (type 1B under the Model Leniency Programme). Coercers would be explicitly excluded from the benefit of immunity but would continue to be eligible for a reduction of fines. However, if a conditional leniency is not finalised because the applicant fails to co-operate or conceals its true role in the infringement, it would benefit from the reduction of fines regime.
- The system for reduction of fines would be made more transparent. The amount of the reduction would depend on the timing and the quality and nature of the information submitted. More precise percentages for reductions would be included. Applicants would be required to provide information which constitutes significant added value with respect to the information already in the FCA's possession. The discretion of the Market Court in determining whether to grant a reduction and the amount of the reduction would be reduced. Reduction of fines other than in cartel cases would be dealt with under new rules on infringement.
- The evidential threshold for leniency will be further aligned with the Model Leniency Programme. The leniency applicant would not automatically be required to immediately end its involvement in the infringement, as it is, in principle, the case today, but it should follow the instructions of the FCA. Information on past or possible future leniency applications to other authorities would be explicitly required. The applicant would not be allowed to disclose information on the

leniency application except to other competition authorities, nor destroy evidence before or after submitting the application.
- It is proposed that a list of information required for a marker and formal summary applications along the lines of the Model Leniency Programme would be introduced.
- Documents submitted to the FCA as a part of a leniency application, including corporate statements, could not be used in private litigation. Transfer of information between competition authorities or the FCA's right to open an investigation on possible abuse of a dominant position on the basis of the information provided would not be affected. It is also proposed that the Openness Act be amended to protect the confidentiality of leniency applications including corporate statements. It would be clarified that documents included in leniency applications or decisions that leniency is not granted would not be considered to be public documents under the Openness Act. Other parties to the investigation would have the right to review leniency documents, but would be bound by relevant confidentiality obligations under the Openness Act.

For further later information about the outcome of the reform, please refer to *www.dittmar.fi*.

France

Herbert Smith Sergio Sorinas & Estelle Jégou

BACKGROUND
1. What is the relevant legislation containing the leniency policy and what is the enforcing body?
The enforcing body is the *Autorité de la Concurrence* (Competition Authority – the *Autorité*) created by the *Loi sur la Modernisation de l'Economie* (Modernisation of the Economy Act – the LME Law) of 4 August 2008 which replaces the former *Conseil de la Concurrence* (Competition Council – the *Conseil*). The *Rapporteur Général* of the *Autorité* (general case-handler) is empowered to receive leniency applications.

Articles L 462-6 and L 464-2 of the French Commercial Code (the Commercial Code) provide the *Autorité* with the power to impose fines on any undertaking which has infringed Articles L 420-1 (anticompetitive agreements) or L 420-2 (abuse of a dominant position or economic dependency) of the Commercial Code and/or Articles 101 and 102 of the Treaty on the Functioning of the European Union (TFEU) prohibiting anticompetitive agreements and abuse of a dominant position.

Although there are no detailed rules or guidelines on the method of setting fines, Article L 464-2 I of the Commercial Code provides that fines must be proportionate to the gravity of the alleged facts, to the extent of the damage caused to the economy, to the situation of the undertaking being penalised or the group to which it belongs and to repeated infringements. The maximum fine undertakings may incur is 10 per cent of the highest worldwide pre-tax turnover reached during the financial year after which the practices were carried out.

Unlike many other jurisdictions, where leniency programmes are the result of notices issued by competition authorities, the French leniency programme was introduced by law. This procedure, introduced into French competition law as part of the modernisation package contained in the *Loi sur les Nouvelles Régulations Economiques* (New Economic Regulation Act – the NRE Law) of 17 May 2001, has been codified in Articles L 464-2 IV and R 464-5 of the Commercial Code.

In response to criticism that the French leniency rules left too much discretion to the competition authorities and did not clearly spell out the conditions for obtaining full or partial immunity, a procedural notice relating to the French leniency programme (the Procedural Notice) was adopted on 11 April 2006 to clarify its application and encourage use of the procedure.

The Procedural Notice was revised on 17 April 2007 in order to comply with the Model Leniency Programme adopted by the European Competition Network in September 2006 (the ECN Model Programme). Besides the introduction of a marker system and of the possibility to file a summary application in cases where the European Commission has authority to handle the case, the conditions for immunity and reduction in fines have been clarified and the guarantees relating to the statements made by the undertakings have been strengthened. The Procedural Notice follows for the large part the European Commission's Notice on immunity from fines and reduction of fines in cartel cases (OJ C298/17, 8.12.2006) (the EC Leniency Notice). On 2 March 2009, the *Autorité* adopted its own Procedural Notice on the French leniency programme, which is entirely similar to the previous one.

Quite separate from the leniency procedure is the availability of a reduction in fine by negotiating a settlement with the *Rapporteur Général* (Article L 464-2 III of the Commercial Code) once a formal proceeding has been initiated (the settlement procedure). In this situation, the *Rapporteur Général* plays a pivotal role by proposing to the *Autorité* a fine reduction that takes into account the fact that the applicant does not challenge the findings set out in the statement of objections. However it is for the *Autorité* and not the *Rapporteur Général* to decide whether an undertaking may benefit from a reduction in fine and the percentage of reduction.

2. What are the basic tenets of a leniency/immunity programme? Is leniency also available for types of competition law violations other than cartel offences?

According to Article L 464-2 IV of the Commercial Code, the leniency programme is available to undertakings which have participated in an infringement of Article L 420-1 of the Commercial Code and who decide to inform the French competition authorities of the existence of such an infringement.

In theory, this position differs from that in many other jurisdictions in which leniency is available only in cartel cases, because Article L 420-1 of the Commercial Code has a wider scope and covers not only cartel practices such as horizontal price fixing, bid rigging and market sharing, but also vertical practices. However, the *Autorité* has clarified the scope of the leniency programme in the Procedural Notice by indicating that the infringements concerned are cartels between undertakings including price-fixing, market sharing, production or sales quota, or any other similar anti-competitive behaviour between competitors, which excludes vertical practices.

Under Article L 464-2 IV of the Commercial Code and the Procedural Notice, the French leniency policy offers both full and partial immunity.

As in many other jurisdictions, the assessment of a leniency application depends in particular on:
- the timing of the leniency application;
- the extent and nature of the evidence provided to the competition authorities (such as evidence enabling the authorities to carry out a

targeted inspection or to establish an infringement, or evidence of significant added value);
- the co-operation of the applicant with the competition authorities; and
- to a limited extent, the role of the applicant in the cartel (if a coercive role excludes the benefit from leniency, a ringleader can be eligible for leniency).

Full immunity is granted to the first undertaking that comes forward and provides the competition authorities with the requisite information (see response to questions 4 and 8 below). As under the EC Leniency Notice, an undertaking may be eligible for full immunity even after the launch of a targeted inspection (a 'dawn raid'). In such a case, the standard of proof will be higher as the undertaking will have to provide the competition authorities with evidence enabling them to find a breach of Article L 420–1 of the Commercial Code and/or of Article 101 TFEU. Leniency applicants that come forward subsequent to the first immunity applicant may be eligible for a reduction of fine up to 50 per cent (partial immunity) if they provide evidence which represents 'significant added value' with respect to the evidence already in the competition authorities' possession.

Applicants eligible for full or partial immunity will also need to meet other conditions such as providing the competition authorities with all the evidence relating to the cartel, making employees or legal representatives available for interview by the competition authorities and not coercing other undertakings to participate in the cartel (see response to question 4 below).

Applicants wishing to apply for leniency need to make a formal written or oral application to the *Rapporteur Général*. Since April 2007, it has been possible for an applicant to make use of the marker system.

3. How many cartels have been unveiled and punished since the adoption of the leniency policy?

The leniency policy came into force on 17 May 2001. Since then, 125 cartels have been unveiled and punished.

The *Autorité* has issued four decisions on leniency cases since this procedure was created (three total immunity and one partial immunity).

Since 2001, 41 leniency applications have been filed with the *Autorité* and it has issued 28 conditional opinions (see response to question 10). Seventy-five per cent of these opinions received a positive response. It is worth noting that in 2008, the *Autorité* received 18 leniency applications, ie roughly the same number as in all the previous years combined.

4. What is needed to be a successful leniency applicant? Is documentary evidence required or is testimonial evidence sufficient?

To be a successful leniency applicant, an undertaking must:
- file a leniency application to the *Autorité* (section 25 of the Procedural Notice);
- meet certain eligibility conditions (sections 12 to 19 of the Procedural Notice); and

- meet certain substantive conditions (sections 20 and 21 of the Procedural Notice).

4.1 The leniency application

In addition to its name and address, an undertaking must provide, orally or in writing, the competition authorities with:
- information on the circumstances which led to its leniency application;
- the name and address of the other cartel participants;
- information on the product(s) and on the territory(ies) on which the alleged cartel is likely to have an impact;
- the nature and estimated duration of the alleged cartel; and
- any leniency application which has been or will be made to other competition authorities in relation to the alleged cartel.

This is simply a first set of information that must be provided and it does not have to be exhaustive. It allows the applicant to place a marker (ie to reserve its place in the queue). The applicant will then be granted a limited period of time to gather evidence meeting the requisite standard to be eligible for leniency.

It is also important to note that the applicant does not have to specify whether it is applying for full or partial immunity. The *Rapporteur* in charge of the case will inform the applicant promptly of the classification of the leniency application (Type 1 A, 1 B or 2 cases).

4.2 Eligibility conditions

An undertaking will be eligible for full immunity if it is the first cartel participant to provide the *Autorité* with sufficient evidence enabling them either to:
- carry out targeted inspections in connection with the alleged cartel (type 1 A case); or
- establish the existence of an infringement of Article L 420-1 of the Commercial Code or of Article 101 TFEU in connection with the alleged cartel (type 1 B case). Type 1 A cases cover the scenario where an undertaking applies for leniency prior to an inspection while type 1 B cases cover the scenario when an inspection has already taken place.

In type 1 A cases, immunity will only be granted if: (i) the competition authorities did not previously have sufficient evidence to be able to carry out a targeted inspection on their own initiative; and (ii) the applicant provides evidence which is sufficient, in the *Autorité's* view, to have the targeted inspection carried out.

In order to meet this evidential threshold, the applicant must provide all the information requested for filing a leniency application (see above) and any pieces of evidence (documentary, testimonial or any other nature) in its possession or that can be made available at the time of the application. These elements may consist of information helping to identify locations, dates and the object of contacts or meetings between participants in the alleged cartel.

In type 1 B cases, immunity will only be granted if: (i) at the time of the application, the competition authorities did not have sufficient evidence to find an infringement of Article L 420-1 of the Commercial Code and/or Article 101 TFEU; (ii) the applicant provides evidence, which in the *Autorité's* view, is sufficient to establish the existence of such an infringement; and (iii) no undertaking has obtained a conditional opinion granting type 1 A full immunity.

Applicants who do not meet the type 1 A or type 1 B conditions may be eligible for a reduction of fine of up to 50 per cent (partial immunity). In order to qualify for partial immunity, an undertaking must provide the *Autorité* with evidence of the alleged infringement which represents 'significant added value' with respect to the evidence already in the competition authorities' possession.

The concept of 'significant added value' refers to the extent to which the evidence provided strengthens, by its very nature and/or its level of detail, the ability of the *Autorité* to prove the existence of the alleged infringement. In this respect, the *Autorité* will generally consider written, contemporaneous evidence to have a greater value than evidence subsequently established, and incriminating evidence directly relevant to the facts at stake to have a greater value than evidence of indirect relevance. Similarly, compelling evidence will be attributed a greater value than evidence which requires corroboration if contested. Hence, even if testimonial evidence is accepted, compelling documentary evidence will give the undertaking a greater chance of securing a reduction in fine.

The level of reduction of fine will depend on the ranking of the application and the time when the evidence was submitted, as well as the extent to which the elements submitted bring significant added value.

The partial immunity granted to an applicant that has provided significant added value cannot in principle exceed 50 per cent of the fine which would have otherwise been imposed, had the applicant not been granted leniency.

4.3 Substantive conditions
In addition to the above conditions, the applicant must meet the following cumulative conditions to qualify for full or partial leniency:
- The applicant must end its involvement in the alleged cartel immediately and at the latest as from the notification of the leniency opinion of the *Autorité* (although this date may be postponed to preserve the confidentiality and the efficiency of the investigation proceedings).
- The applicant must co-operate genuinely, fully, on a continuous basis and expeditiously with the *Autorité*. As part of this application, the applicant must:
  - provide the competition authorities promptly with all information and evidence regarding the alleged cartel;
  - respond promptly to any competition authority request which may contribute to establishing the facts;
  - make current (and if possible, former) employees and legal representatives available for interview by the competition

authorities;
- not destroy, falsify or conceal information relating to the alleged cartel; and
- not disclose the fact or content of its leniency application before the *Autorité* issues a statement of objections, unless otherwise agreed.
- When contemplating making the leniency application, the applicant must not have destroyed or falsified evidence of the alleged cartel, nor disclosed its intention to apply for leniency except to other competition authorities.

TIMING
5. What are the benefits of being 'first in' to co-operate?
Full immunity is only available to the first undertaking to come forward and provide the requisite information relating to the alleged cartel. Undertakings which are not the first to apply for leniency are not eligible for full immunity.

Undertakings may now apply for a marker protecting their place in the queue for a given period of time, such period to be specified on a case-by-case basis. It allows the applicant to complete its internal investigation to gather the required information and items of evidence.

6. What are the consequences of being 'second'? Is there an 'immunity plus' or 'amnesty plus' option?
Undertakings which are not the first to come forward are not eligible for full immunity. However, an undertaking which is second to apply for leniency will be eligible for a reduction in fine if it provides the *Autorité* with evidence of the alleged cartel which represents 'significant added value' and meets the four cumulative substantive conditions set out in response to question 4. The Procedural Notice does not follow the European Commission's practice in adopting a sliding scale of fine reduction depending on the order of application by the cartel participants. Rather, the *Autorité* has kept a certain amount of discretion to determine the level of reduction of fine by indicating that, in principle, the reduction should not exceed 50 per cent.

The Procedural Notice does not provide for an 'amnesty plus' option. However, if the applicant for a reduction of fine is the first to submit compelling evidence which the *Autorité* uses to establish additional facts which have a direct bearing on the amount of the fine, this will be taken into account in the individual setting of the fine which may give rise to partial immunity.

7. Are subsequent firms given any beneficial treatment if they make a useful contribution? How are 'useful contributions' defined?
All undertakings which provide evidence of 'significant added value' with respect to the evidence that the *Autorité* already has and who meet the four cumulative substantive conditions set out in response to question 4 may benefit from a reduction of fine regardless of the time at which they decide to co-operate.

As explained in response to question 4 above, the concept of 'significant added value' refers to the extent to which the evidence provided strengthens, by its very nature and/or its level of detail, the ability of the competition authorities to prove the alleged infringement. In making this assessment, the *Autorité* will generally consider written, contemporaneous evidence to have a greater value than evidence subsequently established. Similarly, incriminating evidence directly relevant to the facts at stake will have a greater value than evidence of indirect relevance, and compelling evidence will be attributed a greater value than evidence such as witness statements which require corroboration if challenged.

The Procedural Notice does not provide a sliding scale of fine reduction depending on the order of application by the cartel participants. It merely indicates that the *Autorité* will take into account both the order and time of application and the extent to which the evidence submitted represents significant added value.

SCOPE/FULL LENIENCY
8. **Is it possible to receive full leniency? And, if so, what are the conditions required to receive full leniency? Can ringleaders/coercers receive full leniency? If there is a requirement to 'co-operate fully and on an ongoing basis' what does it entail? Does the regulatory authority require the applicant to cease participation in the cartel conduct after its application?**

Yes, full immunity will be granted to the first undertaking to provide the requisite information on the alleged cartel. The Procedural Notice contains two different evidential thresholds.

Type 1 A cases cover the scenario where the competition authorities have no information on the alleged cartel, ie, in cases where an inspection has not yet been launched.

In such a case, the applicant may qualify for full immunity if:
- the competition authorities did not previously have sufficient evidence to be able to carry out a targeted inspection (as defined in Article L 450-4 of the Commercial Code) on their own initiative; and
- in the *Autorité's* view, the evidence submitted is sufficient to have the targeted inspection carried out. In order to meet this evidential threshold, the applicant must as a minimum provide, orally or in writing: (i) all the information usually requested for a leniency application which includes *inter alia* a detailed description of the alleged cartel and the identity of its members (see response to question 4 above for further detail); and (ii) any pieces of evidence (documentary, testimonial or of any other nature) in its possession or that can be made available at the time of the application. These elements may consist of information helping to identify locations, dates and the object of contacts or meetings between participants in the alleged cartel.

Type 1 B cases cover the scenario where the competition authorities are already in possession of information on the cartel or have already carried out an inspection. In this case, the applicant may still qualify for full immunity

if all of the following conditions are met:
- At the time of the application, the competition authorities did not have sufficient evidence to find an infringement of Article L 420-1 of the Commercial Code and/or Article 101 TFEU.
- The applicant provides evidence which, in the *Autorité's* view, is sufficient to establish the existence of such an infringement. The standard of proof is significantly higher than for type 1 A cases since the competition authorities already have information on the infringement.
- No undertaking has obtained a conditional opinion granting type 1 A full immunity.

As for type 1 A cases, the applicant must provide, orally or in writing, the information usually requested for a leniency application (see response to question 4 above).

In addition to these eligibility conditions, the applicant must meet the three cumulative substantive conditions set out in detail in response to question 4 above. It must:
- put an end to its involvement in the infringement;
- co-operate genuinely, fully, on a continuous basis and expeditiously with the competition authorities; and
- not have destroyed or falsified evidence, nor disclosed its intention to apply for leniency.

Finally, as under the EC Leniency Notice, the applicant must not have taken steps to coerce other undertakings to participate in the infringement. It is worth noting however that being an instigator or ringleader in a cartel does not exclude the benefit of full immunity (decision 06-D-09 of 11 April 2006/wooden doors cartel).

9. How many companies have received full immunity from fines to date?

As at 31 December 2009, the *Conseil* had issued 125 infringement decisions for cartel activity since the NRE Law came into effect and the leniency policy has been available. The *Conseil* has issued four decisions on leniency cases since the procedure was created, of which two were handed down in 2008 (decision 08-D-12 of 21 May 2008/plywood production sector and decision 08-D-32 of 1 December 2008/steel trading sector). Among these decisions, three granted total immunity to the applicants.

It is worth noting that there are a number of cases where full immunity has been applied for and granted but where an infringement decision is still awaited.

PROCEDURE
10. What are the practical steps required to apply for leniency?
An undertaking applying for leniency will go through three practical steps: filing the application; providing evidence; and attending a hearing.

10.1 Filing the application
The applicant must contact the *Rapporteur Général*. Its contact details are:

Rapporteur Général de l'Autorité de la concurrence, 11 rue de l'Echelle – 75001 Paris, Telephone: +33 (0)155 040 078, Fax: +33 (0)155 040 086.

It should be noted that the *Autorité* accepts anonymous approaches by applicants wishing to obtain guidance on the implementation of leniency proceedings.

The leniency application can be made by registered mail with acknowledgement of receipt or even orally. In the latter case, the date and time of oral application is noted in writing.

The leniency applicant must provide:
- its name and address;
- information on the circumstances which led to its leniency application;
- the name and address of the other cartel participants;
- information on the product(s) and on the territory(ies) on which the alleged cartel is likely to have an impact;
- the nature and estimated duration of the alleged cartel; and
- any leniency application which has been or will be made to other competition authorities in relation to the alleged cartel.

The receipt of the application by the *Rapporteur Général* permits the undertaking to apply for a marker. A marker aims to protect the applicant's place in the queue for a period of time to be specified on a case-by-case basis in order to enable the applicant to gather information and items of evidence relating to the infringement which are necessary for the examination of the leniency application. If the applicant perfects the marker within the period set by the *Rapporteur Général*, the information and evidence provided will be deemed to have been submitted on the date when the marker was granted.

10.2 Examination of the leniency application

Once the leniency application is registered – either by written receipt of the letter sent by recorded delivery or by the drafting of a minute – a written or oral corporate statement is taken from the undertaking's representative by a *Rapporteur* of the *Autorité*. At the applicant's request, the oral statement can be electronically recorded by the *Autorité* (see response to question 13 for further details).

At this stage, the applicant must provide the competition authorities with all the evidence that it considers necessary to support its leniency application (eg, a detailed description of the alleged infringement including information about its nature, duration, operating system and implementation as well as about its members). However, at this stage of the procedure, the applicant does not have to provide all the pieces of evidence it has in its possession, in particular if the provision of such elements would interfere with the confidentiality of its application. Only the leniency opinion will require the transmission of these elements and the compliance with such a request will only be assessed in the final decision of the *Autorité*.

Thereafter, the *Rapporteur* in charge of the investigation of the leniency application drafts a report in which it verifies that all of the eligibility and substantive conditions are fulfilled and prepares, if applicable, proposals for full or partial immunity. It must promptly inform the applicant of whether its application constitutes a Type 1 A case or not. The report is then notified to the applicant and the *Commissaire du gouvernement* (a representative of the Minister of the Economy), at least three weeks before the hearing.

10.3 Leniency opinion of the *Autorité*
On the basis of the report, the applicant is called to attend a hearing (which is not public) before the *Autorité*.

The *Autorité* then adopts a leniency opinion in which it indicates whether it grants the applicant full or partial immunity from fines, and, in the latter case, the rate of reduction, and also specifies the conditions attached to it (see response to question 4). This leniency opinion is confidential.

The *Autorité* does not decide whether the conditions set up by the leniency opinion have been complied with until the end of the procedure. The statement of objections and the final report, drafted by the *Rapporteur* under the control of the *Rapporteur Général*, include an appraisal of the applicant's compliance with these conditions.

The *Autorité*, when judging on the merits, considers whether it grants the total or partial immunity requested. If it considers that the applicant fulfils the conditions set out in the leniency opinion, it grants full or partial immunity from fines, as indicated in the leniency opinion. Otherwise, it determines the exact level of the partial immunity. If it considers that the conditions are not met, it issues a negative opinion and the information and items of evidence are returned to the applicant upon its request.

Parallel to the usual steps to obtain leniency is the 'summary application' procedure which allows an applicant to lodge a short form summary with the *Autorité* in cases where the applicant has also sought full immunity from the European Commission (see response to question 19).

11. Is there an optimal time to approach the regulatory authority?
In common with many other jurisdictions, the French leniency policy encourages undertakings to intervene as soon as possible: the sooner an undertaking provides information and items of evidence to the *Autorité*, the greater the fine reduction may be. Indeed, the first cartel member to provide information may in principle be eligible for full immunity and subsequent applicants for a reduction in fine not exceeding 50 per cent.

The marker system introduced in April 2007 enables the undertakings to protect their rank in the leniency procedure. In order to ensure that it secures a marker as the first in the queue, the applicant should contact the *Rapporteur Général* as soon as possible. If the applicant is not sure whether the evidence it holds is sufficient to qualify for leniency, it can informally and on an anonymous basis seek guidance from the *Rapporteur Général*. However, it has to be noted that such an informal request does not secure a place in the leniency queue for the applicant.

12. What guarantees of leniency exist if a party co-operates?
There is no guarantee of leniency until the final decision is adopted by

the *Autorité*. However, an applicant fulfilling the conditions set out in the opinion of the *Autorité* awarding partial or full immunity will secure leniency.

Among the conditions that a leniency applicant has to comply with are the co-operation obligations.

The *Autorité* has elaborated on the content of the co-operation condition in the Procedural Notice and has prescribed the following requirements that must be met in order for the co-operation condition to be fulfilled. Indeed, as part of its obligation to co-operate genuinely, fully, on a continuous basis and expeditiously with the *Autorité*, the applicant must:
- provide the *Autorité* promptly with all information and evidence it retains regarding the alleged cartel;
- respond promptly to any competition authority request which may contribute to establishing the facts;
- make current (and if possible, former) employees and legal representatives available for interview by the competition authority;
- not destroy, falsify or conceal information relating to the alleged cartel; and
- not disclose the fact or content of its leniency application before the *Autorité* issues a statement of objections, unless otherwise agreed.

Provided all the other substantive conditions (ie, no coercion, ending its involvement in the cartel, not having destroyed or falsified evidence, nor disclosed its intention to apply for leniency) and eligibility conditions (see response to question 4 above) are met, leniency should be guaranteed. However, in practice the *Autorité* has significant discretion in deciding whether the conditions are met, particularly given the subjective nature of terms such as 'significant added value' or 'full' co-operation.

CONSEQUENCES
13. What effects does leniency granted to a corporate defendant have on the defendant's employees? Does it protect them from criminal and/or civil liability?

As the *Autorité* has no power to impose penalties on employees, there is no leniency programme for individuals.

Leniency does however impact on an applicant's employees if they have infringed Article L 420-6 of the Commercial Code. Under this provision, individuals who personally and decisively take part in designing, organising, or carrying out anticompetitive practices with fraudulent intent can be punished with up to four years' imprisonment and a fine of €75,000. The *Autorité* can refer such matters to the public prosecutor (*Procureur de la République*). However, the *Autorité* has undertaken not to do so for individuals who work for an undertaking which has been granted leniency.

Indeed, the Procedural Notice states that where an undertaking has been granted leniency, the *Autorité* will not refer its employees to the public prosecutor for prosecution of a criminal offence pursuant to Article L 420-6 of the Commercial Code. The *Autorité*'s policy not to make criminal referrals is available only to successful leniency applicants. This procedure should alleviate the concerns which would otherwise discourage leniency applicants in cases where there are precedents of criminal sanctions, such as in bid-rigging cases.

14. Does leniency bar further private enforcement?
As regards civil enforcement, the Procedural Notice expressly states that full or partial immunity does not protect the undertaking from any civil law consequences that may result from its participation in a cartel. Leniency is only related to proceedings before the *Autorité* and to possible fine reductions, and not to any awards for damages over which the *Autorité* does not have jurisdiction. In addition, a leniency application has no impact on the applicant's liability nor on the lawfulness of its conduct. Consequently, the courts may award damages to a victim on the basis of an *Autorité* decision sanctioning an undertaking for cartel involvement, even though it was granted leniency and thus is fully or partly exempted from fines.

PROTECTION AGAINST DISCLOSURE/CONFIDENTIALITY
15. Is confidentiality afforded to the leniency applicant and other co-operating parties? If so, to what extent? Is the identity of the leniency applicant/other co-operating parties disclosed during the investigation or in the final decision? Is information provided by the leniency applicant/other co-operating parties passed on to other undertakings under investigation? Can a leniency applicant/other co-operating party request anonymity or confidentiality of information provided?
The French competition authorities are well aware of the importance of confidentiality in regard to the applicant's incentive to co-operate and therefore in relation to the efficiency of the leniency programme. Therefore, different measures have been taken to protect the confidentiality of leniency applications.

Throughout the leniency procedure and until the statement of objections is sent to the other parties to the cartel, the existence of a leniency application is kept absolutely confidential from other cartel participants and any other third parties. In this respect, the leniency applicant is not obliged to provide all the evidence it has in its possession at the corporate statement stage. Similarly, the *Autorité* may postpone the date at which the applicant has to end its involvement in the infringement. The letters exchanged between the *Autorité* and the leniency applicant are kept confidential unless used to establish the prohibited practice and the *Rapporteur's* report proposing the fine reduction and the conditions to be fulfilled is also kept confidential. Only the leniency opinion adopted by the *Autorité* is made available to other parties to the proceeding, once the statement of objections has been issued.

An oral procedure has been introduced into the French leniency programme in order to preserve the confidentiality of the leniency application and to protect leniency applicants from the risk of discovery. Initial anonymous contacts with the *Autorité* can be made before the filing of a formal leniency application and the leniency application can be made

France

orally. The *Autorité* also accepts oral corporate statements. Under this procedure, the applicant does not retain a written statement for its records. It simply provides a verbal statement which will be electronically recorded if the applicant has requested it. Following the notification of the statement of objections, the transcripts will only be available to the parties to the proceedings through a consultation at the premises of the *Autorité*.

16. Is the evidence submitted by the leniency applicant protected from disclosure to other competition authorities with whom the authority in question co-operates? If so, how?
Since 1 May 2004, the *Autorité* has been a member of the ECN, which was created by Regulation 1/2003. Within the ECN, competition authorities co-operate closely. Rules on the efficient division of work and co-operation mechanisms for allocating cases and mutual assistance between authorities have been adopted. These rules, which include principles relating to the protection of persons who apply for leniency, were detailed by the Commission in the Notice on co-operation.

In addition, oral statements made under the leniency programme will only be transmitted by the *Autorité* to other competition authorities, pursuant to Article 12 of Regulation No 1/2003, if the conditions set out in the Notice relating to co-operation are met and provided that the receiving competition authority guarantees a degree of confidentiality that is equivalent to the one guaranteed by the *Autorité*.

17. To what extent can evidence submitted by the leniency applicant (transcripts of oral statements or written evidence) become discoverable in subsequent private enforcement claims? Can leniency information be subjected to discovery orders in domestic or foreign courts? Can leniency information submitted in a foreign jurisdiction be subjected to discovery orders in domestic courts?
With respect to the ability of third parties to obtain information from the *Autorité* in the context of a civil action for damages, it should be kept in mind that the judge in a civil action can request the disclosure of information and documents. According to Article 11 of the Code of Civil Procedure, a judge may on the request of the parties, order the production of all documents held by third parties unless there is a legitimate reason preventing such communication. In this respect, the *Autorité* would be considered a third party to the civil proceeding.

However, in its 2005 annual report the *Autorité* took the position that if such a request pertained to a leniency application, it would refuse to disclose the corporate statement as well as any information provided in support of a leniency application on the grounds that any such disclosure could damage the effectiveness of the leniency programme. The *Autorité* reaffirmed its view of the importance of preserving the effectiveness of leniency programmes when publishing an opinion in 2006 related to the introduction of a 'group action' under French law. Therefore, the *Autorité* decided to adopt the Commission's reasoning set out in the Commission Notice on the co-operation between the Commission and the courts of the EU member states pursuant to Articles 101 and 102 TFEU, and will not disclose information voluntarily submitted by a leniency applicant to national courts (either domestic or foreign) without the consent of that applicant.

Moreover and to address these concerns, the *Autorité* made clear that when implementing the leniency rules, the French authorities will accept oral corporate statements. Under this procedure, the applicant does not retain a written statement for its records, and therefore cannot produce a statement in the event of a discovery order.

18. Are there any precedents in which evidence from a leniency application has been discovered in a private enforcement claim?
There is no precedent for evidence from a leniency application being discovered in a private enforcement claim.

RELATIONSHIP WITH THE EUROPEAN COMMISSION'S LENIENCY NOTICE AND LENIENCY POLICY IN OTHER EU MEMBER STATES

19. Does the policy address the interaction with applications under the Commission Leniency Notice? If so, how?
The Procedural Notice takes into account that a leniency applicant might also file an application to the European Commission. So as to be informed of such parallel proceedings, the Procedural Notice requires the applicant to provide the *Autorité* in its leniency application with any other leniency application which has been or will be made to another competition authority.

More importantly, in order to alleviate the burden associated with multiple parallel applications, the Procedural Notice introduced a 'summary application' procedure which allows an applicant to lodge a short form summary with the *Autorité* in cases where the applicant has also sought full immunity from the European Commission. This procedure was introduced in April 2007 when the Procedural Notice was amended to comply with the ECN Model Programme and is designed to minimise the burden of multiple filings borne by leniency applicants.

The *Autorité* accepts summary applications in type 1 A cases where:
- the Commission is 'particularly well placed' to deal with a case (ie where the cartel has an effect on more than three EU member states);
- the applicant has filed or is about to file an application for full immunity with the Commission; and
- the summary application includes the following information:
  - the name and address of the applicant;
  - the identity of the other parties in the alleged cartel;
  - a short description of the affected products and territories;
  - a short description of the duration and nature of the alleged cartel;
  - the member states where evidence is likely to be located; and
  - information on other past or possible leniency applications in relation to the alleged cartel.

Summary applications must be sent by recorded delivery with written receipt or by oral statement. The *Rapporteur Général* will acknowledge receipt (including the date and the time) of the application and will confirm whether the applicant is eligible for type 1 A immunity.

The date of receipt of the application or the drafting of the oral statement makes it possible to determine the queuing order of the summary application. If it is confirmed that the applicant is the first to seek full immunity, the summary application will be considered by the *Autorité* as having been made in accordance with the conditions provided for type 1 A immunity. However, the applicant is still required to provide the *Autorité* with any additional information which it may request.

If the *Autorité* decides to take action in a case for which a summary application has been submitted, the undertaking must provide all information and evidence necessary to examine the application under the conditions provided for a conventional leniency application.

20. Does the policy address the interaction with applications for leniency in other EU member states? If so, how?
The Procedural Notice does not address the interaction with leniency applications made in other EU member states.

Steps have, however, been taken by the ECN to address the concern that has arisen as a result of the discrepancies between the leniency programmes of the EU member states, via the ECN Model Programme. This sets out the treatment which an applicant can anticipate in any ECN jurisdiction once alignment of all the programmes has taken place.

RELATIONSHIP WITH SETTLEMENT PROCEDURES
21. What is the relationship between leniency and applicable settlement procedures? Are they mutually exclusive?
The settlement procedure, codified in Article L 464-2 III of the Commercial Code, provides that when a company does not contest the statement of objections served upon it, the *Rapporteur Général* may propose that the *Autorité* grant a fine reduction. In this case, the theoretical maximum amount of the fine incurred will be reduced by half (ie 5 per cent of the consolidated worldwide turnover instead of 10 per cent). When the undertaking goes further than simply not contesting the objections and commits to alter its conduct in the future, the *Rapporteur Général* may propose a further reduction of the fine.

Regarding the possibility of combining leniency and settlement procedures, the question is twofold: (i) can the same company benefit from both leniency and settlement procedures in the same proceedings; and (ii) can a company benefit from a settlement procedure when another company (or companies) has applied for leniency?

Regarding the first question, the different features and rationale of the two procedures (and notably the fact that leniency is only available before the statement of objections whereas settlement is only available subsequently) appear to exclude that an undertaking could benefit from both procedures cumulatively. Accordingly, a leniency applicant will not be able to benefit from an additional fine reduction under the settlement procedure. The future guidelines on the settlement procedure to be issued by the *Autorité* will probably provide more guidance in connection with this issue.

In response to the second question, the fact that an undertaking has applied for leniency does not preclude other parties from entering into settlement procedures. In this respect, the *Autorité* applied both leniency and settlement procedures for the first time in its decision relating to a cartel in the international removal sector. To date, the two procedures have been applied concurrently in three cases (decision 07-D-48 of 18 December 2007/ international removal, decision 08-D-12 of 21 May 2008/wood industry and decision 08-D-32 of 16 December 2008/steel trading sector).

REFORM/LATEST DEVELOPMENTS
22. Is there a reform underway to revisit the leniency policy? What are the latest developments?
No reform is currently underway.

Germany

Gleiss Lutz Dr Matthias Karl & Dr Martin Beutelmann

BACKGROUND
1. What is the relevant legislation containing the leniency policy and what is the enforcing body?

The German Act against Restraints of Competition (*Gesetz gegen Wettbewerbsbeschränkungen* or ARC) prohibits collusive agreements between enterprises that restrict competition and that are not exempted under sections 2 and 3 ARC (section 1 ARC). The ARC was amended to correspond to the new EC competition law under Regulation 1/2003 on 1 July 2005. The interpretation of the ARC provisions must, in general, be in accordance with EC competition law.

The wilful or negligent violation of section 1 ARC (as well as of Article 101 TFEU) can be fined as an administrative offence under section 81(1) and 81(2) ARC. The fine can amount to up to €1 million (section 81(4) 1 ARC) and beyond, but for each undertaking and association of undertakings participating in the infringement, the fine shall not exceed 10 per cent of the total turnover in the preceding business year (section 81(4) 2 ARC).

Section 1 ARC is addressed to 'undertakings' and 'associations of undertakings'. These entities are subject to the ARC and can be fined for an infringement under section 81 ARC. An undertaking is legally responsible for any violation of ARC provisions if a person entitled to represent it violates its duty to supervise the competitive behaviour of the overall undertaking with regard to ARC provisions. German law also provides for the possibility of fining certain natural persons (a legal representative or another person in a comparable position) if such a person has personally contributed to the infringement or has not taken appropriate measures to prevent the anticompetitive conduct (sections 130 and 30 of the Administrative Offences Act (*Gesetz über Ordnungswidrigkeiten*). In addition, if a natural person carries out business activities, such person is to be classified as an 'undertaking' and can be an offender within the meaning of section 81 ARC.

The Federal Cartel Office or FCO (*Bundeskartellamt*), which is the national authority enforcing German and European competition law, first adopted a notice containing leniency regulations on 17 April 2000 (Notice 68/2000). This notice has now been replaced by 'Notice no. 9/2006 of the *Bundeskartellamt* on the immunity from and reduction of fines in cartel cases' dated 07 March 2006 (Leniency Guidelines). The notice is available in German, English and French on the website of the FCO (*www.bundeskartellamt.de*). This second notice is understood to be an updated and modernised version of the original leniency notice that takes account of both EC leniency policy and the model leniency programme developed by the European Competition Network (ECN).

The Leniency Guidelines apply to the setting of fines imposed on both natural persons and undertakings which offend against ARC provisions. Since the leniency policy of the FCO is intended to be in line with the leniency notice of the EC Commission, literature and case law which relate to the EC leniency notices of 1996, 2002 and 2006 can provide useful information on the interpretation and application of the Leniency Guidelines.

It should be noted that the ARC provisions as well as Article 101 TFEU are enforced not only by the FCO, but also by the supreme competition authorities (*Landeskartellbehörden*) of the 16 federal states (*Bundesländer*). The FCO will deal with infringement cases only if the effect of the infringement on the market extends beyond the territory of one *Bundesland*. In all other cases, the *Landeskartellbehörden* will conduct the investigations (section 48 ARC). This division of competencies should be taken into account when considering a leniency application since the Leniency Guidelines of the FCO do not directly apply to infringement proceedings conducted by the *Landeskartellbehörden*. Although the FCO and the *Landeskartellbehörden* apply the same substantial and procedural rules (ie the ARC provisions), they are not bodies of the same legal entity. Therefore, the Leniency Guidelines of the FCO, which are administrative principles only binding on itself, do not have binding effect on the *Landeskartellbehörden* and cannot be invoked by a leniency applicant in infringement proceedings before these authorities.

Therefore, the leniency applicant is recommended to apply to the FCO even if a *Landeskartellbehörde* may actually be competent under section 48 ARC. In the application it should be argued that the conditions of the Leniency Guidelines of the FCO are met and that the applicant is willing to fully co-operate in line with these guidelines, but that there is no comparable leniency protection before the competent *Landeskartellbehörde*. The lack of leniency protection before the respective competition authority of the Bundesland should be sufficient justification for applying the mechanism of flexible competence under section 49(3) ARC. According to this provision, the *Landeskartellbehörde* of one *Bundesland* may, at the request of the FCO, refer the case to the FCO if this is required by the specific circumstances of the relevant case.

2. What are the basic tenets of a leniency/immunity programme? Is leniency also available for types of competition law violations other than cartels?

According to the Leniency Guidelines, cartel members can receive (complete) 'immunity from fines' or a 'reduction of fines' of up to 50 per cent. According to the wording of the Leniency Guidelines, they only apply to 'cartels', but not to vertical infringements or cases of unilateral abuse of market power. Yet, the FCO has indicated in its practice that it is prepared to take into account the co-operation of a participant in anti-competitive vertical behaviour and to grant significant reductions comparable to the ones under the Leniency Guidelines. There are, however, no formal, specified rules in this respect.

The qualification of a leniency applicant for one of these options is in particular dependent upon: the timing of the leniency application (see question 5 below); the role the applicant played in the cartel; and the extent and nature of its contribution during the infringement proceedings.

Full immunity will be granted only to the 'first in' and only under certain circumstances (see question 8 below). The first applicant can be granted full immunity even after the FCO has learned of the cartel infringement and even if the FCO was already in a position to obtain a search warrant. Subsequent applicants, or applicants not fulfilling the preconditions for full immunity, can receive at most a 50 per cent reduction. If the applicant played a 'decisive' role in the cartel, they cannot receive full immunity, but are not generally excluded from being granted a reduction of the fine. As a further important condition, co-operation with the enforcement authority must be continuous and without reservation.

The new leniency notice provides for the possibility of placing a marker, ie a cartel member's declaration of its willingness to co-operate. The FCO will acknowledge receipt of the marker, but will generally not decide on the extent of the reduction of the fine until the final decision is adopted. Only if the marker refers to an application for complete immunity will the Commission issue in the course of the proceedings an assurance saying that the applicant will be granted full immunity, provided that the applicant was neither the only ringleader of the cartel, nor coerced other undertakings into participating in the cartel.

The Leniency Guidelines are legally binding on the FCO. They limit the discretionary powers conferred upon it for the setting of fines. However, it should be noted that the Leniency Guidelines do not automatically reduce the prospective fine. There is still some scope left for the final decision by the FCO.

3. How many cartels have been unveiled and punished since the adoption of the leniency programme?

The FCO praises the efficiency of the Leniency Guidelines in detecting and punishing cartels. The number of leniency applications has consistently increased over recent years and is expected to increase further. In the years 2000 to 2008, 210 leniency applications were filed concerning 69 different proceedings. Eighty of these 210 applications, concerning 37 proceedings, were filed in the years 2007 and 2008.

4. What is needed to be a successful leniency applicant? Is documentary evidence required or is testimonial evidence sufficient?

There are no clear-cut requirements for a successful leniency application. The leniency notice requires any applicant to 'co-operate fully and on a continuous basis'. The leniency applicant is expected to provide all 'verbal and written' information available to them, including documents and evidence relating to the cartel. In particular, all information necessary for the calculation of the fine has to be handed over. Furthermore, the identity of all employees involved in the cartel agreement has to be revealed. If the application is intended to be filed for more than one legal entity belonging to the same group, the respective affiliated companies must be named in the application. The duty to hand over information in whatever form does not end with filing the application, but continues throughout the proceedings.

The FCO will not consider the co-operation as fulfilling the above requirements if the leniency applicant merely submits information or documents without any further explanation. In particular, the co-operation requires an oral or written description of the relevant cartel behaviour, including time and place of meetings, details of the illegal behaviour, as well as the identity of the companies involved.

In order to receive full immunity, the leniency application must enable the FCO to initiate further investigatory measures. Full immunity will only be granted if the application enables the FCO to obtain a search warrant. If the FCO had already been in a position to obtain a search warrant due to information available to it, the applicant will be granted full immunity only if the information in the application enables the FCO to prove the offence. Consequently, the leniency applicant is required to gather and present the documents and the factual background of the relevant cartel behaviour in order to increase its chances of meeting these thresholds.

With regard to the reduction of the fine, the Leniency Guidelines require the applicant to hand over 'all the information and evidence available' to the applicant which makes a significant contribution to proving the offence. The value of the contributions to uncovering the illegal agreement will be one decisive aspect relating to the amount of the reduction that will be granted to the applicant. This provision proves to be problematic in practice. Companies not having particularly incriminating documents or information can be provoked into exaggerating the information in their possession and the facts that can be proved with it.

TIMING
5. What are the benefits of being 'first in' to co-operate?
If the leniency applicant is 'first in' to co-operate, such applicant will – subject to the conditions set out in question 8 below – not be fined at all. As this full immunity will be granted only to the 'first in', companies are under significant pressure to evaluate the risk of being uncovered, not only by the competition authority but also by their fellow cartel members. The Leniency Guidelines therefore create an unstable situation between cartel members similar to the 'prisoner's dilemma'. However, even the 'second in' can qualify for full immunity under certain conditions, see below under question 6.

6. What are the consequences of being 'second'? Is there an 'immunity plus' or 'amnesty plus' option?
If the leniency applicant is only 'second' and the first applicant qualifies for full immunity, then the second applicant will be granted a reduction of its fine not exceeding 50 per cent. This leniency position can be achieved even

after an investigation has been initiated. It must be noted that applicants can receive full immunity even if they are not the 'first in'. The German Leniency Guidelines do not exclude the possibility of the second applicant moving into the position of the first applicant. This might be the case if the first applicant was the sole ringleader or does not fulfil its obligation to co-operate. The prospect of overtaking the first applicant intensifies the competition between applicants to offer the most value – and to denounce the first applicant.

No rules exist as to 'immunity plus' or 'amnesty plus'.

7. Are subsequent firms given any beneficial treatment if they make a useful contribution? How are 'useful contributions' defined?

Leniency applicants subsequent to the 'first in', or not qualifying for full immunity under the 'first in' rules, may receive reduced fines. The maximum reduction that can be granted is 50 per cent.

In order to qualify for a reduction, the applicant has to adhere to the following obligations:

- it has to co-operate fully and on a continuous basis for the entire duration of the proceedings;
- it must hand over all the information and evidence available to it (see above question 4) which is likely to make a significant contribution. There is no explicit definition of 'significant contribution' in the Leniency Guidelines. The FCO has a very broad discretion as to whether it grants any reduction at all;
- it must end its involvement in the cartel immediately on request by the FCO;
- it has to maintain confidentiality regarding its co-operation with the FCO until explicitly relieved of it; and
- it must name all employees involved in the cartel and ensure that they all adhere to the co-operation obligation.

Provided that the applicant fulfils these obligations, the FCO will determine the reduction of the fine on the basis of the value of the contribution and the sequence of applications.

An application can be made as long as the proceedings have not been concluded by the FCO by means of a formal decision. In particular, a reduction is not excluded because the initiation of the investigation has become known. However, the later the applicant decides to file an application, and the more information the FCO has already collected, the less 'significant' the applicant's information will be. On the other hand, the sequence of applications as such is not the exclusive determining factor for the amount by which the fine is reduced. If an early applicant is not able to present valuable information, then a later applicant will be able to achieve a more significant reduction by presenting data of higher value.

Apart from the value of the contributions and the sequence of the applications, the Leniency Guidelines do not mention any further provisions that will be taken into account in the course of determining the reduction of the fine. The Leniency Guidelines do not exclude the possibility of a reduction of the fine for the ringleader of a cartel or for an undertaking that coerced other undertakings into participating in the cartel.

SCOPE/FULL LENIENCY
8. Is it possible to receive full leniency? And, if so, what are the conditions required to receive full leniency?
On the basis of the Leniency Guidelines, the conditions for full immunity depend on whether the FCO already has sufficient evidence to obtain a search warrant or not.

Before this is the case, a leniency applicant (automatically) receives full immunity if it: is the first participant in a cartel to contact the FCO before it has obtained sufficient evidence to obtain a search warrant; provides the FCO with verbal and written information and, where available, evidence which enables it to obtain a search warrant; was not the only ringleader of the cartel, nor coerced others into participating in the cartel; and co-operates fully and on a continuous basis with the FCO.

If at the time when the application is filed the FCO was already in a position to obtain a search warrant, full immunity will – as a rule – be granted if the applicant: is the first participant in the cartel to contact the FCO before it has sufficient evidence to prove the offence; provides the FCO with verbal and written information and, where available, evidence which enables it to prove the offence; was not the only ringleader of the cartel, nor coerced others into participating in the cartel; co-operates fully and on a continuous basis with the FCO and; provided no cartel participant is granted immunity before it.

All of the respective conditions must be met.

8.1 Can ringleaders/coercers receive full leniency?
A sole ringleader of a cartel or an undertaking having coerced another undertaking into participating in the cartel will under no circumstances be eligible for full immunity.

8.2 If there is a requirement to 'co-operate fully and on an ongoing basis' what does it entail?
According to the Leniency Guidelines, the obligation to co-operate with the FCO entails at least the obligation to provide any information and evidence that is available to the applicant. This obligation also refers to information that is necessary for calculating the fine if it is available to the applicant or can be procured by it. Furthermore, the applicant has to name all employees involved in the infringement and must ensure that they also co-operate fully and on a continuous basis.

8.3 Does the regulatory authority require the applicant to cease participation in the cartel conduct after its application?
The Leniency Guidelines require that the applicant ceases its participation in the cartel on request by the FCO.

9. How many companies have received full immunity from fines to date?

Several undertakings have received full immunity. There is no official data on the total number of applicants that have received full immunity.

PROCEDURE/CONFIDENTIALITY

10. What are the practical steps required to apply for leniency?

10.1 Initial contact/is there a 'marker' system?

Under the first Leniency Guidelines of 2000, undertakings considering a leniency application to the FCO were faced with a lack of transparency about the whole leniency procedure and, thus, with legal uncertainty. They were required not only to assess the risk of being uncovered by the competition authorities or by other cartel members. In addition they had to examine all information available to them as to whether it would be of sufficient value. The new Leniency Guidelines introduce what is known as a marker system that is intended to give applicants guidance and certainty during the proceedings.

The applicant can initiate the leniency proceedings by contacting the *Sonderkommission Kartellbekämpfung* (special unit for combating cartels) or the chairman of the competent *Beschlussabteilung* (decision-making division) of the FCO. The contact details are: Bundeskartellamt, Sonderkommission Kartellbekämpfung, Mr. Töllner, Kaiser-Friedrich-Strasse 16, 53113 Bonn, Germany, Fax: +49-(0)228-94.99.400.

The applicant can place a 'marker' by announcing its unreserved willingness to co-operate with the FCO. Placing the marker does not require the undertaking to submit a complete application as set out in question 4 above. It has to contain only a summary of the most important identifying features of the cartel including details about the type and duration of the infringement, the product and geographic market affected, the identity of those involved and the other competition authorities to which applications have been, or are intended to be, filed. If the marker is intended to be placed for more than one legal entity belonging to the same group, the respective affiliated companies must be included in the marker. The marker can be placed verbally or in writing. It can be in English or in German.

10.2 Full disclosure

The FCO will then confirm that a marker has been placed and will set a time limit of not more than eight weeks for filing the complete application for leniency containing all the necessary information. The application can be filed in written or verbal form and either in German or in English. In the latter case, a written German translation must also be provided. An application submitted by an undertaking will be treated by the FCO as an application also for its current and former employees, unless otherwise indicated. The FCO can exempt the applicant from filing a complete application if the European Commission is the best placed authority to decide on the case and if the applicant intends to file, or has already filed, an application to the European Commission.

10.3 Conditional reduction of fine
Thereafter, the FCO will confirm receipt of the complete application. It will generally not decide whether and to what extent immunity or a reduction will be granted. The FCO will only state how the applicant is ranked and whether it fulfils its co-operation duties. Only if the undertaking fulfils the conditions for automatic full immunity, ie applies for leniency before the FCO has sufficient information to obtain a search warrant (see above question 8), the FCO will 'assure the applicant in writing that it will be granted immunity from the fine subject to the condition that it was neither the only ringleader of the cartel nor coerced others into participating in the cartel and fulfils its obligations to co-operate'.

10.4 Final reduction
The exact amount of reduction will ultimately be decided in the final decision of the FCO.

11. Is there an optimal time to approach the regulatory authority?
As can be seen from the conditions for receiving full immunity, the optimal time to approach the FCO is before the cartel has become known to it through its own investigations, through customers or suppliers of the cartel, or through a leniency application by another cartel member. However, the leniency applicant will normally not learn whether there has been such contact. Nevertheless, a leniency application should be submitted as soon as possible in order to ensure a strong position. By placing a marker the applicant gains up to eight weeks in which it can gather all the information available to it in order to safeguard its position in the leniency proceedings.

12. What guarantees of leniency exist if a party co-operates?
There is no guarantee of leniency until the final decision is adopted by the FCO at the end of the investigation. The FCO will only confirm receipt of the marker and of the complete application and it will state how the applicant is ranked and whether it fulfils its duties to co-operate. Only if the undertaking fulfils the conditions for automatic full immunity, ie applies for leniency before the FCO has sufficient information to obtain a search warrant, will the FCO issue a written, conditional assurance that it will receive full immunity. The assurance is issued on the condition that the applicant fulfils its co-operation obligations, that it was not the sole ringleader of the cartel and that it did not coerce another undertaking into participating in the cartel.

Apart from that, the leniency applicant might learn of the pre-existing co-operation of another cartel member at a later procedural stage, eg when exercising its right of access to the file. In addition, the reduction of the fine depends to a significant extent on the FCO's assessment of the documents and evidence as a 'significant contribution'. However, the FCO does not clearly communicate during the procedure whether the contribution of a leniency applicant fulfils this criterion. Even if the leniency applicant provides the FCO with all the information available to it, this might not be sufficient to get an acceptable leniency position since another applicant might have provided even more detailed and incriminating documents. Therefore, the leniency applicant cannot really evaluate its position during the course of an investigation.

CONSEQUENCES
13. What effects does leniency granted to a corporate defendant have on the defendant's employees?
In German antitrust law, it is important to distinguish between those employees entitled to represent the undertaking or to exercise managerial functions on the one hand, and those who are not. If the latter engage in antitrust behaviour, they do not violate ARC provisions since they are not classified as 'undertakings' because their actions cannot be attributed directly to their employer. However, if their behaviour was facilitated by lack of internal supervision, the people entitled to represent the undertaking or to exercise managerial functions will have violated their duty to supervise the undertaking within the meaning of section 130 of the Administrative Offences Act. They can, thus, be fined. The violation of this duty is an administrative offence that is imputed to the relevant undertaking under section 30 of the Administrative Offences Act which can then be fined as well.

The Leniency Guidelines explicitly state that a leniency application filed on behalf of an undertaking will also be rated by the FCO as one made on behalf of the natural persons participating in the cartel as former or current employees of the undertaking in question. The undertakings can, however, declare that the application shall not be treated as representing the employees. The FCO leaves open the question of whether an application by a natural person on their own behalf will also be treated as representing the undertaking in question. It is generally assumed that this is not the case.

14. Does leniency bar further criminal or private enforcement?
The Leniency Guidelines have no effect on the consequences that the participation in an illegal cartel might trigger under civil law. Customers of the cartel members can claim damages pursuant to section 33 ARC and section 823 of the Civil Code (*Bürgerliches Gesetzbuch*). In this respect it needs to be borne in mind that customers and other injured parties have access to the file under section 406e of the Code of Criminal Procedure (*Strafprozessordnung*) to the extent described above. The FCO, however, recognises the effect that a broad right of access to the file for third parties has on cartel members' willingness to co-operate and therefore will usually be open to discussion on how the leniency applicants' interests can best be protected.

A violation of ARC provisions is not in itself a criminal offence. However, if the antitrust behaviour includes criminal offences such as bid rigging (section 298 of the Criminal Code, *Strafgesetzbuch*), the FCO must refer proceedings against any natural person to the public prosecutor under section 41 of the Administrative Offences Act. Co-operation with the FCO may be relevant as a mitigating factor in any criminal proceedings, but generally does not prevent them.

PROTECTION AGAINST DISCLOSURE/CONFIDENTIALITY
15. Is confidentiality afforded to the leniency applicant and other co-operating parties? If so, to what extent?
The FCO is well aware that confidentiality is an important asset with regard to the applicant's incentive to co-operate and therefore to the efficiency of a leniency programme. The Leniency Guidelines contain some rules on how the applicants' confidentiality is to be protected. However, although the FCO may be prepared to grant protection to applicants, this often conflicts with the information rights of third parties (for example, other undertakings under investigation, other competition authorities and damaged third parties). As a general rule, the Leniency Guidelines state that, until the statement of objections is issued, and 'within the scope of the statutory limits and regulations on the exchange of information with foreign competition authorities' (among the European Competition authorities, some rules are set out in the Commission notice on co-operation within the network of competition authorities) the FCO will safeguard the applicant's confidentiality by treating as confidential the identity of the applicant and by preserving its trade and business secrets.

15.1 Is the identity of the leniency applicant/other co-operating parties disclosed during the investigation or in the final decision?
The other undertakings under investigation will have access to the file of the FCO at the latest after the issuance of the statement of objections. They will then be able to identify the leniency applicant(s).

The FCO usually publishes on its website a press release and/or a case report after handing down the final decision, in which it reveals the identity of the cartelists and the sum of the fines. There is no coherent practice with regard to the leniency applicant's identity. The FCO has revealed the identity of the leniency applicant in some cases and has kept it secret in others.

15.2 Is information provided by the leniency applicant/other co-operating parties passed on to other undertakings under investigation?
The other undertakings under investigation will have access to the file of the FCO, at the latest after the issuance of the statement of objections. Although business secrets will be deleted, large parts of the leniency application will become accessible at this stage to the other parties under investigation.

15.3 Can a leniency applicant/other co-operating party request anonymity or confidentiality of information provided?
The protection mentioned above is granted irrespective of a request by the applicant. A request for further protection can be brought and may be provided by the FCO if this is within its discretion.

16. Is the evidence submitted by the leniency applicant protected from transmission to other competition authorities with whom the authority in question co-operates? If so, how?
The FCO has signed the 'Statement regarding the Commission notice on co-

Germany

operation within the network of competition authorities'. It thereby agreed to pass on leniency applications and related documents to other authorities of the NCA only in the cases specified in the Commission notice. The most important case in this respect is if the applicant has given its consent to passing on the information to another authority.

17. To what extent can evidence submitted by the leniency applicant (transcripts of oral statements or written evidence) become discoverable in subsequent private enforcement claims?

On the basis of section 406e of the Code of Criminal Procedure any undertaking (including damaged third parties) has the right of access to the file provided that it can show a legitimate interest. These provisions give the FCO discretionary powers to decide on the extent of this right. In the Leniency Guidelines, the FCO states that it will use these discretionary powers to refuse applications by private third parties for file inspection or the supply of information, 'insofar as the leniency application and the evidence provided by the applicant are concerned'.

Whether the approach of the FCO is justified, is currently under judicial review. The FCO has indicated that it will reject all requests by third party claimants for access to the file until this matter has been decided.

For the time after the final decision of the FCO has been issued, the FCO has indicated that it may be prepared to limit access to the file by third parties to certain documents that do not include the leniency application and the associated documents. However, there have not been any decisive precedents so far, therefore, the legal situation is still unclear.

17.1 Can leniency information be subjected to discovery orders in domestic courts? Can leniency information submitted in a foreign jurisdiction be subjected to discovery orders in domestic courts?

German civil procedure law does not provide for rules comparable to those in the US which enable a court to issue discovery orders that oblige a party to disclose certain documents or a certain category of documents for use in civil proceedings. Although section 142 of the German Code of Civil Procedure (*Zivilprozessordnung*) has been claimed by some commentators to offer similar options, it has to our knowledge not been employed to oblige a leniency applicant to disclose a leniency application in civil proceedings. This applies to information submitted to the FCO as well as to information submitted to a competition authority in a foreign jurisdiction.

17.2 Can leniency information be subjected to discovery orders in foreign courts?

Depending on the respective national civil procedural law, leniency information may in principle be subjected to discovery orders in foreign courts. The FCO has indicated – both in the Leniency Guidelines and in its recent practice – that it is willing to protect the confidentiality of applicants' submissions. In order to make leniency applications 'discovery-proof', the Leniency Guidelines allow applicants to submit both the marker and the application in oral form.

18. Are there any precedents in which evidence from a leniency application has been discovered in a private enforcement claim?

There have been requests by third parties for access to the FCO's files in nearly all significant cases. There are several proceedings currently pending. We do not have reliable information on how many requests have actually been successful and enabled a third party to access a leniency applicant's submissions. However, although the legal basis for access to the file (section 406e *Strafprozesordnung*) does not provide for overly strict conditions, the FCO has shown a willingness to protect leniency applicants under the Leniency Guidelines.

RELATIONSHIP WITH THE EUROPEAN COMMISSION'S LENIENCY NOTICE AND LENIENCY POLICY IN OTHER EU MEMBER STATES

19. Does the policy address the interaction with applications under the Commission Leniency Notice? If so, how?

The Leniency Guidelines take into account that an applicant for leniency might also file an application to the European Commission. In order to be informed of such potentially concurrent proceedings, the Leniency Guidelines oblige the applicant to include with the marker details of whether and to which other competition authority an application for leniency has been, or is going to be, filed.

If the applicant has also applied, or intends to apply, to the European Commission and if the Commission is the best placed authority according to the criteria of the Commission notice on co-operation within the network of competition authorities, then the FCO can exempt an undertaking that has placed a marker from submitting a complete application. Whether or not the FCO grants this exemption depends on whether the Commission actually picks up the case. This merely confirms that the FCO respects the priority of the proceedings at EU level in accordance with Article 11 (6) of Regulation 1/2003.

20. Does the policy address the interaction with applications for leniency in other EU member states? If so, how?

The Leniency Guidelines only refer once to the possibility that other national competition authorities might also be addressed by an applicant. In order to be informed of such potentially concurrent proceedings, the Leniency Guidelines oblige the applicant to include with the marker whether and to which other competition authority an application for leniency has been, or is going to be, filed beside the one to the FCO.

The Leniency Guidelines neither contain any indication that the application in another EU member state will have an effect on the applicant's position in the proceedings in Germany nor in what other way the FCO will interpret the relationship between the German and the other proceedings. An applicant will therefore have to file its application in any member state in which it can expect to be liable to a fine. It can be expected that the FCO will apply the Commission notice on co-operation within the network of competition authorities in this respect.

The applicant has to expect that the FCO will share the information contained in the application with other competition authorities. However, it will treat as confidential the identity of the applicant and its trade and business secrets, but only until a statement of objections has been issued to a cartel participant.

RELATIONSHIP WITH SETTLEMENT PROCEDURES
21. What is the relationship between leniency and applicable settlement procedures? Are they mutually exclusive?
The FCO included rules on settlement procedures in a case summary that it published in January 2010 relating to the proceedings against coffee-roasting companies. According to these rules, up to a 10 per cent reduction of the fine can be achieved by agreeing on a settlement with the FCO. The rules do not explicitly state whether this bonus can be cumulated with a leniency reduction. But given the obligations of the undertaking trying to achieve a settlement on the one hand and its obligations as a leniency applicant on the other, there appears to be no reason why a company should not be cumulatively rewarded for both the settlement and the leniency co-operation.

REFORM/LATEST DEVELOPMENTS
22. Is there a reform underway to revisit the leniency policy? What are the latest developments?
The organisational framework within the FCO was changed in October 2008. Efforts to streamline and strengthen the FCO's resources for pursuing hardcore infringements started in 2002 when it set up a special unit for combating cartels (*Sonderkommission Kartellbekämpfung* (SKK)). The task of the SKK is to assist the relevant decision-making divisions in the FCO, which are competent for all antitrust and merger cases relating to specific industrial sectors, in uncovering cartel agreements by deploying specialised personnel resources.

In 2005, the FCO restructured its internal division of competence in order to increase the quota of uncovered cartel agreements and to speed up proceedings. For this purpose, it set up a special unit with competence for all hardcore cartels regardless of the industrial sector affected. In October 2008, the FCO set up a second special unit of that kind.

It is not expected that a revised leniency regulation will be issued within the next two or three years.

One remarkable development concerns the FCO's practice regarding markers. While the FCO has generally requested that undertakings placing a marker complete the application within a specified period of time, it has recently shown a willingness to follow a more flexible approach. Depending on the facts of the case and on the FCO's tendency to open formal proceedings, it appears to be possible to agree with the FCO on a more flexible timeframe including making the option of completion of the marker dependent on events in the future.

Hungary

Bán S. Szabó & Partners Dr Chrysta Bán

BACKGROUND
1. What is the relevant legislation containing the leniency policy and what is the enforcing body?

Competition law in Hungary, including rules on illegal cartel activity, is regulated by Act LVII of 1996 on the Prohibition of Unfair Trade Practices and Restriction of Competition (as amended) (the Competition Act).

The Competition Act grants the Office of Economic Competition (the Competition Office) permission to act as the administrative authority in Hungary on all issues which fall under the scope of the Competition Act. The independent decision-making body of the Competition Office is the Competition Council.

Leniency regulations in Hungary were first introduced in 2003, when the Competition Office issued leniency guidelines about the application of the leniency policy. At that time, the Competition Act itself did not contain regulations about the leniency policy. The entire leniency policy was based on section 78(3) of the Act, according to which the co-operation of an undertaking under investigation which helps the proceedings has to be taken into account when establishing its fine. Nevertheless, there was a need to establish actual guidelines regulating in which cases, under what conditions, and to what extent the Competition Office is authorised to reduce the fine of a cartel participant who promotes the investigation of the authority and provides underlying evidence about the activity of a cartel.

According to section 36(6) of the Competition Act, the president of the Competition Office and the president of the Competition Council together are authorised to issue guidelines with respect to the law enforcement policies followed by the Competition Office. Such guidelines do not create an obligation on the Competition Office or on the Competition Council, their function is merely to provide information to the public on the interpretation and implementation of law as well as the practice followed in the past and to be followed in the future in connection with different key issues of the Competition Act. The leniency guidelines were modified in 2006, but the basic legal character of the leniency regime – namely that leniency is not regulated on a statutory level – did not change.

In this respect, the modification of the Competition Act (Act No. XIV of 2009 on the modification of Act No. LVII of 1996) effective from 1 June 2009 is a significant step towards establishing a much higher standard in the rule of law, while the modification implemented the most important rules of leniency into the Competition Act. The enactment, in addition to elevating leniency to a statutory level, introduced modifications to the previous policy taking into account the Model Leniency Programme issued by the European Competition Network in September 2006 and the Commission notice on immunity from fines and reduction of fines in cartel cases (the Commission Notice).

In addition to the statutory enactment, the president of the Competition Office issued explanatory notes (Explanatory Notes) to the practical implementation and application of the revised rules of the leniency policy.

2. What are the basic tenets of a leniency/immunity programme? Is leniency available also for other types of competition law violations than cartels?

Maintaining secrecy and destroying evidence are basic characteristics of cartel activities. Under these circumstances it is extremely difficult to fight them using just the regular tools of law enforcement. Key to successful actions against cartels is to break such secrecy and establish a different method of collecting evidence. The leniency policy makes cartel members interested in revealing the cartel activity to the authority in exchange for more favourable treatment in the proceedings if they collect and hand over evidence. The assumption behind the leniency policy is that there are cartel members who would like to quit their illegal activity and would be willing to provide information to the authorities about the activity of the cartel so they could rely with certainty on being exempted from the legal consequences of their previous participation or, at least, could expect a reduction of their individual sanctions.

According to the new section 78/A of the Competition Act, the Competition Council exempts the applicant from the entire amount of the fine (or provides for a reduction of the fine) if the applicant reveals satisfactory information on activity constituting a violation of section 11 of the Competition Act (or Article 101 of the TFUE) through an agreement or concerted practice resulting in direct or indirect price fixing, market division (including bid rigging) or establishing quotas in the field of manufacturing or sales.

The regulations provide for two possibilities: complete exemption from the fine or a reduction of the fine. A complete exemption from the fine is possible for the cartel member that arrives first to the authority and provides evidence sufficient so that the Competition Office can obtain a court order for an on-site dawn raid, and/or the establishment of the illegal activity, provided that it also meets other conditions detailed in the Competition Act. Reduction of the fine is possible for cartel members whose assistance significantly contributed to the revelation of the cartel and establishment of the illegal activity, but who were not the first to report it. This latter category covers different levels of fine reduction, ranging between 20-50 per cent, depending on the actual circumstances, timing and content of the information submitted to the authority and the efficiency of the assistance provided to the authority.

3. How many cartels have been unveiled and punished since the adoption of the leniency policy?

There are no public statistics available which state definitively how many cartels have been unveiled since 2003 – the original introduction of the leniency policy. We have been told informally that there have been nine different cases in which the leniency policy rules were applied to a cartel member who provided information before an investigation had begun.

4. What is needed to be a successful leniency applicant? Is documentary evidence required or is testimonial evidence sufficient?

There are no specific requirements in the leniency guidelines with respect to the actual types of evidence required. Evidence deemed acceptable for full immunity or a reduction of fine is assessed on the basis of its novelty and its contribution to the discovery of the case and the establishment of the illegality of the acts under investigation.

Accordingly, the evidence supplied by a 'first in' applicant has to be substantial enough to enable the Competition Office to obtain a court order for a dawn raid, or, for ongoing proceedings, must be new to the Competition Office and sufficient to establish the illegality of the acts under investigation. For second and subsequent applicants the evidence provided has to represent 'substantial added value' with respect to the evidence already in possession of the Competition Office. The filing of additional evidence needs to be made prior to the notification of the preliminary findings of the Competition Office or the first day where the undertakings involved in the proceedings file have access to the file (whichever occurs earlier).

The overall circumstances of the case and the information and evidence already available to the Competition Office will determine whether an applicant is eligible for a fine reduction. The Competition Office places greater weight on direct and contemporaneous evidence over evidence which is indirect or has been compiled or organised later on. The value of the evidence is also influenced by the necessity of finding supporting evidence from outside sources.

The rate of reduction of the fine is 30-50 per cent for the first applicant meeting the above requirements, 20-30 per cent for the second applicant and a maximum of 20 per cent for any further applicant meeting the above requirements, provided in each case that the applicant satisfies further conditions discussed below.

The applicant must also furnish all the evidence it has in its possession in connection with the case. Partial disclosure will not make the candidate eligible for immunity or fine reduction.

In addition to providing evidence at the time and of the value required above, the Competition Act sets forth further requirements and conditions which have to be met by each applicant in order to be eligible for immunity or fine reduction.

Immunity or fine reduction will be granted by the Competition Office only to an undertaking which, in addition to those set out above, meets the

following conditions:
- The applicant must cease its cartel activity immediately following the filing of its application, except in those cases and to the extent where the Competition Office considers the continuation of certain activities necessary to the success of the proceeding. This request by the Competition Office is limited to the successful execution of dawn raids at other undertakings involved in the case, ie the Competition Office may not compel the undertaking to continue its activity in order to collect more evidence.
- The applicant has to fully and continuously co-operate in good faith with the Competition Office. According to the Explanatory Notes, within the frame of the co-operation obligation, the Competition Office primarily expects the applicant:
  (i) to provide all information in its possession in a timely manner;
  (ii) to be available and react immediately to any further information request of the Competition Office;
  (iii) to do its best efforts in order to make its current and past employees and officers available for testimony;
  (iv) not to destroy, falsify or hide any information or evidence;
  (v) not to announce or publish the fact or content of the leniency application before the Competition Office has notified its preliminary opinion or have granted to the undertakings involved access to the file;
  (vi) to act in good faith even prior to filing the application. According to the Explanatory Notes this means, among other things, that the applicant may not destroy evidence immediately prior to the application, may not notify the other undertakings about the fact or content of the leniency application, and may not organise a 'cartel for leniency', for example by sharing evidence with other participants.

As a general rule, those applicants who took steps to coerce another undertaking to participate in the cartel are not eligible for immunity.

TIMING
5. What are the benefits of being 'first in' to co-operate?

There are different benefits attached to the 'first in' status of a leniency applicant. Most importantly, only the leniency applicant who qualifies as 'first in' is eligible to total immunity, (ie exemption from the entirety of the fine) provided that it meets all the other requirements discussed above. Furthermore, only the first leniency applicant is eligible for exemption from criminal sanctions, both as an undertaking and, under certain circumstances, as an individual, provided the conditions for exemption from criminal liability, discussed in detail under question 13 below, are fulfilled.

The Competition Office will grant immunity to the undertaking from the entirety of the fine if:
- the undertaking is the first to submit information and evidence previously unknown to the Competition Office about a cartel which

enables the Competition Office to obtain a court order for a dawn raid; or
- in proceedings already commenced by the Competition Office, the undertaking is the first to submit new evidence and information which enables the Competition Office to find an infringement illegal, on the condition that the Competition Office did not have, at the time of the submission, sufficient evidence to find an infringement.

Even a first applicant is eligible to be exempted from the fine only if it meets all the additional conditions discussed in question 4 above.

6. What are the consequences of being 'second'? Is there an 'immunity plus' or 'amnesty plus' option?

An applicant who co-operates with the authority, but is not eligible for immunity may be entitled to a reduction of the fine if the evidence provided to the Competition Office constitutes significant added value in the proceedings compared with the evidence in the possession of the Competition Office at the time of filing the application. The filing of additional evidence needs to be made prior to the handing out of the preliminary findings of the Competition Office or the first day of opening the file for review for any of the undertakings under proceedings (whichever occurs earlier).

The overall circumstances of the case and the information and evidence already available to the Competition Office will determine whether an applicant is eligible for the reduction of the fine. The Competition Office places greater weight on direct and contemporaneous evidence over evidence which is indirect or has been compiled or organised later on. The value of the evidence is also influenced by the necessity of finding supporting evidence from outside sources.

The rate of reduction of the fine is 30-50 per cent for the first applicant meeting the above requirements, 20-30 per cent for the second applicant and a maximum of 20 per cent for any further applicant meeting the above requirements, provided in each case that the applicant satisfies all the other necessary conditions.

There are no immunity plus or amnesty plus programmes provided by the law.

7. Are subsequent firms given any beneficial treatment if they make a useful contribution? How are 'useful contributions' defined?

An undertaking that provides evidence to the Competition Office as a third applicant may receive a reduction in the amount of the fine of between 20-30 per cent, if the evidence it provided has 'substantial added value' in the proceedings, and the undertaking meets the requirements described in question 4 above. Any subsequent applicant providing evidence of substantial added value for the proceedings and meeting the requirements described in question 4 above may be granted with a fine reduction of up to 20 per cent compared with the fine set in accordance with the general rules.

When an undertaking provides compelling evidence regarding facts already known by the Competition Office which can lead to an increase of the fine, the Competition Office will not rely on them when setting the fine of the undertaking providing such evidence.

SCOPE/FULL LENIENCY
8. Is it possible to receive full leniency? If so, what are the conditions required to receive full leniency? Can ringleaders/coercers receive full leniency? If there is a requirement to 'co-operate fully and on an ongoing basis' what does it entail? Does the regulatory authority require the applicant to cease participation in the cartel conduct after its application?

In order to receive full leniency the applicant has to meet all of the following requirements:
- it has to be first to report to the Competition Office the existence of the cartel, and provide evidence substantial enough to enable the Competition Office to obtain a court order for a dawn raid; or in the case of already pending proceedings it has to be first to provide new evidence substantial enough to establish the illegality of the acts under investigation;
- it has to provide the Competition Office with all information and evidence it has in its possession without altering its content;
- it has to fully co-operate, in good faith, on a continuous basis throughout the entire procedure with the Competition Office (the actual content of such requirement is discussed in question 4 above);
- it has to discontinue its involvement in the cartel following the submission of evidence, no later than the time agreed upon with the Competition Office; and
- it must not have taken steps to coerce other undertakings into participating in the infringement and operating the cartel agreement.

9. How many companies have received full immunity from fines to date?

To our knowledge, so far all companies relying on the leniency rules have received full immunity or a fine reduction.

PROCEDURE
10. What are the practical steps required to apply for leniency?

Technically there are three different ways to file a leniency application: the preferred format is to file an application in full, in which case all required information is included in the file in accordance with the application form put together for this purpose by the Competition Office. If the applicant cannot provide all the information at the time of the filing, it may file an incomplete form (marker application), in which case the Competition Office will set a deadline for the completion of the information. The third possible filing relates to international cartels, where parallel to the local application, the applicant also files a leniency application at the European Commission.

The application must include the name of the applicant and the description of the cartel and must be accompanied by the required attachments including all available evidence.

Anonymous applications are not accepted. The application may be filed in writing, or may be presented orally by the representative of the applicant, in both cases to the cartel department of the Competition Office. Foreign language documents need to be translated into Hungarian.

10.1 Full application for immunity
A full application for immunity includes all information required on the application form prepared by the Competition Office. When designing the application form the Competition Office took into account the Model Leniency Programme of the ECN and the Commission Notice.

A full application has to include information sufficient to justify the court order for an on-site dawn raid, or if filed at a later stage of the proceedings, enough evidence to establish the illegal cartel. Applications for a dawn raid have to be filed prior to a dawn raid and typically has to include the name and address of all undertakings involved in the cartel activity; name, position and address of all private persons who participated in the cartel activity; and a detailed description of the cartel, including its goal, its activity, the affected products and the geographical scope, the timeframe and the estimated market volume affected, the dates and places where meetings were held, their length and participants. All available supporting evidence must be filed along with sufficient explanation.

Applications containing evidence sufficient to establish the cartel may be filed at any time during the proceedings, provided that no one has filed an application for the justification of a dawn raid. The filed documents together with the explanation and the description of the cartel in their entirety have to be sufficient to prove the existence of the cartel.

10.2 Incomplete summary application for immunity: 'marker' application
If the applicant is not able to provide all the required information and evidence at the same time, it may file an incomplete application. A marker application protects the place of the applicant in the potential queue of leniency applicants, while providing additional time for the applicant to prepare a completed application in order to meet the requirements for immunity. At a minimum, it has to include the name of the applicant, the known facts on the cartel and information on the evidence known to the applicant, including its form and content. The Competition Office sets a deadline for the completion of the full application.

10.3 Application for a reduction of the fine
In order to be eligible for the reduction of a fine the applicant has to file evidence with the Competition Office that in its character or detail contributes significant added value relative to the evidence already in the possession of the Competition Office, thereby enhancing the possibility of proving the illegal cartel activity. Application for the reduction of the fine

may be filed at the latest prior to the date of handing out the preliminary opinion of the Competition Office, or the day when the file is made available for review to the participants, whichever occurs earlier.

Companies may not file a joint application except where they are members of the same group. According to the Explanatory Notes the most practical way to do this is if the controlling company files the application, naming all group companies involved in the cartel activity, accompanied by a power of attorney from each company involved. An application at one competition authority will not provide leniency at other competition authorities.

11. Is there an optimal time to approach the regulatory authority?
There is no recipe for how to time a leniency application. Obviously full immunity is only possible for the undertaking which qualifies as 'first in'. If an undertaking receives information about an ongoing investigation, it is worth thinking about whether it could apply for leniency and provide substantial added value to the evidence already held by the Competition Office. It requires a very quick evaluation of the situation and fast decision-making in order to secure a good position in the queue.

12. What guarantees of leniency exist if a party co-operates?
According to the recent modification of the Competition Act, if the applicant meets all the conditions of the Competition Act, the Competition Council must provide the applicant with immunity or a fine reduction, whichever the case may be, provided that the applicant: acts in all respects in accordance with the requirements of the law; fully co-operates throughout the entire proceedings with the Competition Office; provides all evidence it has in its possession; and stops its cartel activity at the time as agreed upon with the Competition Office. In accordance with the process described under question 10 above, the Competition Office deals with each application individually, in the order in which they were received and issues a resolution granting conditional immunity or conditional fine reduction to the applicant whether its application is accepted as 'first in', or second, or as a subsequent application. The granting of immunity, a fine reduction or any other benefit is awarded by the Competition Office only at the end of the proceedings, in the final decision on the merits, when the competition council can already evaluate the actual level of co-operation and fulfilment of all conditions required by law.

CONSEQUENCES
13. What effects does leniency granted to a corporate defendant have on the defendant's employees? Does it protect them from criminal and/or civil liability?
A request for the application of the leniency policy shall be accepted by the Competition Office only from the official representatives of an undertaking. In the event that officers or employees of the undertaking participated in the cartel and want to gain immunity from criminal sanctions, they have to

participate in the reporting personally. Reporting made by the management of an undertaking does not shield the employees or other officers of the company from criminal sanctions. Furthermore, employees and officers of an undertaking receive immunity from criminal sanctions only if the reporting occurs at a time when none of the authorities (Competition Office, financial authorities, public procurement authorities, etc) has knowledge of the criminal act. Consequently, exemption from criminal sanctions will only happen when the reporter was not only 'first in' at the authority, but also, no authority yet had knowledge about the act.

With respect to criminal sanctions, the situation is more complex. Section 296/B of the Criminal Code states that:

'(1) Any person who enters into an agreement aiming to manipulate the outcome of an open or restricted tender published in connection with a public procurement procedure or an activity that is subject to a concession contract by fixing the prices (charges) or any other term of the contract, or for the division of the market, or takes part in any other concerted practices resulting in the restraint of trade is guilty of felony punishable by imprisonment for up to five years.

(2) Any person who partakes in the decision-making process of an association of companies, public body, a society or similar organisation, and adopting any decision that has the capacity for restraining competition aiming to manipulate the outcome of an open or restricted tender published in connection with a public procurement procedure or an activity that is subject to a concession contract shall also be punishable as set forth in subsection (1).

(3) [...]

(4) The perpetrator of a criminal act defined in subsections (1)-(3) shall be exonerated from punishment if it confesses the act to the authorities first hand and reveals the circumstances of the criminal act. Authorities shall also mean the bodies supervising competition and financial operations and the body which reviews procedures in connection with public procurement contracts.'

It is important to point out that only cartels which relate to public procurement tenders and concession contracts are subject to criminal punishment. For cartels in these areas the persons acting on behalf of the undertaking in the cartel, or being involved in the decision-making process, whether an officer or an employee, are punishable. Any person who participates in the decision-making process (directors, members of the board, managing directors, heads of divisions, etc) making the undertaking involved in a cartel is punishable. In order to gain immunity from criminal punishment the person who is punishable has to report the criminal act, individually or together with the management of the company, as 'first in', at a stage when none of the authorities yet has knowledge about the criminal act. Only the first-comer (not only to the Competition Office, but to any authority mentioned in the Criminal Code) may rely on immunity. Reporting by the management of the undertaking does not create immunity from criminal sanctions for the employees and officers involved in the acts. The Competition Office accepts leniency applications only from the official representative of an undertaking. Therefore, it is possible that reporting by an employee may create immunity from criminal sanctions for that employee, but may not exempt the undertaking from either the competition law fine or the criminal sanctions. Undertakings are also subject to criminal sanctions under Hungarian law (the sanctions may be a fine, termination of the company or limitation of its activities for a certain period).

14. Does leniency bar further private enforcement?

The effect of granting immunity is limited to administrative proceedings, it does not provide immunity from civil law liability. Nevertheless, in order to make the leniency regime more attractive, the Competition Act provides that the applicant who received immunity may deny payment of a civil law claim as long as the damages can be collected from other participants in the cartel. The lawsuit for damages against the undertaking enjoying immunity must be suspended until the decision of the Competition Office in the antitrust matter becomes final and binding.

PROTECTION AGAINST DISCLOSURE/CONFIDENTIALITY

15. Is confidentiality afforded to the leniency applicant and other co-operating parties? If so, to what extent? Is the identity of the leniency applicant/other co-operating parties disclosed during the investigation or in the final decision? Is information provided by the leniency applicant/other co-operating parties passed on to other undertakings under investigation? Can a leniency applicant/other co-operating party request anonymity or confidentiality of information provided?

Under the Competition Act anonymous leniency applications are not possible. According to the Competition Act (Article 55(1)), the party under investigation and its representative may have access to the documents relating to the proceedings only after the completion of the investigation, or following the date set by the Competition Council and they may make copies and take notes of them. Specifying the documents concerned, the competition council may give its consent to the party or its representative having access to the documents before the completion of the investigation where this does not jeopardise the effectiveness of the proceedings. This means that, typically, the identity of the leniency applicant and the statements and other evidence made by it are held confidential by the Competition Office until the end of the investigation phase of the proceedings.

In addition to the above rule the leniency applicant may request that certain reports, evidence, statements, etc be handled confidentially during the proceedings. According to Article 55(3) of the Competition Act the party under investigation may request, based on protection of business secrets, the confidential treatment of some documents by establishing why the given document qualifies as a business secret. Leniency applicants may use this opportunity to limit the possibility of other parties to the proceedings reviewing the filed documents and other evidence. In practice confidentiality is granted only to the extent that it does not jeopardise other participants' right of defence. If the request for confidential treatment of certain business secrets is granted by the Competition Office, the applicant typically must file a confidential and a non-confidential version of the same brief.

16. Is the evidence submitted by the leniency applicant protected from transmission to other competition authorities with whom the authority in question co-operates?

In accordance with the Competition Act, the Competition Office may not use the information and evidence provided by the applicant for immunity for any purposes other than the leniency proceedings until the issuance of the decision granting conditional immunity. If the application is rejected, or the applicant withdraws its application prior to such decision, the Competition Office has to give back all documents and evidence to the applicant. Nevertheless, the Competition Act does not provide any other protection to the applicant, nor does it bar the Competition Office from providing information to other authorities. It is a highly controversial issue and will require further legislation in order to clarify its uncertainty and provide a higher level of protection to applicants.

With respect to competition authorities in the European Union, Regulation 1/2003 EC is binding on the Competition Office. In accordance with Article 12, the Competition Office is entitled to share any information or evidence, including confidential information, with other EU authorities.

17. To what extent can evidence submitted by the leniency applicant (transcripts of oral statements or written evidence) become discovered in subsequent private enforcement claims? Can leniency information be subjected to discovery orders in domestic or foreign courts? Can leniency information submitted in a foreign jurisdiction be subjected to discovery orders in the domestic courts?

Discovery, as known and regulated in common law jurisdictions, is not available under the Hungarian legal system. In a private enforcement claim based on cartel activity, the court must notify the Competition Office. The Competition Office may send its comments to the court, or may commence investigation proceedings. The final decision of the Competition Office on the merits of the competition law infringement is binding on the court deciding the civil law matter. Other than that, the law does not regulate how, under what conditions or whether the evidence filed with the Competition Office can be revealed in civil law proceedings.

18. Are there any precedents in which evidence from a leniency application has been discovered in a private enforcement claim?

See answer to question 17.

RELATIONSHIP WITH THE EUROPEAN COMMISSION'S LENIENCY NOTICE AND LENIENCY POLICY IN OTHER EU MEMBER STATES

19. Does the policy address the interaction with applications under the Commission Leniency Notice? If so, how?

If there is the possibility of parallel applications within the European Union, and it seems that the European Commission is the most suitable to carry the case forward, the applicant may file a preliminary application with the

Hungarian Competition Office. A preliminary application may be filed only as an application for immunity by providing enough information to justify a court order for a dawn raid. The application must include the name and address of the applicant, the name of the other participants in the cartel, the products, the geographical area, the timeframe and the nature of the cartel. With respect to the Hungarian market the application has to provide information on the cartel affecting Hungary, the market effect of the cartel on the Hungarian market and the estimated market share of the participants in the Hungarian market.

The applicant also has to inform the Competition Office whether it has filed or plans to file other leniency applications with other competition authorities.

Filing a preliminary application ensures that if the European Commission decides not to pursue the case, but the local authority proceeds with it, the applicant secures its position for leniency with the Hungarian authority at the time of submitting the preliminary filing. Provision of the immunity is subject to the applicant providing all supplementary information and evidence that is requested by the Competition Office when launching its proceedings.

20. Does the policy address the interaction with applications for leniency in other EU member states? If so, how?
The law does not address the interaction with applications made in other EU member states. It states clearly that application of the leniency policy in competition proceedings does not provide the applicant with immunity from any fines that may be imposed by other (foreign) competition authorities.

RELATIONSHIP WITH SETTLEMENT PROCEDURES
21. What is the relationship between leniency and applicable settlement procedures? Are they mutually exclusive?
There are no specific regulations with respect to settlement procedures. Voluntary undertaking of different obligations is known in Hungarian law only in proceedings commenced by the Competition Office *ex officio*. Parallel application of the voluntary undertaking with the leniency filing would be impossible, since the precondition of eligibility for immunity or fine reduction is that the applicant immediately ceases the illegal activity, ie, it is a statutory requirement and not an option or voluntary undertaking.

REFORM/LATEST DEVELOPMENTS
22. Is there a reform underway to revisit the leniency policy? What are the latest developments?
We are unaware of any plans to reform the new regime in the near future.

India

J. Sagar Associates Farhad Sorabjee & Reeti Choudhary

BACKGROUND
1. What is the relevant legislation concerning the leniency policy and what is the enforcing body?

The Competition Act 2002 (the Act) and its implementing regulations also known as the Competition Commission of India (Lesser Penalty) Regulations 2009 (the Regulations) set out the leniency policy in India. The Regulations amended draft regulations previously published by the Commission (Draft Regulations).

Legal challenges to the Act resulted in major amendments in 2007 and the substantive provisions of the Act relating to anti-competitive agreements became effective as of 20 May 2009. These provisions also provide for the imposition of penalties for infringement of the Act and empower the Competition Commission of India (the Commission) to impose penalties lower than prescribed under the Act.

Section 27 of the Act empowers the Commission to impose fines not exceeding 10 per cent of the average turnover for the last three preceding financial years upon any enterprise or person who may be a party to an anti-competitive agreement. However, if such agreement has been entered into by a cartel, a fine may be imposed upon each member of the cartel which may extend to up to three times its profit for each year of the continuance of the agreement or 10 per cent of its turnover for each year of the continuance of such agreement, whichever is higher.

The power to impose a lesser fine as the Commission may deem fit and the requirements for qualification for the imposition of a lesser fine have been provided for under section 46 of the Act. Further details with respect to procedures and requirements are provided for in the Regulations, which also prescribe the benefits available to the applicant.

Applications for leniency are to be made to a designated officer of the Commission. The allowance of a reduction in statutory penalties is given by the Commission. The investigation division of the Commission is the Director-General of Competition (Director-General), which conducts the investigation and presents its report to the Commission.

2. What are the basic tenets of a leniency/immunity programme? Is leniency available also for other types of competition law violations than cartels?

Under the Regulations, the leniency provisions cover undertakings or persons who have been members of a cartel and are willing to provide information to and co-operate with the Commission in order to ensure the termination of the cartel activities. Under the Act, cartel activities include any kind of agreement entered into by undertakings and/or associations of undertakings, which are active in the same sector (ie goods or services).

Cartel activities are defined broadly under the Act and include an agreement whose purpose is to:
- fix purchase or selling prices;
- limit or control production, markets, technical development or investment;
- share markets or source of production; and
- engage in bid rigging or collusive bidding.

Such agreements are presumed to have an appreciable adverse effect upon competition.

To qualify for reductions in fine, applicants are required to comply with the following conditions:
- from the time of disclosure, the applicant must cease its participation in the cartel or its activities;
- the applicant is expected to provide all relevant information, documents and evidence as may be required by the Commission and not conceal, destroy, manipulate or remove documents;
- the applicant is required to co-operate genuinely, fully, continuously and expeditiously throughout the investigation and proceedings before the Commission; and
- in matters under investigation by the Commission, the applicant should have approached the Commission before the investigative division, the Director-General, has submitted its findings to the Commission.

The Commission may also impose other conditions in addition to those above.

If the Commission is of the opinion that the conditions have not been complied with or that the information does not constitute full and vital disclosure, it shall not grant the applicant a reduction in fine. Before dismissal of an application, the Commission will afford a hearing to the applicant. Despite dismissal of an application, the Commission has the right to use the information submitted in the dismissed application in its investigation.

The Regulations provide for full immunity from fine for the first applicant which makes a vital disclosure by submitting evidence enabling the Commission to reach a *prima facie* opinion as to the existence of a cartel, knowing that without such evidence the Commission could not have reached such an opinion. Full immunity is also available to an applicant making a vital disclosure by submitting evidence during an ongoing investigation which establishes a contravention, and without which the Commission would not have been able to establish the contravention. The grant of full immunity is discretionary.

Subsequent applicants may also be granted reductions in penalties by making disclosures and submitting evidence providing significant added value to the evidence already available to the Commission or the Director-

General to establish the existence of a cartel. The term 'added value' means evidence that enhances the ability of the Commission or the Director-General to establish the existence of a cartel. Pursuant to this, the applicant marked second is entitled to a fine reduction of up to 50 per cent of the full fine, and the applicant marked third is entitled to a fine reduction of up to 30 per cent of the full fine. Again, the partial leniency provisions are also discretionary and the manner of exercise of this discretion remains to be tested.

When the cartel is established, the fines imposed upon each member of the cartel may reach three times its profit for each year of participation in the cartel or 10 per cent of its turnover for each year of participation in the cartel, whichever is higher.

3. How many cartels have been unveiled and punished since the adoption of the leniency programme?

The provisions of the Act were brought into effect on 20 May 2009, and the Regulations were only issued in August 2009. During this short period, no effective leniency application has been filed with or processed by the Commission.

4. What is needed to be a successful leniency applicant? Is documentary evidence required or is testimonial evidence sufficient?

An applicant is required to provide information in accordance with the requirements of regulation 10 of the Competition Commission of India (General) Regulations 2009 (as amended) (the General Regulations). This requires that an applicant submitting information provides details of the alleged contravention along with a list of all documents, affidavits and evidence in support of the contravention. Procedures for filing additional information and paper books are also set out. Further, the General Regulations also provide that an applicant seeking lesser fine must provide all relevant information, documents and evidence as may be required by the Commission. The Schedule to the General Regulations also requires the applicant to provide a descriptive list of evidence regarding the nature and content of the evidence provided in support of the application for lesser fine and any other material information as may be directed by the Commission. It is therefore clear that it is expected that documentary evidence would also be provided. Whether or not testimonial evidence *simplicitor* would be considered to be sufficient evidence remains unclear and there is no specific guidance or provision to suggest that this would be the case.

As mentioned elsewhere, for an applicant to successfully obtain full leniency, it must make a vital disclosure by submitting evidence which enables the Commission to reach a *prima facie* opinion as to the existence of a cartel, knowing that without such evidence the Commission could not have reached such an opinion. Full immunity is also available if an applicant makes a vital disclosure by submitting evidence during an ongoing investigation which establishes a contravention, without which the Commission may not have been able to establish the contravention. Further, an applicant is required to fulfil the obligations mentioned in the answer to question 2 above.

TIMING
5. What are the benefits of being 'first in' to co-operate?
The first enterprise to make a vital disclosure pertaining to cartel activity or contravention of the provisions of the Act is the only enterprise eligible to receive the benefit of reduction in fines up to or equal to 100 per cent.

Interestingly, under the earlier Draft Regulations, full immunity from the fine would have been automatic upon fulfilment of the requirements mentioned above. The revised Regulations, however, appear to make the granting of full immunity discretionary even if the disclosure and evidence meets all other requirements. This suggests that immunity is no longer automatic upon fulfilment of the requirements. As the provisions have not been applied so far, it remains to be seen as to whether and how the Commission will exercise its discretionary power.

6. What are the consequences of being 'second'? Is there an 'immunity plus' or 'amnesty plus' option?
An enterprise making a disclosure after the first applicant, pertaining to cartel activity or contravention of the provisions of the Act, and that provides significant added value to the evidence already in possession of the Commission or the Director-General, may be granted the benefit of a reduction in fines up to or equal to 50 per cent.

There is currently no specific provision, guidance or precedent for 'immunity plus' or 'amnesty plus' options. However, it is possible that if an applicant provides requisite information and material, knowingly or unknowingly, with respect to a related contravention, the Commission may seek to obtain further information and open an investigation in connection with this contravention. There is nothing in the provisions of either the Act or the Regulations that precludes the Commission from treating the disclosure as a marker should it decide to investigate such a contravention, and it is possible that these options may arise and be acknowledged by the Commission in future.

7. Are subsequent firms given any beneficial treatment if they make a useful contribution? How are 'useful contributions' defined?
Yes. Under the Regulations the third applicant in an investigation being conducted by the Commission or Director-General may also be granted the benefit of a reduction in fine of up to 30 per cent of the fine leviable under the Act.

Further markers providing for reductions of 10 per cent of the penalties imposed, which were envisaged under the earlier Draft Regulations, have been removed in the revised Regulations.

To be eligible for leniency, disclosures by applicants subsequent to the first are required to significantly add value to the evidence already in the possession of the Commission or the Director-General for the purpose of establishing the existence of a cartel. The added value of the evidence submitted will depend on the ability of the Commission or the Director-General to establish the existence of a cartel on the basis of such evidence.

Again, there is no guidance or precedent as yet as to how this provision will be interpreted.

SCOPE/FULL LENIENCY
8. Is it possible to receive full leniency?
Yes, as mentioned in the answer to question 5, full leniency may be granted to the first applicant making a vital disclosure. The vital disclosure should involve a full and true disclosure of information enabling the Commission to reach a *prima facie* opinion about the existence of a cartel, or to establish the existence of cartel activities.

8.1 If so, what are the conditions required to receive full leniency?
The conditions required to be fulfilled have been detailed in the answers to questions 2 and 4.

8.2 Can ringleaders/coercers receive full leniency?
Full leniency is available to the first applicant making a complete and vital disclosure. The Act and the Regulations do not distinguish between ringleaders, coercers or other members of a cartel.

8.3 Does the regulatory authority require the applicant to cease participation in the cartel conduct after its application? If there is a requirement to 'co-operate fully and on an ongoing basis' what does it entail?
Yes, one of the prerequisites for being eligible for leniency is to cease all participation in the cartel, unless expressly otherwise requested by the Commission and to co-operate fully, continuously and expeditiously. This is provided for in Regulation 3 of the Regulations. The applicant is also required to:
- provide all relevant information, documents and evidence as may be required by the Commission;
- not conceal, destroy, manipulate or remove relevant documents in any manner that may contribute to the establishment of a cartel.

The applicant is also expected to co-operate with the Commission until the conclusion of the proceedings. Section 46 of the Act expressly states that an applicant who fails to co-operate accordingly shall not be eligible for the grant of a lesser fine. It remains to be seen how the requirement to '... co-operate genuinely, fully, continuously and expeditiously throughout the investigation and proceedings...' will be treated and interpreted.

9. How many companies have received full immunity from fines to date?
So far, no company has received full immunity from fines. The Commission has yet to process a leniency application.

PROCEDURE
10. What are the practical steps required to apply for leniency?
The Regulations do not provide for private consultation/informal guidance prior to the initial contact/filing of the application. Since the leniency programme is as yet untested, it is unclear whether this will be required in the future.

The Regulations set out a marker system. The earlier Draft Regulations provided that markers would be set in accordance with the dates of written communications of the offence. The new Regulations permit markers to be set orally, to be followed up by submission of evidence and material within 15 days.

The Commission will assign a priority status to the applicants in the order of their initial contact with it. Initial contact may be made by the applicant either directly or through its authorised representative by providing the prescribed written application in accordance with the Schedule to the Regulations or by fax or email. The application can also be made orally. If the applicant has made initial contact through email, fax or orally, it will need to ensure that the prescribed written application is received by the Commission within 15 days of the initial contact. Failure to do so will result in the applicant losing its status, with subsequent applicants, if any, moving up the rank.

Within three working days of the receipt of the prescribed written application, the designated authority shall put up the application before the Commission. The Commission shall mark the priority status of the applicant.

In the case of applications received via fax, email or orally, the date and time of receipt of the application by the Commission for the purpose of the marker shall be the date and time as recorded by the designated authority or as recorded on the server or the facsimile transmission machine of the designated authority. In the event that the prescribed written application is not received within the stipulated period, the applicant may also forfeit its claim for priority status, affecting its eligibility for the grant of lesser fine. On completion of the evaluation of the first applicant's evidence, the Commission shall form an opinion about whether the applicant has provided full, true and vital disclosure of information and evidence.

When the Commission is considering the dismissal of the application for leniency, it shall conduct an oral hearing. Until such evaluation of the evidence submitted by the first applicant has been completed, the next applicant shall not be considered by the Commission.

In the event that the priority status is not granted to the first applicant, the subsequent applicants move up the rank and the procedure mentioned above for the first applicant shall apply *mutatis mutandis*.

Orders passed by the Commission reducing or waiving the fine that may be imposed under the Act are conditional upon compliance with conditions and restrictions set out in the Regulations and in the order. If the Commission subsequently finds that the applicant is not eligible for the benefit, it may revoke the benefit granted. In such a case, the applicant shall be liable to pay the full fine under the Act and may be tried for the offence with respect to which the leniency had been sought.

The Commission may, however, continue to rely on the information gathered in the context of the leniency application in order to proceed with its investigation.

11. Is there an optimal time to approach the regulatory authority?

Reduction of up to 100 per cent of the fine is only available to the applicant 'first in' ie, where this benefit has not already been granted to another applicant. Further, until the Commission has evaluated the information received from the applicant with first priority, it will not process or evaluate information or evidence received subsequently.

If a disclosure is made after the Commission receives the report of the Director-General in an investigation, a lesser fine will not be available. It is not possible to accurately predict or know when the Director-General is likely to provide its report to the Commission.

Given the current resources available to the Commission, the practical feasibility of *suo motu* investigations is questionable. However given the size of the market in many areas, it is quite possible that multi-jurisdiction international cartels will need to make leniency filings, and issues of timing in such cases will be driven by the need for co-ordination.

In addition, in cases where no investigation has commenced – given the current levels of resource and data availability – it is unlikely that the Commission would already have in its possession evidence that would enable it to disregard the information provided by an informant and therefore deny leniency under the Act.

12. What guarantees of leniency exist if a party co-operates?

The grant of leniency is discretionary. After the issuance of the amended Regulations, this discretion remains even if the party co-operates, and as such, leniency is not guaranteed by the provisions of law. The development of the jurisprudence and precedents in this area will provide useful guidance as to how the Commission will exercise its discretion. The Commission may choose to grant leniency broadly and as a matter of principle, thereby only using its discretionary power in unforeseen or extraordinary cases.

CONSEQUENCES
13. What effects does leniency granted to a corporate defendant have on the defendant's employees? Does it protect them from criminal and/or civil liability?

The law does not protect employees of undertakings which have been granted leniency from either criminal or civil liability. In fact, under section 48 of the Act, every person who is in charge of and was responsible to the company for the conduct of its business at the time is deemed to be guilty of the contravention. This presumption is rebuttable. If a contravention takes place as a result of the connivance or consent or neglect of a director, manager, secretary or other officer, that person shall also be deemed guilty of the contravention. In the case of a firm, this includes a partner.

While the Act does not extend criminal jurisdiction to the Commission, regular criminal prosecutions may be adopted on the basis of a finding of guilt. Any such finding of guilt may have serious consequences under ancillary laws including, for instance, the disbarment of a person from directorships.

14. Does leniency bar further private enforcement?

The leniency policy does not prevent private enforcement against a person or enterprise found guilty of contravening the provisions of the Act.

Section 53N of the Act provides for compensation to be awarded by the Competition Appellate Tribunal to any person or enterprise for losses or damages that may arise out of the finding of a contravention of (i) the Act by the Commission, or (ii) the orders of the Commission or the Competition Appellate Tribunal.

The person or company claiming the award of damages has not to prove afresh the violation of the Act or the contravention of the order passed. The enquiry to be conducted shall be limited to the determination of the eligibility to and quantum of compensation to be awarded.

PROTECTION AGAINST DISCLOSURE/CONFIDENTIALITY

15. Is confidentiality afforded to the leniency applicant and other co-operating parties? If so, to what extent? Is the identity of the leniency applicant/other co-operating parties disclosed during the investigation or in the final decision? Is information provided by the leniency applicant/other co-operating parties passed on to other undertakings under investigation? Can a leniency applicant/other co-operating party request anonymity or confidentiality of information provided?

Under the Regulations, an informant shall be afforded confidentiality. The Commission shall also maintain confidentiality of the identity of the applicant or the information obtained from it and shall not disclose the identity of the informant or the information obtained unless:
- the disclosure is required by law; or
- the applicant has agreed to such disclosure in writing; or
- there has been a public disclosure by the applicant.

Further, the General Regulations permit an informant to request the Commission to treat its identity as confidential.

Additionally where publicly disclosing documents will result in a disclosure of business secrets, or destruction or appreciable diminution of the commercial value of any information, or can reasonably be expected to cause serious injury, an informant may request the Commission or the Director-General to maintain the confidentiality of such documents. In the event that such documents form part of the informant's written submissions, the public version of the submissions shall be an exact copy of the confidential version with the confidential information redacted.

The confidentiality to be granted upon the documents shall be decided at

the discretion of the Commission or the Director-General and shall be granted for such period as specified. Factors that the Commission or Director-General may consider before reaching a decision of confidentiality include:
- the extent to which the information is known to the public;
- the extent to which the information is known to the employees, suppliers, distributors and others involved in the party's business;
- the measures taken by the party to maintain the secrecy of the information; and
- the ease or difficulty with which the information could be acquired or duplicated by others.

Documents that the Commission has agreed to treat as confidential shall be removed from the public file and secured in a sealed envelope bearing, *inter alia*, the mention 'Confidential record under Regulation 35' (of the General Regulations), and the date on which confidential treatment expires.

If the Commission includes in any order or decision or opinion, information that has been granted confidential treatment under this regulation, the Commission shall file two versions of the order or decision or opinion. The public version shall omit the confidential information that appears in the complete version and be marked 'Subject to confidentiality requirements under Regulation 35 (of the General Regulations)'. This version shall be served upon the parties, and shall be included in the public file of the proceeding.

Any person or party, including any officer, employee, expert appointed or engaged by the Commission who is privy to the contents of such confidential documents shall ensure that they maintain their confidentiality.

These provisions of the Regulations and the General Regulations may be in conflict with those of the Right to Information Act 2005 (Information Act). The Information Act was enacted to provide a mechanism enabling persons to secure access to information which is under the control of public authorities.

The Information Act empowers a person seeking to obtain any information to secure access to it by making a request. No reason for requesting the information or any personal details (except as may be necessary for contacting them) are required to be given.

Information so requested has to be provided to the person within 30 days from the date of its request. The Information Act has set out certain grounds on the basis of which the concerned authority may reject such a request for information. These include, *inter alia*:
- information which has been expressly forbidden to be published by any court of law or tribunal or whose disclosure may constitute contempt of court;
- information including commercial confidence, business secrets or intellectual property, whose disclosure would harm the competitive position of a third party, unless the competent authority is satisfied that larger public interest warrants the disclosure of such information; and
- information which would impede the process of investigation or apprehension or prosecution of offenders.

16. Is the evidence submitted by the leniency applicant protected from transmission to other competition authorities with whom the authority in question co-operates? If so, how?

There are no specific provisions in the Act or the Regulations governing the exchange of information between the Commission or the Director-General and other competition authorities. How this develops remains to be seen. It is also significant that the Commission has in the past co-operated closely and in great detail with other competition authorities and continues to do so.

The confidentiality of the documents *per se* is envisaged in detail as mentioned under question 15 above in both the General Regulations and *qua* the identity of the informants in the Regulations. The maintenance of confidentiality appears to be time-bound, as confidential documents are separately maintained and are required to have a date on which confidential treatment expires.

There is also a significant overlap in connection with the matters covered by the Commission and sectoral regulators such as the electricity or telecommunications regulatory authorities. Co-operation and referrals for opinions are provided for between these authorities. There is insufficient information yet as to how this will be construed by the Commission and the Director-General.

17. To what extent can evidence submitted by the leniency applicant (transcripts of oral statements or written evidence) become discoverable in subsequent private enforcement claims? Can leniency information be subjected to discovery orders in domestic or foreign courts? Can leniency information submitted in a foreign jurisdiction be subjected to discovery orders in the domestic courts?

Evidence submitted and claimed by the leniency applicant as confidential is required to be treated as such and the Commission is expressly required by law to determine the validity and areas of confidentiality in the evidence submitted. A sanitised public version may be made available. Information already known to the public and the ease of access to such information by others are factors to be considered when assessing confidentiality.

A person may seek discovery by invoking the provisions of the Information Act or by obtaining a court order directing the authority to make disclosure.

The Information Act permits an authority to reject a request for disclosure on grounds of commercial confidentiality, among others, and it is unlikely that the Commission will disclose confidential information easily and breach *inter se* confidentiality obligations.

While it is possible in theory to obtain an order for discovery from domestic courts, it is again unlikely that the Indian courts would easily grant such orders, and they would certainly not do so during the course of a pending investigation or proceedings under the Act.

An order by a foreign court for discovery would have to be enforced in India. Such enforcement would need to be ensured by an Indian court, where it may be resisted on the ground that it is contrary to the public policy of India, which includes the general provisions of Indian law (including the Act).

It is also improbable that a domestic court would pass orders for discovery of documents submitted outside its jurisdiction.

The answer above is based on the general principles of enforcement of Indian civil law and is unrelated to specific situations concerning the Commission. There is no specific law which requires the Commission, as a statutory authority in India, to provide such information upon request.

18. Are there any precedents in which evidence from a leniency application has been discovered in a private enforcement claim?
The leniency regime has only been operational in India over the past few months. To date, no leniency application has been filed or processed by the Commission.

RELATIONSHIP WITH THE EUROPEAN COMMISSION'S LENIENCY NOTICE AND LENIENCY POLICY IN OTHER EU MEMBER STATES
19. Does the policy address the interaction with applications under the Commission Leniency Notice? If so, how?
Not applicable.

20. Does the policy address the interaction with applications for leniency in other EU member states? If so, how? Does the authority accept summary applications in line with the ECN Model Leniency Programme?
Not applicable.

RELATIONSHIP WITH SETTLEMENT PROCEDURES
21. What is the relationship between leniency and applicable settlement procedures? Are they mutually exclusive?
Under Indian competition law there is no settlement procedure.

REFORM/LATEST DEVELOPMENTS
22. Is there a reform underway to revisit the leniency policy? What are the latest developments?
As mentioned earlier, the leniency policy itself is a new development. The Regulations were brought into force in the latter half of 2009. The current final Regulations are a revised version of the earlier published Draft Regulations. There are certain significant differences between the earlier Draft Regulations and the Regulations.

The earlier Draft Regulations stated that the Commission would provide a reduction in fine under the Act to the applicants making a disclosure in accordance with the conditions given, in the following order:
- the first applicant would receive full waiver of the fine;
- the second would receive a waiver of 50 per cent of the fine;
- the third would receive a waiver of 30 per cent of the fine; and
- any subsequent applicant would receive a waiver of 10 per cent of the fine.

Under the current regulations, the last class mentioned above has been done away with. Further, with respect to the earlier classes, the Commission now

India

appears to have discretion with respect to the actual percentage of fine that it may waive. How – and whether – this discretion is exercised by the Commission will have a significant influence upon the efficacy of the leniency regime in India.

Italy

Bonelli Erede Pappalardo Massimo Merola & Luciano di Via

BACKGROUND
1. What is the relevant legislation concerning the leniency policy and who is the enforcing body?
The Italian Law Decree 223 issued on 4 July 2006, better known as the Bersani Decree, updated the Italian Antitrust Act (Law No. 287 of 1990), and introduced a number of important changes to align Italy's national regulations with the provisions set out in EC Regulation 1/2003. In particular these concern: (i) the power of the Italian Competition Authority (the Authority) to grant provisional injunctions; (ii) the Authority's power to adopt a programme aimed at reducing sanctions imposed on companies that voluntarily report the existence of restrictive agreements; and (iii) the option granted to companies charged with infringements, to commit themselves to the removal of the anti-competitive effects of their unlawful practices, so as to bring an investigation to an early end and obviate the imposition of any sanctions. The Bersani Decree was codified in Law 248/2006 (the Bersani-Visco Law).

The Bersani Decree also empowers the Authority to adopt an implementing act, setting out the general rules and criteria that the Authority can apply in order to reduce sanctions imposed by antitrust laws, for any company which reports a secret arrangement that restricts competition.

After the completion of a wide-ranging public consultation, the Authority approved the definitive operational guidelines (the Notice). On 15 February 2007, it enacted the antitrust leniency programme for companies intending to co-operate with the Authority, by assisting it to identify the most serious anti-competitive arrangements. The Notice introduced a system of partial or total exoneration from penalties that would apply to cartel members that report their cartel membership. Indeed, this leniency programme provides immunity for the cartel member that is the first to withdraw from the agreement and reveals the existence of the cartel. A considerable reduction of fines (between 20 and 50 per cent) is also granted to those who offer additional information to substantiate the presence of these types of agreements. The Leniency Notice is largely inspired by the European Commission's leniency programme and by the Model Leniency Programme adopted by the European Competition Network on 29 September 2006.

2. What are the basic tenets of the leniency/immunity programme? Is leniency available also for other types of competition law violations than cartels?

In accordance with EC principles, the leniency programme is applied to all horizontal agreements, as well as tender procedures and especially in cases of price-fixing cartels, market sharing, sales and production limitation agreements, since these are particularly capable of damaging both consumers and competitors. Furthermore, it is applied to violations that are particularly difficult to ascertain. The leniency programme applies to agreements that fall under Article 101 of the TFUE (Treaty on the Functioning of the European Union), or under Article 2 of the Italian Antitrust Act.

The programme allows for a sliding scale of reductions according to the usefulness of the collaboration offered by the 'repentant' company. This ranges from total immunity for a company that is first to spontaneously provide the Authority with decisive proof of a secret cartel, particularly when the information is not already available to the Authority.

At the other end of the scale, it is possible for a company, whose collaboration contributes significantly to the evidence available to the Authority, to benefit from a reduction in its fine, usually of not more than 50 per cent. Obviously, the timeliness of a company's collaboration and the value of the evidence produced is taken into account.

It is worth noting that, as opposed to the Commission's programme, the Italian leniency programme does not require the second (and third, etc) applicant to provide evidentiary documents or information with further 'added value' to those already gathered by the Authority, but simply to provide evidence that is able to 'strengthen' the evidence already at the Authority's disposal. Such a semantic difference might certainly give room to different approaches in the practical treatment of applications for reduction in fines, in that the 'strengthening' of the collected evidence is more quantitative in nature, compared to the slightly more qualitative requirement of 'added value'.

Full collaboration with the Authority is an essential requirement in order to benefit from the leniency programme. Therefore, on risk of exclusion, a company must present all of its available relevant information and must not reveal its participation in the leniency programme to third parties.

A company wishing to take part in the leniency programme must present an application to the Authority, with all the relevant information and documents attached. In some cases, a company may not be in a position to immediately produce the elements of proof necessary to obtain immunity but may be able to obtain them within a short period of time. In this event, it may present an incomplete application and request that the Authority fix a deadline to produce the relevant information and documents to complete its application (ie, a marker).

Lastly, in order to lighten the administrative burden on companies, it is possible to present an application for immunity in a simplified form in cases where the European Commission is best placed to carry out the investigation into the cartel in question.

3. How many cartels have been unveiled and punished since the adoption of the leniency programme?

As already mentioned, the leniency programme was introduced in 2007. To date the Authority has delivered only two decisions applying its leniency notice: Decision 16835, *Produttori di Pannneli Truciolari in Legno*, 30 May 2007 and Decision 20931, *Prezzo del GPL per riscaldamento regione Sardegna*, 24 March 2010. In the first case the Authority unveiled a cartel whose aim was to share the market, partition customers and fix prices in the chipboard panels market. This infringement had occurred between January 2004 and November 2005. The undertakings concerned represented 80 per cent of the market. This was accomplished due to the decisive information received from Gruppo Trombini, one of the undertakings active in that market and (partially) involved in the cartel. The investigation began after receiving information at the end of 2005, and following an extensive investigation, a statement of objections was delivered on 15 January 2007. Gruppo Trombini was totally exempted from the fine. The Authority imposed fines on all the other cartel members. Once the proceedings had begun, the other undertakings concerned also collaborated with the Authority. As a consequence, the basic amount was reduced by 30 per cent for all undertakings fined (except for Gruppo Frati's basic amount, which was reduced by 40 per cent due to financial difficulties, since the imposition of a higher amount could irreparably damage a company); nevertheless, the total amount of fines imposed was more than €31 million. A point to note which was applied in this case is that according to paragraph 29 the basic amount may be reduced if the Commission finds that mitigating circumstances exist. One of the circumstances explicitly mentioned is: 'where the undertaking concerned has effectively collaborated with the Commission outside the scope of the Leniency Notice and beyond its legal obligation to do so'.

The second case was about a cartel among LPG wholesalers aimed at co-ordinating price list increases and, in so doing, maintaining stable market shares and customer allocation among the three companies involved. The cartel members were the three largest Italian LPG wholesalers, representing about 40 per cent of the market (Eni, Butangas and Liquigas). The collusion lasted for more than a decade (1995-2005). Initially started with reference to the Sardinian market only, the investigations were later widened to the whole Italian market due to the information provided by Eni (the market leader and former State incumbent), which submitted a number of statements by current and former employees disclosing the way the agreement was organised and monitored. The applicant also submitted a limited number of documents concerning meetings among competitors and data exchange among them. Eni was granted immunity from fines, while the Authority imposed fines on the other two companies involved totalling almost €24 million. Butangas and Liquigas have appealed the decision and the case is pending before the administrative court competent for antitrust matters.

Up to now two other on-going cartel investigations have been triggered by leniency applications (namely Case I-701, *Personal care products;* I-722, *Goods terrestrial shipping*).

Furthermore, in the Authority's decisional practice, there is evidence of reduction and immunity treatments even before the leniency programme was introduced (see *Operatori nel settore degli esplosivi da mine*, Decision 26 June 1997 No 5161).

The latter case is of great significance because it was the first time the Authority did not fine a company for being part of a cartel. This decision was taken because the undertaking concerned had abandoned the unlawful practice and had informed the Authority of the existence of the cartel. Before this disclosure, the Authority had been unaware of the existence of the cartel. Following the application, the Authority initiated proceedings against the main Italian firms producing and distributing explosives for the mining industry. They were alleged to have implemented agreements with the aim of sharing production and sales, as well as fixing prices.

In this case, *Italesplosivi*, one of the companies involved in the proceedings, which distributes explosives in the Italian market on behalf of firms competing among themselves, could have been the means by which to co-ordinate the commercial policies of its stockholders and the represented undertakings. Given the importance of the parties involved in the agreements, restriction on competition was considered substantial. Indeed, they represented more than 90 per cent of the Italian explosives market for the mining industry. Taking into account the significant market shares of the parties, the Authority ruled that the agreement had substantially restricted competition, leading to a reduction in the range of available products and to higher prices. In view of the seriousness of the offence and considering the different roles played by the companies with respect to the agreement, the Authority imposed fines ranging from 2 to 3 per cent of the companies' turnover (totalling L1,406 million). No fine, however, was imposed against the compliant company, since it had voluntarily ceased breaking the law before the Authority's intervention, and had played a decisive role in the detection of the agreement.

4. What is needed to be a successful leniency applicant? Is documentary evidence required or is testimonial evidence sufficient?

Full collaboration with the Authority is an essential requirement to benefit from the leniency programme.

The programme allows for a sliding scale of reductions according to the usefulness of the collaboration offered by a penitent company. This ranges from total immunity for a company that is first to spontaneously provide the Authority with decisive evidence of a secret cartel, where this information is not already available to the Authority; to a reduction of at most 50 per cent for a company whose collaboration significantly contributes to the evidence available to the Authority.

Usually, the decrease is proportional to the timeliness of a company's collaboration and the value of the evidence produced. Therefore, so as not to risk exclusion, a company must present all the relevant information it has available and must not reveal its participation in the leniency programme to third parties.

The 'first in' condition requires that the application, which may be oral or in writing, is submitted by a person who is empowered to act on behalf of a company for that purpose and that this notification is made individually.

When a company makes an oral application, its representative's statements are recorded on a hard disk and then written out by Authority employees. However, the oral application does not avoid the obligation of providing any documentary evidence that is at the company's disposal. Access to oral application is postponed until the statement of objections is issued (see Article 13(10) DPR 217/1998: *'The office may, giving reasons therefore, defer access to the documents requested until it has been ascertained that they are relevant for the purposes of acquiring evidence of infringements, but not beyond the date of the service of notice of the results of the investigation referred to in section 14'*).

A company must provide all the information at its disposal, which is relevant to prove the infringement. Consequently a company must, as far as possible, state:
- the name of its company and its registered office;
- the names and registered offices of the undertakings that have participated in the cartel;
- a detailed description of the anti-competitive cartel including: (i) nature, purpose and modalities of the cartel; (ii) the goods or services involved; (iii) the geographical area of the agreements; (iv) when the agreements were initiated and when they were concluded; (v) the names of the persons within the undertakings who were, or are involved in the infringement;
- copies of documents relating to the reported infringement and that a company has access to; and
- if the infringement has also been reported to another competition authority within the European Union. In this case, a company should provide the information sent to the other authority.

TIMING
5. What are the benefits of being 'first in' to co-operate?
Only a company that is 'first in' can apply for full immunity. To receive immunity, a company must provide enough information to meet the following requirements:
- based on the Authority's discretionary assessment, the nature and the quality of the information and evidence gained are critical in ascertaining the infringement or in carrying out an inspection;
- the Authority does not already have enough information or evidence to prove the existence of that infringement;

and the following conditions are met:
- a company withdraws from the cartel, unless the Authority asks it not to do so, as the other cartel members might suspect something;
- a company fully and consistently co-operates, which means: (i) providing any relevant information that may be required; (ii) being at the Authority's disposal, replying promptly to any request that may help

Italy

to ascertain the infringement; (iii) allowing the Authority to interview all the employees; (iv) not destroying or hiding any documents related to the infringement; (v) keeping the application for leniency secret until the statement of objections is released; and
- a company applying for leniency must not tell anyone except other national competition authorities of its intention.

6. What are the consequences of being 'second'? Is there an 'immunity plus' or 'amnesty plus' option?

A company that is 'second' can apply for a reduction in fine as long as it provides significant evidence. Other companies whose collaboration contributes significantly to the evidence available to the Authority, may benefit from a reduction in their fines of not more than 50 per cent.

To qualify for the reduction, a company should provide enough information, which strengthens in 'a significant manner', with regard to the nature or extent of detail, the evidence already obtained by the Authority, and this information should meet the following requirements:
- the collaboration should be prompt and complete;
- the Authority should regard as significant the way in which the information and evidence provided strengthens the body of evidence already collected.

Furthermore, the following conditions must be met:
- a company must leave the cartel, unless the Authority asks it not to do so, as in doing so might raise the suspicions of the other cartel members; and
- a company must fully and consistently co-operate, which means: (i) providing any relevant information that may be required; (ii) being at the Authority's disposal, replying promptly to any request that may help to ascertain the infringement; (iii) allowing the Authority to interview all the employees; (iv) not destroying or hiding any documents relevant to the infringement; and (v) keeping the application for leniency secret until the statement of objections is released.
- a company applying for leniency must not tell anyone except other national competition authorities of its intention.

The reduction of fines is subject to respecting the full collaboration requirements. Therefore, if the Authority discovers that these requirements are not being met, it will promptly communicate this to a company.

When the Authority obtains new incriminating evidence from a company, this evidence is not taken into consideration when assessing the amount of the final fine to be imposed on the company.

In any case, the Italian leniency notice does not provide for an 'immunity plus' or 'amnesty plus' option.

7. Are subsequent companies given any beneficial treatment if they make a useful contribution? How are 'useful contributions' defined?

According to the Notice, other companies may subsequently submit evidence that enriches the information and the documents the Authority already has had access to, in order to strengthen its ability to fully establish

Italy

the facts of the investigation. The information and evidence will be evaluated according to the nature and extent of the detail that it is able to provide.

SCOPE/FULL LENIENCY
8. Is it possible to receive full leniency? And, if so, what are the conditions required in order to receive full leniency? Can ringleaders/coercers receive full leniency? If there is a requirement to 'co-operate fully and on an ongoing basis' what does it entail? Does the regulatory authority require the applicant to cease participation in the cartel conduct after its application?

It is possible to receive full leniency if a company is the first to make an application and it meets the following conditions:
- based on the Authority's discretionary assessment, the nature and the quality of the information and evidence gained is critical in ascertaining the infringement or in carrying out an inspection;
- the Authority does not already have enough information or evidence to prove the existence of that infringement;

and the following conditions must be met:
- a company must leave the cartel, unless the Authority asks it not to do so, if by so doing, it might raise the suspicions of the other cartel members;
- a company must fully and consistently co-operate, which means: (i) providing any relevant information that may be required; (ii) being at the Authority's disposal, replying promptly to any request that may help to ascertain the infringement; (iii) allowing the Authority to interview all the employees; (iv) not destroying or hiding any documents related to the infringement; and (v) keeping the application for leniency secret until the statement of objections is released;
- a company applying for leniency must not tell anyone except other national competition authorities of its intention.

The possibility to apply for leniency is granted regardless of the role the company played in the cartel. Accordingly, also the cartel ringleader is allowed to ask for immunity.

9. How many companies have received full immunity from fines to date?
As already mentioned in question 3, up until now only Gruppo Trombini (Decision 16835, *Produttori di Pannneli Truciolari in Legno*, 30 May 2007) and Eni (Decision 20931, *Prezzo del GPL per riscaldamento regione Sardegna*, 24 March 2010) have received full immunity from fines. It is interesting to point out that, in both cases, the Italian Competition Authority gave an extensive and clear explanation of the reasons for granting full immunity which were, obviously, compliant with its leniency notice requirements. The wording of the Authority's reasoning should be emphasised. First of all, it remarked on the decisive contribution made to the proceedings by the leniency applicant. Then it pointed out that the undertaking was the first participant that spontaneously gave crucial information, such

Italy

as documentary evidence pertaining to the existence of the cartel, and specifically, information concerning the identity of the undertakings involved and their representatives. Moreover, it gave the Authority all the relevant information it could get before and after the proceedings had started, and was willing to provide extensive and detailed clarifications in relation to the documents found during the dawn raids, in the light of the cartel's structure. Finally, the quality of the information provided further enriched the factual framework, which was the object of the Authority's investigation.

Furthermore, as also mentioned in question 3, in June 1997 the Authority completed an investigation into a horizontal agreement between the nine leading mine explosives manufacturers. The Authority ruled that the agreement had substantially restricted competition, leading to a reduction in the range of available products and to higher prices in the market. In view of the seriousness of the offence and considering the different roles played by the companies with respect to the agreement, fines ranging from 2 to 3 per cent of the companies' turnover (totalling L1,406 million) were imposed. No fine, however, was imposed on the compliant company, since it had voluntarily left the cartel before the Authority took action, and played a decisive role in the discovery of the agreement.

PROCEDURE
10. What are the practical steps required to apply for leniency?
A company wishing to take part in the leniency programme must present an application to the Authority, with the relevant information and documents attached. If so requested by a company, the Authority can issue a receipt that states the date and time when the application was submitted.

In some cases, a company may not be in a position to immediately produce the elements of proof necessary to obtain immunity, but it may be able to obtain them within a short period of time. In this case, it may lodge an incomplete application and request that the Authority fix a deadline for the relevant information and documents to complete the application to be produced (ie, a marker).

Furthermore, if a company requesting the marker does not complete its application, the documentation provided may be used in order to consider a reduction of the fine.

11. Is there an optimal time to approach the regulatory authority?
If a company has decided to apply for leniency, then it should approach the Authority as soon as possible in order to be considered the 'first in' to collaborate. Probably, the best moment to apply is when the Authority has no knowledge of the existence of a cartel, or before it has begun to carry out any inspections.

However, prior to applying, a company should contact the Authority under the cover of confidentiality to find out if any other undertakings have already applied for immunity.

12. What guarantees of leniency exist if a party co-operates?

The only kind of formal guarantee granted to a company willing to co-operate is that of being the 'first in' to report an infringement. In fact, the Authority believes that restricting full exemption from fines only to the 'first in' to report an infringement significantly undermines the stability of a cartel, by increasing the uncertainty of its participants about which of them would be the first to 'snitch'. Therefore, this limitation would trigger the undertakings involved to try to be the first to co-operate with the Authority. However, being the first to report an infringement might not in itself be enough, as the Authority also evaluates whether the other requirements for immunity have been met. It accepts the application and grants conditional immunity subject to the condition of full collaboration. Therefore, the Authority only assesses immunity when it makes its final decision.

If a company refuses to co-operate fully, it loses its conditional immunity and this would promptly be communicated by the Authority. A company would also lose any chance of applying for a reduction in fine.

In the case where an application for immunity has been rejected, a company may either ask for a reduction in fine (up to 50 per cent), or for the full retraction of all information and evidence provided. As for immunity, the decision regarding the reduction of fines is only made at the time of the final decision.

CONSEQUENCES
13. What effects does leniency granted to a corporate defendant have on the defendant's employees? Does it protect them from criminal and/or civil liability?

This is not applicable in Italy, since no sanctions can be imposed on individuals for infringements of competition law.

14. Does leniency bar further criminal or private enforcement?

Under the Italian Antitrust Act, the only sanctions that can be imposed on companies infringing competition rules are pecuniary fines.

Furthermore, the leniency programme does not bar private civil actions for damages. Nonetheless, an oral application can be filed in order to avoid potential interested third parties from accessing the file and copying any written statement by the leniency applicant that admits involvement in a cartel and discloses details of how it functions.

PROTECTION AGAINST DISCLOSURE/CONFIDENTIALITY
15. Is confidentiality afforded to the leniency applicant and other collaborating parties? If so, to what extent? Is the identity of the leniency applicant/other co-operating parties disclosed during the investigation or in the final decision? Is information provided by the leniency applicant/other co-operating parties passed on to other undertakings under investigation? Can a leniency applicant/other co-operating party request anonymity or confidentiality of information provided?

If the Authority so decides, access to the information and evidence

Italy

provided by the leniency applicant can be postponed until the statement of objections is served. Nonetheless, this postponement is mandatory only when a company applies orally; whereas if a written application is made, a company is only entitled to request a postponement.

If an oral statement is made, those who may access cannot obtain a copy of the recording, but may only listen to it and take notes.

16. Is the evidence submitted by the leniency applicant protected from transmission to other competition authorities with whom the authority in question co-operates? If so, how?
The Italian leniency notice does not provide for any specific rule on the possible exchange of information with other competition authorities. Subsequently, general rules on co-operation within the European Competition Network apply.

To our knowledge, the applicant – either of its own motion, or subsequent to a request by the Authority – can give its written or oral consent to allow the Authority to enter into possible consultations with the Commission and/ or the other members of the ECN interested in the content of the leniency application.

17. To what extent can evidence submitted by the leniency applicant (transcripts of oral statements or written evidence) become discoverable in subsequent private enforcement claims? Can leniency information be subjected to discovery orders in domestic or foreign courts? Can leniency information submitted in a foreign jurisdiction be subjected to discovery orders in the domestic courts?
There is no discovery system in the Italian civil judicial system. Therefore, judges cannot order the discovery of evidence during a civil procedure on their own motion. Nonetheless, a party, allegedly damaged by the cartel, can ask the judge to order the defendant or a third party (that might well be the Authority) to disclose any document relevant to the case if it is able to identify the requested documents with a sufficient degree of accuracy (see, Article 210 of the Civil Procedural Ccode).

18. Are there any precedents in which evidence from a leniency application has been discovered in a private enforcement claim?
Because the leniency notice has only recently been introduced into the Italian system, to our knowledge, there are still no cases of evidence discovery before the civil judge in a private enforcement claim.

19. Does the policy address the interaction with applications under the Commission's Leniency Notice? If so, how?
In order to lighten the administrative burden on companies, it is possible for a company to present an application for immunity in a simplified form, where the European Commission is best placed to carry out the investigation of the cartel in question. For a simplified form, companies have to, at the very least, provide the following information:

- name of the company and registered office;
- names and registered offices of the undertakings that have participated in the cartel;
- a detailed description of the anti-competitive cartel including: (i) nature of the agreement; (ii) goods or services involved; (iii) the geographical area of the agreements; and (iv) when the agreements were initiated and when they were concluded;
- an indication of where, in other member states, it is possible to find evidence of the infringement; and
- if the infringement has also been reported to another competition authority within the European Union, the information sent to the other authority.

Finally, it is also worth noting that, on request, the Authority will issue a receipt stating the time of application and will inform a company if it is still possible to apply for immunity. When the Authority needs more information, it will fix a deadline for a company to provide it. Furthermore, when the Authority wants to intervene in a case, it will give the applicant a term to complete the immunity application. In this case, the moment of application would be the time when the simplified application was lodged.

20. Does the policy address the interaction with applications for leniency in other EU member states? If so, how?
See answer to question 19 above.

RELATIONSHIP WITH SETTLEMENT PROCEDURES
21. What is the relationship between leniency and applicable settlement procedures? Are they mutually exclusive?
Not applicable. There is no settlement procedure under Italian competition rules.

REFORM/LATEST DEVELOPMENTS
22. Is there a reform underway to revise the leniency policy? What are the latest developments?
Since its recent introduction, the Notice has not been subject to any amendments or reform.

The authors would like to thank their colleague Francesco Russo for useful discussions and comments to an earlier version of this paper. They remain solely responsible for any opinion expressed in the paper.

Japan

Anderson Mōri & Tomotsune Hideto Ishida,
Shigeyoshi Ezaki, Yusuke Nakano & Koya Uemura

BACKGROUND
1. What is the relevant legislation containing the leniency policy and what is the enforcing body?
The leniency policy is contained in the Anti-monopoly Act (AMA) at paragraphs 10 to 18, Article 7-2 and the Rules on reporting and submission of materials regarding immunity from or reduction of surcharges (Leniency Guidelines). This leniency policy became effective from 4 January 2006, following an amendment to the AMA.

The Fair Trade Commission of Japan (JFTC) is responsible for enforcing the AMA.

2. What are the basic tenets of a leniency/immunity programme? Is leniency available also for other types of competition law violations than cartels?
Under the leniency programme, a maximum of five companies (or groups of companies) may declare their participation in a cartel to the JFTC. Following their compliance with certain other conditions, these companies (or groups of companies) may receive immunity or a reduction in the applicable administrative fines which may apply to the participants due to their illegal behaviour. The leniency programme is available only for unreasonable restraint of trade (typically cartels) and not for other types of violation such as private monopolisation and unfair trade practices.

3. How many cartels have been unveiled and punished since the adoption of the leniency policy?
According to the JFTC, as of 31 March 2009, 264 applications for leniency had been filed under the programme. The identities of successful leniency applicants in 30 cartel cases have been publicly disclosed.

4. What is needed to be a successful leniency applicant? Is documentary evidence required or is testimonial evidence sufficient?
The applicant, among other things, must 'independently' submit reports (Forms 1, 2 or 3) as well as documentary and other evidence of the anti-competitive conduct to the JFTC. Documentary evidence is required, sole testimonial evidence is insufficient. For further requirements (including the obligation to fully co-operate with the JFTC during the course of its investigation), see questions 8 and 10.

TIMING
5. What are the benefits of being 'first in' to co-operate?
The first qualifying applicant who comes forward before the start of the JFTC's investigation will be entitled to total immunity from administrative fines. In principle, the leniency programme in Japan only purports to offer leniency with respect to administrative fines and, strictly speaking, does not offer express immunity from criminal prosecution. However, the JFTC has stated that it will not request the indictment of the first leniency applicant (including its officers and employees, provided that they fully co-operate with the applicant in regard to its internal investigation and subsequently co-operate with the JFTC) and will consider subsequent applicants on a case-by-case basis. In this regard, the Japanese Ministry of Justice has also issued a statement that the public prosecutors' office will 'pay due respect' to the policy of the JFTC.

For further details, see questions 10 and 13.

6. What are the consequences of being 'second'? Is there an 'immunity plus' or 'amnesty plus' option?
The second qualifying applicant who comes forward before the start of the JFTC's investigation will only be entitled to a fixed 50 per cent reduction. The programme also offers a guaranteed 30 per cent reduction in fines to the third, fourth and fifth qualifying applicants who come forward before the start of the JFTC's investigation. Application for leniency after the start of JFTC's investigation can still be filed. However, those applicants who seek leniency after the commencement of the JFTC's investigation may only seek a 30 per cent reduction in fines, provided that those applicants are: (i) within the fifth position among itself and any prior applicants (either before or after the start of the JFTC's investigation); and (ii) within the third position among itself and prior applicants after the start of the JFTC's investigation, and that certain other conditions are met (see question 10). 'Immunity plus' or 'amnesty plus' options are not available under the AMA.

For further details, see questions 10 and 13.

7. Are subsequent firms given any beneficial treatment if they make a useful contribution? How are 'useful contributions' defined?
The JFTC has no discretion to offer any kind of leniency to parties that co-operate after the first five slots have been taken whether or not they make a useful contribution. Therefore, 'useful contributions' are not defined in the AMA.

SCOPE/FULL LENIENCY
8. Is it possible to receive full leniency? And, if so, what are the conditions required to receive full leniency?
Full immunity from fines is available to the first applicant provided that all of the following conditions are met:
- the applicant has 'independently' submitted reports (Forms 1 and 2) as well as documentary and other evidence of the anti-competitive conduct

to the JFTC;
- the reports and documents are submitted before the start of the JFTC's investigation;
- the applicant stops the conduct before the start of the JFTC's investigation;
- the applicant provides additional information as requested by the JFTC;
- the reports and evidence provided by the applicant are not false; and
- the applicant has not previously coerced another party to participate in the illegal conduct or prevented it from ceasing such conduct.

For further details see question 10.

9. How many companies have received full immunity from fines to date?

As of 31 May 2009, 15 companies have received full immunity from fines in 23 cases.

On 8 September 2006, the JFTC released its policy concerning public announcement of the results of leniency applications. The policy states that, if the successful applicant requests a public announcement be made, the JFTC will announce the name, address, name of representative and grant of immunity or reductions in terms of percentage. It is unlikely that an applicant would not request this public announcement because without it the company will not have access to a shorter period of 'suspension of nomination' by various governmental authorities (a '*de facto* punishment' against cartel participants which prevents them from tendering for contracts).

PROCEDURE/CONFIDENTIALITY

10. What are the practical steps required to apply for leniency?

The practical steps which must be taken to apply for leniency will depend on whether the application is made before or after the JFTC has commenced its investigation (ie the JFTC's dawn raid or criminal inspection). However, regardless of the time at which the application is made, the following principles are applicable to an application for leniency:
- the reports (Form 1, 2 or 3) shall be written in Japanese;
- evidence written in a foreign language shall be translated into Japanese; and
- applications can be prepared and submitted by an attorney.

Applicants are not required to fully disclose facts relevant to a cartel at the time of the submission of Form 1, 2 or 3, but are required to fully answer inquiries by the JFTC during the course of JFTC's investigation after the submission of Form 2 or 3.

10.1 Before the start of JFTC's investigation

An application for leniency which is made before the start of the JFTC's investigation can result in full immunity (first applicant only) or reduction in fines (50 per cent for second applicant and 30 per cent for third, fourth and fifth applicants).

Practically, the following summarises typical steps for making an application prior to the JFTC's commencement of an investigation.

Step 1: Internal investigation and informal consultation/ guidance
After detecting a cartel, the company should conduct an internal investigation to determine whether it should file an application. The company may hold prior consultation with the Senior Officer for the Leniency Programme to seek informal guidance. This consultation and guidance can be made on an anonymous basis.

Step 2: Submission of Form 1
Form 1 should be sent to the JFTC using a specified facsimile number. Roughly speaking, Form 1 requires the products or services involved to be listed in addition to a brief description of the relevant violation, and the period of violation. There is no need for any evidence to be attached to Form 1. The ranking of each applicant will be determined based on the timing of the submission of Form 1. The submission of Form 1 functions as so-called 'marker'.

Step 3: Submission of Form 2 and the JFTC's notice of acceptance
The applicant must submit Form 2 to the JFTC within the period specified by the JFTC (normally two weeks). Form 2 requires more detailed information than Form 1, including specific details of the conduct, applicant's executives or employees involved, co-violators, etc. Evidence including witness statements signed by relevant employees should be attached to Form 2 in compliance with the required evidentiary standards. A few weeks or months after receiving Form 2, the JFTC will issue a notice of acceptance of Form 2. The notice of acceptance of Form 2 acts as a confirmation by the JFTC that the application has been accepted and is complete.

Step 4: Investigation of the co-violators and applicant(s) by the JFTC
Typically, the JFTC investigates the co-violators as well as applicant(s) a few months following the submission of Form 2.

Step 5: Continued co-operation with additional requests by JFTC
The applicant must continue to co-operate with the JFTC in response to requests for additional information. In our experience, the JFTC makes repeated requests for substantial numbers of reports and large amounts of evidence.

Step 6: Grant of immunity/ reduction of surcharge
The JFTC grants immunity or reduction of fines to applicants about six to 12 months after the start of the JFTC's investigation. Upon finding infringement, the JFTC issues a cease and desist order and a fines payment order against each of the undertakings that are the subject of its investigation. Successful immunity applicants receive a notice of immunity from fines instead of the payment order. We note that the JFTC often refrains from issuing cease and desist orders to successful leniency applicants who have applied for leniency before the start of the JFTC's investigation, because of an appreciation of the sound functioning of their compliance system.

10.2 After the start of JFTC's investigation
Even after the start of the JFTC's investigation, applications for leniency can still be filed to seek a 30 per cent reduction in fines as long as the applicant is: (i) within the fifth position including the applicant itself and all the prior applicants; and (ii) within the third position including the applicant itself and prior applicants after the start of the JFTC's investigation.

11. Is there an optimal time to approach the regulatory authority?
Because the JFTC has no discretion in determining the order of application and percentage of reduction, it should be approached as soon as possible. Spending substantial time on the collection of detailed information makes little sense under the leniency programme in Japan.

This early approach is especially relevant in the case of Form 1, because a company who submits a small amount of information in Form 1, followed by Form 2 containing the minimum amount of sufficient information, will beat another company even if they submitted a large amount of information in Form 1 (of greater value than all the information submitted by the first company in Forms 1 and 2). In that sense, Form 1 can work as a 'marker'.

12. What guarantees of leniency exist if a party co-operates?
Where leniency applications are submitted both before and after the commencement of the JFTC's investigation, the JFTC should issue a notice of acceptance of Form 2 or 3 to leniency applicants promptly after receipt of the reports and evidence (Article 7-2, paragraph 15 of the AMA). This notice should be issued in a few weeks or months. While this notice of acceptance does not legally guarantee the grant of immunity or leniency, practically speaking this means that leniency is granted.

As a final step, a successful immunity applicant will receive a notice of immunity from fines from the JFTC when it issues surcharge payment orders against all other violators in the same case (Article 7-2, paragraph 18 of the AMA). Other successful leniency applicants (who can receive 50 per cent or 30 per cent reductions) will be able to confirm the grant of leniency and the result of their leniency application once they receive a draft of a surcharge payment order from the JFTC.

CONSEQUENCES
13. What effects does leniency granted to a corporate defendant have on the defendant's employees? Does it protect them from criminal and/or civil liability?
Nothing in the AMA refers to the effects that leniency granted to a corporate defendant may have on the defendant's employees. However, if employees of a corporate defendant may be subject to criminal liability even where the corporate defendant is the first applicant for leniency before the start of the JFTC's investigation, the corporate defendant may feel reluctant to apply for leniency, fearing that its employees (including senior management) may be subject to a criminal charge. Taking this potential concern into account, the JFTC has officially announced its policy not to file criminal charges against

employees of a corporate defendant who is the first applicant for leniency before the start of a JFTC investigation, provided that the employees fully co-operate with the applicant in regard to its internal investigation and subsequently co-operates with the JFTC during its investigation (the JFTC Policy on Criminal Charges and Investigations on the Violation of the Antimonopoly Act, issued by the JFTC on 7 October 2005). Because the JFTC's filing of criminal charges is a requirement for the criminal prosecution of a violation of the AMA by the public prosecutors' office, this JFTC policy not to file criminal charges against employees of first applicants effectively releases such employees from criminal liability.

The Ministry of Justice has also expressed its intention during a Diet session regarding the leniency programme that, if the JFTC decides not to file criminal charges against a corporate defendant or its employees because the corporate defendant is the first applicant for leniency before the start of the JFTC investigation, the public prosecutors' office will 'pay due respect' to the JFTC's decision.

It should be noted that this protection from criminal liability can be afforded only to employees of the first leniency applicant before the start of the JFTC investigation. Some critics suggest that the JFTC should also refrain from filing criminal charges against co-operative individuals of other successful leniency applicants, because second to fifth leniency applicants could face difficulties in asking officers and employees for co-operation if the JFTC were able to file criminal charges nominating them. The JFTC makes decisions on these matters on a case-by-case basis.

Contrary to criminal liability, employees of a corporate defendant will not be protected from civil liability at all, even when the corporate defendant is eligible for the full immunity from the surcharge as the first applicant before the start of the investigation.

14. Does leniency bar further private enforcement?
Leniency does not bar private enforcement, at least from a legal viewpoint. In theory, companies that apply for leniency expose themselves to the risk of subsequent private actions. Nonetheless, the risk might not be a significant disincentive to apply for leniency, because Japan does not allow for class actions or treble damages.

PROTECTION AGAINST DISCLOSURE/CONFIDENTIALITY
15. Is confidentiality afforded to the leniency applicant and other co-operating parties? If so, to what extent? Is the identity of the leniency applicant/other co-operating parties disclosed during the investigation or in the final decision? Is information provided by the leniency applicant/other co-operating parties passed on to other undertakings under investigation? Can a leniency applicant or other co-operating party request anonymity or confidentiality of information provided?
Neither the AMA nor the Leniency Guidelines explicitly state whether or to what extent the JFTC may disclose the information submitted by leniency

applicants to third parties. However, in practice, the JFTC has a general policy of not disclosing information to third parties.

The JFTC does not in practice disclose leniency application forms or other evidence provided by applicants in the course of leniency application to other defendants or interested parties, or even to Japanese courts. However, information obtained by the JFTC through its own investigations, including interviews with key employees and executives (see question 10), can be submitted as evidence at the hearings and is disclosed to other defendants.

The JFTC will not disclose the identity of a successful leniency applicant unless the applicant requests that a public announcement (see question 9) be made.

After consideration of the US comments made on the draft version in 2005, the Leniency Guidelines specifically provide for oral statements from the applicant's employees and executives instead of written evidence required under Form 2 or 3, in order to reduce the risk of discovery in foreign courts.

On the other hand, Article 8 of the Leniency Guidelines explicitly states that leniency applicants (who have submitted Forms under the Leniency Guidelines to the JFTC) must not disclose the facts of such a submission to third parties unless a justifiable reason exists. Disclosure to a foreign competition authority for the purpose of an application for leniency in the relevant jurisdiction is considered to constitute a justifiable reason.

16. Is the evidence submitted by the leniency applicant protected from transmission to other competition authorities with whom the authority in question co-operates? If so, how?

The JFTC will not transmit evidence submitted by a leniency applicant to other competition authorities, even where it is co-operating with such authorities.

The amendment to the AMA in 2009 introduced a new Article 43-2 regarding the provision of information to foreign competition authorities. Article 43-2 provides that the JFTC may provide foreign competition authorities with information that the JFTC considers useful for the performance of the duties of such authorities. However, the JFTC expressed a position that it would not disclose the evidence submitted by the leniency applicants to any third parties. Moreover, Article 43-2 specifically states that the JFTC must not disclose information to foreign competition authorities if such disclosure is likely to hinder due performance of the JFTC's duties under the AMA. The disclosure by the JFTC of leniency information to foreign competition authorities will become a serious disincentive for defendants who are considering filing for leniency, and will hinder the performance of JFTC's duties. As a result, the JFTC is unlikely to transmit evidence submitted by leniency applicants even under the new Article 43-2.

17. To what extent can evidence submitted by the leniency applicant (transcripts of oral statements or written evidence) become discoverable in subsequent private enforcement claims? Can leniency information be subjected to discovery orders in foreign or domestic courts? Can leniency information submitted in a foreign jurisdiction be subjected to discovery orders in the domestic courts?

The JFTC will not disclose leniency information to Japanese courts even if it is ordered to disclose such information. Under the Code of Civil Procedure, Japanese courts are granted a power to order the holder of a document to produce the document. However, the holder of a document may refuse to produce the document if its submission is likely to harm the public interest or substantially hinder the performance of public officials' duties. The JFTC's position is that the disclosure of leniency information will substantially hinder its performance and it should refuse such court orders on that basis. Similarly the JFTC does not disclose leniency information to foreign courts. However, foreign courts may order defendants, rather than the JFTC itself, to submit evidence that the defendants submitted to the JFTC. To mitigate such a risk, the JFTC allows applicants to give some of the statements in oral form to the JFTC in leniency applications (see question 15).

Japanese courts are considered to have no power to request document holders in a foreign country to submit documents, as such a request would be in conflict with the sovereignty of the foreign country. Therefore, it is unlikely that a document production order will be issued against foreign competition authorities. However, we cannot deny the possibility that a copy of a written leniency application as held by the applicant will be subject to a document production order.

18. Are there any precedents in which evidence from a leniency application has been discovered in a private enforcement claim?

There is no precedent in which evidence from a leniency application has been discovered in a private enforcement claim.

RELATIONSHIP WITH THE EUROPEAN COMMISSION'S LENIENCY NOTICE AND LENIENCY POLICY IN OTHER EU MEMBER STATES

19. Does the policy address the interaction with applications under the Commission Leniency Notice? If so, how?

Not applicable.

20. Does the policy address the interaction with applications for leniency in other EU member states? If so, how? Does the authority accept summary applications in line with the ECN Model Leniency Programme?

Not applicable.

RELATIONSHIP WITH SETTLEMENT PROCEDURES
21. What is the relationship between leniency and applicable settlement procedures? Are they mutually exclusive?
There is no settlement procedure applicable to anti-competitive practices in Japan.

REFORM/LATEST DEVELOPMENTS
22. Is there a reform underway to revisit the leniency policy? What are the latest developments?
Before the amendment, the first applicant was granted full immunity from fines, the second was granted a 50 per cent reduction, and the third was granted a 30 per cent reduction, before the start of the JFTC's investigation. After the start of the JFTC's investigation, an applicant within the third position (including itself and any prior applicants) was granted a 30 per cent reduction.

Under the amended leniency policy, before the start of a JFTC investigation, the first applicant is granted full immunity, the second 50 per cent and the third 30 per cent, and the fourth and fifth applicants are also granted a 30 per cent reduction. After the start of the JFTC's investigation, an applicant who is: (i) within the fifth position including itself and any other applicants (either before or after the start of the JFTC's investigation); and (ii) within the third position including itself and any other applicants after the start of the JFTC's investigation, will be granted a 30 per cent fine reduction.

Another amendment to the leniency programme relates to so-called group filing. Before the amendment, leniency had to be applied for by a company with an independent legal personality, and therefore, two or more companies within the same group were not allowed to jointly apply for leniency. This meant that companies within the same group were never granted full immunity. After the amendment, companies within the same group can jointly apply for leniency, and if such joint application is the first application before the start of the JFTC's investigation, the companies within the same group will be granted full immunity.

Luxembourg

Elvinger Hoss & Prussen Léon Gloden & Stéphanie Damien

BACKGROUND
1. What is the relevant legislation concerning the leniency policy and what is the enforcing body?
The law of 17 May 2004 on competition came into force on 30 May 2004 (Mémorial L 2004, page 111), (the 2004 Law) having abrogated the law of 17 June 1970 on anti-competitive practices. It basically mirrors Council Regulation EC 1/2003 of 16 December 2002 on the implementation of the rules on competition laid down in Articles 81 and 82 of the Treaty (the EC Regulation 1/2003).

The 2004 Law set up the relevant competition authorities – the Council for Competition Matters (*Conseil de la concurrence* (the Council)) and the Investigation Division for Competition Matters (*Inspection de la concurrence* (the Investigation Division)).

The powers of the Investigation Division are very similar to the powers of the European Commission and are subject to the same conditions as set out in EC Regulation 1/2003. The Council is the decision-making body.

Article 19 of the 2004 Law provides for a leniency regime for competition law infringements. The statutory rules are very scarce. On its website, the Council undertakes to apply the Model Leniency Programme as provided for by the European Competition Network (the ECN) as far as it does not conflict with Luxembourg law.

2. What are the basic tenets of a leniency/immunity programme? Is leniency available also for other types of competition law violations than cartels?
Leniency only applies to agreements between undertakings, decisions by associations of undertakings and concerted practices (the cartel). Other infringements to competition law are not covered by Article 19 of the 2004 Law.

The principles laid down in Article 19 of the 2004 Law are as follows.

The Council may grant an undertaking immunity from any fine which would otherwise have been imposed if the undertaking is the first to denounce the existence of a cartel of which neither the Council nor the Investigation Division have knowledge. The Council may reduce the fine imposed on an undertaking if that undertaking denounces the existence of a cartel prior to the notification of a complaint. According to the Council's website, bringing additional information unknown to the competition authorities is sufficient in this case.

The cumulative conditions to be met in order to benefit from immunity or a reduction of fines are:
- the concerned undertaking provides the Council or the Investigation Division with all evidence and information in its possession regarding the suspected cartel and co-operates fully and on a continuous basis until the Council has reached its final decision;
- the concerned undertaking has ended its involvement in the suspected infringement no later than the time it denounces the infringement to the Council or the Investigation Division; and
- neither the Council, nor the Investigation Division is in possession of evidence that the concerned undertaking has coerced other undertakings by its economic market power or by any other means to participate in the infringements.

Even if those conditions are fulfilled, the Council's power to grant immunity or leniency is still discretionary.

3. How many cartels have been unveiled and punished since the adoption of the leniency programme?
As of today, no cartels have been found to exist. See below question 9.

4. What is needed to be a successful leniency applicant? Is documentary evidence required or is testimonial evidence sufficient?
Article 19 of the 2004 Law does not specify whether only documentary evidence, or even testimonial evidence, will be accepted by the Investigation Division and/or the Council. As the involved undertakings have to fully co-operate with the competition authorities, one may assume that the authorities will accept any proof enabling the Council to take a decision.

Form a general point of view, the Council states on its website that the probative value of the information to be provided with respect to an application for immunity may be lower than with respect to an application for a reduction of fines.

TIMING
5. What are the benefits of being 'first in' to co-operate?
Only the 'first in' may benefit from immunity provided that it meets the cumulative conditions as set out in Article 19 of the 2004 Law (see question 2).

6. What are the consequences of being 'second'? Is there an 'immunity plus' or 'amnesty plus' option?
The second undertaking which denounces the existence of a cartel cannot benefit from immunity but only from a reduction of fines provided that the conditions set out in Article 19 of the 2004 Law are met (see question 2).

7. Are subsequent firms given any beneficial treatment if they make a useful contribution? How are 'useful contributions' defined?
Any subsequent undertaking meeting the conditions set out in Article 19 of the 2004 Law may benefit from a reduction of fines.

The 2004 Law does not refer to the concept of 'useful contribution'. However in a decision of the Council and in its annual report for 2006, the Council expressly refers to the test of 'added value'. On its website, the Council explains that the information provided to the competition authorities must strengthen by its nature or its precision the competition authorities' capacity to establish the existence of the presumed cartel. A simple denunciation or admission of participation in a cartel will not be sufficient. It also specifies that the added-value of the information provided by the leniency applicant will be appreciated in relation to the information already at the disposal of the competition authorities at the moment of the application for leniency.

SCOPE/FULL LENIENCY
8. Is it possible to receive full leniency? If so, what are the conditions required to receive full leniency?
Full leniency may be granted provided that the conditions laid down in Article 19 of the 2004 Law are met (see question 2).

8.1 Can ringleaders/coercers receive full leniency?
Immunity or reduction of fines can only be granted if the undertaking has not compelled other undertakings to participate in the prohibited activity.

8.2 If there is a requirement to 'co-operate fully and on an ongoing basis' what does it entail?
Article 19 of the 2004 Law only provides for a total and permanent co-operation. The few decisions rendered by the Council are silent on the ongoing co-operation obligations.

8.3 Does the regulatory authority require the applicant to cease participation in the cartel conduct after its application?
To benefit from immunity or reduction of fines, Article 19 of the 2004 Law requires that the concerned undertaking has ended its involvement in the suspected infringement no later than the time it denounces the infringement to the Council or the Investigation Division.

9. How many companies have received full immunity from fines to date?
The decisions rendered by the Council on leniency applications (the 'leniency opinions') are not published. In its report for 2008, the Council reports that between the creation of the Council in 2004 and 2008 five leniency applications have been filed. Three of them led to a conditional leniency opinion and two of them to a negative leniency opinion. Because, as yet, the Council has never found the existence of a cartel, we do not know whether these undertakings would have finally been granted full immunity or not.

PROCEDURE
10. What are the practical steps required to apply for leniency?
In order to benefit from the leniency regime, an undertaking must file an application with the Council or the Investigation Division (which will transmit the application to the Council). No particular form is required for the application. Even oral applications are accepted as long as the undertaking provides all elements and information of which it is aware. Following the application of the concerned undertaking, the Council, at the request of the Investigation Division, may take a leniency opinion which lays down the conditions under which the immunity or leniency is granted. The undertaking may present its observations prior to the leniency opinion. Such leniency opinion is notified to the undertaking and is not published.

10.1 Full disclosure
The leniency applicant must disclose and provide all the elements, evidence and information, of which it is aware and/or has in its possession.

10.2 Initial contact/is there a 'marker' system?
The first contact with the competition authorities is very important as it will guarantee the rank of the leniency applicant (and thus whether it may be granted immunity or a reduction of fines) if several undertakings apply for leniency with respect to the same cartel.

No marker system is provided by the 2004 Law. Nevertheless, pursuant to published information on the Council's website, the Luxembourg competition authorities will apply the marker system model as provided by the ECN Model Leniency Programme. To obtain a marker, the undertaking must, during its first contact, provide a minimum amount of information (its corporate name, address, the circumstances that lead to the leniency application, the participants in the presumed cartel, the market(s) involved, the affected territory(ies), the total duration of the presumed cartel and information on any other leniency application which has been or will be made to other competition authorities (EU or non-EU)). The undertaking will then receive an acknowledgement containing the date and time of the first contact. From such acknowledgement, the undertaking has two weeks to complete the file and provide the Council and the Investigation Division with all the information and evidence in its possession.

10.3 Conditional reduction of fine
Article 19 of the 2004 Law provides that the Council's opinion on leniency lays down the conditions under which the immunity or leniency is granted. After the investigation, the Council, when deciding on the existence of a cartel, will verify whether the conditions have been met and if so will grant immunity or leniency.

10.4 Final reduction
The 2004 Law does not provide for any scale according to which fines may be reduced. However, on its website, the Council states that the reduction

will depend on the information provided to the competition authorities at the time and the extent and utility of such information.

11. Is there an optimal time to approach the regulatory authority?
The 2004 Law does not provide for any deadline, but Article 19(2) of the 2004 Law provides that the Council may reduce fines imposed on an undertaking if such undertaking denounces the existence of the cartel prior to the notification of a complaint.

12. What guarantees of leniency exist if a party co-operates?
The 2004 Law does not provide for any guarantees of leniency. As stressed under question 2, the Council is not obliged to grant immunity or reduce fines.

In a recent judgment, the administrative court of first instance rejected an action brought against a negative leniency opinion of the Council by arguing that any opinion which lays down the conditions is only a preliminary act which does not cause harm to the applicant. It is only the final decision which may cause harm to the applicant and hence only the final decision may be challenged before the administrative court (*tribunal administratif, 13 juin 2007, no. de rôle 21870*). This judgment has been confirmed by the administrative court of appeal (*cour administrative, 24 janvier 2008, no. de role 23178C*).

CONSEQUENCES
13. What effects does leniency granted to a corporate defendant have on the defendant's employees? Does it protect them from criminal and/or civil liability?
The 2004 Law only provides for immunity or leniency granted to undertakings. Fines may not be levied against employees. Consequently leniency should have no impact on employees.

14. Does leniency bar further private enforcement?
The legal framework does not provide for any effect on private enforcement.

PROTECTION AGAINST DISCLOSURE/CONFIDENTIALITY
15. Is confidentiality afforded to the leniency applicant and other co-operating parties? If so, to what extent?
Even if the 2004 Law does not address the issue of the confidentiality of leniency applicants and other co-operating parties, it may nevertheless be assumed that the competition authorities will not refuse confidentiality to the leniency applicant.

Furthermore Article 19(4) of the 2004 Law provides that the leniency opinion is not published (see question 10).

15.1 Is the identity of the leniency applicant/other co-operating parties disclosed during the investigation or in the final decision?
The 2004 law does not address this issue. It is likely that unless

confidentiality has been requested and granted, the identity of the leniency applicant and/or other co-operating parties might be disclosed during the investigation and/or final decision. However, in its report for 2008, the Council states that in the interests of the investigation and the leniency applicant, the competition authorities will guarantee during the investigation a high degree of confidentiality when dealing with a leniency application.

15.2 Is information provided by the leniency applicant/other co-operating parties passed on to other undertakings under investigation?

In principle, after the notification of the communication of the claim, all parties have access to the file including information provided by the leniency applicant or other co-operating parties.

15.3 Can a leniency applicant/other co-operating party request anonymity or confidentiality of information provided?

Pursuant to Article 24 of the 2004 Law, undertakings or interested persons may request to the chairman of the Council that information or documents used in the investigation remain partially or totally confidential (ie, business secrets). They must prove that divulging such information or documents would cause them prejudice. If confidentiality is granted, then the information or documents in question will be removed from the file. The 2004 Law expressly excludes documents and information necessary to the proceedings or the exercise of the rights of the parties from the scope of confidentiality.

16. Is the evidence submitted by the leniency applicant protected from transmission to other competition authorities with whom the authority in question co-operates? If so, how?

The 2004 Law provides for the co-operation between the Luxembourg competition authorities and the European Commission and the competition authorities of the other member states of the European Union. Nothing prevents the Luxembourg competition authorities from transmitting the evidence submitted by the leniency applicant to the European Commission or other national competition authorities in the European Union.

17. To what extent can evidence submitted by the leniency applicant (transcripts of oral statements or written evidence) become discoverable in subsequent private enforcement claims? Can leniency information be subjected to discovery orders in foreign or domestic courts? Can leniency information submitted in a foreign jurisdiction be subjected to discovery orders in the domestic courts?

As explained above, the 2004 Law and the case law do not provide any information on this issue. It is likely that no specific protection exists and thus evidence might be requested to be disclosed in subsequent private enforcement claims.

18. Are there any precedents in which evidence from a leniency application has been discovered in a private enforcement claim?
No, there are not.

RELATIONSHIP WITH THE EUROPEAN COMMISSION'S LENIENCY NOTICE AND LENIENCY POLICY IN OTHER EU MEMBER STATES

19. Does the policy address the interaction with applications under the Commission Leniency Notice? If so, how?
The 2004 Law does not address this issue. However, when an undertaking has applied or intends to apply for total exemption to the European Commission, a summary leniency application, as provided for by the ECN Model Leniency Programme, can be filed with the Luxembourg competition authority in order to benefit from leniency at national level if the case is reallocated to national authorities. If this occurs, the application will have to be completed.

20. Does the policy address the interaction with applications for leniency in other EU member states? If so, how? Does the authority accept summary applications in line with the ECN Model Leniency Programme?
The 2004 Law does not address this issue. As explained in question 18, summary applications are accepted by Luxembourg competition authorities, but only with respect to applications for total exemption with the European Commission. Consequently, when a cartel affects markets in several EU member states, a leniency application will have to be filed with the competition authorities of each EU member state affected by the cartel.

RELATIONSHIP WITH SETTLEMENT PROCEDURES

21. What is the relationship between leniency and applicable settlement procedures? Are they mutually exclusive?
The 2004 Law does not provide for a settlement procedure.

REFORM/LATEST DEVELOPMENTS

22. Is there a reform underway to revisit the leniency policy? What are the latest developments?
The 2004 Law will be amended by the Bill of Law n°5816, which was filed with Parliament on 20 December 2007. It provides for the adaptation of the leniency regime to the ECN Model Leniency Programme. The Bill of Law n°5816 may be amended during the course of the parliamentary process.

Mexico

Ríos-Ferrer, Guillén-Llarena, Treviño y Rivera, SC
Ricardo Ríos-Ferrer & Alejandro González Muñoz

BACKGROUND
1. What is the relevant legislation concerning the leniency policy and what is the enforcing body?

The Federal Economic Competition Law (the FECL) and the Regulations of the Federal Economic Competition Law (the RFECL) contain the substantial legislation applicable to the leniency programme available in Mexico.

The legislation is federal and applicable throughout Mexico in all states and municipalities. There is no local law relating to leniency or antitrust issues. Any aspect not expressly covered by the FECL is governed by the Federal Civil Procedures Code.

Specifically, Article 33 *bis* 3 defines the leniency programme. Article 33 *bis* 2 provides for reduction of sanctions applicable to relative monopolistic practices and prohibited concentrations, whereas Article 33 *bis* 3 defines the leniency programme.

In order to benefit from the leniency programme, the procedure laid down under Articles 43 and 44 RFECL must be followed.

For guidance on the implementation of the leniency programme, the Federal Competition Commission (the FCC) has published on its website (*www.cfc.gob.mx*) a document (*Proyecto de Guía del Programa de Inmunidad*) which provides clear information as to the criteria to be applied by the FCC when applying the provisions of the leniency programme under the FECL and RFECL (the leniency guidelines). However, this document is intended only for information purposes and is not intended to reflect jurisdictional criteria, nor be considered as a mandatory interpretation of the existing legislation.

The enforcing body of the FECL and the RFECL is the FCC, which is an administrative agency specifically created within the Ministry of Economy to combat monopolistic practices and prohibited concentrations, and which has technical and operative autonomy. The FCC's main purpose is to prevent and fight competition law violations and thus it is in charge of enforcing Mexican competition law within an administrative competence.

The FCC is governed by a board of five commissioners who adopt the decisions of the FCC collectively.

2. What are the basic tenets of a leniency/immunity programme? Is leniency available also for other types of competition law violations than cartels?

Under the FECL, the leniency programme is mainly focused on and available to cartels. Anti-competitive practices such as price fixing, market sharing, production or sales quotas, bid rigging and other absolute monopolistic practices are covered by the programme. Leniency is also available for other practices such as monopolistic practices and prohibited concentrations. In any case, leniency under Mexican law is limited to fine reduction only. The programme does not cover any other criminal or civil penalties that might be applicable.

Mexican competition law divides anti-competitive practices into absolute monopolistic practices, relative monopolistic practices and prohibited concentrations.

Under Article 9, the FECL identifies absolute monopolistic practices as the execution of contracts, agreements, arrangements, or combinations among competing economic agents, whose purpose or effect are any of the following:
- to fix, raise, agree upon or manipulate the sale or purchase price of goods or services offered or demanded in the markets, or to exchange information with the same purpose or effect;
- to establish the obligation to refrain from producing, processing, distributing, commercialising or acquiring a restricted or limited amount of goods, or to render services limited or restricted to a specific number, volume or frequency;
- to divide, distribute, allot or impose portions or segments of the current or potential market for goods and services, by means of clients, suppliers, timing or spacing determined or to be determined; or
- to establish, agree upon or co-ordinate bids or to abstain from bids, tenders, public auctions or bidding.

Pursuant to Article 33 *bis* 3 of the FECL, in order to benefit from the leniency provisions for absolute monopolistic practices, the following conditions must be met:
- the undertaking must be the first among the cartel to provide evidence that, in the opinion of the FCC, is sufficient to prove the existence of the collusive conduct;
- to co-operate fully and on an ongoing basis with the FCC during the investigation procedure and in any subsequent proceedings;
- take the necessary steps in order to terminate its participation in the violation of the competition law; and
- the application to benefit from the leniency programme must be filed by the applicant before the FCC has issued its resolution concluding an investigation for absolute monopolistic practices.

In any case, a minimum fine of the equivalent of a minimum daily wage in Mexico City must be imposed against the applicant. The minimum daily wage for Mexico City has been set at approximately $4.35 dollars for 2010.

All other undertakings that do not meet the first condition (ie, second and subsequent applicants), but that meet all the other conditions might be entitled to a reduction of 50, 30 or 20 per cent of the maximum amount of the fine that would otherwise be imposed pursuant to the law. In addition, to become eligible to receive leniency, any subsequent applicant must provide additional or new evidence not already in the possession of the FCC that is sound enough to prove the existence of the absolute monopolistic practice.

In any case, the FCC is obliged to protect the identity of all undertakings applying under the leniency programme.

As stated above, the leniency programme is focused on cartel practices, but the FECL also includes fine reductions for relative monopolistic practices and prohibited concentrations where collusion with other undertakings and competitors is not always present.

The FECL identifies in Article 10, the following relative monopolistic practices:

'Those acts, contracts, agreements, procedures or combinations, whose purpose or effect is or may result in unlawfully displacing other agents from the market; substantially hindering their access to it; or which establish exclusive advantages in favour of one or several economic agents, in the following cases:

- among economic agents that do not compete among themselves: fixation, imposition, or establishment of the exclusive distribution or commercialisation of goods or services, by means of subject, geographic location, or specific periods of time, including the division, distribution or allotment of customers and suppliers; as well as the imposition of the obligation not to manufacture or distribute certain goods or to provide services for a certain period of time to be determined;
- setting the prices or other conditions that a distributor or supplier has to abide by when commercialising or distributing goods or providing services;
- the sale or transaction conditioned on buying, acquiring, selling or providing another additional good or service, normally distinct or distinguishable, or on the basis of reciprocity;
- the sale, purchase or transaction subject to the condition of not using, acquiring, selling, marketing or providing goods or services produced, processed, distributed or commercialised by a third party;
- the unilateral action consisting of refusing to sell, commercialise or provide to specific individuals, goods or services available and normally offered to third parties;
- the agreement reached among several economic agents or the invitation to them to exert pressure against an economic agent or to refuse to sell, commercialise or acquire goods or services to such other economic agent, in order to discourage it from a specific behaviour, as retaliation, or to force it to act in a specific manner;
- the systematic sale of goods or services below their average total cost or their occasional sale below their average variable cost, when there are elements to presume that those losses will be recovered in future price increases, as determined in the regulations of this Law. Regarding different goods or services produced jointly or that might be divided for their commercialisation, the total average cost and the variable average cost shall be distributed among all the sub-products or by-products, as

determined in the regulations of this Law.
- granting discounts or incentives by producers or suppliers to the buyers, with the condition of not using, acquiring, selling, commercialising or providing goods or services produced, processed, distributed or commercialised by a third party, or the purchase or transaction subject to the condition of not acquiring, commercialising or providing to a third party, those goods or services acquired under such sale or transaction;
- using the profits obtained by an economic agent in the sale, commercialisation or supplying of goods or rendering of services, to finance losses suffered in the sale, commercialisation or rendering of other goods or services;
- to establish different prices or different sale or purchase terms and conditions for different buyers or sellers that are in equal condition; or
- the action by one or several economic agents whose aim or effect, direct or indirect, is to increase the costs or create difficulties in the productive process, or reduce the demand faced by their competitors.

In order to determine if the practices referred to in this Article should be penalised in accordance with this Law, the Commission shall analyse any efficiency gains deriving from such conduct, that the economic agents involved demonstrate, and that have a favourable incidence in the economic competition and free market process. Such efficiency gains may include the following: the introduction of new products; the distribution of discontinued products, defective or perishable products; costs savings deriving from the creation of new techniques and production processes, the integration of assets, any increases in the scale of production, and the production of different goods or services using the production factors; the introduction of technological improvements that produce new or improved goods or services; the combination of productive assets or investments, and their return improving the quality or expanding the benefits of goods or services; any improvements in the quality, investments and their return, opportunity and service that have a favourable impact on the distribution chain; that do not cause a significant price increase, or a significant reduction in the options available to consumers, or an important inhibition in the degree of innovation existing in the relevant market; as well as other efficiency gains that demonstrate that the net benefits for the consumers deriving from such practices, are greater than their anticompetitive effects.'

The cases of relative monopolistic practices above are subject to verification that the undertaking has substantial power in the relevant market, and that the conduct is carried out with respect to goods or services that correspond to the relevant market.

Pursuant to Article 33 *bis* 2 of the FECL, in order to benefit from the leniency available for relative monopolistic practices and prohibited concentrations, the following conditions must be met:
- a written petition must be submitted by the economic agent committing to suspend, suppress, correct or refrain from the relative monopolistic practices or prohibited concentration, before a final resolution has been

issued by the FCC declaring that the economic agent participated in the relative monopolistic practices or prohibited concentration;
- the free competition process can be restored once the prohibited concentration or relative monopolistic practice has ceased to have effect; and
- the measures proposed by the economic agent are suitable and economically feasible in order to suspend or cease the effects of the relative monopolistic practice or the prohibited concentration.

If the conditions are met, the FCC will suspend the proceedings and anticipate the conclusion of the investigation and then issue a final resolution imposing a fine only equivalent to one day of the minimum wage in Mexico City.

The undertaking can only benefit from leniency under Article 33 *bis 2* once every five years and there is no 'first' applicant. All applicants that meet the conditions referred to above are entitled to the same fine reductions – as opposed to the leniency programme applicable to cartels, where first and subsequent applicants are entitled to different fine reductions as explained above.

3. How many cartels have been unveiled and punished since the adoption of the leniency programme?

Only one cartel has been unveiled and punished since the introduction of the leniency programme. The investigation started in 2007 and on 9 July 2009, the FCC imposed a fine of MXN$24,373,975 (approximately $1,860,600) which was allotted in different amounts among all the 33 members of the cartel.

The Mexican leniency programme entered into effect on 28 June 2006. However, the programme was scarcely regulated at that time and since only the basic principles of the programme were known, there was no procedure laid down to apply for the benefits of the programme. Regulations for the programme were not issued until more than a year after its enactment. It was not until 12 October 2007 that the RFECL laid down the applicable procedure under which an applicant could file a petition to be eligible to participate in the leniency programme.

Pursuant to the 2008 annual report of the FCC, during that year, 152 cases were initiated. Of those 152 cases, only 24 were related to anti-competitive practices and just two out of the 24 cases related to cartels engaged in absolute monopolistic practices. None of them were sanctioned.

During 2009, the FCC started seven investigations. In three out of those seven the FCC issued sanctions, but there were no leniency applicants in those cases.

4. What is needed to be a successful leniency applicant? Is documentary evidence required or is testimonial evidence sufficient?

For absolute monopolistic practices, Article 33 *bis* 3 of the FECL provides that the applicant must provide the FCC with sufficient evidence to verify the existence of the cartel. It is not specified whether documentary or testimonial evidence is required. Instead, the FCC evaluates any kind of evidence provided by the applicant and then determines if the evidence is sound enough to prove the existence of the cartel and, thus, if the applicant is eligible for leniency.

The applicant must request the benefits of the programme before a decision concluding the investigation has been issued by the FCC. In fact, the applicant can be eligible even if the investigation has not yet started.

The applicant will be granted leniency only if – once the two conditions above are met – it continues to co-operate fully on an ongoing basis with the FCC during the investigation and any subsequent proceedings and the applicant also takes the necessary steps to disengage from the cartel and any illegal practices.

TIMING
5. What are the benefits of being 'first in' to co-operate?
The successful first applicant is entitled to a reduction of the fine so that the final sanction is equivalent to a minimum daily wage in Mexico City ($4.35 dollars). Without the leniency programme a condemned undertaking may receive a fine equivalent to 1.5 million times the minimum daily wage in Mexico City (approximately $6,579,389) (see response to question 22). All subsequent successful applicants are entitled to a lesser reduction of the potential applicable fine.

6. What are the consequences of being 'second'? Is there an 'immunity plus' or 'amnesty plus' option?
Second and subsequent applicants to the leniency programme are entitled to reductions of 50, 30 and 20 per cent of the maximum fine applicable. However, the policy of the FECL as to how to apply the fine reduction in the case of second, third and subsequent successful applicants is not clear. The wording of Article 33 *bis* 3, allows different ways in which the fine reduction may apply. For example, second, third and fourth successful applicants might receive a 50, 30 and 20 per cent reduction. But if the third applicant provides better evidence than the second and fourth applicants, the FCC may grant a 50 per cent reduction of the potential fine to the second and third applicants and may grant a 30 or 20 per cent reduction to the fourth applicant. Therefore the extent of the fine reduction is not necessarily linked to the chronological order of the applications; instead the reduction might be decided by the FCC based on a combination of different factors, namely, the chronological order of the application, the quality of the evidence and the fulfilment of the obligation to co-operate fully and on an ongoing basis.

7. Are subsequent firms given any beneficial treatment if they make a useful contribution? How are 'useful contributions' defined?
All applicants are eligible for reductions of the potential fines as long as they meet the conditions listed under question 4 above.

There is no definition of the concept of 'useful contribution' in the FECL or in the RFECL. Nevertheless, the existing legal provisions and the criteria of the FCC laid down in the leniency guidelines suggest that 'useful contribution' should be understood as meaning the addition of new evidence not already in the possession of the FCC which can be used to establish the existence of the cartel and which further supports the evidence already available to perfect or extend the investigation of the collusive conduct. However, it should be noted that the FCC has discretionary power to determine whether or not any potential evidence is sufficient to prove the existence of the cartel. Therefore, the first applicant is more likely to be eligible for leniency than the second, third, fourth or subsequent applicants.

SCOPE/FULL LENIENCY
8. Is it possible to receive full leniency? If so, what are the conditions required to receive full leniency?

The FCC is entitled to grant leniency under the FECL only in order to reduce the potential fines applicable for violations of the FECL. In fact, the first successful applicant under the leniency programme is entitled to almost a complete fine reduction. However, the reduction of the fine to a minimum ($4.35 dollars equivalent to one minimum daily wage in Mexico City) still constitutes a sanction with potentially severe effects in the case of recidivism. If the collusive conduct is repeated, the reduced original fine imposed shall be taken into account and the undertaking would therefore be sanctioned with the equivalent of up to 10 per cent of its total annual sales or the equivalent of 10 per cent of the value of its total assets.

The leniency programme does not entitle the successful applicant to receive leniency for losses and damages caused to third parties. Also criminal penalties incurred are not within the scope of the leniency programme. The undertaking that is found to be responsible for carrying out absolute monopolistic practices shall be subject to civil and criminal actions derived from the same investigation conducted by the FCC, however, before a final penalty is imposed, the corresponding civil or criminal action before a competent court must be followed.

8.1 Can ringleaders/coercers receive full leniency?
Both ringleaders and coercers are eligible for leniency. Article 33 *bis* 3, makes no exception and provides that any undertaking that has participated or is participating in an absolute monopolistic practice can acknowledge it before the FCC and receive leniency pursuant to the law, provided that the eligibility conditions are met.

8.2 If there is a requirement to 'co-operate fully and on an ongoing basis' what does it entail?
The leniency guidelines expressly state that 'co-operate fully and on an ongoing basis' requires all undertakings applying for leniency under the programme to '…honour their commitment and legal obligation to co-operate, in order for their potential sanctions to be reduced'. The leniency guidelines further state that when the FCC:

'…*considers that the undertaking is not duly complying with its obligation, it shall notify the applicant in order to request compliance in a reasonable time, at the discretion of the Commission.*

'If the Commission deems that the lack of co-operation fully and on an ongoing basis is not justified, or that the necessary measures have not been taken in order to cure the breach, it shall evaluate such issue in the corresponding resolution and might refrain from granting leniency. In that respect, the protection granted by the immunity programme is deemed to be subject to a suspensive condition. No fine reduction will be applied until the co-operation of the undertaking is deemed sufficient to prove the monopolistic practice in trial proceedings and until there is enough evidence to serve notice on the members of the identified cartel.'

Considering the foregoing, what the obligation of co-operation fully and on an ongoing basis entails shall be determined at the reasonable discretion of the FCC. However, the objective element is that the co-operation should result in having enough evidence to establish the existence of the cartel. The FCC will have discretionary power to determine if the elements contributed by the applicant are sufficient to prove the monopolistic practice or not.

8.3 Does the regulatory authority require the applicant to cease participation in the cartel conduct after its application?

Pursuant to section III of Article 33 *bis* 3 of the FECL, the undertaking must carry out all actions necessary to terminate its participation in the illegal practice. This condition must be met before receiving leniency.

9. How many companies have received full immunity from fines to date?

Only one of the undertakings that participated in the cartel referred to in question 6 received full immunity from fines under the Mexican programme. A fine of just MXN$54.80 (approximately $4.18), which was the equivalent of the minimum daily wage in Mexico City during 2009, was imposed on this undertaking. The reduction applied is the maximum permitted under the FECL.

PROCEDURE
10. What are the practical steps required to apply for leniency?

10.1 Full disclosure

Full disclosure of the relevant information to be submitted by the applicant may not take place at the time the application is submitted, as this is not a requirement to apply for leniency. Full disclosure will occur once a formal and personal meeting between the applicant and the FCC has been agreed. During this meeting, the undertaking should be reasonably capable of explaining the background and current situation of the case, and present the evidence that might prove the existence of the cartel.

Pursuant to question 6 of section 5 of the leniency guidelines the information expected by the FCC to be submitted by the applicant in the first meeting includes:

- official identification and the document to evidence representation (if applicable);
- name of the members of the relevant cartel;
- thorough information about the facts that constitute violation of the FECL;
- relation of the evidence that is being offered by the applicant and information to identify the market in which the applicant participates;
- information to identify the products or services that are subject to the anticompetitive practice; and
- any other evidence that the applicant deems relevant, and if the applicant has no legal access to it, the place where the documents are to be found.

10.2 Initial contact/is there a 'marker' system?

Pursuant to Article 43 of the RFECL the applicant should submit its application by means of a voicemail or by electronic mail. The leniency guidelines provide the telephone number +52 552789-6632 or the electronic address *inmunidad@cfc.gob.mx*.

The application can be filed both ways, ie either by voicemail or by electronic mail. However, the application which will be considered for formality purposes will be the one that was submitted first. All applications filed in a different manner shall be considered as a denunciation, and shall not be subject to the benefits of the leniency programme.

The leniency guidelines state that in its application, the undertaking should include at least the following:
- a statement in a clear and express manner of the intention to benefit from the leniency programme; and
- the contact information with enough data to make sure the undertaking or its representatives can be contacted effectively, including the complete name of the person with whom the communication and meetings will be held, telephone number and their address. In addition, the FCC recommends providing alternative electronic mail and physical addresses, and if possible, the same information relating to the applicant's attorneys or advisers.

If the applicant is an entity, the decision should be understood as a corporate decision, not the unilateral decision of any of its officers. To prove the foregoing, any and all actions taken under the programme must be carried out by an attorney-in-fact with a power of attorney with a general power for administration or a special power to execute legal acts before the FCC.

Once the application has been filed in compliance with all the requirements, the FCC will issue a code to identify the application and will inform the applicant by phone or via electronic mail.

The code given by the FCC constitutes the 'marker system' of the Mexican leniency programme. Voicemail and electronic mail were the two methods chosen for contacting the FCC in order to make it easy to determine the chronological order of the applications and accurately secure the position of the first applicant.

The code is alphanumeric. It will allow the FCC to know the order and timing of all the applications submitted in each case in order to determine the first and subsequent applicants, and to determine, at the corresponding resolution, the degree of leniency once all the conditions are met.

The leniency guidelines indicate that within the two days following the date the application was filed, the General Director of Investigation of Monopolistic Practices and Restrictions to Interstate Commerce of the FCC should contact the applicant to inform him of the day and time on which he should appear at the FCC to submit the relevant information.

At this meeting, the applicant shall disclose all the information referred to in the first section of this question. The purpose of this meeting is for the applicant to explain the case and provide the FCC with the evidence needed to prove the existence of the cartel. Such evidence will be assessed by the FCC to determine if it is sound enough in order to decide whether or not to start an investigation or whether the elements provided are convincing for determining the existence of a cartel if an investigation has already started.

The leniency guidelines provide that at the time of the formal meeting, the applicant may wish to extend the benefits of its application to its officers or employees who have participated in the collusive conduct. To that effect it is required that the applicant submits the application of its officers or employees by means of written letter signed by each of them. Neither the RFECL nor the leniency guidelines clarify whether or not the officers and employees to which the protection is purported to be extended are also entitled to share the same chronological order of the principal application, that is to say, if for example, the principal applicant is the first applicant, whether the officers and employees would be also considered as first applicants and, therefore, entitle them to the maximum leniency permitted under the FECL.

We have no knowledge of whether the situation described above has occurred so far, but it is our opinion that the protection of the officers and employees should be considered to be in the same chronological order as it is implied in the guidelines, ie, that the application for officers and employees is an extension of the principal application, thus, the employees' applications should be treated with the same benefits as the main application.

Pursuant to section II of Article 43 of the RFECL, the FCC should not evaluate any other application before making a decision about a prior application. That means that the FCC must conclude if an applicant is eligible for leniency and if this is the case, the extent of the leniency to be granted before another application can be assessed.

Once the application has been filed and the meeting has taken place, section III of Article 43 of the RFECL imposes on the FCC a 15 working-day term to evaluate and decide whether or not the application has been successful and to notify the applicant of the order of its application and the percentage of the applicable fine reduction. If the applicant did not succeed, the FCC will cancel the application and the code and will give back to the applicant the information submitted.

10.3 Conditional reduction of fine

The fine reduction will always be conditional upon the applicant meeting all the requirements as explained in question 4 above. A Sanctions Reduction Decision shall be issued and notified to the applicant by the FCC if the conditions are preliminarily met. The Sanctions Reduction Decision shall include the order of the application and the percentage of the reduction applicable to the potential fine to which the applicant is entitled.

Considering that the obligation of the applicant to co-operate fully and on an ongoing basis remains effective until trial proceedings take place, and that such proceedings start after the investigation has been concluded, the Sanctions Reduction Decision should be understood to be conditional upon fulfilment of the applicant's obligation to co-operate fully and on an ongoing basis during the investigation and subsequent proceedings.

The trial proceedings are neither followed in a court, nor a procedure of a jurisdictional nature, rather, it is an administrative procedure conducted by the FCC following due process. The proceedings are provided for in Article 33 of the FECL and are started after the investigation has concluded. The purpose of such proceedings is to determine the responsibility of all the undertakings involved in the cartel if during the investigation, enough evidence was gathered against it.

10.4 Final reduction

Final reduction of the fine is deemed to be confirmed if the FCC does not revoke the Sanctions Reduction Decision, which would only occur if the applicant failed to co-operate fully and on an ongoing basis.

11. Is there an optimal time to approach the regulatory authority?

The optimal time to approach the FCC is before the investigation has started. Otherwise there is a good chance that the evidence to be provided by the applicant is already in the possession of the FCC.

Once the FCC decides to start an investigation, a summary of such decision must be published in the Official Gazette of the Federation, which is a journal used by the federal government to publish facts of public interest. As a result, undertakings that may be involved in the cartel may have notice that the investigation has started and may start considering applying for leniency to become the first applicant and receive full leniency.

12. What guarantees of leniency exist if a party co-operates?

There are no specific guarantees that leniency will be given even if a party co-operates. As has been explained above, to co-operate is only one of the conditions necessary to be entitled to receive leniency. It is therefore essential that the undertaking meets all the conditions explained in question 4 above. Once the conditions have been met, the undertaking should receive leniency.

CONSEQUENCES

13. What effects does leniency granted to a corporate defendant have on the defendant's employees? Does it protect them from criminal and/or civil liability?

The effects of leniency granted to a corporate defendant do not cover *ipso iure* the corporation's officers or employees. As explained in the answer to question 10 the corporate defendant that has applied for leniency must expressly request the FCC to extend the benefits of the principal application under the leniency programme in favour of its officers and employees, otherwise, the employees and officers are not protected. The same rule applies to employees of an individual.

In any event, leniency under the FECL does not grant protection against civil or criminal liability incurred by any employee or the principal applicant since the leniency programme is limited to fine reductions only (see response to question 22).

14. Does leniency bar further private enforcement?

Article 33 *bis* 2 expressly states that leniency granted in connection with relative monopolistic practices or prohibited concentrations is without prejudice to the liability that might be incurred for losses and damages caused to third parties. Furthermore, Article 38 of the FECL provides that:

'Once the resolution of the Commission is definitive without any recourse, the economic agents that have suffered damages or losses resulting from the monopolistic practice or prohibited concentration, may file a legal claim to obtain compensation for the damages and losses sustained. In such event, the court may request the Commission to estimate the amount of said damages and losses'.

PROTECTION AGAINST DISCLOSURE/CONFIDENTIALITY

15. Is confidentiality afforded to the leniency applicant and other co-operating parties? If so, to what extent?

All applicants under the leniency programme are entitled to confidentiality of their identity pursuant to Article 33 *bis* 3 of the FECL. The FCC is not authorised by law to reveal the identity of the applicants. However, only applicants under the leniency programme are entitled to confidentiality of their identity. The FECL does not afford confidentiality to other co-operating parties if they are not successful applicants.

15.1 Is the identity of the leniency applicant/other co-operating parties disclosed during the investigation or in the final decision?

Pursuant to the leniency guidelines the identity of the leniency applicant is never disclosed explicitly during the investigation or in any subsequent trial proceedings. All applicants are identified by the code referred to in the answer to question 10 above in order to keep their identity confidential. Only the General Director of Investigation of Monopolistic Practices and Restrictions to Interstate Commerce of the FCC is empowered to administer the leniency programme and the codes, this ensures that no other person has access to the confidential information of the applicant, thus preventing information being leaked.

15.2 Is information provided by the leniency applicant/other co-operating parties passed on to other undertakings under investigation?

Pursuant to the final paragraph of Article 43 of the RFECL, the information provided by the leniency applicant to the FCC can only be used by the FCC in the investigation and during the development of the trial proceedings to determine the responsibility of the members of a cartel.

Pursuant to Article 31 *bis* of the FECL, during the investigation the FCC will not allow anybody to have access to the file. Once the trial proceedings have started, only the undertakings involved in the proceedings will have access to the information in the file, except to information classified as confidential.

The information provided by the leniency applicant might be passed on to other undertakings during the trial proceedings if the leniency applicant did not request the FCC to classify the information provided as confidential pursuant to second paragraph of section II of Article 31 *bis* of the FECL. Otherwise, the FCC has the obligation to keep the confidentiality of the information provided by the leniency applicant.

15.3 Can a leniency applicant or other co-operating party request anonymity or confidentiality of information provided?

Pursuant to the second paragraph of section II of Article 31 *bis*, the information provided to the FCC will only be classified as confidential when the undertaking so requests and provides evidence that such information is in fact confidential. In such a case, the undertaking must submit a summary of the information to the satisfaction of the FCC, in order to be incorporated into the investigation file, or alternatively the reasons for which such summary cannot be done. If the undertaking does not submit the summary, the FCC shall again require the undertaking to deliver the summary; if the undertaking does not comply, the FCC will be deemed authorised to do the summary.

16. Is the evidence submitted by the leniency applicant protected from transmission to other competition authorities with whom the authority in question co-operates? If so, how?

In accordance with the leniency guidelines the FCC will not share the applicant's identity nor the information provided by it with other competition authorities in other jurisdictions. However, in certain cases of international relevance or when the FCC deems so advisable, the FCC might request the applicant to grant its consent for the FCC to share the identity or the information provided, with the sole purpose of supporting any investigation or procedure in foreign jurisdictions. The applicant might refuse to grant its consent for the FCC to share the information provided and, as long as the applicant's disagreement is justified, the FCC will not consider the refusal as a breach of its obligation to co-operate fully and on an ongoing basis under the leniency programme.

17. To what extent can evidence submitted by the leniency applicant (transcripts of oral statements or written evidence) become discoverable in subsequent private enforcement claims?

Pursuant to the second paragraph of Article 31 *bis* of the FECL, any information that has been classified as confidential shall not be disclosed by the FCC. Furthermore, if a competent authority requests the FCC to provide information, both the FCC and the requesting authority should take all necessary measures to keep the applicable information confidential.

17.1 Can leniency information be subjected to discovery orders in the domestic courts?

All Mexican competent courts are empowered to request any information, including leniency applications, and to use that information in court proceedings, as long as such information is relevant to the case.

Article 79 of the Federal Code of Civil Procedures provides that in order to know the truth, the judge may avail himself of any person, whether a party to the trial or a third party, or anything or document, whether or not such thing or document belongs to the contending parties or to a third party, provided that the kind of evidence is permitted by the law and has relevance to the case.

An example would be a party to a trial having no legal access to the relevant information. That party would then try to use the leniency information as evidence in order to sustain its position and would request the court to order the FCC to provide the information available in its files. The court would then decide, based on the merits of the case, if the petition is justified. If the court so decides, any information may be used as evidence and be made known to the parties in the trial.

17.2 Can leniency information be subjected to discovery orders in foreign courts?

The third paragraph of Article 31 *bis* of the FECL, provides that all public officers are subject to liability for releasing information in their custody. However, when a competent authority issues an order to show leniency information, the FCC and the ordering authority should take the appropriate measures to maintain the confidentiality of the information so classified.

Pursuant to Article 559 of the Federal Code of Civil Procedures, the agencies of the Mexican Federation are not authorised to show documents or copies of documents existing in official archives that are under their control. An exception is made to those cases related to private interest, personal documents or personal archives allowed by law, provided in these cases that a Mexican court previously so authorises.

17.3 Can leniency information submitted in a foreign jurisdiction be subjected to discovery orders in the domestic courts?

As explained above, any competent Mexican court has the authority to request any information – including leniency information – and to use it in court proceedings, as long as the information has immediate relevance to the case.

18. Are there any precedents in which evidence from a leniency application has been discovered in a private enforcement claim?

Currently there are no known precedents in which evidence from a leniency application has been discovered in a private enforcement claim.

RELATIONSHIP WITH THE EUROPEAN COMMISSION'S LENIENCY NOTICE AND LENIENCY POLICY IN OTHER EU MEMBER STATES

19. Does the policy address the interaction with applications under the Commission Leniency Notice? If so, how?

Not applicable.

20. Does the policy address the interaction with applications for leniency in other EU member states? If so, how? Does the authority accept summary applications in line with the ECN Model Leniency Programme?

Not applicable.

RELATIONSHIP WITH SETTLEMENT PROCEDURES

21. What is the relationship between leniency and applicable settlement procedures? Are they mutually exclusive?

Settlement procedures are not regulated under the FECL.

REFORM/LATEST DEVELOPMENTS

22. Is there a reform underway to revisit the leniency policy? What are the latest developments?

A reform is currently underway as the House of Representatives has recently passed a bill which will become effective once approved by the Senate and the President.

This bill significantly enhances the ability of the FCC to fight cartels and clarifies specific points of the leniency programme.

Firstly, the leniency programme would apply to individuals or economic agents which, despite having supported, promoted, induced or participated in absolute monopolistic practices are not directly responsible for such practices.

Secondly, the method of settling fines has been modified. Under the current rules, the maximum amount of the fine is 1.5 million times the minimum daily wage in Mexico City (approximately $6,579,39) which is not sufficiently dissuasive. Pursuant to the bill currently being approved the maximum amount of the fine will be 10 per cent of the annual income achieved during the relevant undertaking for the relevant fiscal year, ie when the infringement was committed. The purpose of such a change is to grant the FCC the power to impose heavy fines on economically powerful cartels in order to prevent them from engaging in anticompetitive practices.

Lastly, under the bill, the leniency programme will also grant protection against criminal sanctions.

The Netherlands

Loyens & Loeff N.V. Maurice Essers, Gert Wim van de Meent, Robin A. Struijlaart & Marc Wiggers

BACKGROUND

1. What is the relevant legislation concerning the leniency policy and what is the enforcing body?

On 11 September 2009 the Minister of Economic Affairs published policy rules on reducing administrative fines with regard to cartels (the Leniency Policy Rules), which replaced Leniency Guidelines of the *Nederlandse Mededingingsautoriteit* (the Competition Authority) of 9 October 2007 (and earlier versions since July 2002). The Competition Authority is the enforcing body in the Netherlands and decides whether leniency will be granted.

2. What are the basic tenets of a leniency/immunity programme? Is leniency available also for other types of competition law violations than cartels?

Category	Ranking	Coercing of another undertaking	Investigation started	Reduction of the fine (%)
A	First	No	No	100
B	First	No	Yes	60-100
C	Second and subsequent or first and coercing	Possible	Possible	10-40

Leniency is only available for cartels. A cartel is defined in the Leniency Policy Guidelines as *'an agreement or concerted practice between two or more competitors with the object of restricting competition contrary to European and Dutch cartel prohibition'*. Thus, purely vertical infringements, even if these are hardcore, are outside the scope of the Leniency Policy Rules.

3. How many cartels have been unveiled and punished since the adoption of the leniency programme?

Since the adoption of the Dutch leniency programme in 2002 several hundreds of fines have been imposed by the Competition Authority for cartels in a plethora of sectors of the Dutch economy. In the vast majority of cases a leniency application, if any, was not the trigger for the Competition Authority to start its investigation.

4. **What is needed to be a successful leniency applicant? Is documentary evidence required or is testimonial evidence sufficient?**
A leniency application can be submitted by email, fax, post, telephone or in person. Therefore, testimonial evidence can be sufficient. However, in practice the Competition Authority will ask for testimonial evidence to be substantiated with documentary evidence.

TIMING
5. **What are the benefits of being 'first in' to co-operate?**
Only the first applicant to submit a leniency application can be granted full immunity from a fine.

6. **What are the consequences of being 'second'? Is there an 'immunity plus' or 'amnesty plus' option?**
The second and subsequent parties to submit a leniency application – before the Competition Authority has issued a report to any of the cartel members – can be granted a reduction of 10 per cent and up to a maximum of 40 per cent, if: (i) the leniency application contains information with significant added value; and (ii) the applicant complies with the duty of full co-operation (see question 8).

7. **Are subsequent firms given any beneficial treatment if they make a useful contribution? How are 'useful contributions' defined?**
'Information with significant added value' as referred to in the Leniency Policy Rules means evidence which, by its very nature and its level of detail and in view of the information known to the Competition Authority at the time when the information is provided, significantly strengthens the Competition Authority's ability to prove the existence of the cartel.

The Competition Authority has a discretionary power to grant a reduction of between 10 per cent and 40 per cent to the second and subsequent applicants (see question 5). The level of the reduction will mainly be based on the significance of the information provided by the applicant to the Competition Authority.

SCOPE/FULL LENIENCY
8. **Is it possible to receive full leniency? If so, what are the conditions required to receive full leniency? Can ringleaders/coercers receive full leniency? If there is a requirement to 'co-operate fully and on an ongoing basis' what does it entail? Does the regulatory authority require the applicant to cease participation in the cartel conduct after its application?**

8.1 If no investigation has been started
The Competition Authority shall reduce the fine by 100 per cent in response to a leniency application if:
- the applicant is the first to submit a leniency application;

- the leniency application relates to a cartel which the Competition Authority has not yet started to investigate;
- the applicant provides information with the leniency application that enables the Competition Authority to conduct a targeted inspection;
- the applicant did not coerce any other undertaking into participating in the cartel; and
- the applicant complies with the duty of full co-operation.

8.2 Investigation has been started
The Competition Authority shall reduce the fine by at least 60 per cent and up to a maximum of 100 per cent in response to a leniency application if:
- the applicant is the first to submit a leniency application;
- the leniency application relates to a cartel that is being investigated by the Competition Authority, but it has not yet issued a report to the members of the cartel;
- the leniency application contains information with significant added value;
- the applicant did not coerce any other undertaking into participating in the cartel; and
- the applicant complies with the duty of full co-operation.

The Competition Authority shall reduce the fine by 100 per cent if a leniency applicant is the first to provide the Competition Authority with information previously unknown to it which enables it to prove the existence of the cartel.

Ringleaders can receive full leniency, as long as they did not coerce any undertaking into participating in the cartel. Coercers cannot receive full immunity. However, they can still receive a reduction of their fine (10-40 per cent).

Until the decision to impose an administrative fine becomes final in respect of all the cartel members, a leniency applicant will need to co-operate fully, as required in the interests of the investigation or the proceedings. The requirement of full co-operation implies that the leniency applicant shall:
- desist from any conduct that may impede the investigation or the proceedings;
- provide the Competition Authority as soon as possible, from the moment of submission of the leniency application, on the applicant's own initiative or at the Competition Authority's request, with all information regarding the cartel which the applicant has or may reasonably obtain;
- cease all involvement in the cartel immediately after submission of the leniency application, except and insofar as the Competition Authority considers the continuation of it to be reasonably necessary in order to guarantee the effectiveness of inspections; and
- ensure that persons working for the applicant and, where reasonably possible, persons who previously worked for the applicant are at the Competition Authority's disposal to provide statements.

9. How many companies have received full immunity from fines to date?

There are only few cases publicly known in which full immunity from fines has been received.

PROCEDURE

10. What are the practical steps required to apply for leniency?

A prospective leniency applicant may contact the Competition Authority in order to discuss a body of facts and the applicability of the Leniency Policy Rules in that context. The contact may take place anonymously or through the agency of a lawyer and may concern a hypothetical body of facts.

A leniency applicant that submits an incomplete leniency application may be eligible for a marker if:
- the Competition Authority considers the application to offer a concrete basis for a reasonable suspicion of the applicant's involvement in a cartel; and
- the leniency applicant provides at least information in respect of:
  - the name and address of the leniency applicant;
  - the cartel members;
  - the products or services involved;
  - the geographical scope of the cartel;
  - the duration of the cartel;
  - the nature of the conduct of the cartel; and
  - whether the leniency applicant has approached or may approach other competition authorities or the European Commission with regard to the cartel.

If the Competition Authority sets a marker for a leniency applicant, it shall specify a period within which the applicant must complete the leniency application. If the incomplete leniency application is completed within this period the application shall be deemed to have been complete from the moment when the marker became applicable. If the incomplete leniency application is not completed within this period, the Competition Authority shall reject the application.

Having received a leniency application that is in accordance with these Policy Rules, the Competition Authority shall draw up a leniency agreement as soon as possible. The leniency applicant shall sign the leniency agreement. If a leniency applicant fails to fulfil the obligations of the leniency agreement, it shall become null and void. If the leniency agreement becomes null and void, the Competition Authority may use the information it received from the leniency applicant as evidence. The Competition Authority shall inform a leniency applicant of the percentage by which the fine will be reduced at the latest with the report to the applicant. The Competition Authority shall determine the fine with due observance of the leniency agreement, provided that the leniency applicant fully complies with the obligations of the leniency agreement.

11. Is there an optimal time to approach the regulatory authority?
In general, the sooner a leniency request is submitted the better it is, as it will increase the chance of being the first applicant and, therefore, of full immunity (and a higher fine reduction). As time goes by, the chance of providing information with significant added value decreases. From the moment the Competition Authority issues a report, leniency will no longer be possible.

A prospective leniency applicant may ask the Competition Authority by telephone, and exclusively through the agency of a lawyer, whether the prospective applicant may be eligible for full immunity. If the Competition Authority answers the question in the affirmative, the lawyer will need to submit a leniency application immediately.

12. What guarantees of leniency exist if a party co-operates?
No guarantees are given by the Competition Authority at the moment of submission of the leniency request.

A leniency agreement is drawn up by the Competition Authority as soon as the leniency application has been submitted entirely in accordance with these Leniency Policy Rules. The leniency agreement is a document that sets out the rights and obligations of both the Competition Authority and the leniency applicant. The leniency agreement is signed by the leniency applicant. If the leniency applicant fulfils its obligations under the leniency agreement (including the duty of full co-operation), the Board will take into account the leniency agreement when determining the fine. If the leniency applicant fails to fulfil its obligations, the leniency agreement will become null and void.

CONSEQUENCES
13. What effects does leniency granted to a corporate defendant have on the defendant's employees? Does it protect them from criminal and/or civil liability?
The Dutch Competition Act provides for administrative fines to be imposed by the Competition Authority on private individuals who have given instructions or have exercised *de facto* leadership with respect to infringements of the cartel prohibition of Article 6(1) Competition Act by the undertakings by which they are or were employed (or for which they otherwise worked).

Under the Dutch Leniency Policy Rules, private individuals who have given instructions or have exercised *de facto* leadership with regard to a cartel may apply for leniency under the same conditions and pursuant to the same procedure as undertakings (Article 9(b) and (c) of the Leniency Policy Rules).

An undertaking may include its current (but not its former) employees in its leniency application, but an individual (or a group) may only apply for leniency on its own behalf (Article 10 (1) and (3) of the Leniency Policy Rules). Therefore the undertaking applying for leniency should explicitly state in its application that it intends to cover certain designated employees. If such a reasoned request to cover employees is omitted, the Competition

Authority is at full liberty to impose fines on the employees while the undertaking that employs them may very well qualify for full immunity. Former employees may only be covered by their former employer's leniency application with the express consent of the Competition Authority. A request to include former employees shall be rejected if the Competition Authority (in practice the Leniency Officer) fears that such an inclusion may jeopardise the interests of the investigation (Article 10(1)(b)). In the explanatory notes to the Leniency Policy Rules, the Minister of Economic Affairs states that the Board of the Competition Authority (again, in practice, the Leniency Officer) must judge each case on its own merits. It is our experience that in practice, the Competition Authority readily accepts the inclusion of retired employees, but that it is extremely reluctant to accept the inclusion of individuals who are still active. In our experience, the inclusion of individuals who have moved to competitors that are or may be involved in the same cartel will be rejected in any event.

Dutch competition law does not (yet) provide for criminal sanctions to be imposed on either companies or private individuals. There is, however, a parliamentary debate ongoing about whether or not to impose these. With the fall of the Dutch coalition government on 20 February 2010, this debate is likely to be suspended until after the June 2010 elections and the subsequent formation of a new government.

Furthermore, if a private individual indeed qualifies for leniency, this is entirely without prejudice to any civil liabilities they may face for their conduct. It is, however, observed in this respect that we are not aware of any precedents under Dutch law in which private individuals were held liable for competition law infringements they helped to commit.

14. Does leniency bar further private enforcement?
Under Dutch law, leniency does not in any way bar further private enforcement, neither for undertakings nor for private individuals.

PROTECTION AGAINST DISCLOSURE/CONFIDENTIALITY
15. Is confidentiality afforded to the leniency applicant and other co-operating parties? If so, to what extent? Is the identity of the leniency applicant/other co-operating parties disclosed during the investigation or in the final decision? Is information provided by the leniency applicant/other co-operating parties passed on to other undertakings under investigation? Can a leniency applicant/other co-operating party request anonymity or confidentiality of information provided?
A leniency application cannot be submitted anonymously. The Competition Authority is however barred from using information submitted to it in: (i) anonymous consultations; and (ii) leniency applications that were rejected prior to the award of a conditional grant of leniency, without the express consent of the applicant (Article 25 of the Leniency Policy Rules).

In addition, the Competition Authority may not reveal, unless it is bound to do so by law or the applicant has explicitly agreed to it, the identity of a leniency applicant prior to issuing a statement of objections (Article 26 of the Leniency Policy Rules).

After the issuing of a statement of objections, the Competition Authority will reveal the identity of a leniency applicant as a matter of law. If that leniency applicant is a company rather than a private individual, its identity will also be disclosed to the general public once the Competition Authority adopts a formal decision. In addition, the other addressees of a statement of objections will also acquire access to the leniency application, save those parts that qualify for confidential treatment (in particular business secrets). If, however, a leniency application was made orally, the other addressees shall only be granted access to the transcripts of the oral statements, provided that the addressee or its legal representative commits in writing not to make a copy, and to use the information contained in that statement in the administrative procedure only (Article 27(1) of the Leniency Policy Rules). The Explanatory Notes to the Leniency Policy Rules specify that such an addressee or its legal representative may, however, make handwritten notes or a handwritten copy. It is not clear from the Explanatory Notes whether or not the Competition Authority would also allow the addressee or its legal representative to read the transcript out loud and record this (which recording could subsequently be used to manufacture a factual copy of the transcript more efficiently than by making a handwritten copy).

16. Is the evidence submitted by the leniency applicant protected from transmission to other competition authorities with whom the authority in question co-operates? If so, how?
The conditions on confidentiality as described above apply. Only with regard to oral applications, the Leniency Policy Rules explicitly provide in Article 27(2) that the Board of the Competition Authority will transmit a transcript of an oral statement to other authorities or the European Commission in accordance with Article 12 of Regulation 1/2003, provided that: (i) the conditions of the Commission's Notice on Co-operation within the Network of Competition Authorities (OJ 2004. C 101) are met; and (ii) the level of protection offered against disclosure by the recipient competition authority or the European Commission is equivalent to the protection offered by the Competition Authority.

17. To what extent can evidence submitted by the leniency applicant (transcripts of oral statements or written evidence) become discoverable in subsequent private enforcement claims? Can leniency information be subjected to discovery orders in foreign or domestic courts? Can leniency information submitted in a foreign jurisdiction be subjected to discovery orders in the domestic courts?
In the absence of any case law to suggest the opposite, it must be assumed that the regular provisions on discovery (*bijzondere exhibitieplicht*) contained in Article 843a of the Civil Procedure Code (*Wetboek van Burgerlijke Rechtsvordering; 'Rv'*) can in principle apply to leniency applications (whether domestic or foreign). We are, however, unaware of any precedents in which

it was attempted to apply the procedure of Article 843a Rv in order to obtain discovery of a leniency application. Whether or not Dutch leniency applications could become discoverable in foreign jurisdictions would depend on the law of the applicable foreign jurisdiction. We are equally unaware of any relevant precedents.

Article 843a Rv provides that a natural or legal person able to demonstrate a 'legitimate interest' may demand access to specified documents which it knows exist (the existence of a leniency application will be mentioned in the public version of a decision by the Competition Authority; see question 15 above) and which relate to a legal relationship to which the claimant is a party. An action under Article 843a is lodged by a writ of summons/ subpoena (*dagvaarding*) addressed to the natural or legal person with whom the requested documents reside. 'Documents' are to be understood in the widest sense and can also include computerised data and sound or image recordings (Parliamentary Documents, Explanatory Memorandum relating to the Revision of the Civil Procedure Code, at page 553). A tort action, which would form the basis of any action for damages pursuant to competition law infringements, constitutes such a legal relationship (Parliamentary Documents, Explanatory Memorandum relating to the Revision of the Civil Procedure Code, at page 554). However, the (former) leniency applicant will, of course, normally dispute the existence of the tort and therefore equally the existence of the legal relationship.

It is also observed that the text of Article 843a Rv remains unclear on whether or not it is not required that the natural or legal person with whom the documents rest is a party to the aforementioned legal relationship. The Supreme Court (*Hoge Raad*) has, however, ruled that this is indeed required (Supreme Court 18 February 2000, NJ 2001, 259, *News c.s. vs. ABN AMRO*). Hence, it seems excluded that an applicant could successfully subpoena the Competition Authority in order to obtain (parts of) a leniency application or transcriptions of it.

A party could, however, attempt to invoke the Openness of Public Information Act (*Wet Openbaarheid van Bestuur* or Wob) to obtain these from the Competition Authority. This is an administrative rather than a civil proceeding. The Competition Authority is legally obliged to delete all business secrets from the relevant documents (Article 10(1)(c) Wob) if it were to grant access to these. For the other information in the application, the Competition Authority must balance the interests of the applicant in obtaining the information against the legitimate interest of the leniency applicant of that information remaining secret. Therefore, an action under the Wob is unlikely to provide an applicant with more details and facts than the public version of a Competition Authority decision.

A 'legitimate interest' is deemed present if a party in a dispute enjoys either a disproportionate disadvantage (the claimant) or a disproportionate advantage (the opponent). Such could be the case where a leniency application would be required for the claimant to sufficiently substantiate its claim for damages. In addition, the documents in question must be necessary for a 'proper distribution of law'. This means that a court may reject a claim pursuant to Article 843a Rv if liability for damages could also be proven on the basis of other evidence, eg, the public version of a Competition Authority decision or through other means, eg an interrogation of witnesses (see on the latter Supreme Court 31 May 2002, NJ 2003, 589, *K. v. Aegon*).

The defendant in an Article 843a Rv procedure may refuse to provide access to documents if it can demonstrate 'severe interests' (*gewichtige redenen*). These may include business secrets and financial information (Supreme Court 20 December 2002, NJ 2004, 4, *Lightning Casino*). However, unlike under Article 10(1)(c) Wob, this ground of refusal is far from absolute. In fact, courts tend to be highly reluctant to assume the existence of severe interests. The Hague Court of Appeals (*Gerechtshof*) for example refused to accept endangerment of a company's competitive position as a severe interest (Hague Court of Appeals 20 May 2003, S&S 2004, 59).

In view of the above, one may cautiously conclude that by orally making a company statement in the context of a leniency application, an applicant may reduce the risk of successful discovery, since the applicant might then successfully claim not to be in possession of the application. This theory remains to be tested in court. In addition, such an oral statement should always be provided by a lawyer in the absence of company representatives, since the latter could be summoned to testify in court. Whether it would be possible to successfully summon Competition Authority officials to testify in civil proceedings on the content of oral statements or transcriptions of which these officials have knowledge, or whether such officials could or even should invoke professional secrecy, remains equally unclear.

18. Are there any precedents in which evidence from a leniency application has been discovered in a private enforcement claim?
As becomes clear from the above answer to question 17, we are unaware of any such precedent.

RELATIONSHIP WITH THE EUROPEAN COMMISSION'S LENIENCY NOTICE AND LENIENCY POLICY IN OTHER EU MEMBER STATES

19. Does the policy address the interaction with applications under the Commission Leniency Notice? If so, how?
Article 15 of the Leniency Policy Rules provides that the Competition Authority shall assign a marker to a leniency applicant if:
- the leniency applicant is the first to submit a leniency application;
- the European Commission is particularly well placed to investigate the cartel;
- the leniency applicant has submitted a leniency application, or intends to do so soon, with the European Commission; and
- the applicant provides the information required to obtain a marker in purely domestic proceedings (see the reply to question 10 above), as well as a list of EU member states in which evidence on the cartel is likely to be located.

Paragraph 2 of Article 15 provides that the Competition Authority may set the applicant a timeframe within which to complete the application. Thus, the Competition Authority may also refrain from setting a timeframe and simply wait for the Commission to take action. It is our experience that in practice, the Competition Authority will wait for one to two weeks in order to see whether or not the Commission will further handle the case before deciding on whether or not to set a timeframe.

If a timeframe is indeed set, the normal provisions of completing a marker in purely domestic cases apply (see the reply to question 10 above).

20. Does the policy address the interaction with applications for leniency in other EU member states? If so, how? Does the authority accept summary applications in line with the ECN Model Leniency Programme?

This is not explicitly addressed in the Leniency Policy Rules. It is, however, our experience that the Competition Authority accepts summary applications as described in the ECN Model Leniency Programme under the conditions specified in it.

RELATIONSHIP WITH SETTLEMENT PROCEDURES
21. What is the relationship between leniency and applicable settlement procedures? Are they mutually exclusive?

Pursuant to Article 49a Competition Act, the Competition Authority may consider settlements until a formal decision has been adopted (although the Competition Authority in practice prefers to negotiate on settlements before a statement of objections has been issued). Cases in which leniency applications have been submitted are not formally excepted from settlement proceedings. In fact, settlements are always agreed by the Competition Authority with multiple undertakings. Thus, parties to a settlement will not be aware of the fact that one of them applied for leniency. Of course, if a settlement is eventually reached, this implies that no fines shall be imposed and that any conditional grant of leniency shall not be consummated.

REFORM/LATEST DEVELOPMENTS
22. Is there a reform underway to revisit the leniency policy? What are the latest developments?

We are not aware of any plans to revise the policy. We observe in this respect that the current Leniency Policy Rules are very recent.

South Korea

Kim & Chang Kyung Taek Jung, Han Woo Park
& Michael H. Yu

BACKGROUND
1. What is the relevant legislation concerning the leniency policy and what is the enforcing body?
The applicable provisions implementing the Leniency Policy of the Korea Fair Trade Commission (FTC) are provided for in Article 22-2 (Mitigation of Informants) of the Monopoly Regulation and Fair Trade Law (the FTL) and in Article 35 (Criteria for the Mitigation of or Exemption from Punishment for Informants, etc.) of the Enforcement Decree (the Enforcement Decree) promulgated under the FTL.

In addition, the FTC has enacted the Notification on Corrective Orders Regarding Voluntary Reporters of Improper Concerted Acts and the Leniency Programme (the Notice), dated 1 April 2005 which contains specific rules regarding the reporting process and the standards governing the grant of total or partial exemptions of applicable sanctions.

2. What are the basic tenets of a leniency/immunity programme?
If the FTC concludes that a respondent was involved in price-fixing or other cartel-like behaviour in violation of the FTL, then the FTC may impose the sanctions described below. In addition, the specific individuals who actually conducted the acts in violation of the FTL may also be subject to sanctions. The FTC has the power to issue the following orders and penalties:
- Cease and desist or corrective order: The FTC usually issues a corrective order in which the offending party or parties are ordered to bring the infringement to an end.
- Public announcement of the violation: The FTC may also order the offending party or parties to publish a public announcement concerning the violation of the FTL (such as a public apology). The FTC will designate the number of daily newspapers in which the announcement must be published, the size of the announcement and will usually dictate its contents as well.
- Fine: The violating party or parties may be subject to up to a 10 per cent surcharge on the gross sales derived from the business activities relating to the cartel activity ('affected sales') during the period of the cartel activity. Note, however, that the maximum surcharge on cartel activity which ceased prior to 1 April 2005, or which commenced prior to 1 April 2005 and ended prior to 4 December 2007 is five per cent of the affected sales made by the offending party or parties. In the case where

the violating party has no sales, it may be subject to up to KRW 2 billion of the fine.
- Complaint for criminal sanctions: Criminal sanctions are the most severe penalties available under the FTL. In the case of criminal sanctions, the FTC will file a complaint with the prosecutors' office for indictment under the FTL. Criminal proceedings can be commenced only if the FTC files the complaint. In the case of a conviction: (i) for corporate entities, the offending party may be subject to a criminal fine of up to KRW 200 million (approximately $160,000 or €110,000); or (ii) for individuals, the offending party may be subject to imprisonment for up to three years or a criminal fine of up to KRW 200 million – although imprisonment is reserved for only the most exceptional cases.

In general, the FTC will issue one of the first three above penalties or, more often, a combination of the three. Only in the most severe and blatant cases of violation of the FTL or where the offending party continues to engage in the illegal activities despite the cease and desist order, will criminal sanctions be imposed. If the FTC concludes that the respondent(s) violated the FTL, then such finding may be used by South Korean customers to commence a civil action for damages attributable to such cartel behaviour. In such a case and under South Korean law, the claimant is only required to prove damages (and proximity with the cartel activity), as the conclusions of the FTC that a cartel existed and that such cartel had an adverse impact on competition in South Korea will be relied on by South Korean courts.

The leniency programme as provided under the FTL, the Enforcement Decree and the Notice are intended to encourage co-operation with the FTC and to facilitate their investigation with respect to potential violations of the FTL. The leniency programme is available to companies who co-operate with the FTC's investigation (such as through admission of involvement in a cartel, co-operation through every stage of the FTC's investigation, etc).

2.1 Is leniency available also for other types of competition law violations than cartels?

The leniency programme applies only to violations of provisions relating to cartel activities prescribed in Article 19 of the FTL.

3. How many cartels have been unveiled and punished since the adoption of the leniency programme?

According to a report prepared by the FTC in August 2009, the statistics with respect to general cartel enforcement in South Korea are as indicated in the table below.

South Korea

Classification	Criminal prosecution (*1)	Surcharge	Corrective order (*2)	Surcharge	Warning	Total
2008	5	5	45	38	15	65
2007	7	6	22	18	15	44
2006	3	2	31	25	12	46
2005	4	2	28	19	14	46
2004	3	2	21	10	11	35
2003	5	3	11	6	7	23

Note *1. Cases counted under this heading include:
(i) cases where only a sanction consisting of criminal prosecution was imposed;
(ii) cases where not only criminal prosecution but also corrective orders were imposed; and
(iii) cases where the sanctions imposed were a combination of the following: criminal prosecution; corrective order; and fines.
Note *2. Cases counted under this heading include:
(i) cases where only the sanction of a corrective order was imposed; and
(ii) cases where not only a corrective order, but also fines were imposed.
(Source: White Paper on Fair Trade, published by FTC on August 2009.)

The leniency programme in South Korea was introduced in 1997, one of the first countries in Asia to do so after similar programmes were introduced in the US, Canada and the EU. In its initial stages, there were relatively few applicants under the leniency programme as indicated in the table below. However, after its revision in 2005 to exclude the FTC's discretion in determining the level of fine reduction, there has been a noticeable increase of not only the number but also the proportion of cases involving leniency applicants as indicated below during the period between 2005 and 2008.

Number of leniency applications

Year	99	00	01	02	03	04	05	06	07	08	Total
No. of cartel cases levied surcharges	15	15	8	14	11	14	23	27	24	43	194
No. of cases of leniency applicants	1	1	–	2	1	2	7	7	10	21	52
Ratio (%)	6.7	6.7	–	14.3	9.1	14.3	30.4	25.9	41.7	48.8	27

(Source: as above)

4. What is needed to be a successful leniency applicant? Is documentary evidence required or is testimonial evidence sufficient?

Under the Enforcement Decree, the applicant has to meet certain

requirements and provide certain evidence in order to succeed. The level of fine reduction that will be granted will depend on whether and to what extent these conditions are met. Generally, there are four parameters which are taken into account:
- Priority in reporting. What level of leniency the applicant will qualify for will depend on whether the applicant is the first such applicant to report 'exclusive' information to the FTC.
- Timing of leniency. The determination of the exemption or the reduction of the fine will also depend on: (i) whether the FTC had already commenced investigating the matter prior to the applicant's provision of information; and (ii) whether the applicant for leniency is the first, second or subsequent applicant to do so with regard to the improper concerted acts.
- Degree of co-operation. The amount and duration of the co-operation that the applicant provides during the FTC's investigation will also be considered for determining the exemption or the relevant reduction level.
- Continued participation. Lastly, the FTC will also review whether the applicant is currently conducting the improper behaviour being investigated or has ceased to do so.

As to the form of the evidence to be submitted at the time of reporting, the Notice indicates that such evidence may be in the form of documentary evidence, recorded tapes, computer files, or any other type of media.

TIMING
5. What are the benefits of being 'first in' to co-operate?
Subject to the satisfaction of all four of the criteria prescribed in Article 35(1)(i) of the Enforcement Decree, an applicant who firstly and only reports illegal cartel activities to the FTC may be assured of receiving 100 per cent leniency on all applicable sanctions.

More specifically, an applicant who has reported to the FTC prior to the commencement of the investigation and fulfils each of the following criteria will be exempt from fines and corrective orders:
- an applicant who first provides exclusively the information which was necessary to evidence the improper concerted act;
- the report shall have been made at a time when the FTC had either no knowledge of the improper concerted acts or the FTC was not able to obtain sufficient evidence necessary to prove the improper concerted acts;
- all facts relevant to the improper concerted acts shall have been provided, and co-operation shall have been provided, including the submission of relevant documents, until the completion of the FTC's investigation; and
- the applicant shall have ceased all activity which could be deemed improper concerted acts.

In addition, under Article 35(1)(ii) of the Enforcement Decree, after the commencement of investigations by the FTC, an applicant who has

co-operated with the FTC and fulfils each of the following criteria shall be exempt from fines and exempt or partially exempt from the corrective orders:
- an applicant who first provides information which was necessary to evidence the improper concerted act;
- the co-operation shall have been provided at a time when the FTC had either no knowledge of the improper concerted acts or the FTC was not able to obtain sufficient evidence necessary to prove the improper concerted acts;
- all facts relevant to the improper concerted acts shall have been provided, and co-operation shall have been provided, including the submission of relevant documents, until the completion of the FTC's investigation; and
- the applicant shall have ceased all activity which could be deemed improper concerted acts.

6. What are the consequences of being 'second'? Is there an 'immunity plus' or 'amnesty plus' option?

Even if the applicant was not the first to provide the relevant evidence, the Enforcement Decree provides that the applicant can still qualify for partial leniency. Under Article 35(1)(iii) of the Enforcement Decree, a 'second reporter', who reports to the FTC prior to the commencement of investigations or co-operates with the FTC after the commencement of investigations can qualify for a 50 per cent reduction in fines and partial exemption from the corrective orders if such person fulfils all of the following criteria:
- an applicant who, as the second person to do so, provides information which was necessary to evidence the improper concerted act;
- all facts relevant to the improper concerted acts shall have been provided, and co-operation shall have been provided, including the submission of relevant documents, until the completion of the FTC's investigation; and
- the person shall have ceased all activity which could be deemed improper concerted acts.

In addition, the FTL also includes an 'amnesty plus' provision under Article 35(1)(v) of the Enforcement Decree. More specifically, an applicant who was under an ongoing investigation regarding an allegation of one area of cartel activity ('first cartel') can seek amnesty or full leniency with respect to other improper concerted acts ('second cartel') which were not the subject of the FTC's initial investigations. In this case, the applicant for 'amnesty plus' may be partially exempt from the corrective order and be fully or partially exempt from the surcharge with respect to the first cartel, depending on the relative importance of the first cartel and second cartel prescribed in Article 16 of the Notice as follows:
- if the scale of the second cartel is not greater than 100 per cent of the scale of the first cartel, then the applicant will receive a 20 per cent reduction with respect to the first cartel;

- if the scale of the second cartel is greater than 100 per cent but less than 200 per cent of the scale of the first cartel, then the applicant will receive a 30 per cent reduction with respect to the first cartel;
- if the scale of the second cartel is greater than 200 per cent and less than 400 per cent of the scale of the first cartel, then the applicant will receive a 50 per cent reduction with respect to the first cartel; and
- if the scale of the second cartel activity is greater than 400 per cent of the scale of the first cartel, then the applicant will receive full lenience with respect to the first cartel.

Under Article 16(3) of the Notice, for purposes of the foregoing measurement, the 'scale' shall be computed based on the relevant amount of sales of the relevant products or services.

7. Are subsequent firms given any beneficial treatment if they make a useful contribution? How are 'useful contributions' defined?

Even if an applicant fails to meet the conditions prescribed in Article 35(1) of the Enforcement Decree (ie the third or subsequent applicants), the FTC may regard the applicant to be a 'collaborator' if the FTC determines in its sole discretion that the applicant has fully co-operated with the FTC's investigation and provided the evidence necessary to prove the cartel activities under the Article 2(2) of the Notice.

SCOPE/FULL LENIENCY

8. Is it possible to receive full leniency? And, if so, what are the conditions required to receiving full leniency?

With regard to the availability of full indemnity please refer to question 5.

8.1 Can ringleaders/coercers receive full leniency?

Under Article 35(1)(v) of the Enforcement Decree, in spite of the fulfilment of the qualifications for leniency, an applicant who has coerced other co-operating parties into participating in the improper concerted acts or not stopping the improper concerted acts in question after their commencement, shall be disqualified from applying for leniency (ie the full or partial exemption of both the corrective order and the surcharge).

However, with regard to ringleaders, subject to the satisfaction of the qualifications prescribed in Article 35(1)(i) or (ii) of the Enforcement Decree, ringleaders may receive full exemption with respect to the applicable sanctions.

8.2 If there is a requirement to 'co-operate fully and on an ongoing basis' what does it entail?

As mentioned above, to obtain leniency, the applicant should fully co-operate with the FTC, including submitting relevant documents, until the completion of the FTC's investigation under Article 31 of the Enforcement Decree.

More specifically, under Article 5 of the Notice, whether a party has 'co-operated fully and on an ongoing basis' shall be determined together with all the circumstances including consideration of the following:
- whether the applicant immediately stated all facts relating to the

improper concerted act under investigation;
- whether the applicant immediately and promptly provided all materials relating to the improper concerted act (including but not limited to the relevant documents) which the applicant possessed or could gather;
- whether the applicant promptly explained the inquiries and co-operated with the FTC at its request;
- whether all employees and directors of the applicant endeavoured to fully co-operate with the FTC in the course of the investigation and at the decision of the FTC;
- whether the applicant destroyed, manipulated, damaged or hid evidence or the information relating to the improper concerted act in question; and
- whether the applicant disclosed or leaked information relating to the improper concerted act or the submission of the application for leniency with the prior consent of the FTC before notification of the examiner's report.

8.3 Does the regulatory authority require the applicant to cease participation in the cartel conduct after its application?

Under Article 13 of the Notice, if the applicant fails to stop the improper concerted act immediately after the submission of the application for leniency, the applicant could be disqualified from obtaining leniency pursuant to the FTL.

9. How many companies have received full immunity from fines to date?

The FTC does not make this data available. The reason for this is that the FTC is required to take precautions against identifying anyone who has benefitted from leniency from being disclosed through media reports, as provided under Article 19(4) of the Notice.

PROCEDURE

10. What are the practical steps required to apply for leniency?

The flowchart on the following page has been provided by the FTC to explain the relevant steps in the leniency application process.

South Korea

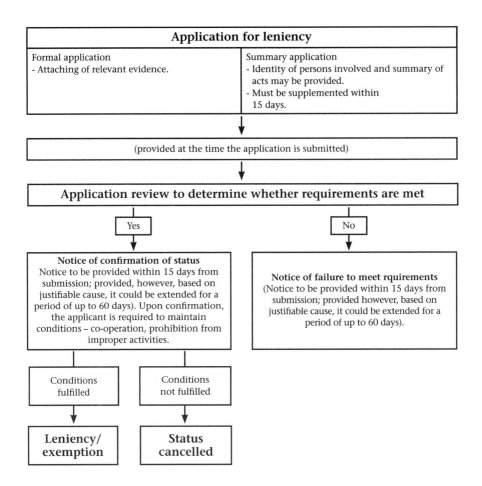

In connection to 'markers', given the relative ease with which a full application can be filed, there has been no need for a separate marker system.

11. Is there an optimal time to approach the regulatory authority?
There is no particular consideration in terms of when the application for leniency should be submitted. However, given that the benefits of the leniency programme will only be provided to first and second applicants, an application should be submitted as quickly as possible.

12. What guarantees of leniency exist if a party co-operates?
Based on the application, a determination of whether the applicant qualifies under the conditions provided under Article 35 of the Enforcement Decree will be made within 15 days from the date of submission. If the FTC confirms that the applicant has qualified under the conditions, then the FTC is prohibited under Article 12 of the Notice from cancelling such a determination, unless any one of the following conditions exist:
- the applicant has failed to provide complete co-operation until the end of the investigation of the FTC;
- the evidence submitted is determined to be fraudulent or false; or

- the applicant has failed to cease the improper acts by the time the FTC has made its final determination in the case.

CONSEQUENCES
13. What effects does leniency granted to a corporate defendant have on defendant's employees?
Under the FTL, the employees of a corporate defendant are not subject to the sanctions imposed by the FTC.

14. Does leniency bar further criminal or private enforcement?
No. The intent of the leniency provisions is to restrict the enforcement powers of the FTC only in its administration of the FTL, without affecting the rights of other authorities or third parties. As such, the extent of the remedies provided under the leniency provisions is limited only to reducing the scope of monetary fines and corrective orders that can be imposed by the FTC on an applicant.

At the same time, one additional measure that the FTC can implement in the event that an improper concerted act is found, is to recommend the case to the Office of the Prosecutor General for criminal sanctions to be imposed on the relevant participants. Under Article 20 of the Notice, the FTC should refrain from referring applicants, who have been granted leniency under Article 31(1) of the Enforcement Decree, to the criminal authorities if their status has been confirmed under the leniency provisions, except where the applicants are engaged in certain types of egregious violations or the prosecutor general has already made a request that the FTC should submit a criminal complaint.

PROTECTION AGAINST DISCLOSURE/CONFIDENTIALITY
15. Is confidentiality afforded to the leniency applicant and other co-operating parties? If so, to what extent? Is the identity of the leniency applicant/other co-operating parties disclosed during the investigation or in the final decision? Is information provided by the leniency applicant/other co-operating parties passed on to other undertakings under investigation? Can a leniency applicant/other co-operating party request anonymity or confidentiality of information provided?
Under Article 22(2) of the FTL and Article 35(2) of the Enforcement Decree, the FTC and its officials shall neither provide nor disclose the identity and reported information of an applicant who co-operated in the investigation, except with the prior consent of the applicant or when necessary for lawsuits pursuant to the relevant laws.

More specifically, Article 19 of the Notice provides the details of the confidentiality obligations which are imposed on FTC official(s) who review the application submitted by the applicant:
- the FTC shall use an alias for the applicant for examination reports and decisions;
- to prevent the identity of the applicant from being disclosed, the FTC shall take necessary measures to remove or redact parts containing

identifying information even in the evidential materials attached to examination reports;
- regarding any case that is subject to confirmation of status of the applicant pursuant to the Notice, the FTC shall take measures to prevent the identity of the applicant from being disclosed. For example, writing a separate examination report and decision for each applicant in the course of deliberations and resolutions and conducting deliberation for each applicant; and
- the FTC shall take precautions to prevent the identification of anyone who benefits from the leniency programme from being disclosed through media reports.

16. Is the evidence submitted by the leniency applicant protected from transmission to other competition authorities with whom the authority in question co-operates? If so, how?

Other than being provided when necessary for lawsuits pursuant to Article 35(2) of the Enforcement Decree, there is no obligation on the FTC and its procedures to transmit the information relevant to the application for leniency. The FTC is the sole competition authority in South Korea.

In addition, there is no procedure under the relevant laws or regulations which govern the provision of findings or materials by the FTC to competition authorities in foreign countries. In this regard, although the FTC has recently embarked on an effort to increase inter-jurisdictional co-operation by executing memorandums of understanding (MOUs) or entering into co-operation agreements with other foreign competition authorities, there is no specific provision in any relevant MOU or treaty which addresses the provision of information relating to leniency to the counter party of the MOU or treaty.

17. To what extent can evidence submitted by the leniency applicant (transcripts of oral statements or written evidence) become discoverable in subsequent private enforcement claims?

As mentioned above, under Article 35(2) of the Enforcement Decree, when the documents relating to the application for leniency are requested for filing or litigating lawsuits, it can be disclosed by the FTC without any consent of the applicant. In this regard, Article 19(5) of the Notice also indicates that when an administrative lawsuit is filed against the improper concerted act, the FTC may submit to a court of law evidentiary material containing the identity of the applicant.

17.1 Can leniency information be subjected to discovery orders in the domestic courts?

There is no convention under the civil procedure of South Korea which is the same as discovery orders in the US. However, the procedure of 'entrusting forwarding the documents' prescribed in the Civil Procedure Act (the CPA) can be considered a *de facto* equivalent of 'discovery orders' which could have the effect of resulting in the disclosure of information relating to leniency granted by the FTC.

More specifically, under Article 352 and 352-2 of the CPA, if a request for submission of documentary evidence applicable to a civil procedure (including private enforcement claims) is made by filing a request to forward the document, the addressee who maintains custody of such documents is obliged to comply with such request unless there are justifiable reasons for not doing so. As such, in a subsequent private enforcement claim, if the plaintiff requests the delivery of the documents relating to the decision on the improper concerted act, including the application for leniency, the FTC may co-operate with the request pursuant to the CPA.

17.2 Can leniency information be subjected to discovery orders in foreign courts?
In this regard, there is no specific regulation or procedure in South Korea to determine whether discovery orders in foreign courts can be enforced in South Korea.

17.3 Can leniency information submitted in a foreign jurisdiction be subjected to discovery orders in the domestic courts?
As mentioned above, there is no provision under the relevant laws and regulations to provide US-style 'discovery orders' in South Korea.

18. Are there any precedents in which evidence from a leniency application has been discovered in a private enforcement claim?
Not to our knowledge.

RELATIONSHIP WITH THE EUROPEAN COMMISSION'S LENIENCY NOTICE AND LENIENCY POLICY IN OTHER EU MEMBER STATES
19. Does the policy address the interaction with applications under the Commission Leniency Notice? If so, how?
Not applicable.

20. Does the policy address the interaction with applications for leniency in other EU member states? If so, how? Does the authority accept summary applications in line with the ECN Model Leniency Programme?
Not applicable.

RELATIONSHIP WITH SETTLEMENT PROCEDURES
21. What is the relationship between leniency and applicable settlement procedures? Are they mutually exclusive?
There is no official settlement procedure in South Korea.

REFORM/LATEST DEVELOPMENTS
22. Is there a reform underway to revisit the leniency policy? What are the latest developments?
The most recent revisions to the leniency policy were implemented and took effect as of 19 May 2009. The main purpose of these revisions is to

adopt the concept of joint application for leniency. Under Article 22-2 of the FTL and Article 4-2 of the Notice, in cases where the relationship between the applicants is one where one party is an affiliate which is substantially controlled by the other party or one party is an entity which was spun-off from or acquired a business from the other party, the two parties may be deemed joint applicants and treated as one applicant for leniency.

Spain

Herbert Smith LLP Pedro Suárez

BACKGROUND
1. What is the relevant legislation concerning the leniency policy and what is the enforcing body?
The Competition Act (Law 15/2007 dated 3 July on the defence of competition) and its implementing regulation (Royal Decree 261/2008 dated 22 February 2008 adopting the regulation on the defence of competition) are the pieces of legislation governing the leniency policy.

Articles 65 and 66 of the Competition Act are the particular provisions dealing with the leniency policy and provide the legal basis for the exemption from payment of fines and the reduction of the amount of fines. The corresponding provisions in the implementing regulation are Articles 46 to 53, which set out the procedure applicable to leniency applications.

The National Competition Commission (the Commission) has published provisional guidance on the leniency programme (provisional guidelines on the handling of applications for exemption and reduction of the amount of fines). These guidelines intend to clarify and give practical recommendations on certain aspects of the legislation governing the leniency programme.

The Commission is the primary enforcer of the leniency programme. However, regional competition authorities also enforce the provisions in the Competition Act concerning the leniency policy in those cases where the scope of the conduct is limited to the territory of their respective region.

2. What are the basic tenets of a leniency/immunity programme? Is leniency available also for other types of competition law violations than cartels?
The leniency programme set out in the Competition Act and its implementing regulation provides for the exemption from payment of fines in those cases where a person who would otherwise have had to pay a fine is the first person to provide evidence which, in the opinion of the Commission, is sufficient to order an inspection or prove an infringement of the cartel prohibition in Article 1 of the Competition Act, provided that, when such evidence is handed in to the Commission, it does not already have sufficient evidence for these purposes.

The leniency programme also provides for the reduction of the amount of fines where a person who does not comply with the requirements to obtain an exemption from payment of fines provides evidence in connection with an alleged infringement that is of significant added value with respect to the evidence already available to the Commission.

Spain

Leniency is only available to persons providing evidence in connection with cartel behaviour.

3. How many cartels have been unveiled and punished since the adoption of the leniency programme?

It is widely believed that several ongoing cartel investigations have been triggered by leniency applications submitted since the leniency programme entered into force in February 2008. However, at the time this contribution is prepared, the Commission has not adopted a final decision on any of these investigations.

4. What is needed to be a successful leniency applicant?

Exemption from payment of fines requires that the applicant satisfies the following conditions:
- the applicant must co-operate fully, continuously and diligently with the Commission throughout the proceedings;
- the applicant must bring its participation in the alleged infringement to an end at the moment when it provides the Commission with evidence of such infringement, except in those situations where the Commission considers that such participation should continue in order to preserve the effectiveness of an inspection;
- the applicant must not have destroyed any evidence relating to the infringement or disclosed its intention to apply for an exemption from payment of fines to a third party other than the European Commission or other competition authorities; and
- the applicant must not have adopted any measures to coerce other persons to participate in the infringement.

Reduction of the amount of fines requires that the applicant satisfies the first three conditions.

The duty to co-operate fully, continuously and diligently throughout the proceedings has been defined by the implementing regulation. This duty requires the fulfilment of the following obligations:
- to provide the Commission without delay with all relevant information and evidence relating to the infringement which is in the possession or otherwise available to the applicant;
- to remain available to the Commission and respond without delay to all requests from the Commission that can contribute to establishing the factual background to the infringement;
- to make current company employees and executives available for interviews with the Commission and, if relevant, also former executives;
- to abstain from destroying, falsifying or concealing relevant information or evidence in relation to the infringement;
- to abstain from disclosing the fact that the applicant has filed a leniency application or the contents of such application until the statement of objections is issued or before any other moment which might be agreed with the Commission.

Spain

4.1 Is documentary evidence required or is testimonial evidence sufficient?
There is no statutory provision that requires a leniency applicant to provide the Commission with documentary evidence of an infringement. Any type of evidence which is admissible in court, including testimonial evidence, can also be produced before the Commission.

TIMING
5. What are the benefits of being 'first in' to co-operate?
Only the person who is the first to provide the Commission with relevant evidence of an infringement and complies with the remaining statutory conditions can expect to be granted an exemption from payment of fines.

6. What are the consequences of being 'second'?
A person coming forward after a leniency applicant, even if it fulfils all the requirements to qualify for exemption from payment of fines, is ineligible for such an exemption.

Such person will, however, be eligible for a reduction of the amount of fines if it provides evidence of an infringement that is of significant added value with respect to the evidence already available to the Commission and meets the remaining statutory conditions.

6.1 Is there an 'immunity plus' or 'amnesty plus' option?
The Spanish competition rules do not provide for an 'immunity plus' or 'amnesty plus' option.

However, where a person provides evidence that enables the Commission to establish additional facts having a direct impact on the amount of the fine, this will be taken into account by the Commission when determining the amount of the fine imposed on such person.

7. Are subsequent firms given any beneficial treatment if they make a useful contribution?
Any person who does not meet the requirements to qualify for an exemption from payment of fines – among them the requirement to be the first person to provide relevant evidence of the infringement – may, however, qualify for a reduction of the amount of fines.

Such person will be eligible for a reduction of the amount of fines if it provides evidence of an infringement that is of significant added value with respect to the evidence already available to the Commission and meets the remaining statutory conditions.

The reduction of the amount of fines is to be calculated by the Commission according to the following rules: the first person to meet the requirements to qualify for a reduction of the amount of fines will benefit from a reduction of between 30 and 50 per cent of the amount of the applicable fine; the second person to meet the requirements will benefit from a reduction of between 20 and 30 per cent; and any subsequent persons meeting the requirements will benefit from a reduction of up to 20 per cent.

Also, where a person provides evidence that enables the Commission to establish additional facts having a direct impact on the amount of the fine, it will be taken into account by the Commission when determining the amount of the fine imposed on such person.

7.1 How are 'useful contributions' defined?
According to the implementing regulation, evidence will be considered to be of 'significant added value' when it, whether by its nature or by its level of detail, reinforces the ability of the Commission to prove the facts giving rise to an infringement.

SCOPE/FULL LENIENCY
8. Is it possible to receive full leniency?
Full leniency (ie, exemption from payment of fines) is available to any person who would otherwise have been subject to a fine and is the first person to provide evidence which, in the opinion of the Commission, is sufficient to order an inspection or prove an infringement of the cartel prohibition in Article 1 of the Competition Act, provided that, when such evidence is handed in to the Commission, it does not already have sufficient evidence for these purposes.

8.1 If so, what are the conditions required to receive full leniency?
Apart from the applicable evidentiary thresholds, exemption from payment of fines requires that the applicant satisfies the following conditions:
- the applicant must co-operate fully, continuously and diligently with the Commission throughout the proceedings;
- the applicant must bring its participation in the alleged infringement to an end at the moment when it provides the Commission with evidence of such infringement, except in those situations where the Commission considers that such participation should continue in order to preserve the effectiveness of an inspection;
- the applicant must not have destroyed any evidence relating to the infringement or disclosed its intention to apply for an exemption from payment of fines to a third party other than the European Commission or other competition authorities; and
- the applicant must not have adopted any measures to coerce other persons to participate in the infringement.

8.2 Can ringleaders/coercers receive full leniency?
Ringleaders who coerce other persons to participate in a cartel cannot qualify for an exemption from payment of fines since they do not meet the last condition.

8.3 If there is a requirement to 'co-operate fully and on an ongoing basis' what does it entail?
The duty to co-operate fully, continuously and diligently throughout the

proceedings has been defined by the implementing regulation to require the fulfilment of the following obligations:
- to provide the Commission without delay with all relevant information and evidence relating to the infringement which is in the possession or otherwise available to the applicant;
- to remain available to the Commission and respond without delay to all requests from the Commission that can contribute to establishing the factual background to the infringement;
- to make current company employees and executives available for interviews with the Commission and, if relevant, also former executives;
- to abstain from destroying, falsifying or concealing relevant information or evidence in relation to the infringement; and
- to abstain from disclosing the fact that the applicant has filed a leniency application or the contents of such application until the statement of objections is issued or before any other moment that might be agreed with the Commission.

8.4 Does the regulatory authority require the applicant to cease participation in the cartel conduct after its application?
The leniency applicant must bring its participation in the alleged infringement to an end at the moment when it provides the Commission with evidence of such infringement, except in those situations where the Commission considers that such participation should continue in order to preserve the effectiveness of an inspection.

9. How many companies have received full immunity from fines to date?
It is widely believed that several ongoing cartel investigations have been triggered by leniency applications submitted since the leniency programme entered into force in February 2008. However, at the time this contribution was prepared, the Commission has not adopted a final decision on any of these investigations and therefore no person has been granted an exemption from payment of fines to date.

PROCEDURE
10. What are the practical steps required to apply for leniency?
The procedural steps required to apply for exemptions from payment of fines are the following:
- The procedure will be initiated at the request of the applicant, who must submit to the Commission a formal application for exemption along with all the relevant information and evidence available to the applicant in connection with the infringement.
- The Commission may allow the application to be made orally at the request of the applicant. The oral statement will be recorded at the premises of the Commission. The transcript of the oral statement, along with all relevant information and evidence submitted by the applicant, will be entered into the registry of the Commission.

- The applicant must provide the Commission with the following information and evidence:
  - name and address;
  - names and addresses of the participants in the cartel;
  - a detailed description of the cartel which includes references to the following issues: cartel aims, activities and organisation; products and territories affected by the cartel; and estimated duration and nature of the cartel activities;
  - evidence relating to the cartel in the possession of the applicant or available to it within a reasonable time period; in particular, contemporaneous evidence of the cartel which allows the Commission to verify any ongoing activities; and
  - if applicable, a list of any other applications for exemption from payment of fines or for a reduction of the amount of fines which the applicant has filed or intends to file with other competition authorities in relation to the same cartel.
- Applications will be handled according to the order in which they are entered into the registry of the Commission. The applicant may request that the Commission acknowledges receipt of the application and that a document indicating the date and time of registration is issued.
- The Commission may grant, following a reasoned request from the applicant, additional time for submitting evidence in relation to the cartel. If such evidence is submitted within the time limit established by the Commission, the relevant date and time of the application will be deemed to be that of the initial submission.
- The Commission will examine the evidence submitted by the applicant and consider whether it is sufficient to order an inspection or to prove a cartel infringement. In such case, the Commission will adopt a decision granting the applicant conditional exemption from payment of fines. This decision will be communicated to the applicant.
- If the Commission considers that the evidence submitted by the applicant is not sufficient to order an inspection or to prove a cartel infringement, the Commission will adopt a decision dismissing the application which will be communicated to the applicant. The applicant may then withdraw the application or request that it is re-examined as an application for reduction of the amount of fines. If the evidence is withdrawn, this will not prevent the Commission from using its powers of investigation in relation to any evidence that has been submitted with the application.
- Applications for exemption from payment of fines will be examined according to the order in which they are received by the Commission.
- Applications for exemption from payment of fines can be made up to the moment at which the statement of objections is issued. The Commission will dismiss any application submitted after that moment.
- The Commission (Directorate of Investigation) will include in its proposal for a final decision on the proceedings its preliminary opinion on the granting of an exemption from payment of fines.

Spain

- If the applicant has complied throughout the proceedings with all the applicable statutory conditions, the Commission (Board) will grant an exemption from payment of fines in its final decision on the proceedings. If the conditions for an exemption have not been met by the applicant, it may still benefit from a reduction of the amount of fines if it has complied with the conditions to obtain such a reduction. Otherwise, the applicant will not benefit from any favourable treatment.

The procedural steps required to apply for reductions of the amount of fines are fundamentally the same as those required to apply for exemptions from payment of fines. However, the following differences should be noted:
- Applications for reduction of the amount of fines may be accepted by the Commission after the statement of objections has been issued in those cases where the Commission considers that this is justified having regard to the information already available to it and the nature and contents of the evidence submitted by the applicant.
- Applications for reduction of the amount of fines will always be handled after the Commission has reached a decision on whether conditional exemption should be granted to any prior applicant for exemption from payment of fines.
- The Commission (Directorate of Investigation) will inform the applicant of its preliminary decision on the application for reduction of the amount of fines no later than at the moment when the statement of objections is issued. Such preliminary decision will be favourable to granting a reduction where the evidence submitted by the applicant in connection with the infringement is of significant added value and the remaining statutory conditions have been complied with by the applicant. Otherwise, such preliminary decision will be contrary to granting a reduction.
- If the application for reduction of the amount of fines is submitted after the statement of objections has been issued, the Commission (Directorate of Investigation) will inform the applicant of its preliminary decision on a reduction of the amount of fines in its proposal for a final decision on the proceedings.
- The Commission (Directorate of Investigation) will include in its proposal for a final decision on the proceedings its preliminary opinion on the granting of any reductions of the amount of fines.
- If the applicant has complied throughout the proceedings with all the applicable statutory conditions, the Commission (Board) will grant a reduction of the amount of fines in its final decision on the proceedings. Such reduction will be calculated according to the percentage ranges applicable to the first, second and successive persons to fulfil the conditions.

10.1 Full disclosure
The duty to co-operate fully, continuously and diligently throughout the proceedings, as defined by the implementing regulation, requires that all leniency applicants provide the Commission without delay with all the

relevant information and evidence relating to the infringement in the possession of or otherwise available to the applicant.

10.2 Initial contact/is there a 'marker' system?
The Spanish leniency programme does not provide for a 'marker' system. However, in the case of applications for exemption from payment of fines, the Commission may grant, following a reasoned request from the applicant, additional time for submitting evidence in relation to the cartel. If such evidence is submitted within the time limit established by the Commission, the relevant date and time of the application will be deemed to be that of the initial submission.

As regards initial contact with the Commission in connection with a leniency application, it should be noted that the Commission has set up two dedicated telephone lines (+34 91 536 9058 and +34 91 536 9024) through which prospective applicants may contact the staff of the sub-directorate for cartel and leniency and discuss any issues related to the presentation of a leniency application.

10.3 Conditional reduction of fine
As opposed to the conditional exemption granted by the Commission to an applicant for exemption from payment of fines whose application is supported by evidence that is considered sufficient to order an inspection or to prove a cartel infringement, no conditional reduction is granted by the Commission to applicants for reduction of the amount of fines at any stage during the proceedings.

10.4 Final reduction
If an applicant for reduction of the amount of fines has complied throughout the proceedings with all the applicable statutory conditions, the Commission (Board) will grant the reduction in its final decision on the proceedings. The reduction will be calculated according to the different percentage ranges applicable to the first, second and successive persons to qualify for the reduction.

In particular, the following rules apply: the first person to meet the requirements to qualify for a reduction of the amount of fines will benefit from a reduction of between 30 and 50 per cent of the amount of the applicable fine; the second person to meet the requirements will benefit from a reduction of between 20 and 30 per cent; and any subsequent persons meeting the requirements will benefit from a reduction of up to 20 per cent.

11. Is there an optimal time to approach the regulatory authority?
Leniency applications will be handled according to the order in which they are entered into the registry of the Commission. It should be noted in this regard that the relevant time and date will be that of the corresponding entry made into the registry.

If the application is filed with any other public registry, the relevant time and date for the purposes of the leniency programme will not be that of entry into such registry, but the time and date of entry into the registry of the Commission. It is important to note in this connection that there may be a difference of several days between the two entries, as the application will typically be sent from the first public registry to the registry of the competition authority by administrative mail.

The applicant may request that the Commission acknowledges receipt of the application and that a document indicating the date and time of registration is issued.

Given that exemption from payment of fines is only available to the first person that provides relevant evidence of an infringement and that applications for exemption are considered according to the order in which they are handed in to the Commission, there is an obvious incentive for any person interested in such exemption to file an application as soon as possible.

The same is true for any person with an interest in a reduction of the amount of fines, since applications for reduction are also considered by the Commission according to the registration date and time. In this regard, it should be noted that applications for reduction of the amount of fines will always be handled after the Commission has reached a decision on whether conditional exemption should be granted to any prior applicant for exemption from payment of fines.

Applications for exemption from payment of fines can be filed until the moment when the statement of objections is issued. Applications for reduction of the amount of fines may be accepted by the Commission after the statement of objections has been issued in those cases where the Commission considers that this is justified having regard to the information already available to it and the nature and contents of the evidence submitted by the applicant.

12. What guarantees of leniency exist if a party co-operates?
Provided that the applicable statutory conditions are fulfilled, the Commission must grant the exemption from payment of fines or the reduction of the amount of fines applied for.

It should be noted, however, that compliance with these conditions is often far from being a clear-cut issue since it depends on the interpretation of concepts that are inherently subjective, such as 'sufficient to order an inspection' or 'sufficient to prove an infringement', which are the relevant thresholds that must be met by evidence submitted with an application for exemption from payment of fines.

Although the implementing regulation has gone some way towards clarifying their meaning, a similar problem exists with concepts such as 'significant added value', which is the relevant threshold applicable to evidence submitted with applications for reduction of the amount of fines, or 'full, continuous and diligent co-operation', which is a condition that any leniency applicant must comply with throughout the proceedings.

CONSEQUENCES
13. What effects does leniency granted to a corporate defendant have on the defendant's employees?
An exemption from payment of fines granted to a company will also benefit its representatives or the members of its management bodies who have participated in the cartel, provided that these persons have collaborated with the Commission.

Similarly, the reduction of the amount of fines granted to a company will also be applicable, in the same percentage, to the fines imposed on its representatives or on the members of its management bodies who have participated in the cartel, provided that these persons have collaborated with the Commission.

13.1 Does it protect them from criminal and/or civil liability?
Companies and natural persons qualifying for favourable treatment under the leniency programme can only expect protection from administrative fines imposed by the Commission under the competition rules. The leniency programme offers no protection from eventual criminal or civil liability flowing from cartel conduct that has been declared to infringe the competition rules.

14. Does leniency bar further private enforcement?
Companies and natural persons qualifying for favourable treatment under the leniency programme can only expect protection from administrative fines imposed by the Commission under the competition rules. The leniency programme offers no protection from private claims seeking redress in court from cartel conduct that has been declared to infringe the competition rules.

PROTECTION AGAINST DISCLOSURE/CONFIDENTIALITY
15. Is confidentiality afforded to the leniency applicant and other co-operating parties? If so, to what extent?
The Commission will treat as confidential the fact that an application for an exemption from payment of fines or for reduction of the amount of fines has been submitted. The Commission will also maintain a separate confidential file in which the application and any other documents submitted by the applicant in connection with its application will be kept. The identity of the applicant will also be kept confidential.

15.1 Is the identity of the leniency applicant/other co-operating parties disclosed during the investigation or in the final decision?
The implementing regulation provides that the Commission (Directorate of Investigation) will include in its proposal for a final decision on the proceedings its provisional opinion on whether an exemption from payment of fines or of any reductions of the amount of fines should be granted to applicants.

The practice of the Commission is to mention the names of the applicants already at the statement of objections stage, as the identity of the applicants is thought to be an element that the addressees of the statement of objections must have access to in order to prepare an adequate response to the charges directed against them.

15.2 Is information provided by the leniency applicant/other co-operating parties passed on to other undertakings under investigation?

General administrative procedure rules provide that any person interested in the proceedings must have access to all evidentiary elements on which the statement of objections is grounded and are necessary to prepare an adequate response to the charges directed against such person.

Therefore, as will normally be the case in proceedings where leniency applications have been submitted, if the Commission relies on evidence provided by a leniency applicant in its statement of objections, the persons charged with an infringement will have access to such evidence. The evidence will cease to be confidential *vis-à-vis* these persons, at the latest, from the moment when the statement of objections is communicated to them. However, the implementing regulation restricts the right of these persons to obtain copies of any statement made by leniency applicants specifically for the purposes of the application.

15.3 Can a leniency applicant/other co-operating party request anonymity or confidentiality of information provided?

It is not necessary for a leniency applicant to request anonymity or confidentiality for the information provided in connection with its application, as the leniency programme provides that the Commission will give anonymous and confidential treatment to such information of its own motion.

16. Is the evidence submitted by the leniency applicant protected from transmission to other competition authorities with whom the authority in question co-operates? If so, how?

The leniency programme does not contain any rules on the transmission of the information provided by a leniency applicant between the Commission and other competition authorities.

In the case of exchanges within the European Competition Network, the provisions on exchange of information in Council Regulation (EC) No 1/2003 and the guidelines on exchange and use of confidential information in the European Commission's notice on co-operation within the network of competition authorities apply.

17. To what extent can evidence submitted by the leniency applicant (transcripts of oral statements or written evidence) become discoverable in subsequent private enforcement claims?

The civil procedure rules impose a general obligation on all administrative bodies (among them the Commission) to comply with any court order which requests that the documents in their files are shown to the court or that a certified copy of such documents is provided to the court. The sole exception to this obligation is where the documents in question are legally classified as secret (ie, documents whose disclosure could compromise national security).

Since a leniency application and any evidence submitted along with it will only rarely be considered to compromise national security, the Commission would be obliged to show and to issue certified copies of the information submitted by the leniency applicant, if a court so ordered in the context of private enforcement proceedings.

However, a specific civil procedure rule enabling the Commission to intervene in court proceedings dealing with issues related to the enforcement of Article 1 of the Competition Act (which contains the cartel prohibition) states that the Commission will not provide the court with information or documents obtained as a result of a leniency application.

It remains to be seen whether this specific rule will be used by the Commission to avoid providing the court with evidence submitted by leniency applicants in cases where a court so orders and the Commission is not (or is not yet) an intervener in the court proceedings. The absence of precedent, at least to our knowledge, prevents the giving of a clear answer about this issue.

17.1 Can leniency information be subjected to discovery orders in domestic courts?

Spanish civil procedure does not contemplate the type of discovery which is usual before courts in common law jurisdictions. However, Spanish courts do have the power to order that parties before the court and third parties disclose documents in their possession.

There is in principle no obstacle to a court ordering a person who is known to have applied for leniency to produce before the court any copies of the leniency application and of any evidence submitted along with it which are in its possession.

17.2 Can leniency information be subjected to discovery orders in foreign courts?

There are no specific rules on the discovery of information submitted to the Commission under the Spanish leniency programme as a result of an order issued by a foreign court.

In the case of discovery orders issued by courts of other member states in relation to evidence located in Spain, the rules on the taking of evidence in civil or commercial matters in Council Regulation (EC) No 1206/2001 would apply.

17.3 Can leniency information submitted in a foreign jurisdiction be subjected to discovery orders in domestic courts?

There are no specific rules on the discovery of information submitted to a competition authority under a foreign leniency programme as a result of an order issued by a Spanish court.

In the case of discovery orders issued by Spanish courts in relation to evidence located in other member states, the rules on the taking of evidence in civil or commercial matters in Council Regulation (EC) No 1206/2001 would apply.

18. Are there any precedents in which evidence from a leniency application has been discovered in a private enforcement claim?
There is no such precedent to our knowledge.

RELATIONSHIP WITH THE EUROPEAN COMMISSION'S LENIENCY NOTICE AND LENIENCY POLICY IN OTHER EU MEMBER STATES

19. Does the policy address the interaction with applications under the Commission Leniency Notice? If so, how?
Where a person has filed or is going to file an application for immunity from fines with the European Commission because the latter is particularly well placed to deal with the case, an abbreviated application for exemption from payment of fines may be made to the Commission.

The following rules apply in the case of abbreviated applications:
- They may only be made in those cases where the applicant is submitting evidence that is intended to enable the Commission to order an inspection.
- The European Commission will be considered to be particularly well placed to deal with the case if it has an effect on competition in more than three member states.
- Abbreviated applications must contain at least the following information:
  - name and address of the applicant;
  - names and addresses of the companies participating in the cartel;
  - products and territories affected by the cartel;
  - estimated duration and nature of the cartel;
  - member states in whose territory evidence may be found in relation to the cartel; and
  - information on the applications for exemption from payment of fines or for reduction of the amount of fines which the applicant has submitted or is going to submit to other competition authorities in relation to the same cartel.
- The Commission may require the applicant to submit additional information and set a time limit for such submission.
- Abbreviated applications will be handled according to the order in which they are entered into the registry of the Commission. The applicant may request that the Commission acknowledges receipt of an abbreviated application and that a document indicating the date and time of registration is issued.
- In the event that the Commission is eventually designated as the competition authority that is to deal with the case, the applicant will need to submit a complete application for exemption of payment

of fines, including all information and evidence required by the Spanish leniency programme. The applicant will have 10 days to prepare a complete application from the date on which the European Commission informs the applicant that the case has been assigned to the Commission.

20. Does the policy address the interaction with applications for leniency in other EU member states? If so, how?

The Spanish leniency programme does not provide for specific rules for cases where a person has already filed or intends to file leniency applications in other member states.

20.1 Does the authority accept summary applications in line with the ECN Model Leniency Programme?

The Spanish leniency programme does not contemplate the possibility of filing abbreviated leniency applications apart from cases where a person has filed or is going to file an application for immunity from fines with the European Commission because it is particularly well placed to deal with the case.

RELATIONSHIP WITH SETTLEMENT PROCEDURES
21. What is the relationship between leniency and applicable settlement procedures?

The Competition Act provides for a settlement procedure in cases where the participants in an alleged infringement offer commitments that solve any potentially negative effects on competition resulting from the conduct being investigated. In such cases, the Commission may order closure of the proceedings without finding an infringement or imposing fines, provided that the public interest is sufficiently guaranteed by the settlement.

Although the use of this settlement procedure is in principle unrestricted and therefore available without respect to the type of conduct being investigated, in the past the Commission has not considered it appropriate to make use of the settlement procedure in the case of naked cartels. Given that the leniency programme targets precisely this type of conduct, the interaction between the settlement procedure and the leniency programme, although possible in theory, is highly unlikely in practice.

21.1 Are they mutually exclusive?

The settlement procedure and the leniency programme are not mutually exclusive, in the sense that the filing of a leniency application does not in principle exclude the opening of a settlement procedure in the same proceedings.

However, in the past the Commission has not considered it appropriate to make use of the settlement procedure in the case of naked cartels, which all but excludes in practice its use where the Commission has already obtained evidence of a cartel infringement through a leniency application.

REFORM/LATEST DEVELOPMENTS
22. Is there a reform underway to revisit the leniency policy? What are the latest developments?

No reform is expected in relation to the Spanish leniency policy in the near future.

It is widely believed that several ongoing cartel investigations have been triggered by leniency applications submitted since the leniency programme entered into force in February 2008. At the time this contribution is prepared, the Commission has not adopted a final decision on any of these investigations.

However, final decisions of the Commission on some of these investigations are likely to be adopted very soon, which will provide companies and practitioners with additional guidance on the practical enforcement of the Spanish leniency programme.

Sweden

Mannheimer Swartling Tommy Pettersson, Dr Johan Carle & Elin Gilmark

BACKGROUND
1. What is the relevant legislation concerning the leniency policy and what is the enforcing body?

1.1 Relevant legislation
All aspects of Swedish competition law are governed by the Swedish Competition Act (SFS 2008:579) (the Act). The Act came into force on 1 November 2008, replacing the previous competition act of 1993. The general prohibition against anti-competitive co-operation between undertakings in chapter 2 section 1 of the Act is modelled on Article 101 of the Treaty on the Functioning of the European Union (TFUE) (former Article 81 of the EC Treaty).

In Sweden, a leniency and immunity programme has existed since 2002. The rules are applied by the Swedish Competition Authority (the SCA), in accordance with statements in the White Paper and in the general guidelines on immunity from fines and reduction of fines (KKVFS 2009:2) issued by the SCA in 2009. The guidelines are modelled on the European Commission's 2006 notice on immunity from fines and reduction of fines in cartel cases. In the guidelines, the SCA provides information on how it interprets and applies the Act's rules on immunity from fines and reduction of fines under chapter 3 sections 12-14 of the Act. The guidelines cover the immunity from fines and reduction of fines only in relation to infringements of the prohibition against restrictive agreements in chapter 2 section 1 of the Act and Article 101 TFUE, and only concerning co-operation between competitors. The guidelines are without prejudice to the interpretations made by the courts in relation to fines under the Act.

English versions of the Act and the guidelines can be found on the SCA's website *www.kkv.se*, although only the Swedish versions are authentic.

1.2 The SCA
The SCA is the enforcing body responsible for implementing and administering the Act. Although the SCA has the power to order an undertaking to terminate an infringement, it does not have the power to impose fines on companies for infringements of the Act. The SCA must apply to the Stockholm District Court for a fine to be imposed on the undertaking. Where the undertaking in question does not dispute the fines, the SCA has the right to impose binding fines on the undertaking.

2. What are the basic tenets of a leniency/immunity programme? Is leniency available also for other types of competition law violations than cartels?

Under the Act, only the undertaking first in can qualify for immunity. For participants who do not qualify for immunity, there is a chance to have their fines reduced by up to 50 per cent under chapter 3 sections 13-14 of the Act.

Leniency is available for all infringements of the prohibition against restrictive agreements (chapter 2 section 1 of the Act/Article 101 TFUE). However, undertakings that have infringed the prohibition against abuse of a dominant position (chapter 2 section 7 of the Act/Article 102 TFUE) may not be granted immunity from a fine. There is no legal definition of cartels in Swedish competition law. Although the guidelines only cover horizontal issues, all violations of chapter 2 section 1 of the Act or Article 101 TFUE may be notified to the SCA under the leniency programme.

In addition to fines, the Act introduced the possibility of imposing an injunction to prevent trading in Sweden against persons who have participated in serious breaches of chapter 2 section 1 of the Act or Article 101 TFUE, provided such an injunction is necessitated by the public interest.

In assessing whether an injunction against trading is necessitated by the public interest, special consideration is given to whether the conduct was systematic or intended to produce significant personal gain, whether such conduct caused or was intended to cause significant harm, whether the person in question has previously been convicted of criminal acts in respect of business activities and whether the conduct was intended to seriously prevent, restrict or distort competition. Therefore the cartel must have been of a serious nature and of relatively long duration for an injunction to be imposed. The SCA has recently published guidelines on leniency from injunctions against trading.

Furthermore, where the person against whom an injunction is considered has participated in giving significant assistance to the SCA's investigation of the infringement, an injunction shall not be considered necessary in the public interest. An injunction against trading may be issued against members and alternate members of the board of directors, the managing director and the deputy managing director, provided that such a person committed the previous crime in respect of business activities or was serving in such a post at the time of the infringement of the competition rules.

An injunction against trading can also be imposed against persons who, in another capacity, have in fact conducted the management of a business, or who have held themselves out to third parties as responsible for a business. Negligence in appointing, instructing and supervising staff is normally not sufficient for an injunction against trading to be imposed. The board of directors and the management are, however, obliged to take corrective action if they learn that persons within the company are engaged in cartels with competitors. If such action is not taken immediately, infringements that are committed thereafter may be relevant when assessing whether an injunction should be imposed.

Sweden

3. How many cartels have been unveiled and punished since the adoption of the leniency programme?
To our knowledge, five cartels have been unveiled and punished since the adoption of the leniency programme in 2002.

4. What is needed to be a successful leniency applicant? Is documentary evidence required or is testimonial evidence sufficient?
There are two possibilities for obtaining full leniency. Firstly, an applicant can receive immunity if it submits information not previously accessible to the SCA, which enables the SCA to take action against the infringement. Secondly, when the SCA already has sufficient material to take action against the infringement, full leniency may be granted provided that: (i) the applicant is the first to provide information that establishes infringement; or (ii) the applicant in some other way has to a very significant extent facilitated the investigation of the infringement. In either case, the applicant must also fulfil the following criteria:
(i) the applicant must provide all the information and documents available to it about the infringement to the SCA;
(ii) the applicant must actively co-operate with the SCA during the investigation of the infringement;
(iii) the applicant must not destroy evidence or in other ways hinder the investigation of the infringement; and
(iv) the applicant must stop its participation in the infringement as soon as possible after submitting the application or after it has provided the information.

The information that needs to be provided by the applicant includes the following:
- what the co-operation concerns;
- the goods or services and the geographical area the co-operation encompassed;
- which undertakings have participated in the co-operation;
- when the co-operation was initiated and when it was concluded;
- the contacts that have been established between the undertakings who have taken part in the co-operation and the contents of these meetings;
- when the contacts occurred;
- what the participating undertakings have done to facilitate and implement the infringement;
- who within the undertaking is able to provide information about the infringement; and
- who in competing undertakings has participated in the infringement.

Furthermore, undertakings that are not first in and thus do not qualify for immunity may benefit from a reduction of any fine that would otherwise have been imposed. In order to qualify for a reduction of fines, the undertaking must provide the SCA with information that facilitates the investigation of the infringement to a significant extent. In order to qualify for a reduction, the undertaking in question must fulfil the above conditions ((i)-(iv)). It is necessary that the undertaking provides the information, which may be written or verbal, voluntarily. Verbal information should be documented, eg, through tape recordings or signed statements.

TIMING
5. What are the benefits of being 'first in' to co-operate?
Only the first applicant can qualify for full leniency (see question 8 below).

6. What are the consequences of being 'second'? Is there an 'immunity plus' or 'amnesty plus' option?
As described above (see question 4), undertakings that are not first in do not qualify for immunity, but may benefit from a reduction of any fine that would otherwise have been imposed. Only one undertaking may be granted full immunity and the undertaking in second place may receive a reduced fine under chapter 3 section 13 of the Act if the undertaking fulfils the conditions that apply for immunity as mentioned in question 4. The SCA decides in its writ of summons whether the information an undertaking has provided has added considerable value, and the level of reduction. The reduction for the first undertaking to provide information adding considerable value will be between 30 and 50 per cent and for the second undertaking the reduction will be 20 to 30 per cent. For other undertakings the reduction will be up to 20 per cent.

7. Are subsequent firms given any beneficial treatment if they make a useful contribution? How are 'useful contributions' defined?
Fines will be reduced by 20-30 per cent for the second undertaking to fulfil the conditions for reduction of fines. Fines for other undertakings that fulfil the relevant conditions will be reduced by up to 20 per cent. In determining the level of reduction within these categories, the SCA will take into account at what time the information was provided, to what extent the information added value, and to what extent and with what continuity the undertaking has co-operated with the SCA subsequent to the information being provided.

SCOPE/FULL LENIENCY
8. Is it possible to receive full leniency? If so, what are the conditions required to receive full leniency?
Full leniency may be granted to the first applicant that fulfils the criteria described above (see question 4).

8.1 Can ringleaders/coercers receive full leniency?
No, undertakings that have compelled others to participate in the infringement may not be granted leniency from fines according to chapter 2 section 12 paragraph 3 of the Act.

8.2 If there is a requirement to 'co-operate fully and on an on-going basis' what does it entail?
Chapter 3 Article 14 point 2 states that in order to be granted full leniency a company must actively co-operate with the SCA during the investigation

Sweden

of the infringement. According to the SCA's guidelines on immunity from fines and reduction from fines the requirement to 'actively co-operate with the Competition Authority during the investigation of the infringement' entails that the applicant must place its employees and, if possible, previous employees, at the disposal of the SCA. The applicant must also, without reminder from the SCA and without delay, submit such information and documentation that concerns the infringement and that the applicant becomes aware of after the notification has been made. This requirement also encompasses the processing of the matter in court.

Applicants for leniency or reduction of fines must also comply with four conditions:
(i) to provide the SCA with all information and evidence about the infringement available to it;
(ii) to actively co-operate with the SCA during the investigation;
(iii) not to destroy evidence or in another way hinder the investigation of the infringement; and
(iv) to stop its participation in the infringement as soon as possible after an application or after it has provided the information.

8.3 Does the regulatory authority require the applicant to cease participation in the cartel conduct after its application?
Yes. As described above (see question 4), in order to qualify for immunity or reduction of fines, the applicant must cease its participation in the infringement as soon as possible after submitting the application.

9. How many companies have received full immunity from fines to date?
To our knowledge, two companies have received full immunity from fines since the adoption of the leniency programme.

PROCEDURE
10. What are the practical steps required to apply for leniency?
If an undertaking wishes to take advantage of the leniency programme, it should contact the SCA for an assessment of its chances of qualifying for immunity from, or a reduction of, fines. An undertaking may contact the SCA anonymously and describe the infringement in hypothetical terms. If the information submitted by the undertaking is not sufficient for the SCA to be able to assess whether the undertaking fulfils the conditions for obtaining immunity, the SCA will inform the undertaking of this fact. The undertaking may then take a decision on whether to provide more precise information. Based on the information submitted by the undertaking, the SCA will take a preliminary position as to whether the conditions for immunity have been fulfilled at the time of the anonymous contact. This position is not legally binding on the SCA. Neither can the SCA guarantee that another undertaking will not report the infringement before the anonymous undertaking has made its report. The contact must be made by a person empowered to represent the undertaking. The undertaking cannot

qualify for immunity until a formal application has been filed with the SCA. The notification should contain the information stated under question 4 above. This application should normally be made in writing and signed by a person empowered to represent the undertaking. However, the SCA has, in practice, recently accepted oral applications since undertakings have hesitated to file written applications owing to the risk that the material will be used in proceedings for damages in the US. The undertaking should provide the name, address and telephone number of a contact. The undertaking should also state whether it has reported the infringement to another competition authority within the European Union.

Leniency applicants may contact the SCA in any of the following ways: Tel: +46 8 700 15 99, Fax: +46 8 700 15 98, email: *eftergift_kkv@kkv.se,* and for further information refer to *www.kkv.se.*

There is no marker system in Sweden. As stated above, the undertaking contemplating notification of a cartel may initially contact the SCA anonymously and present information in hypothetical terms to clarify with the SCA whether it is in a position to qualify for immunity. However, a formal application is required for the undertaking to qualify for immunity from, or reduction of, fines. Undertakings that consider themselves to be entitled to reduction of fines should notify the SCA of this fact when they approach the SCA to voluntarily submit evidence on the infringement. Regarding the final reduction, see question 12.

11. Is there an optimal time to approach the regulatory authority?

Please also refer to question 11 in the EU chapter of this book, since similar factors and considerations are relevant in the context of the Swedish leniency programme. In order to improve the chances of being granted full immunity from fines under the Swedish leniency programme, the undertaking should file an application with the SCA as soon as it has gathered the necessary information. Otherwise, it runs the risk that one of the other participants may 'blow the whistle' first, considerably limiting the undertaking's chance of qualifying for leniency.

12. What guarantees of leniency exist if a party co-operates?

If the SCA finds that qualification for immunity is a possibility, it will notify the undertaking. The applicant then has the right to apply for the SCA to make a written statement as to whether it submitted its report before the SCA had sufficient evidence to take measures against the infringement, and if the undertaking has been the first to report the infringement. Such a decision is binding on the SCA as well as the Stockholm District Court and the Market Court. However, in order to receive immunity, the applicant must still fulfil the conditions described above (see question 4). Moreover, whether these conditions have been fulfilled is officially guaranteed when the SCA sends its preliminary assessment, and immunity is officially granted when the SCA submits its summons application regarding the infringement to the Stockholm District Court.

CONSEQUENCES
13. What effects does leniency granted to a corporate defendant have on the defendant's employees? Does it protect them from criminal and/or civil liability?
There are no criminal sanctions for any violation of the Act. As stated under question 2, persons who have participated in serious breaches of chapter 2 section 1 of the Act or Article 101 TFUE may be subject to injunction against trading in Sweden. The SCA may apply for an injunction against trading either in conjunction with an action for administrative fines or in separate proceedings in a district court. The SCA's guidelines on injunction against trading for breaches of the competition provisions (to be found at *www.kkv.se*) states that employees are embraced by the company's application for leniency or reduction of fines. Persons who are no longer employees of the company will not be included in the application, nor will employees who actively oppose the company's leniency application or the company's filing of information to obtain leniency or reduction of fines. Moreover, the SCA will not make individual declarations for the employees of the applicant. The SCA will apply the same rules to companies that have been granted immunity or reduction of fines by other EU member states or by the European Commission.

14. Does leniency bar further private enforcement?
No, leniency does not prevent claims for private damages.

PROTECTION AGAINST DISCLOSURE/CONFIDENTIALITY
15. Is confidentiality afforded to the leniency applicant and other co-operating parties? If so, to what extent?
In Sweden, there is a principle of public access to official records, laid down in the Swedish Press Act and the Secrecy Act (2009:400). Consequently, the public has the right to access all non-classified information. Confidentiality applies to investigations by the SCA into infringements of chapter 2 section 1 of the Act or Article 101 TFUE if, considering the object of the investigation, it is of 'exceptional importance' that the information is not disclosed. The normal secrecy rules apply after an investigation is closed and confidentiality applies to information concerning an individual's business or operational circumstances, if it can be assumed that the individual would suffer damage if the information is disclosed.

15.1 Is the identity of the leniency applicant/other co-operating parties disclosed during the investigation or in the final decision?
Besides the provisions mentioned above, the Secrecy Act ensures confidentiality for informants and information submitted to the SCA by such persons if the individual in question will suffer substantial damage or considerable detriment if the information is disclosed.

15.2 Is information provided by the leniency applicant/other co-operating parties passed on to other undertakings under investigation?

Confidentiality will always be subject to the parties' right of access to the SCA's file. Parties have full access unless it is of particular importance from a public or individual perspective that the information is not revealed.

15.3 Can a leniency applicant/other co-operating party request anonymity or confidentiality of information provided?

Requests for confidentiality made by the submitting party are not legally binding and cannot release the SCA from considering a third party's request to access the information. However, such request or confidentiality markings on documents may informally function as a 'warning signal' to the authority. If the SCA's decision to classify the documents is appealed, disclosure of documents is finally to be decided by a court.

16. Is the evidence submitted by the leniency applicant protected from transmission to other competition authorities with whom the authority in question co-operates? If so, how?

It follows from paragraph 40 of the Commission's Notice on co-operation within the network of competition authorities that information voluntarily submitted by a leniency applicant will only be transmitted to another member of the network pursuant to Article 12 of Council Regulation 1/2003 with the consent of the applicant. Similarly, other information that has been obtained during or following an inspection or by means of or following any other fact-finding measures which, in each case, could not have been carried out except as a result of the leniency application, will only be transmitted if the applicant has consented to the transmission to that authority of information it has voluntarily submitted in its application for leniency. Once the leniency applicant has given consent to the transmission of information to another authority, that consent may not be withdrawn.

17. To what extent can evidence submitted by the leniency applicant (transcripts of oral statements or written evidence) become discoverable in subsequent private enforcement claims? Can leniency information be subjected to discovery orders in domestic courts?

Firstly, the principle of public access to official records (see question 15 above) enables any third party to request access to the documents directly from the SCA. The authority must however, before disclosing any document, always consider whether the information at hand shall be deemed classified.

Secondly, there is no Swedish equivalent to the extensive, US- and UK-style, discovery/disclosure procedures. A request for production of documents in Swedish courts must contain a description of the requested document which is sufficient to identify it, or, if the request concerns a category of documents, a description in sufficient detail of a narrow and specific requested category of documents. The ability to request documents by reference to a category does not preclude the requirement for the request to be narrow and specific. These rules are designed to prevent extensive document production and 'fishing expeditions'. Moreover, the requesting party must submit a description of how the documents requested are relevant and material to the outcome of the case. However, there seems to be no obvious practical reason for a document request to be brought against a Swedish authority (even though this should be possible from a formal perspective). If documents are to be requested from a Swedish authority the most apparent way to do so is by claiming that it contains public information. Should an authority deny a document request, this decision may be overruled by a court if it can be assumed that the documents could be used as evidence in litigation. In other words, documents containing business secrets may be recovered, but the court must find that there are exceptional reasons why the documents should be delivered.

17.1 Can leniency information be subjected to discovery orders in foreign courts? Can leniency information submitted in a foreign jurisdiction be subjected to discovery orders in domestic courts?

As pointed out above, there is no Swedish equivalent to the extensive, US- and UK-style, discovery/disclosure procedures. Discovery orders by foreign courts may not immediately be executed in Sweden. Instead the Swedish court will try the case and apply Swedish law. As stated above, Swedish law prohibits 'fishing expeditions' and in this context it is noticeable that when signing the Hague Convention of 18 March 1970, Sweden expressly declared that it would not confirm a request ordering someone to 'produce any documents other than particular documents specified in the [request]'. However, this may mean that if the document request is specific and in other regards meets the legal requirements, a Swedish court may order that the documents be delivered to the applicant. Furthermore, as stated above, if documents are held by a Swedish authority, it is recommended to request access to the documents directly from the authority.

Through the international agreements that Sweden is party to, it is formally possible for Swedish courts to ask foreign courts for assistance with taking evidence. It is not possible to give a general comment on the actual outcome of such requests as they depend greatly on the other country and the applicable international treaty. The jurisdiction of Swedish courts is in all other respects limited to the Swedish territory.

18. Are there any precedents in which evidence from a leniency application has been discovered in a private enforcement claim?

To the best of our knowledge there are no Swedish precedents in which evidence from a leniency application has been discovered in a private enforcement claim. However, if a third party has requested and been granted access to documents held by a Swedish authority, the authority in question is not allowed to ask for the party's identity. Hence, it is not possible to know whether evidence in subsequent private enforcement claims derive from the SCA.

RELATIONSHIP WITH THE EUROPEAN COMMISSION'S LENIENCY NOTICE AND LENIENCY POLICY IN OTHER EU MEMBER STATES

19. Does the policy address the interaction with applications under the Commission Leniency Notice? If so, how?

The policy does not explicitly address the interaction with applications under the Commission Leniency Notice or with policies adopted in other EU member states.

20. Does the policy address the interaction with applications for leniency in other EU member states? If so, how? Does the authority accept summary applications in line with the ECN Model Leniency Programme?

See question 19.

RELATIONSHIP WITH SETTLEMENT PROCEDURES

21. What is the relationship between leniency and applicable settlement procedures? Are they mutually exclusive?

Under certain circumstances, the SCA may impose a fine on an undertaking without applying to the Stockholm District Court, provided that the undertaking in question does not dispute the fine. This procedure may also be used for reduction of fines.

REFORM/LATEST DEVELOPMENTS

22. Is there a reform underway to revisit the leniency policy? What are the latest developments?

When the new Swedish Competition Act entered into force in November 2008, the rules on leniency were amended in order to adjust them to the model used on a European level. The SCA has recently published guidelines on its interpretation and application of the provision on leniency regarding injunctions against trading.

Switzerland

Homburger Dr Franz Hoffet, Dr Marcel Dietrich & Dr Gerald Brei

BACKGROUND
1. What is the relevant legislation concerning the leniency policy and what is the enforcing body?
The relevant legislation in Switzerland is the Federal Act on Cartels and other Restraints of Competition of 6 October 1995 (ACart). Despite substantial improvements to the substantive and procedural rules, the enforcement instruments under ACart were not sufficiently effective. In particular, when both the United States and the European Commission imposed substantial fines after the vitamins cartel was discovered, Switzerland, which did not have a policy on imposing fines for first-time infringements, could not impose fines against the companies involved in the cartel in Switzerland. This situation triggered an additional amendment to ACart in 2003 which entered into force on 1 April 2004. This amendment introduced the Competition Commission's power to order substantial fines against first-time infringements of the most important substantive rules and a leniency system.

Unlawful agreements are subject to the provisions of Article 5 ACart. In terms of the intensity of the restraint of competition, three types of unlawful agreements are to be distinguished:
- agreements that do not significantly affect competition – such agreements are lawful;
- agreements that significantly affect competition – such agreements may be justified on grounds of economic efficiency; and
- agreements which eliminate effective competition – such agreements are unlawful.

Article 5(3) and (4) ACart defines types of agreements which are presumed to lead to the elimination of effective competition. Only these types of agreements, apart from illegal practices by market-dominant companies (Article 7 ACart), can be directly sanctioned according to Article 49a(1) ACart. In contrast, first-time infringements in the case of agreements that significantly affect competition and which cannot be justified on grounds of economic efficiency can arguably not be sanctioned. This view, however, is controversial; it has not yet been tested in court. Members of the Swiss competition authorities have published articles defending the opposite viewpoint. The maximum fine may amount to up to 10 per cent of the turnover achieved in Switzerland during the last three business years. The amount shall be calculated on the basis of the duration and severity of the illegal conduct and the presumed profit resulting from it shall be duly taken into account (Article 49a(1) ACart).

Under Article 5(3), ACart the following horizontal agreements among actual or potential competitors are presumed to lead to the elimination of effective competition:
- agreements directly or indirectly fixing prices;
- agreements restricting the quantities of goods or services to be produced, bought or supplied; and
- agreements allocating markets geographically or according to trading partners.

According to Article 5(4) ACart, agreements between undertakings on different market levels (ie, vertical agreements) regarding minimum or fixed prices as well as clauses in distribution agreements regarding the allocation of territories, provided distributors from other territories are prohibited from sales into these territories, are presumed to eliminate effective competition. The latter provision regarding exclusive distributorship agreements has to be seen in the context of the debate in Swiss Parliament. Prior to the 2003 amendment, there were political and public controversies regarding the price level in Switzerland, quite often referred to as 'high-price island' within Europe. The reason for these allegedly high prices has been attributed, among others, to certain vertical restraints.

A company that acts illegally according to Article 7 ACart can also be fined according to Article 49a(1) ACart. Article 7(1) ACart provides that practices of undertakings holding a dominant position are deemed unlawful when such undertakings, through the abuse of their position, prevent other undertakings from entering or competing in the market, or when they injure trading partners. As a consequence, under this provision both the abuse of dominance against competitors and against down-stream or up-stream trading partners may be unlawful. This is further confirmed by a list of examples of such abuses in Article 7(2) ACart which includes refusals to deal, discrimination between trading partners, the imposition of unfair prices or conditions, predatory pricing, restrictions of production, outlets or technical developments or tying. The definition of abuses of dominant positions is very similar to the one in Article 102 of the Treaty on the Functioning of the European Union (formerly Article 82 EC). As in other jurisdictions, conduct of dominant companies may be justified on the basis of legitimate business reasons. If the conduct of a dominant undertaking is held to be unlawful, it is subject to first-time infringement fines based on Article 49a(1) ACart.

The 2003 amendment also introduced a clear legal basis for coercive measures in connection with investigations by the competition authorities and a leniency programme. According to Article 49a(2) ACart, the sanction may be waived, in whole or in part, if the enterprise co-operates in uncovering and eliminating the restraint of competition. The conditions and the procedure for full or partial exemption from sanctions under Article 49a(2) ACart are contained in the Ordinance on Sanctions regarding illegal restraints of competition of 12 March 2004 (OS ACart). In addition, this Ordinance contains provisions regarding the rules for the calculation of fines.

In Switzerland, apart from private enforcement before civil courts, only federal administrative bodies (the Competition Commission and its Secretariat) have the power to implement ACart. The main administrative body enforcing ACart is the Competition Commission which is elected by the federal government (Article 18(1) ACart). The Competition Commission is composed of a number of between 11 and 15 members. Its majority has to consist of so-called independent experts who are usually either legal or economic scholars (Article 18(2) ACart). The remaining members of the Competition Commission are usually recruited from among the leading members of trade associations, unions, consumer groups, representatives of retailers and of agricultural production associations. The Competition Commission is independent of the federal government (Article 19(1) ACart). For administrative purposes, it is attached to the Federal Department of Economic Affairs. The Competition Commission is the sole administrative body having power to issue decisions prohibiting certain conduct, agreements or concentrations of undertakings. It is also the only administrative body having power to impose fines (Article 53(1) ACart).

The Secretariat of the Competition Commission conducts investigations and preliminary investigations and prepares the Competition Commission's decisions (Article 23(1) ACart). The Secretariat has no power to open investigations by itself, rather it may only do so with the consent of a member of the presiding body of the Competition Commission (Article 27(1) ACart). Equally, procedural decisions must be issued by a member of the presiding body of the Competition Commission (Article 23(1) ACart). The Competition Commission's Secretariat consists of more than 50 professionals (lawyers and economists) and is divided into three services (product markets, services, and infrastructure). In addition, the Secretariat consists of six competence centres (law, economics, internal market, international affairs, communications and investigations). The Secretariat is led by an executive management board consisting of a Director, a Deputy Director, two Vice Directors, and the Head of Resources and Logistics (*www.weko.admin.ch/sekretariat*).

Decisions rendered by the Competition Commission, including decisions on leniency, are subject to an appeal to the Federal Court for Administrative Matters (Article 33 lit. f of the Federal Act on the Court of Administrative Matters in conjunction with Article 39 ACart). Its decisions may be subject to an appeal to the Federal Supreme Court (Article 86(1) lit. a of the Federal Act on the Federal Court).

2. What are the basic tenets of a leniency/immunity programme? Is leniency available also for other types of competition law violations than cartels?

The leniency rules were introduced through the 2003 amendment to ACart, although initially there was strong opposition in Parliament to this regime because it allegedly puts a premium on denunciations, contrary to Swiss legal traditions. According to Article 49a(2) ACart, a company taking part in the disclosure and removal of a restraint of competition may benefit from a full or partial waiver of fines. Although OS ACart explicitly regulates the application of a full or partial waiver of fines only in cases of horizontal and vertical agreements according to Article 5(3) and 5(4) ACart, it is widely held, based on the wording of Article 49(a) ACart, that a waiver is also available in the case of illegal practices by market-dominant companies according to Article 7 ACart, if the necessary requirements are fulfilled.

The OS ACart specifies that full waivers are available to first-movers only, for information leading to the opening of an investigation based on Article 5(3) and (4) ACart or for submitting evidence permitting the discovery of an infringement of these provisions (Article 8 OS ACart, also with additional prerequisites – see question 8 for all prerequisites). The provisions referred to define the types of horizontal and vertical agreements which are presumed to lead to the elimination of effective competition (see question 1 for further details).

Partial waivers of fines are available to companies participating voluntarily in an investigation and which, at the time the evidence is submitted, have ceased their participation in the anti-competitive practice. The reduction may amount to a maximum of 50 per cent. It is determined based on the role played by the enterprise in the success of the proceeding (Article 12(2) OS ACart). If additional infringements of Article 5(3) or (4) ACart are discovered on the basis of its participation, the reduction can be up to 80 per cent of the amount calculated according to Articles 3 through 7 OS ACart if a company submits, on an unsolicited basis, information or evidence on these additional anti-competitive practices (Article 12(3) OS ACart). Leniency applications may be made orally and anonymously (Article 9 OS ACart).

The calculation of the fine shall be based on the duration and severity of the illegal conduct. The presumed profit resulting from the illegal conduct shall be duly taken into account (Article 2 OS ACart). Depending on the severity and type of infringement, the basic amount of the fine shall be up to 10 per cent of the turnover which the enterprise concerned achieved in the relevant markets in Switzerland during the last three business years (Article 3 OS ACart). This basic amount of the fine can be increased by up to 50 per cent if the competition infringement lasted between one and five years. If the infringement lasted more than five years, the basic amount of the fine shall be increased by up to 10 per cent for each additional year (Article 4 OS ACart).

In the case of aggravating circumstances, the basic amount of the fine can be increased. This is in particular the case if the enterprise has repeatedly infringed ACart, has achieved a particularly high profit through an infringement or has refused to co-operate with the authorities or has otherwise attempted to obstruct the investigation (Article 5(1) OS ACart). In cases of restraints of competition according to Article 5(3) and (4) ACart, the amount can be additionally increased if the enterprise has instigated the restraint of competition or played a leading role in connection with it, or, in order to enforce the understanding affecting competition, has ordered or carried out retaliatory measures against others involved in the restraint of competition (Article 5(2) OS ACart).

In the case of mitigating circumstances, the basic amount of the fine can be reduced. This is particularly the case if the enterprise has terminated the restraint of competition after the first intervention by the Competition Commission's Secretariat, but no later than prior to the opening of a proceeding (Article 6(1) OS ACart). In the case of a restraint of competition according to Article 5(3) and (4) ACart, the basic amount of the fine can be reduced if the enterprise has only played a passive role or has not carried out retaliatory measures agreed upon in order to enforce the understanding affecting competition (Article 6(2) OS ACart).

3. How many cartels have been unveiled and punished since the adoption of the leniency programme?

The Revised Act on Cartels effective on 1 April 2004 contained a transitional provision according to which no fine could be levied if an existent restriction of competition was notified or cancelled within a year following the enactment of Article 49a ACart. This grace period ended on 31 March 2005 so that an application for leniency only made sense after that date. Since then, several cartels have been unveiled and punished. With respect to full or partial waivers of fines, three cases are worth mentioning:

- On 18 September 2006, the Competition Commission found that the Airport Zurich AG (Unique) abused its dominant position by preventing other companies from offering 'off airport valet parking' services, thus violating Article 7 ACart. It penalised Unique according to Article 49a ACart. As Unique co-operated with the Competition Commission during the later stage of the investigation and allowed the involved companies to offer their parking services again, the Competition Commission partially reduced the fine. However, the reduction was not granted on the basis of a leniency application. Rather, it was based on the fact that Unique co-operated with the competition authorities, leading to an amicable settlement of the matter between the Competition Commission and Unique.
- On 15 August 2007, Felco SA, a company producing, *inter alia*, scissors for gardening purposes, contacted the Secretariat and made a leniency application concerning a vertical agreement between Felco SA and a retailer, Landi, on minimum prices (resale price maintenance). The Competition Commission initiated an investigation and considered this agreement to be unlawful, violating Article 5(4) ACart. Felco SA requested that a full waiver of fines be granted on the basis of its leniency application. The Competition Commission, however, fined both companies involved, including Felco SA. It acknowledged that Felco SA informed the competition authorities about the unlawful agreement and, subsequently, co-operated in the investigation, leading to an amicable settlement of the matter. However, the Competition Commission refused to fully waive the fine as Felco SA had taken a leading role in acting contrary to the ACart (Article 8(2) lit. a OS ACart).
- On 31 January 2008, the Secretariat of the Competition Commission conducted dawn raids against various companies in the electric

Switzerland

installation sector in order to investigate allegedly illegal arrangements (bid riggings) among competitors in public procurement biddings in the Berne region. After the investigation was concluded, the Competition Commission decided that the practices violated Article 5(3) ACart, and it fined the companies involved accordingly. The enterprise, which had been the first to announce full co-operation after the dawn raid was started, was granted a reduction of 100 per cent, whereas the other companies were given a reduction of 40 per cent. Thus, the waiver, and the reductions were not granted on the basis of a leniency application before the investigation was initiated by the Competition Commission. Rather, they were approved because the companies fully co-operated in uncovering and eliminating the restraint of competition in question after the investigation was already underway.

Moreover, there are certain indications that a number of pending investigations have been triggered by leniency applications.

4. What is needed to be a successful leniency applicant? Is documentary evidence required or is testimonial evidence sufficient?

The kind of evidence that is needed for a successful leniency application is dependent on the information and evidence the Competition Commission already has at the time of the application. For a full waiver of fines, therefore, one of the following requirements must be met:

- If the competition authorities have no previous knowledge of the restraint of competition, the enterprise seeking leniency should deliver information which enables the competition authorities to open an investigation under Article 27 ACart (Article 8(1) OS ACart). The waiver of the sanction, however, shall in this case only be granted if the competition authority does not already have information sufficient to open proceedings regarding the restraint of competition (Article 8(3) OS ACart).
- If the competition authorities already have knowledge of the restraint of competition, the enterprise seeking a full waiver of sanctions should submit evidence which enables the competition authorities to establish a competition infringement under Article 5(3) or (4) ACart. The waiver of the sanction in this case shall only be granted if no other enterprise already fulfills the prerequisites for a waiver according to Article 8(1) OS ACart and the competition authority does not already have evidence sufficient to prove the anti-competitive practice (Article 8(4) OS ACart).

Oral information may thus be sufficient if it brings the competition restriction to the competition authority's attention (cf Article 9(1) OS ACart according to which the leniency application can also be stated orally for the record). If the competition authority is already aware of the reported infringement, the submission of documentary evidence, or witness testimony, is needed for a successful leniency application, provided that no other enterprise has previously co-operated with the competition authority.

TIMING
5. What are the benefits of being 'first in' to co-operate?
The benefits of being 'first in' to co-operate are a full waiver of the sanction provided that all prerequisites for such a waiver are fulfilled (for further details see question 8).

A corporate leniency statement should contain the necessary information regarding the notifying enterprise, the type of anti-competitive practice notified, the companies participating in such practice and the relevant markets affected. The corporate leniency statement may also be made orally for the record (Article 9(1) OS ACart). The enterprise may even submit the corporate leniency statement by presenting the information in anonymous form (Article 9(2) OS ACart). The Secretariat can define the modalities of the corporate leniency statement on a case-by-case basis with the consent of a member of the presiding body of the Competition Commission (Article 9(2) OS ACart). As general guidance, the Secretariat has issued an application form that is available (also in English) on its website (see question 10).

Since time is of the essence for leniency applications, the Secretariat shall confirm receipt of the corporate leniency statement ('marker'), including the date and time of receipt. It shall communicate to the notifying enterprise, with the consent of a member of the presiding body of the Competition Commission, as to:
- whether it considers the prerequisites for a complete waiver of the sanction according to Article 8(1) OS ACart to be fulfilled; however, a leniency applicant should take into consideration that this communication may contain an important caveat, ie, that a complete waiver is subject to the condition that the applicant has neither forced any other enterprise to participate in the alleged cartel nor played an instigating or leading role in it;
- the additional information which the notifying enterprise should submit, in particular in order to fulfill the prerequisites according to Article 8(1) OS ACart; and
- in the case of an anonymous corporate leniency statement, the time period within which the enterprise should disclose its identity (see Article 9(3) OS ACart).

In the case of multiple corporate leniency statements, the competition authority shall examine subsequent corporate leniency statements only upon having decided according to Article 9(3) OS ACart on the earlier corporate leniency statements (Article 10 OS ACart). The Competition Commission decides on the full waiver of the sanction. It may only deviate from a communication of the Secretariat according to Article 9(3)(a) OS ACart if it subsequently becomes aware of facts preventing the waiver of the sanction (Article 11 OS ACart). The fact that the ultimate decision on a full waiver of the fine will be made only at the very end of the proceedings is a considerable drawback for leniency applicants. Until then, there may be quite a long period of uncertainty without any full guarantee from the competition authority.

6. What are the consequences of being 'second'? Is there an 'immunity plus' or 'amnesty plus' option?

As set out under question 5, the full exemption from sanctions can only be granted to one single enterprise, the one who first reports to the authorities. When another enterprise meets the requirements stated in Articles 8 and 9 OS ACart but does not qualify for full exemption due to the lack of priority in the timing or for other reasons, it can still benefit from a reduction of the fine in the context of partial exemption provisions.

The Competition Commission can reduce the sanction if a company has participated on an unsolicited basis in a proceeding, and, at the time the evidence is submitted, has ceased participation in the anti-competitive practice (Article 12(1) OS ACart). The fine can be reduced by up to 50 per cent, depending on the extent to which the enterprise contributes to the success of the proceedings (Article 12(2) OS ACart). The reduction may even be up to 80 per cent of the amount of the sanction when a company provides information or evidence on an unsolicited basis regarding further competition infringements pursuant to Article 5(3) or (4) ACart (Article 12(3) OS ACart).

The enterprise seeking a partial exemption from sanctions has to contact the Secretariat of the Competition Commission and submit the necessary information regarding its identity and activities, the type of anti-competitive practice denounced, the companies participating in such practice, and the relevant markets affected. The Secretariat shall confirm receipt of the evidence, including the date and time of receipt (Article 13 OS ACart). It is the Competition Commission which will decide on the amount of the reduction granted to the co-operating enterprise. Should the co-operating enterprise submit to the Competition Commission evidence on the duration of the anti-competitive practice of which the Commission was unaware until then, the latter shall calculate the sanction without taking this time period into consideration (Article 14 OS ACart).

7. Are subsequent firms given any beneficial treatment if they make a useful contribution? How are 'useful contributions' defined?

The reduction of the sanction is not an option that is limited to the second enterprise which co-operates with the Competition Commission. As long as the enterprise concerned participates on an unsolicited basis in a proceeding and has ceased participation in the anti-competitive practice when starting the co-operation with the authority, the benefit of a reduced sanction can be granted (see question 3). Of course, the more participants in an anti-competitive practice which are co-operating with the Competition Commission, the more difficult it will become to play a substantial role in the success of the proceeding (Article 12(2) OS ACart). This is why it might be difficult to reach the same level of reduction as a previous co-operating enterprise. At the same time, however, if a subsequent firm voluntarily submits information or evidence on further anti-competitive practices, the option of a reduction of up to 80 per cent of the amount of the sanction would be fully available to this enterprise coming forward later than the other participants (Article 12(3) OS ACart). The 'useful contributions' may thus be defined along the lines of whether they enable the Competition Commission to better prove the illegal behaviour already under scrutiny or to start a new investigation.

SCOPE/FULL LENIENCY
8. Is it possible to receive full leniency? If so, what are the conditions required to receive full leniency? Does the regulatory authority require the applicant to cease participation in the cartel conduct after its application? Can ringleaders/coercers receive full leniency? If there is a requirement to 'co-operate fully and on an ongoing basis' what does it entail?

A full exemption from sanctions is possible. As already set out in question 4, a full waiver of the sanction is possible if the enterprise notifies its participation in an unlawful restraint of competition and is the first to provide information enabling the Competition Commission to open proceedings or is first to submit evidence enabling the Competition Commission to discover an illegal restraint of competition according to Article 5(3) and (4) ACart (Article 8(1) OS ACart).

In both cases, the following further requirements must be cumulatively satisfied (Article 8(2) OS ACart). The enterprise:
- should not have forced any other enterprise to participate in the infringement of competition and should not have played the instigating or leading role in it;
- should submit to the Competition Commission on an unsolicited basis all information and evidence concerning the infringement of competition in its possession;
- should co-operate continuously, without reservations and delay with the competition authority during the entire duration of the proceeding; and
- should cease its participation in the infringement of competition no later than at the time of its leniency application or upon first order by the competition authority.

Moreover, the waiver of the sanction is not possible if the competition authority already has sufficient information to open an investigation regarding the restraint of competition according to Articles 26 and 27 ACart (Article 8(1)(3) OS ACart) or has already sufficient evidence to prove the anti-competitive practice (Article 8(1)(4) OS ACart). However, the Competition Commission made it clear that it is not impossible for a company to receive full leniency even in a case where the leniency application is filed only at the time of a dawn raid (see question 3). Whereas it is excluded by the very fact of the dawn raid to provide information enabling the Competition Commission to open a proceeding, it is still possible to submit evidence enabling the authority to prove an illegal restraint of competition, unless the authority already has sufficient evidence. The company being raided may still opt to provide suitable evidence voluntarily and unsolicitedly. A company is only obliged to endure the house search, but not forced to actively support it. The company representatives do, however, have the possibility to apply for full leniency during a dawn raid and to offer full co-operation with the authorities. Even if full leniency is excluded because there has been a previous applicant, the voluntary handing over of evidence may lead to a reduction of the fine (see questions 6 and 7).

It is evident from the above list of prerequisites, which have to be cumulatively fulfilled, that it might be difficult for a company to know whether or not it could be barred from being qualified for full leniency. An 'instigating' or 'leading' role may well be debatable depending on the specific circumstances. In case of serious doubts in that respect, a company may decide to abstain from applying for leniency, at least if only a full waiver of the sanction is an acceptable outcome.

Staff members of the Secretariat have publicly stated that appealing against a dawn raid or a sequestration may put at risk the advantages of a leniency application. The Secretariat takes the position that the duty of continuous and unreserved co-operation without delay can hardly be reconciled with raising a complaint or bringing an appeal against investigation measures. Companies may thus be prevented from having recourse to legal remedies after having filed a leniency application. The legality of the position taken by the secretariat has, however, not yet been tested in court.

9. How many companies have received full immunity from fines to date?

At the time of writing, only in one case has a company received full immunity from fines. This case concerned the illegal arrangements (bid rigging) among competitors in public procurement biddings. The company, which was the first to announce full co-operation after the dawn raid had started, was granted a full waiver of fines (see question 3).

PROCEDURE
10. What are the practical steps required to apply for leniency?

The Competition Commission provides on its website (*www.weko.admin. ch*) a leniency application form in which it summarises the necessary information for filing an application (setting out in more detail the information indicated in Articles 9(1) and 13 OS ACart). The headings in the form mention the enterprise seeking leniency, the type of the restraint of competition, the companies that participated in the restraint of competition, a description of the affected markets and the evidence to be submitted. The application form is also available in English (*www.weko. admin.ch/dienstleistungen/00106/index.html?lang=en*).

The Competition Commission advises that leniency applications should be made to the Secretariat by sending the form by fax, by hand delivery, or by submitting it orally for the record. The reason for this is that it could be difficult for the Secretariat to determine the exact order of receipt of applications sent by post. Applications which are sent by email or made by phone will not be considered as having been validly filed. The application must be filed at:

Secretariat of the Swiss Competition Commission
Monbijoustrasse 43
CH-3003 Bern
Fax: +41 31 322 20 53

For the sake of clarification, the Competition Commission expressly notes that a leniency application can only be filed individually, ie, by one enterprise alone and/or its representative, and not by two or several companies jointly.

Attention should be paid to the necessary procedural safeguards when making a leniency application. This holds particularly true for the leniency regime in Switzerland as access to documents during an investigation in general is granted on broader terms than is the case in the European Union. According to Article 43 ACart in conjunction with Article 6 of the Federal Act on Administrative Procedures, all parties who are formally allowed to take part in an investigation have, in principle, access to the relevant evidence. Only business secrets are excluded. Contrary to its former practice, the Competition Commission no longer differentiates between general evidence of the investigation and specific evidence which is related to the leniency application. It does not assign the leniency submission a separate, confidential file with a different file number.

The Secretariat nevertheless acknowledges that special safeguards regarding confidentiality should be maintained. Therefore, the Competition Commission states on its website that the corporate leniency statement will only be used in the proceedings of the Competition Commission and shall not be disclosed to other companies or for other proceedings. Similar to the practice of the European Commission, access to the corporate leniency statement is only granted to other defendants, and at a rather advanced stage of the investigation (usually when the statement of objections is issued). Moreover, the other defendants are only allowed to read the corporate leniency statement at the premises of the Competition Commission. The making of photocopies is prohibited. In so doing, the Competition Commission undertakes to strike a balance between confidentiality protection and the rights of the defence.

It is not clear whether such restricted access to the corporate leniency statement is consistent with Article 43 ACart. This provision sets out, in general, the requirements under which individuals, legal entities and associations can participate in an investigation concerning a restraint of competition as third parties. In principle, a third party has the right to obtain access to the case file. According to its wording, Article 43 ACart does not exclude corporate leniency statements. The question whether access to the corporate leniency statements can be limited to other defendants has not yet been tested in court.

11. Is there an optimal time to approach the regulatory authority?

The optimal time to approach the Secretariat of the Competition Commission may vary depending on the respective restraint of competition. As a general rule, however, one may argue the sooner the better. Since only the first one who knocks at the door of the Competition Commission will benefit from a full exemption from sanctions, it is recommended to come forward as soon as possible. Otherwise, the Competition Commission might obtain knowledge about the illegal restraint of competition from other participants or through its own investigations. If this is the case, a full waiver will no longer be available. In multi-jurisdictional cases, a co-ordination of the Swiss leniency application with leniency applications submitted in other countries concerned is advisable. In such cases, the Swiss competition authorities may ask the leniency applicant for a waiver, permitting contact with other competition agencies in order to coordinate the timing of dawn raids.

12. What guarantees of leniency exist if a party co-operates?

Apart from the legal prerequisites set out in Articles 8 and 12 ACart for a full or partial waiver of the sanction, there are no guarantees of leniency if a party co-operates. It remains to be seen in practice whether, despite the lack of any guarantees, the leniency system will encourage companies to come forward and to co-operate with the Competition Commission.

In the case of a sanction despite a leniency application (or a fine which has not been reduced), the sanctioned enterprise may file an appeal to the Federal Court for Administrative Matters (Article 33 lit. f of the Federal Act on the Court for Administrative Matters). In the appeal procedure, the decision of the Competition Commission will be reviewed as to the facts and the legal rules applied in order to find out whether a full or partial waiver of the sanction should have been granted. The decision of the Federal Court for Administrative Matters may be subject to an appeal to the Federal Supreme Court.

CONSEQUENCES

13. What effects does leniency granted to a corporate defendant have on the defendant's employees? Does it protect them from criminal and/or civil liability?

Leniency granted to a company does not have an immediate effect on its employees because, according to Article 49a ACart, only companies participating in illegal restraints of competition can be sanctioned with first-time infringement fines of up to 10 per cent of the turnover achieved in Switzerland during the last three business years. Employees cannot be sanctioned for first-time infringements.

Criminal enforcement against individuals in Switzerland is limited to certain infringements of amicable settlements with, and orders by, the authorities. Leniency does not bar these criminal sanctions against individuals, but they would only become relevant in the case of a leniency application in a repeated infringement case in which an individual has responsibility for a repeated infringement which violates an order or an amicable settlement. Whoever intentionally violates an amicable settlement, a final order of the competition authorities, or a decision by the appeals authorities shall be punished with a fine of up to CHF 100,000 (Article 54 ACart). An individual may also be punished with a fine of up to CHF 20,000 for intentionally disregarding, or only partially complying with, decisions of the competition authorities regarding the duty to provide information (Articles 55 and 40 ACart).

14. Does leniency bar further private enforcement?
Leniency does not bar private enforcement. Whoever is impeded by an unlawful restraint of competition from entering or competing in a market may request removal or cessation of the obstacle, damages and reparation in accordance with the Swiss code of obligations, or remittance of illicitly earned profits in accordance with the provisions on conducting business without a mandate (Article 12(1) ACart). Other market participants may therefore sue a company that has successfully applied for leniency. The instrument of a class action, as seen in the United States, does not exist in Switzerland.

PROTECTION AGAINST DISCLOSURE/CONFIDENTIALITY
15. Is confidentiality afforded to the leniency applicant and other co-operating parties? If so, to what extent? Is the identity of the leniency applicant/other co-operating parties disclosed during the investigation or in the final decision? Is information provided by the leniency applicant/other co-operating parties passed on to other undertakings under investigation? Can a leniency applicant/other co-operating party request anonymity or confidentiality of information provided?
The enterprise seeking leniency may apply confidentially by filing the information anonymously (Article 9(2) OS ACart). In its information on the leniency application form, the Competition Commission notes that by confirming the receipt of the application, the Secretariat will inform the enterprise about the deadline within which it must disclose its identity. The extent to which confidentiality is afforded will thus be dependent on the circumstances of the specific case. As set out in Article 9(2) OS ACart, the Secretariat shall define the modalities of anonymous applications on a case-by-case basis with the consent of a member of the presiding board of the Competition Commission. Given that there have not been any cases of an anonymous application so far which have come to the public attention, no practical experience with the Competition Commission can be reported.

Confidential treatment of a leniency application in non-anonymous form is usually afforded, at least until dawn raids have been conducted (see also question 10). Once an investigation has been opened, there will come a point in time when the confidentiality of the leniency applicant may not be kept any longer. Possible defendants are entitled to a due process and thus must be granted access to the file and be given the opportunity to comment on the alleged infringements, at the latest when the statement of objections is issued. At this stage of the investigation, the identity of the leniency applicant will become publicly known, if the respective company has not disclosed the fact of a leniency motion itself by then.

Switzerland

16. Is the evidence submitted by the leniency applicant protected from transmission to other competition authorities with whom the authority in question co-operates? If so, how?

Under Swiss law, there is no legal basis allowing the Competition Commission to co-operate with other competition authorities and to deliver to them evidence obtained during an investigation. This holds also true for information which has been brought to the attention of the Competition Commission by a leniency applicant. Moreover, Switzerland did not conclude any international treaties with other countries/competition authorities on the exchange of such evidence. The only exception is provided for in the bilateral Agreement on Civil Aviation with the European Union, which entered into force on 1 June 2002. According to Article 19 of this agreement, each contracting party shall give the other all necessary information and assistance in the case of investigations on possible infringements of the agreement. This includes the exchange of relevant evidence. It is unclear, however, whether confidential information delivered in the course of a leniency application, including the corporate leniency statement, is also covered by this provision. So far, no cases can be reported in this respect (see also questions 10 and 15).

Currently, ACart is under review. In early 2009, a special evaluation group issued an evaluation report on the efficiency of ACart, the main reform prospects being the independence of the Competition Commission, harmonisation of the merger control regime with that of the EU, and review of the rules on the restrictions on vertical agreements. Moreover, the evaluation report also considered unsatisfactory the lack of a legal basis to co-operate with competition authorities in other countries, in particular with the European Commission. Therefore, it proposed to examine whether Switzerland should negotiate a bilateral agreement with the European Union to this effect, and/or whether Switzerland should autonomously set up a legal basis enabling the Competition Commission to co-operate with other competition authorities. The Federal Council is expected to present its recommendations to the Parliament as to proposals for revisions and amendments by 2010. Only then will it become clear whether a proposal to introduce the possibility to co-operate with other competition authorities will be among the recommendations.

17. To what extent can evidence submitted by the leniency applicant (transcripts of oral statements or written evidence) become discoverable in subsequent private enforcement claims? Can leniency information be subjected to discovery orders in domestic or foreign courts? Can leniency information submitted in a foreign jurisdiction be subjected to discovery orders in the domestic courts?

As outlined under question 10, the Competition Commission restricts access to evidence submitted by the leniency applicant, including the corporate leniency statement, to those companies which allegedly participated in the cartel and thus are defendants in the investigation. Other individuals and companies are not normally granted access to the evidence concerning the leniency application. Therefore, they normally do not possess such evidence which they could use, as complaining parties, in subsequent private enforcement claims. It is, however, unclear, due to the lack of precedent, whether a potential plaintiff in a private enforcement claim, who was a party to the Competition Commission's investigation based on Article 43 ACart, might successfully claim access to the file, including the corporate leniency statement.

Furthermore, due to the lack of precedent, it is not clear whether a plaintiff, who was not a party to the Competition Commission's investigation, can, in a subsequent private enforcement claim, successfully demand the disclosure of the evidence concerning the leniency application. In principle, a plaintiff can, based on the applicable Cantonal law, request to the court that the relevant evidence be disclosed. Thus, a plaintiff may request the court to order the Competition Commission to disclose the corporate leniency statement. Moreover, a plaintiff may request the court to order the leniency applicant to disclose the relevant evidence relating to the leniency application in its possession. The court would decide such a request by balancing all public and private interests involved. In so doing, the court might also ask the Competition Commission for its opinion on the legitimacy of the disclosure of evidence relating to the leniency application. If the court decides in favour of the plaintiff, the Competition Commission or the leniency applicant would be obliged to disclose the evidence, including the corporate leniency statement. As mentioned above, however, the requirements for potential disclosure have not yet been tested in court. To date, no precedents in which evidence from a leniency application has been discovered in a private enforcement claim are publicly known (see question 18).

18. Are there any precedents in which evidence from a leniency application has been discovered in a private enforcement claim?
As of the date of writing, no precedents in which evidence from a leniency application has been discovered in a private enforcement claim are publicly known.

RELATIONSHIP WITH THE EUROPEAN COMMISSION'S LENIENCY NOTICE AND LENIENCY POLICY IN OTHER EU MEMBER STATES

19. Does the policy address the interaction with applications under the Commission Leniency Notice? If so, how?
Not applicable.

20. Does the policy address the interaction with applications for leniency in other EU member states? If so, how? Does the authority accept summary applications in line with the ECN Model Leniency Programme?
Not applicable.

RELATIONSHIP WITH SETTLEMENT PROCEDURES
21. What is the relationship between leniency and applicable settlement procedures? Are they mutually exclusive?
There is no provision in the ACart stating that leniency and applicable settlement procedures are mutually exclusive. Leniency and applicable settlement can be combined.

In practice, the small number of cases, in which full or partial waivers of fines have been granted to date, were all concluded based on an amicable settlement of the matter between the Competition Commission and the companies involved (see question 3).

REFORM/LATEST DEVELOPMENTS
22. Is there a reform underway to revisit the leniency policy? What are the latest developments?
Currently, the ACart is under review. In early 2009, a special evaluation group issued a report on the efficiency of the ACart (see question 16). On the basis of it, the Federal Council is expected to present, in 2010, recommendations to Parliament as to proposals for revisions and amendments in order to remedy identified weaknesses and to render the Competition Act more effective. The leniency system, however, is not likely to be affected by this envisaged revision.

Turkey

Hergüner Bilgen Özeke Attorney Partnership
Kayra Üçer & Derya Genç

BACKGROUND

1. What is the relevant legislation concerning the leniency policy and what is the enforcing body?

The main relevant legislation on leniency policy is Law No. 4054 on the Protection of Competition (Competition Law). Following the enactment of an amendment in February 2008, pursuant to Article 16 of the Competition Law, full immunity from or reduction of monetary fines is possible for undertakings or associations of undertakings or their executives and employees who actively co-operate, depending on the quality, effectiveness and timing of the co-operation. In line with the same Article, the conditions for full immunity from fines or a reduction of them, as well as the procedures and principles for effective co-operation, have been set out in a separate regulation, the Regulation on Active Co-operation in Detecting Cartels (the Leniency Regulation), which came into force in February 2009.

The national authority that enforces the Competition Law is the Turkish Competition Authority (the Authority). The Competition Board (the Board) which is the decision-making body of the Authority, is responsible for, *inter alia*, reviewing and deciding on leniency applications. The Board has formed a separate division, the Leniency Division, and assigned this division the task of applying the Leniency Regulation.

2. What are the basic tenets of a leniency/immunity programme? Is leniency available also for other types of competition law violations than cartels?

Leniency applications made in accordance with Article 16 of the Competition law and the Leniency Regulation have to satisfy the Authority's requirements in terms of the quality, effectiveness and timing of the co-operation. Undertakings, associations of undertakings, their executives and employees are the relevant parties who can make a leniency application. Leniency is not available for types of violations other than cartels. Cartels are dealt with under Article 4 of the Competition Law.

Full immunity from fines is regulated under Articles 4 (for undertakings) and 7 (for executives and employees of undertakings) of the Leniency Regulation, whereas reduction of fines is regulated under Articles 5 (for undertakings) and 8 (for executives and employees of undertakings). The conditions for obtaining full immunity from and/or reduction of fines are regulated under Articles 6 (for undertakings) and 9 (for executives and employees of undertakings) of the Leniency Regulation.

3. How many cartels have been unveiled and punished since the adoption of the leniency programme?

As noted above, the Leniency Regulation came into effect on February 2009. In light of the information obtained from the relevant division of the Authority, we understand that since February 2009, four leniency applications have been made. In connection with these applications, one investigation and one preliminary investigation were initiated, and both are currently pending. Other than these, the Board closed two preliminary investigations due to lack of any findings indicating a 'local' cartel.

4. What is needed to be a successful leniency applicant? Is documentary evidence required or is testimonial evidence sufficient?

The conditions for benefiting from full immunity and/or fine reduction are regulated under Article 6.1 for undertakings and Article 9.1 for executives and employees. Although regulated under separate provisions, the conditions listed for both applicant groups are almost identical. In order to submit a successful leniency application, the applicant must:
- submit information and evidence with respect to the alleged cartel, including the products affected, the duration of the cartel, the names of the undertakings party to the cartel, specific dates, locations and participants in cartel meetings;
- not conceal or destroy information or evidence related to the alleged cartel;
- cease its involvement in the alleged cartel, except when otherwise requested by the assigned unit on the grounds that detecting the cartel would be complicated;
- keep the application confidential until the end of the investigation, unless otherwise requested by the assigned unit; and
- maintain active co-operation until the Board takes the final decision upon completion of the investigation.

In addition to the above, if an applicant has coerced other participants of the cartel to engage in the violation, it cannot benefit from full immunity regardless of whether all the above conditions are met. However, such an applicant – having met the listed conditions – can still benefit from a reduction in fines.

Testimonial evidence can be given in which case the Authority produces a written form of such information and receives confirmation from the applicant. The aim of testimonial evidence is to provide safety in relation to private actions for damages.

TIMING
5. What are the benefits of being 'first in' to co-operate?
The applicant who is 'first in' to co-operate can obtain full immunity depending on: (i) the fulfilment of the requirements set forth in Article 6

of the Leniency Regulation (as listed under question 4 above): and (ii) the timing of the submission.

When such conditions are fulfilled, immunity from fines is automatic before the Board initiates a preliminary investigation, whereas an additional requirement is imposed if the Board has already initiated a preliminary investigation.

More specifically, provided that the conditions laid down in Article 6 of the Leniency Regulation are met, the first applicant who submits the information and evidence (independently from other participants of the cartel and/or their executives and employees) before the Board decides to carry out a preliminary inquiry, is granted immunity from fines. In other words, the first in to co-operate is automatically immune from fines if the application is made before the preliminary investigation is initiated. The only requirement in such a case is the fulfilment of the conditions.

That said, where the Board has already started a preliminary investigation at the time of the application, there is still a chance to benefit from full immunity. The first applicant who independently submits information and evidence before the notification of the investigation report, is granted immunity from fines if the Authority does not have, at the time of the submission, sufficient evidence to conclude that there has been a violation of Article 4 of the Competition Law. In this latter case, the additional requirement is that the Board, at the time of the application, should not be able to conclude on its own that there has been a violation.

The executives and employees of undertakings satisfying the conditions of being first-in to co-operate are also immune from fines.

In addition to the above, being first in to co-operate also brings benefits in relation to reduction of fines. An applicant who submits information and evidence and meets the conditions stated in Article 6 (following the decision by the Board to carry out a preliminary inquiry but before the notification of the investigation report) but who cannot benefit from full immunity (because the Board may already have information/evidence sufficient to decide on the violation), can still benefit from a fine reduction. In this case, managers and employees of undertakings admitting the existence of a cartel and actively co-operating also benefit from a reduction of the fine. In this framework, the fine to be imposed on the first applicant is reduced by one-third to half. In case of corporate defendants, the fines to be imposed on the undertaking's managers and employees who admit the cartel and actively co-operate may be reduced by at least one-third or may not be imposed at all.

6. What are the consequences of being 'second'? Is there an 'immunity plus' or 'amnesty plus' option?

Once a successful application is made which deserves to benefit from full immunity, subsequent applicants also have the possibility of benefiting from a reduction in fines according to the sequence of the applications. In this regard, the second applicant receives the highest reduction: the fines are automatically reduced by a quarter to one-third of the original fine. The fines to be applied to the executives and employees of the applicant (where this is an undertaking) who actively co-operate are also reduced by at least a quarter or full immunity may be given to these executives and employees.

7. Are subsequent firms given any beneficial treatment if they make a useful contribution? How are 'useful contributions' defined?

'Useful contribution' is not defined in the Leniency Regulation. The reduction in fines to be given to the subsequent firms is automatic, provided that the applications for leniency – made independently from competitors – by these firms satisfy the general requirements listed in Article 6 of the Leniency Regulation (see question 4 above). Useful contribution is not specifically awarded any beneficial treatment.

SCOPE/FULL LENIENCY
8. Is it possible to receive full leniency? If so, what are the conditions required to receive full leniency?

Yes, it is possible to receive full leniency for the applicants first in to co-operate and meeting the conditions laid down in Article 6 of the Leniency Regulation. Please see questions 4 and 5, above.

8.1 Can ringleaders/coercers receive full leniency?
No, they can only benefit from a reduction in fines (by one-third to half of the fine) having met other conditions listed in Article 6 or Article 9 of the Leniency Regulation.

8.2 If there is a requirement to 'co-operate fully and on an ongoing basis', what does it entail?
According to Article 6 and 9 of the Leniency Regulation: (i) all available information and documents that relate to the cartel should be submitted to the Authority; (ii) no documents should be destroyed/shredded; and (iii) the applicant should actively co-operate until the Board grants its final decision. As far as the third condition is concerned, if the applicant gets hold of new information/documents after the Board concludes its investigation and before the final decision is issued, such information/documents must also be submitted to the Authority. In addition to this, the applicant should provide assistance to the Authority, within the limits of their capabilities, in relation to requests by the Authority for additional explanations. Lastly, the applicant should provide the Authority with the opportunity to resort to the affidavits of its executives/employees.

8.3 Does the regulatory authority require the applicant to cease participation in the cartel conduct after its application?
Yes, according to paragraph c of Article 6 (for undertakings) and 9 (for executives and employees), the applicant must cease participation in the cartel after its application except when the Authority requests otherwise for evidence collection purposes.

9. How many companies have received full immunity from fines to date?
No companies have received full immunity from fines to date. However, as indicated above under question 3, one preliminary investigation and one fully-fledged investigation are pending where leniency applications were made.

PROCEDURE
10. What are the practical steps required to apply for leniency?
The procedure to be followed in relation to leniency applications is regulated under Articles 6 and 9 of the Leniency Regulation. The applications are made to the Leniency Division of the Competition Authority via telephone, fax or email. Upon submission of the minimum required information (the products affected by the cartel, the duration of the cartel and the names of the participants in the cartel) the applicant is given a sequence number and granted a certain period of time for the completion of the application. Upon submission of the complete application, the Board adopts an interim decision and sends it to the applicant. In this interim decision, the Board undertakes to provide full leniency or reduction in fines on the condition that the applicant does not violate the conditions for being a successful applicant (laid down in Articles 6.1. and 9.1).

10.1 Full disclosure
In order to satisfy the first condition for being a successful applicant, the applicants are obliged to disclose all information and evidence with respect to the alleged cartel, including the products affected, the duration of the cartel, the names of the undertakings party to the cartel, specific dates, locations and participants of cartel meetings. However, at the time of initial contact, full disclosure may not be required as described below.

10.2 Initial contact/is there a 'marker' system?
There is a marker system under Articles 6 and 9 of the Leniency Regulation, according to which the applicant is given a time period by the Leniency Division for the completion of its application. In order for the Leniency Division to grant such time period, the applicant should submit the information regarding the products affected by the cartel, the duration of the cartel and the names of the participants in the cartel.

10.3 Conditional reduction of fine
Unlike the EU and US regimes, reduction in fines is not conditional upon the provision of evidence representing significant added value relative to the evidence already in the Authority's possession at the time of application. Reduction is provided automatically at various levels depending on the sequence of applications and on the mere condition that the general conditions listed in Articles 6.1 and 9.1 are met.

10.4 Final reduction
The final reduction is decided at the stage of the final decision of the Board.

The Board's decision in this regard is based on the quality, effectiveness and timing of the co-operation. Upon review of these three criteria, the level of reduction is determined within the fixed range of the minimum and maximum percentages set forth in Articles 5 and 8 of the Leniency Regulation. If the fine is subject to an increase due to evidence submitted (eg the duration of the cartel is found to be longer), the applicant who had submitted such evidence will not be affected by the increase in the fine.

11. Is there an optimal time to approach the regulatory authority?
Yes. The optimal time to approach the Authority is before the Board adopts a decision to initiate a preliminary investigation. Please see question 5 above.

12. What guarantees of leniency exist if a party co-operates?
The Board, by way of an interim decision following the submission of the complete application, undertakes to provide full immunity or reduction in fines to a fully co-operative party that does not violate the conditions laid down in Articles 6.1 and 9.1. Therefore, the interim decision taken by the Board right after the completion of the application is a guarantee that the applicant will benefit from leniency by the time of the final decision of the Board.

CONSEQUENCES
13. What effects does leniency granted to a corporate defendant have on the defendant's employees? Does it protect them from criminal and/or civil liability?
The executives and employees of a corporate defendant held to be fully immune from fines also benefit from such immunity. In the case of reductions, the executives and employees benefit from the reduction (which cannot be less than the original reduction) or may obtain full immunity.

According to the Civil Code, the organs of the corporate entities are liable for the compensation claims, and it is unlikely that the liability would be placed on employees unless they are found not to be acting on behalf of the corporate entities. Regarding criminal liability, although Turkish criminal law includes a specific provision that can be applied to cartels, it has not yet been enforced. That said, prosecution is likely for cartels related to public tenders. In any case, leniency would not yield protection in court as the Competition Law does not include any such provision.

14. Does leniency bar further private enforcement?
There is no specific provision under the Competition Law and the Leniency Regulation preventing further private enforcement.

PROTECTION AGAINST DISCLOSURE/CONFIDENTIALITY
15. Is confidentiality afforded to the leniency applicant and other co-operating parties? If so, to what extent?
Confidentiality is afforded to the leniency applicant and other co-operating parties until the Board sends its investigation report to the concerned parties

Turkey

(in other words until the investigation phase is over). Following service of the investigation report, the parties subject to the investigation receive access to the Authority's files and are allowed to examine any information/document used as evidence in relation to the investigation.

15.1 Is the identity of the leniency applicant/other co-operating parties disclosed during the investigation or in the final decision?
Yes. The identity of the leniency applicant/other co-operating party is disclosed in the final decision.

15.2 Is information provided by the leniency applicant/other co-operating parties passed on to other undertakings under investigation?
In order to secure the right of defence, the information/documents used as evidence can be accessed by the other participants upon request once the Investigation Report of the Authority has been notified to the concerned parties.

15.3 Can a leniency applicant/other co-operating party request anonymity or confidentiality of information provided?
No. This is because the Board can use the information/documents as evidence in its decisions only if it has informed the concerned parties of such information/documents and given the parties the right of defence in relation to such information/documents.

16. Is the evidence submitted by the leniency applicant protected from transmission to other competition authorities with whom the authority in question co-operates? If so, how?
Yes. None of the reciprocal co-operation protocols signed with other competition authorities includes sharing such information.

17. To what extent can evidence submitted by the leniency applicant (transcripts of oral statements or written evidence) become discoverable in subsequent private enforcement claims?
The applicants can submit evidence through oral statements (which will be kept as internal administrative documents by the Authority) in which case third parties and complainants cannot access the information/documents regarding the cartel.

17.1 Can leniency information be subjected to discovery orders in domestic courts?
Yes, the Authority is legally obliged to deliver any and all information/documents if requested by Turkish courts.

17.2 Can leniency information be subjected to discovery orders in foreign courts?
The Board cannot provide any information/document submitted to it to any

court in other jurisdictions. Such information can only be requested from submitting parties.

17.3 Can leniency information submitted in a foreign jurisdiction be subjected to discovery orders in domestic courts?
Turkish courts may ask a Turkish leniency applicant to provide any and all documents/information submitted to Turkish and foreign authorities.

18. Are there any precedents in which evidence from a leniency application has been discovered in a private enforcement claim?
No.

RELATIONSHIP WITH THE EUROPEAN COMMISSION'S LENIENCY NOTICE AND LENIENCY POLICY IN OTHER EU MEMBER STATES
19. Does the policy address the interaction with applications under the Commission Leniency Notice? If so, how?
Not applicable.

20. Does the policy address the interaction with applications for leniency in other EU member states? If so, how? Does the authority accept summary applications in line with the ECN Model Leniency Programme?
Not applicable.

RELATIONSHIP WITH SETTLEMENT PROCEDURES
21. What is the relationship between leniency and applicable settlement procedures? Are they mutually exclusive?
The Competition Law does not provide for an institutionalised settlement procedure.

REFORM/LATEST DEVELOPMENTS
22. Is there a reform underway to revisit the leniency policy? What are the latest developments?
Since the Leniency Regulation is quite recent, no reform is expected in the near future. The leniency process is yet to be explored in Turkey and the two current investigations concerning leniency applications will provide more guidance in this respect when tied to a final decision and made known to public.

According to statements of the Authority officials, a guideline is expected to be issued by the end of 2010.

United Kingdom

Herbert Smith LLP Stephen Wisking & Kim Dietzel

BACKGROUND
1. What is the relevant legislation containing the leniency policy and what is the enforcing body?
Section 36 of the Competition Act 1998 provides the Office of Fair Trading (OFT) with the power to impose a financial penalty on any undertaking which has intentionally or negligently infringed the competition provisions in the Competition Act 1998 or the Treaty on the Functioning of the EU (TFEU) (previously the EC Treaty).

The OFT is required to prepare and publish guidance on the application of penalties (section 38 of the Competition Act 1998). The OFT must have regard to this guidance when setting the amount of the penalty. The leniency policy was introduced on 1 March 2000 at the same time as the Competition Act 1998 came into effect, as part of the penalty guidance.

A revised OFT guidance as to the appropriate amount of a penalty, OFT 423 (the OFT's Penalty Guidance), which sets out the OFT's revised leniency policy was approved by the Secretary of State for publication on 21 December 2004.

There is an equivalent policy offering individual immunity from prosecution for individuals who may be exposed to the criminal cartel offence under section 188 of the Enterprise Act 2002. The offence covers dishonestly agreeing with one or more other persons that undertakings will fix prices, limit supply or production, share markets or be involved in bid rigging arrangements in the United Kingdom. The offence only covers horizontal infringements and only the OFT or the Director of the Serious Fraud Office is able to prosecute individuals for cartel conduct. The immunity available to individuals takes the form of no-action letters which are issued by the OFT under the OFT Guidelines *The cartel offence: Guidance on the issue of no-action letters for individuals, OFT 513*. Section 190(4) of the Enterprise Act 2002 prevents proceedings for the cartel offence being brought against a person who has received notification from the OFT that proceedings will not be brought within the description specified in the notification.

In December 2008, the OFT published *Leniency and no-action: OFT's guidance note on the handling of applications, OFT 803* (the Leniency Guidance Note). The Leniency Guidance Note sets out the detail of how the OFT handles leniency and immunity applications and in this respect supplements and elaborates on the procedures set out in the OFT's Penalty Guidance and the OFT Guidance on the issue of no-action letters for individuals. The Leniency Guidance Note does not replace these documents. The Leniency Guidance Note follows an Interim Note published by the OFT in July 2005 and a draft Leniency Guidance Note published in November 2006, and substantially adds to (and in some cases amends) the guidance previously given. The OFT has stated that this is to take account of its growing experience with leniency applications, including in the context of criminal prosecutions.

The principal enforcement agency is the OFT, however non-criminal leniency applications can be submitted to the relevant sector regulator if the cartel activity occurs in one of the sectors subject to sector-specific regulation (broadcasting and telecommunications, electricity and gas, water, rail and air traffic control services).

The European Commission's leniency policy operates in parallel with the OFT's leniency policy in respect of cartel activity which amounts to a breach of Article 101 of TFEU.

Where an infringement has an effect on trade between states, prospective applicants will need to consider whether a leniency application should be submitted to the European Commission under the European Commission's notice on immunity from fines and reduction of fines in cartel cases (OJ C298/17, 08/12/06) (the EC Leniency Notice) instead of, or simultaneously with, an application to the OFT and/or another EU member state's national competition authority.

Quite separate from the OFT's leniency policy, is the availability of a reduction in fines for mitigating factors, including co-operation which enables the enforcement process to be concluded more effectively and/ or speedily. The OFT has, however, stated in its Penalty Guidance that undertakings benefiting from the leniency programme (a condition of which is their full co-operation) will not receive an additional reduction in financial penalties under this head to reflect general co-operation.

2. What are the basic tenets of the leniency/immunity programme? Is leniency available also for other types of competition law violations than cartels?

The OFT leniency programme covers undertakings which have participated in cartel activities and wish to terminate their involvement and inform the OFT of the existence of the cartel activity. It is not available for other types of competition law violations other than cartels. The concept of cartel activity is defined very broadly as an agreement which infringes Article 101 of TFEU and/or the Chapter 1 prohibition in the Competition Act 1998. The following agreements are classified as cartel activity (and can hence be the subject of a leniency application):
- 'classic' horizontal price fixing;
- vertical price fixing/resale price maintenance (the availability of leniency for resale price maintenance under the UK leniency policy is a key difference between the UK and EC leniency policies. The OFT's policy is not intended to cover other stand-alone vertical restrictions apart from vertical behaviour which facilitates horizontal collusion);

- bid rigging (collusive tendering);
- the establishment of output restrictions or quotas;
- market sharing; and
- market division.

In order to be eligible for full immunity (ie, full leniency), the undertaking must be the first to provide the OFT with evidence of cartel activity and must also satisfy the following cumulative conditions. The undertaking must:

- provide the OFT with all the information, documents and evidence available to it regarding the cartel activity;
- maintain continuous and complete co-operation throughout the investigation;
- refrain from further participation in the cartel activity, from the time of disclosure of the cartel activity to the OFT (except as may be directed by the OFT); and
- not have taken steps to coerce another undertaking to take part in the cartel activity.

Full immunity will be automatic if the information is provided before the OFT has begun an investigation and the OFT does not already have sufficient information to establish that a cartel exists. The OFT describes this as a 'Type A' case. A successful applicant in a Type A case will need to supply the OFT with information that provides the OFT with a sufficient basis to take forward a credible investigation. All current and former employees and directors of a Type A applicant who may be implicated in the cartel will benefit from blanket immunity from the criminal cartel offence.

Type A immunity will be available until the OFT has commenced a civil or criminal investigation, the OFT has 'sufficient information' to establish the existence of an infringement of the Competition Act 1998 or another undertaking has applied for Type A immunity (or in some circumstances subject to the OFT's exercise of its discretion, an individual has applied for Type A individual immunity).

Full immunity is discretionary if the OFT has already commenced a civil or criminal investigation, but does not yet have sufficient information to establish the existence of a cartel infringement (or, in the case of a criminal investigation is not in the course of gathering sufficient information to bring a successful prosecution). The OFT describes this as a 'Type B' case. In practice, approaches to the OFT in Type B cases are most likely to be triggered by inspections (including 'dawn raids'). In order to qualify for Type B immunity, an applicant must be the first undertaking to apply for immunity and must provide information that adds 'significant value' to the OFT's investigation. In Type B cases, all current and former employees and directors of the successful applicant who may be implicated in the cartel will benefit from blanket immunity from the criminal cartel offence.

While the OFT has indicated that the grant of full immunity will be the norm rather than the exception in Type B cases, Type B immunity is less likely to be available where there is a pre-existing criminal investigation. This is because the OFT believes that the blanket individual immunity, which follows a grant of Type B civil immunity is less likely to be in the public interest where there is a pre-existing criminal investigation. In light of this, when there is an existing criminal investigation, the OFT may contemplate the grant of civil immunity (full leniency) to the undertaking without the automatic blanket immunity to its current or former employees or directors.

Partial leniency (a reduction in financial penalty of up to 50 per cent) may be available where the undertaking is not the first to come forward with information and there is a pre-existing civil or criminal investigation. The OFT has described this as a 'Type C' case. Partial leniency may also be available where the undertaking would have qualified for full immunity had it not coerced other undertakings to join the cartel. Employees and directors of a Type C applicant do not receive blanket immunity from the criminal cartel offence and the OFT will assess whether to grant immunity on an individual-by-individual basis.

In order for an individual to be eligible to obtain immunity via the grant of a no-action letter, the individual must meet the following conditions:

- admit participation in the criminal offence including dishonesty, where this is considered appropriate (where this is not considered appropriate or necessary, the OFT may issue a 'comfort letter' instead, see response to question 4 below);
- provide the OFT with all information available to them regarding the existence and activities of the cartel;
- maintain continuous and complete co-operation throughout the investigation and until the conclusion of any criminal proceedings arising as a result of the investigation;
- not have taken steps themselves to coerce another undertaking to take part in the cartel; and
- refrain from further participation in the cartel from the time of its disclosure to the OFT (except as may be directed by the investigating authority).

Immunity will be automatic for current and former employees and directors of an undertaking which has qualified for Type A or Type B immunity. Current and former employees and directors of an undertaking which has qualified for Type C leniency will not benefit from automatic immunity and the OFT will consider whether to grant immunity on a case-by-case basis.

An individual is also able to request a no-action letter directly from the OFT. An individual will be granted immunity if they are the first to talk to the OFT. If there is already a criminal investigation, but the individual informs the OFT before any other individual or undertaking, the individual will still be granted individual immunity provided they add value to the investigation and so long as they meet the cumulative conditions set out above.

An application for leniency to the OFT will not count as an application for leniency to any other national competition authority within the European Community or to the European Commission. If the infringement has or had an effect on another EU member state, prospective applicants should consider whether to apply for leniency to the national competition authority of the other EU member state, in addition to the OFT and/or to the European Commission. Given the importance of timing in most leniency programmes, the applicant will also need to consider whether it would be appropriate to file leniency applications with the relevant authorities simultaneously.

Where the effects of the cartel activity are felt in more than three EU member states, the European Commission's Notice on co-operation within the network of competition authorities (OJ C101, 27/4/04) (the EC Network Notice) indicates that the European Commission is likely to be considered best placed to carry out the investigation. A leniency application should therefore be submitted to the European Commission under the EC Notice on Immunity when this is the case. However, while a leniency application to the European Commission may address a potential Article 101 TFUE infringement, the applicant may still be exposed under UK competition law (or the competition law of another EU member state), and its employees to potential criminal sanctions if they committed the UK cartel offence, and simultaneous applications to the national competition authorities of the EU member states where the cartel activity has had an effect may be advisable.

3. How many cartels have been unveiled and punished since the adoption of the leniency policy?

The leniency policy was adopted when the Competition Act 1998 came into force in March 2000. There have been 18 infringement decisions of the OFT relating to cartel activity, including resale price maintenance infringements (as at 1 January 2010). In the majority of these cases where leniency was sought and obtained, the application for leniency followed the commencement of an investigation by the OFT (Type B immunity). However, there have also been a number of Type A cases, the most recent example of this is the *Construction Recruitment Forum* case in which the OFT reached its decision on 29 September 2009. (In that case, the leniency application had been made on 20 December 2005, suggesting that the passing of a time period in excess of three-and-a-half years between leniency application and decision would not be unusual and that there may therefore be other cases still before the OFT based on leniency applications).

4. What is needed to be a successful leniency applicant? Is documentary evidence required or is testimonial evidence sufficient?

The conditions for obtaining leniency and individual immunity are set out in question 2. The OFT will offer an undertaking a 'marker', reserving the undertaking's place in the 'leniency queue' following an oral request for immunity. In order to perfect the marker in a Type A case the information provided by the applicant must provide the OFT with a sufficient basis to take forward a credible investigation. In a Type B case, the undertaking must provide information to the OFT that adds value to the OFT's investigation. In all cases, the applicant is required to provide the OFT with all information, documents and evidence available to it regarding the cartel activity. The OFT will normally advise the applicant as to the broad categories of information which it considers likely to be relevant. Generally copies of any agreement, file note or correspondence which contain details of the cartel activity, to the extent such documents exist, must be provided in order to 'perfect' the marker. The applicant will normally be required to produce this evidence promptly. The applicant will need to make every effort to ensure that relevant current and former employees make themselves available for interview by the OFT.

The entire application for leniency can be oral, but if it is an oral request, all pre-existing written evidence of the cartel will need to be provided to the OFT. All witnesses will also need to be made available for interview and, if desired by the OFT, to sign witness statements setting out their evidence.

Individuals who have sought immunity (or on whose behalf immunity is sought) will need to be available for interview and, where the involvement in the cartel makes this appropriate, will need to admit to the criminal conduct for which the no-action letter is granted – including an admission of dishonesty. However, individuals who performed only a peripheral role may instead be granted a comfort letter (for which an admission of dishonesty will not be required) or, in some circumstances may not be thought to require either letter if they are viewed as not facing any risk of prosecution.

If the OFT determines that the conditions for individual immunity have not been fully complied with or that the applicant knowingly or recklessly provided information that is false or misleading, the OFT may revoke the grant of immunity from prosecution. On revocation, the grant of immunity will cease to exist, as if the immunity had never been granted and any information provided by the applicant may be used against them in criminal proceedings.

TIMING
5. What are the benefits of being 'first in' to co-operate?
Full immunity is only available to the first undertaking to come forward and provide the OFT with information relating to the cartel activity. Undertakings which are not the first to come forward are not eligible for full immunity. Current and former employees and directors of an undertaking that has obtained Type A or Type B immunity are also guaranteed individual immunity from prosecution for the criminal cartel offence. This creates another incentive to come forward and seek leniency prior to another cartel member.

6. What are the consequences of being 'second'? Is there an 'immunity plus' or 'amnesty plus' option?
Undertakings which come forward and provide evidence of cartel activity before a statement of objections but which are not the first to come forward (Type C case) may be granted partial leniency – a reduction of up to 50 per cent in the amount of the financial penalty which would otherwise be imposed. Partial leniency is also available where an undertaking does not

qualify for full immunity, for example, if the undertaking is found to have coerced another undertaking to participate in the cartel activity. Current and former employees and directors of an undertaking which has received partial leniency are not guaranteed immunity from the criminal cartel offence, and the OFT will assess the position of the employee or director on an individual basis, taking into account the value that would be added by the applicant and whether the grant would be in the public interest.

The UK leniency programme does offer a 'leniency plus' option. The OFT Penalty Guidance provides that an undertaking co-operating with the OFT in relation to cartel activities in one market which informs the OFT about a separate cartel in another market, will receive a reduction in fines in relation to its activities in the first market if the undertaking obtains full leniency in relation to activities in respect of the cartel in the second market. In the Leniency Guidance Note, the OFT makes clear that there should not be undue focus on market definition and the key issue is whether the novel evidence relates to a 'completely separate cartel activity' (or conspiracy). The fact that the activity is in a separate market is a good indicator but not decisive. The reduction in fines under the 'leniency plus' option is additional to the reduction which the undertaking would have received for its co-operation in relation to the first cartel activity alone.

There are at least three examples of undertakings receiving the benefit of the 'leniency plus' programme. In the *Replica Football Kit* price fixing case (1 August 2003), one undertaking received a 25 per cent reduction in penalty as it had been granted full immunity from financial penalties with respect to other infringements while Pirie Group received an additional reduction under the 'leniency plus' programme in both the *Scottish Mastic Asphalt Flat Roofing* collusive tendering case (15 March 2005) and the *Flat Roof/Car Park Surfacing* collusive tendering case (22 February 2006). The total reduction in penalty Pirie received in both cases was 55 per cent, but the exact amount of the uplift that Pirie Group received as a result of obtaining full immunity with respect to other infringements is not set out in either decision. These decisions were all taken prior to the publication of the current Leniency Guidance Note.

It is not clear if the OFT's approach to identifying separate cartel activity has become easier to meet since the introduction of the Leniency Guidance Note (in its draft and final forms) where the OFT has indicated that it will not unduly focus on the market definition in identifying separate cartel activity. The OFT states that its 'leniency plus' programme is intended to mirror the US practice which engages its 'amnesty plus' programme in cases which are based on information relating to a 'second, unrelated conspiracy' and information which lead to investigations in 'a completely separate industry'.

7. Are subsequent firms given any beneficial treatment if they make a useful contribution? How are 'useful contributions' defined?

All undertakings which provide evidence of cartel activity to the OFT before a statement of objections is issued may be granted partial leniency: a reduction of up to 50 per cent in the amount of the financial penalty which would otherwise be imposed (a Type C case).

The grant of partial leniency is discretionary and the OFT must be satisfied that the undertaking should benefit from a reduction taking into account the stage at which the undertaking comes forward, the evidence the OFT already has, and the evidence provided by the undertaking. In the *Public Schools* case (20 November 2006), the OFT declined to grant leniency to a number of schools which approached it during the later stages of the investigation.

Further, in certain instances it appears that the OFT may, once a significant amount of evidence has been received, close the door on leniency investigations. This was the case in respect of the OFT's largest cartel investigation relating to bid rigging in the construction industry (which culminated in the OFT's decision of 21 September 2009). The OFT announced on 22 March 2007 that in view of the extent and quality of evidence received so far, no further applications for leniency in connection with that investigation would be accepted. However, the OFT offered a reduced penalty to all those companies implicated in the bid rigging investigation, but which had not yet applied for leniency, but were willing to co-operate with the OFT under a fast track procedure. This was taken up by a number of the companies under investigation (41 out of 112 firms received up to a 25 per cent discount under the March 2007 'fast track' procedure, in addition to the 33 firms benefiting from a reduction in fine under the usual leniency programme).

The employees or directors of an undertaking which obtains partial leniency will not benefit from automatic immunity from the criminal cartel offence and the OFT will consider, on a case-by-case basis whether to grant immunity to such individuals, taking into account the value that they add to the assessment of the case and whether the grant of immunity would be in the public interest. However, as the OFT points out in the Leniency Guidance Note, in many cases where a Type C approach is made, the OFT is not pursuing a criminal investigation and has no intention of initiating one, and the OFT suggests that an applicant for Type C leniency could seek confidential guidance from the OFT (on a no-names basis if required) to ascertain whether there is in fact any criminal exposure for the undertaking's current and former employees and directors.

As at 1 January 2010 partial leniency had been granted in 14 decided cases. The lenient treatment granted ranged in most cases from a 20 per cent to 50 per cent reduction in the financial penalty that would have been imposed. However, a reduction of up to 55 per cent has been granted where the undertaking also qualified for a reduction under the 'leniency plus' policy and in the *Construction Industry* bid rigging case an undertaking received an initial 40 per cent reduction and an additional 25 per cent reduction in financial penalty, making a total leniency discount of 65 per cent, due to the fact that it was the first undertaking to apply for leniency after the commencement of the OFT's investigation.

SCOPE/FULL LENIENCY
8. Is it possible to receive full leniency? And, if so, what are the conditions required to receive full leniency? Can ringleaders/coercers receive full leniency? If there is a requirement to 'co-operate fully and on an ongoing basis' what does it entail? Does the regulatory authority require the applicant to cease participation in the cartel conduct after its application?

The conditions for receiving full leniency (and individual immunity) are set out under questions 2 and 4.

The Leniency Guidance Note provides further guidance on the application of the conditions and makes it clear that an applicant can still meet the condition relating to full co-operation even if a current or former individual employee or director fails to co-operate with the OFT's investigation. However, an applicant will need to be able to show that it used its best endeavours to secure the co-operation of the individual, and that it overall continues to be able to provide the OFT with sufficient evidence of the reported cartel activity to pass the threshold. It should also be noted that an applicant's general obligation to co-operate includes a positive duty to inform the OFT immediately if it has any concerns as to the level of co-operation provided by any current or former employees or directors, and in particular, if it has concerns regarding the completeness and/or accuracy of any statements made.

In respect of the condition requiring the applicant not to have been a coercer the Leniency Guidance Note provides that there must be evidence of clear, positive and ultimately successful steps from a participant (the 'coercer') to pressurise an unwilling participant to take part in a cartel (therefore this differs significantly from a ringleader issue).

The OFT has indicated that there may be coercion in the following situations:
- there was a provable threat of, or actual, physical violence or blackmail which has a realistic prospect of being carried out (this applies equally to horizontal or vertical arrangements); or
- such strong economic pressure as to make market exit a real risk, where for example, a large participant organises a collective boycott of a small participant or refuses to supply key inputs to a small participant. The OFT notes that these scenarios are more likely to apply in cases where there is a 'significant vertical element' and are less likely to be relevant when the arrangement is horizontal and there is no significant cross supply between the parties.

The bar is high in relation to both the 'coercive behaviour' and the evidence necessary to prove that behaviour and the OFT has indicated that there is no coercion in the following scenarios:
- harmful market pressure which falls short of risking market exit but which may reduce profit margins;
- mere agreed enforcement or punishment mechanisms to enforce the operation of the cartel; and
- the use of standard contracts in a resale price maintenance case even

where there is significant inequality of bargaining power.

The OFT has, to date, never refused corporate immunity on coercion grounds. Even if an undertaking were to lose automatic corporate immunity as a result of being found to be a 'coercer', the undertaking will still be eligible for up to a 50 per cent reduction in penalty; and the undertaking's current and former employees or directors (except for the rogue coercing employee(s)) would remain eligible for individual immunity in both Type A and Type B immunity cases.

Where immunity for individuals is concerned, given that the cumulative conditions also apply to such applicants, it will be clear that there is also a coercer condition which could prevent an individual from obtaining immunity by virtue of their role in coercing another undertaking to take part in the cartel. The coercer test for individual immunity is aligned with that of the undertaking seeking civil immunity and requires there to have been an undertaking which was coerced and, in most cases, an undertaking (rather than individual) which carried out the coercion. The OFT has confirmed that if an undertaking is not found to be a coercer, no employee or director of the undertaking will be refused individual immunity on the coercer ground, save in any exceptional circumstances where somehow an employee or director enjoyed a position of power independent of their position within the undertaking and used it to coerce another undertaking. If an undertaking is found to be a coercer, it is only those individuals within the undertaking who themselves play a coercing role who will be unable to obtain individual immunity. Employees and directors who did not perform a coercing role will not be denied individual immunity on coercer grounds.

9. How many companies have received full immunity from fines to date?

As at 1 January 2010 the OFT had issued 18 infringement decisions for cartel activity (including resale price maintenance) since the Competition Act 1998 came into effect and the leniency policy has been available. Of the 18 infringement decisions, full immunity was granted to an undertaking in 12 cases. One company received full immunity in three cases involving flat roofing cartels.

Partial leniency was granted to an undertaking in 11 out of the 12 cases where full immunity was obtained, and in three other cases where full immunity was not obtained by any undertaking subject to the infringement. In at least three cases a company received the benefit of the 'leniency plus' regime.

Even when a leniency application triggers an investigation by the OFT, it may decide not to proceed to a formal decision. It is possible that a number of undertakings may have sought leniency but no infringement decision was reached. In addition, there will be a number of cases where leniency has been applied for and granted but an infringement decision is still awaited.

PROCEDURE
10. What are the practical steps required to apply for leniency?
Prior to seeking leniency, the legal representative of an undertaking or an

individual can request confidential guidance from the OFT. Guidance can be sought as to:
- whether certain conduct, on hypothetical facts, amounts to coercion;
- whether an investigation has commenced in a particular industry and hence whether Type A automatic immunity is still available;
- whether another undertaking or individual has sought immunity and hence whether Type B immunity is available; or
- whether an individual's behaviour is likely to lead to prosecution under the criminal cartel offence.

This initial approach is always on a no-names basis and involves a discussion based on hypothetical facts. The OFT will give its view by which it will consider itself bound as long as a leniency application follows in a reasonable period of time, no false or misleading information is provided and there is no material change of circumstances.

A legal adviser seeking to ascertain (on a confidential basis) whether Type A immunity is still available will need to provide oral confirmation to the OFT that they have obtained conditional instructions to apply for a marker if the OFT informs them that Type A immunity is available to the undertaking (a professional undertaking will not however be required). The legal adviser will need to provide sufficient information to allow the OFT to determine whether there is a pre-existing civil or criminal investigation.

If the OFT confirms that Type A immunity is available, the legal adviser must disclose the identity of their client and apply for immunity then and there, providing the information that is necessary to secure the marker (the details of the suspected infringement and the evidence that has been uncovered). If, on the other hand, the OFT indicates that Type A immunity is not available, the legal adviser and their client are free to consider other options.

If the OFT is already conducting a civil or criminal investigation, a legal adviser may also seek to ascertain whether another undertaking has already sought immunity (or whether Type B immunity is still available). The OFT will inform the legal adviser whether Type B immunity is available in principle without requiring the legal adviser to identify the undertaking or that the undertaking make an immediate application for immunity.

The OFT will not use information provided in connection with obtaining confidential guidance and will not try to 'reverse engineer' the information in order to establish the undertaking's identity. Where, however, an applicant acted in bad faith (eg, a manifest failure to co-operate), the OFT reserves the right to use that information against the failed applicant.

After an undertaking has obtained confidential guidance or otherwise decided to apply for leniency, the undertaking should obtain a marker in order to secure its place in the leniency queue.

When an undertaking's legal adviser has been informed that Type A immunity is available, this step must be taken immediately by the undertaking's legal representative on its behalf. An undertaking may also request a marker during or immediately after a 'dawn raid' but the OFT may have to defer providing a definite answer. However, if requested, the OFT could provisionally mark the undertaking's position in the queue. Where an application is made during a 'dawn raid' or other inspection, the inspection will continue in its normal way.

In other circumstances it is usual for an undertaking to contact, by telephone, the Director of Cartels at the OFT (or if the cartel activity occurred in one of the regulated markets, contact can be made with the equivalent to the Director of Cartels at the relevant regulator). This step needs to be taken by an individual who has the authority to represent the undertaking.

In order to obtain the marker the representative must identify the concrete basis for the suspicion that the undertaking has engaged in cartel activity, specify the nature and emerging details of the potential infringement and the evidence that has been uncovered.

Crucially, in nearly all cases, the representative will be required to identify the undertaking seeking immunity. As an exception to this general rule, the OFT will allow a 'no-names' marker where the undertaking's representative confirms that it intends to apply to the European Commission for immunity under the EC Leniency Notice. The undertaking's representative will need to identify themselves, their firm, and sufficient details of the affected sector in order to enable the OFT to determine whether there is a pre-existing UK civil or criminal investigation. Once the no-names marker is obtained, the applicant will be required to revert to the OFT by an agreed date to confirm that an application has been made to the Commission, the identity of the applicant and the details of the suspected infringement and underlying evidence. If Commission immunity is no longer available, the applicant may withdraw the request for the no-names marker, without revealing its identity. Alternatively, the applicant may decide to keep its OFT marker (which would need to be perfected in the normal way). In other cases, the applicant will need to provide strong justification for obtaining a no-names marker.

The OFT will reserve the undertaking's place in the queue following this initial contact. A discussion as to the timing and provision of information to 'perfect' the marker will also take place. The OFT has indicated that it will be realistic about what information can sensibly be provided at this early stage and the scope of the information to be provided may be specified at a later point.

Once a marker has been obtained, the undertaking needs to 'perfect' the request for immunity or leniency. The undertaking will usually be given a limited time in which to do this.

In order to 'perfect' an application for Type A immunity, the information supplied by the leniency applicant must provide the OFT with a sufficient basis for taking forward a credible investigation. The OFT has indicated that in practice this means that the information is sufficient to allow the OFT to exercise its formal powers of investigation (ie, provide the OFT with reasonable grounds to suspect undertakings are engaging in cartel activity).

When there is already a pre-existing civil or criminal investigation (a Type B case), the applicant will need to provide information which adds 'significant value' to the OFT's investigation. An undertaking can explore whether the information it can provide would advance the OFT's investigation by making a 'proffer' specifying the form and substance of the information it is likely to provide. The OFT will then confirm whether Type B immunity would be given if such evidence were provided. While this could be done on a 'no-names' basis, the undertaking would not secure a marker in the leniency queue until its identity had been disclosed. The OFT has indicated that it will accept some variation in comparing the information actually received with the information outlined in the 'proffer', provided the 'proffer' does not turn out to be misleading and the OFT's investigation has been genuinely advanced.

The OFT has made it clear in the Leniency Guidance Note that it will not rely on incriminating information submitted during a marker approach, against an undertaking which despite having acted in good faith, failed to qualify for immunity (eg, if the information provided was insufficient to provide the OFT with a basis for taking forward an investigation).

However, the OFT reserves the right to use the information against an applicant if the applicant acted in bad faith, for example, if it manifestly failed to co-operate with the OFT.

The OFT is flexible and it is possible for the entire application to be oral. The applicant needs to provide the details of the cartel activity, in so far as established, setting out the reasons why the conditions for leniency have been fulfilled. A copy of any agreement which records the cartel activity (which may be the case with a resale price maintenance infringement) or a file note or any correspondence or other evidence which details the cartel activity, to the extent that they exist, must be provided. The OFT may request, or the applicant may voluntarily offer the OFT, interviews with the key personnel involved in the potential infringement. The OFT considers that it sets a relatively low evidential threshold for the granting of a marker and prefers leniency applications early on and prior to exhaustive internal investigations having been conducted as it may wish to direct such investigations. The OFT makes clear that it may require information on all internal investigatory steps taken by the applicant, including steps taken prior to the placing of a marker. Controversially, the OFT can require the waiver of any legal privilege pertaining to the lawyers' notes of any internal witness interviews and the disclosure of such notes, including to the third parties being prosecuted for the cartel offence.

Provided that the undertaking is the first cartel member to approach the OFT, the OFT is likely to enter into a standard form leniency agreement with the applicant once the marker has been perfected. (A copy of the pro-forma leniency agreement is included in the Leniency Guidance Note and the OFT has indicated that it will not generally expect to negotiate amendments.) The leniency agreement will grant the applicant provisional leniency – a grant of leniency subject to the condition that the OFT does not at a later stage of the investigation conclude that the applicant does not meet the eligibility conditions, for example the applicant is found to have coerced another undertaking to take part in the cartel or the applicant has failed to provide the OFT with all relevant information. Were the OFT to conclude that the applicant had coerced other cartel members, the applicant would only be eligible to receive partial leniency. If the applicant fails to meet the other conditions (ie, does not co-operate or provide all relevant information), the applicant will not be eligible for any immunity or leniency.

If the undertaking discovers any innocent omissions after the perfection of the marker, the undertaking should inform the OFT immediately and satisfy the OFT that the omission was innocent (the relevant audit of information had been thorough) and that the complete information was subsequently provided without delay. If the information is relevant, the OFT will amend the scope of the leniency agreement and no-action letter. There is no obligation to submit information that is outside the scope of the application. However, if information relating to other cartel conduct is discovered, the undertaking should seek to take advantage of the 'leniency plus' option. When an undertaking obtains Type A or Type B immunity, all current and former employees and directors of the undertaking will automatically receive immunity. The undertaking does not need to produce upfront a list of names of its current and former employees and directors who may be implicated in the cartel. Rather, it can be taken as definite that any former director or employee will receive a no-action letter if they need it. The OFT will assess on an individual-by-individual basis whether to grant immunity to the current and former employees and directors of an undertaking which receives Type C leniency.

In addition, an individual can also approach the OFT on their own account to seek individual immunity. That individual will be guaranteed a no-action letter, if they require this, provided the individual tells the OFT about the cartel activity before any other individual or undertaking and there is no pre-existing criminal or civil investigation. If there is a pre-existing criminal or civil investigation, the individual may still be granted individual immunity provided they add value to the OFT's investigation and the OFT is not already in the course of gathering sufficient information to bring a successful prosecution of the individual.

The legal adviser may also call the OFT and ask if a given 'hypothetical' scenario would, or would be likely to, lead to prosecution for the cartel offence. The OFT has indicated that in many cases it will be able to give an assurance that a prosecution would not be contemplated in a given scenario. The OFT can also be asked for an initial indication of whether it might be prepared to issue a no-action letter. If the OFT is prepared to issue a no-action letter, the individual will be interviewed. Individuals benefiting from automatic immunity as a current or former employee of an undertaking which has qualified as a Type A or Type B applicant will be interviewed in order for the OFT to obtain all relevant information. In other cases where the grant is discretionary, the interview will also enable the OFT to assess whether it is in the public interest to grant the individual immunity.

The interview may extend over several sessions. Any information the individual provides in the interviews will not be used against them in criminal proceedings unless the individual knowingly or recklessly provides false or misleading information or if a no-action letter was issued and subsequently revoked. A copy of the pro-forma no-action letter, which will need to be signed by the individual applicant, is included in the Leniency Guidance Note.

Individuals who co-operate fully with the OFT will not be penalised if other employees or directors of the undertaking fail to co-operate and the undertaking fails to deliver information that matches its 'proffer' (Type B cases).

On completion of the interview(s) the OFT will advise the applicant in writing whether it is prepared to issue a no-action letter. In cases where the OFT concludes that the applicant is not at risk of criminal prosecution for the cartel offence, it will not issue a no-action letter and will confirm this in writing. If an individual, who was initially discounted as irrelevant to the investigation, later assumes more significance, then the individual will be given a no-action letter provided they meet the conditions for obtaining individual immunity.

Parallel to the usual steps to obtain leniency is the 'summary application' route which allows an applicant to lodge a short form summary application with the OFT in cases where the applicant has also sought immunity from the European Commission. This route reflects the uniform summary application model proposed in the ECN Model Leniency Programme in September 2006 and is designed to minimise the burden of multiple filings on leniency applicants.

The OFT has indicated that it will accept short form 'summary applications' where:
- the Commission is 'particularly well placed' to deal with a case (ie, the cartel has effects on more than three EU member states);
- the OFT is also 'well placed' to act in the case (ie, the cartel has a substantial direct actual or foreseeable effect on competition within the UK and is implemented within or originates from the UK; the OFT is able to effectively terminate and sanction the infringement; and the OFT can gather the necessary evidence);
- the applicant has made an application for immunity (full leniency) to the Commission; and
- the applicant is in a Type A position in the UK (ie, the OFT has not commenced an investigation and the applicant is the first undertaking to seek leniency).

A summary application may in many cases follow a no-names marker obtained by an applicant seeking immunity from the Commission. Once the applicant is able to confirm to the OFT that it has in fact sought immunity from the Commission and has perfected the marker (via the identification of the applicant and the description of the marker), the applicant should file the summary application. There is no prescribed form of a summary application in the Leniency Guidance Note but the OFT has indicated that it will follow the procedure set out in the ECN Model Leniency Programme which suggests that a summary application should include the following:

- the name and address of the applicant;
- the other parties to the alleged cartel;
- a short description of the affected products and territories;
- a short description of the duration and nature of the alleged cartel conduct;
- the member states where the evidence is likely to be located; and
- information on other past or possible leniency applications in relation to the alleged cartel.

The OFT will acknowledge receipt of the application and will confirm whether the applicant is the first to seek immunity from it. The OFT will then determine whether it will decide to take up the case. If the OFT does decide to take up the case, it will specify a date by which the applicant needs to make a full submission of relevant evidence and information to meet the threshold. If the applicant submits the required information by the specified date, the information provided will be deemed to have been submitted on the date when the summary application was made.

11. Is there an optimal time to approach the regulatory authority?

Full immunity is only available to the first cartel member to provide information to the OFT in relation to the cartel activities. In addition, full leniency is only automatically available when the undertaking provides information to the OFT before it has commenced its investigation and does not already have sufficient information to establish the existence of the alleged cartel activity (Type A immunity). The applicant will also need to supply the OFT with information that provides it with sufficient basis to take forward a credible investigation.

While the grant of full immunity to an undertaking which is the first to come forward in a pre-existing investigation is discretionary (Type B immunity), the OFT has indicated that full immunity will be the norm rather than the exception in these cases, provided that the information offered genuinely advances the investigation.

In order to ensure an undertaking secures a marker as the first in the queue, the undertaking should make contact with the Director of Cartels at the OFT (or the relevant sector regulator) as soon as possible identifying the basis for the suspected infringement, specifying the nature and details of the infringement and the evidence uncovered to date. The information required to 'perfect' the marker can be provided at a later date as agreed with the OFT at the time the marker is obtained.

12. What guarantees of leniency exist if a party co-operates?

Immunity is only guaranteed if the undertaking seeking immunity is the first undertaking to come forward with information, the information is provided before the OFT has begun an investigation and the OFT does not already have sufficient information to establish that a cartel exists (a Type A case). The applicant will also have to comply with the four cumulative conditions for obtaining immunity.

The OFT has a discretion to grant full immunity when it is sought after an investigation has commenced (Type B) although the OFT has indicated that the grant of full immunity will be the norm not the exception, provided the information the applicant provides genuinely adds value to the investigation. The OFT is able to grant partial leniency when another undertaking has already sought leniency, or when the undertaking has been found to have taken steps to coerce another undertaking to participate in the cartel activity, but again the grant of leniency in these circumstances is discretionary. An applicant will also have to comply with the conditions for obtaining leniency.

Individual immunity will be automatic for those current and former employees and directors of an undertaking which successfully obtains Type A corporate immunity and in most Type B cases, provided the individuals meet the conditions for obtaining individual immunity.

CONSEQUENCES
13. What effects does leniency granted to a corporate defendant have on the defendant's employees? Does it protect them from criminal/civil liability?

Individual immunity will be automatic for all implicated current and former employees and directors of an undertaking which obtained Type A or Type B immunity. However, an applicant should be aware that neither individual nor corporate immunity will be granted where the OFT believes that it has, or is in the course of gathering sufficient information to bring a successful prosecution. Where the OFT's investigation has already been referred to the Serious Fraud Office (the SFO), the OFT will consult the SFO about the possible grant of criminal immunity. The OFT has indicated that in such cases, the grant of immunity may no longer be in the public interest.
It will not be necessary for the applicant to produce a list of names of its current and former employees and directors who may have been implicated in the cartel. The OFT has stated that it can be taken as 'definite' in Type A cases that any current or former employee and director, wherever they are in the world and whatever their role in the cartel activity, will receive a no-action letter where they need it.

When another individual or undertaking has already obtained a marker in the leniency queue (ie, a Type C case), blanket criminal immunity is not available. The OFT will however consider, on an individual-by-individual basis whether one or more employees or directors of an undertaking qualifying for Type C leniency should be granted individual immunity. The OFT's assessment will take into account the overall value added by the Type C applicant and whether such a grant would be in the public interest. A legal adviser could seek confidential guidance from the OFT on a no-names basis as to whether the OFT would be minded to grant immunity to an individual on hypothetical facts.

An employee or director involved in cartel activity may also wish to seek immunity on their own account. The OFT has indicated that individual immunity is most likely to be granted when an individual makes an approach for criminal immunity entirely separately from an approach by an undertaking. If that individual seeks immunity before any other individual or undertaking and there is no pre-existing criminal or cartel investigation, that individual will be guaranteed a no-action letter.

If there is already a criminal investigation, but the individual tells the OFT about the cartel activity before any other individual or undertaking, the individual will still be granted individual immunity, if they provide 'added value' to the OFT's investigation (the OFT will however retain a discretion to determine whether the individual adds value).

When an individual seeks immunity before their undertaking, the undertaking loses the possibility of guaranteed corporate and blanket individual immunity for all employees and directors. However, full immunity is still possible at the discretion of the OFT.

The OFT may, however, still grant corporate and individual immunity to others in the undertaking depending on how much the evidence offered by the undertaking is likely to advance the OFT's investigation and the stage of the investigation at which the undertaking made its approach.

When individual immunity is discretionary (ie, where the applicant does not qualify for Type A or Type B immunity), the OFT will interview the applicant to determine whether it is in the public interest to exercise its discretion to grant a no-action letter in principle and to obtain information from the individual in order to advance the investigation. Even where an immunity applicant benefits from guaranteed individual immunity, the OFT will interview the individual in order to obtain all relevant information. In both scenarios, the interview will be carried out under the protections laid out in the OFT's Guidance on the issue of no-action letter for individuals: information provided by individuals in the interviews will not be used against them in criminal proceedings provided the information is not false or misleading or, exceptionally, if the no-action letter is revoked. Information provided by an individual could, however, be used against the undertaking if the undertaking has failed as a whole to satisfy the co-operation criteria.

Individuals will not be penalised by the failure of other employees to co-operate which may render the undertaking with which they are associated in breach of its co-operation condition of immunity.

14. Does leniency bar further criminal or private enforcement?

Full immunity granted to an undertaking does not bar criminal enforcement against an individual directly involved in the cartel activity. However, the OFT has indicated that in cases where an undertaking has been granted full immunity in accordance with the OFT Penalty Guidance or the EC Leniency Notice, the employees and directors of the undertaking will automatically receive immunity, provided the conditions for individual immunity are met. The OFT Guidance Note sets out the protection from the UK criminal cartel offence that will be afforded current and former employees and directors of an undertaking which has received immunity from the European Commission. This is further detailed below in response to question 19.

The OFT is unable to shield undertakings who have obtained leniency from potential private enforcement claims made by third parties.

While private enforcement claims have historically not been common in the UK, such claims are now on the increase, particularly in cases following an infringement decision by a competition authority.

Section 18 of the Enterprise Act 2002 (which inserted a new section 47A into the Competition Act 1998) provides for 'follow on actions' for damages to be brought before the Competition Appeals Tribunal (the CAT) where there has been an infringement decision of the OFT, the CAT or the European Commission. Section 58A of the Competition Act 1998 (inserted by section 20 of the Enterprise Act 2002) further provides that certain competition law infringement findings are binding on courts. This means that if the OFT has made an infringement decision, a third party claimant bringing a case for damages can rely upon that decision and need only establish causation and quantum.

PROTECTION AGAINST DISCLOSURE/CONFIDENTIALITY
15. Is confidentiality afforded to the leniency applicant and other co-operating parties? If so, to what extent? Is the identity of the leniency applicant/other co-operating parties disclosed during the investigation or in the final decision? Is information provided by the leniency applicant/other co-operating parties passed on to other undertakings under investigation? Can a leniency applicant/other co-operating party request anonymity or confidentiality of information provided?

The OFT has indicated that it will endeavour to keep the identity of the undertaking disclosing information and seeking immunity or leniency confidential throughout the course of its investigation until the statement of objections (SO) is issued. However, the undertaking's interest in keeping its identity secret must be balanced against the OFT's statutory obligations, including its obligation to exchange information within the European Competition Network, the network of the national competition authorities of member states and the European Commission (the ECN), and also its obligation to set out all the facts in the statement of objections and to provide access to the investigation file, if requested.

If a person has sought immunity from prosecution on their own account and can provide valuable information to the OFT as to a cartel they have arguably participated in, the individual may be granted immunity, but remain a secret source. However, the OFT has indicated that an individual immunity source will only be treated as a secret source where the safety of the individual would be in serious jeopardy or other very serious adverse consequences would follow if the individual's approach to the OFT became known.

The OFT has stated that, in the course of a civil investigation it may be necessary, directly or indirectly, to disclose information provided by a leniency application to third party witnesses or those suspected of direct involvement in the cartel. Consequently the OFT recognises that there is a risk that parties will conclude that information has been supplied by a leniency applicant, which may in turn reveal the identity of the applicant.

A similar risk may arise when the OFT is conducting a criminal investigation as, prior to interviewing suspects, the OFT is required to provide disclosure of any material to which the OFT wishes to refer or allude during an investigation.

In a civil investigation, the fact that a party has applied for leniency, together with the information it has submitted and on which the OFT intends to rely, will be set out in the SO issued to the other parties to the proceedings. Similarly, subject to the Competition Act 1998 (OFT's Rules) Order 2004 (the OFT's Rules) on the protection of confidential information, material submitted as part of the leniency application will be disclosed to the parties during the course of access to the file. Before making any such disclosure, however, the OFT will give the leniency applicant a reasonable opportunity to make representations as to whether the OFT should treat any or all of the information as confidential within the meaning of the OFT's Rules. Any person to whom information is disclosed in an SO or as part of access to the file will be bound by the restrictions on further disclosure as set out in Part 9 of the Enterprise Act 2002.

If the OFT's investigation results in an infringement decision, the fact that a party has been granted leniency will become apparent from the infringement decision and thus public. Undertakings applying for leniency must therefore accept that at this stage, the fact that a party has been granted leniency, together with the nature of at least some of the evidence provided will become public.

With regard to disclosure of materials to support private civil proceedings, the OFT has stated that it would firmly resist requests for disclosure of leniency material, or the fact that leniency has been sought, where such requests are made, for example, in connection with private civil proceedings whether in the UK or overseas. However, leniency applicants must be aware that their identity will enter the public domain through any published infringement decision or through any criminal proceedings held in open court.

16. Is the evidence submitted by the leniency applicant protected from transmission to other competition authorities with whom the authority in question co-operates? If so, how?

In its Leniency Guidance Note, the OFT has stated that information supplied as part of an application for corporate immunity or leniency will never be passed to an overseas agency without the consent of the applicant bar one exception. The information may be disclosed to the European Commission and/or the competition authority of an EU member state but only in accordance with the provisions and safeguards set out in the European Commission's Network Notice. The European Commission's Network Notice provides that information voluntarily submitted by a leniency applicant can only be transmitted to another ECN member where the applicant has consented to the transfer, the applicant has also sought leniency in respect of the same infringement from the authority to which the information is to be given, or where the authority to which the information is to be given has given certain guarantees regarding the use of the information.

The OFT has also stated that information supplied as part of an application for individual immunity will never be passed to an overseas agency without the consent of the provider bar one exception. The OFT may provide information to the European Commission to pursue administrative proceedings against two or more undertakings under Article 101 TFEU, in which case the European Commission would be required to guarantee to the OFT that the information would not be provided to any other agency. When the OFT contemplates providing such information to the European Commission, the OFT will consult the individual who provided the information.

The OFT has indicated that, if it were to pass information deriving from an immunity applicant to another UK agency such as the SFO, it would always discuss this with the applicant or their legal adviser first.

17. To what extent can evidence submitted by the leniency applicant (transcripts of oral statements or written evidence) become discoverable in subsequent private enforcement claims? Can leniency information be subjected to discovery orders in foreign or domestic courts? Can leniency information submitted in a foreign jurisdiction be subjected to discovery orders in the domestic courts?

This question raises whether evidence provided by the leniency applicant can be obtained, for the purposes of civil litigation, from: (i) the OFT; (ii) the leniency applicant; and/or (iii) a fellow cartelist who has had access to this evidence, for example through access to the OFT's file in order to exercise its rights of defence.

(i) The OFT has indicated in the Leniency Guidance Note that it would strongly resist requests for disclosure of leniency material, or the fact that leniency has been sought, where such requests are made in connection with private civil proceedings, whether in the UK or overseas. However, where a court has made an order with which the OFT is bound to comply, it has confirmed that it would discharge its duty to the court. Furthermore, it is the case that the identity of leniency applicants, and certain information that they have provided, will enter the public domain through any published infringement decision or through any criminal proceedings held in open court.

(ii) The issue is whether evidence provided by the leniency applicant would have to be disclosed by the leniency applicant, for example as defendant in civil litigation, through the usual disclosure process (or if appropriate pre-action disclosure). While this has not been tested, it would appear likely that at least the underlying historic evidence (ie, not material specifically prepared for any oral leniency application which may potentially be protected, for example, by legal professional privilege) would need to be disclosed in the ordinary way.

(iii) The issue is whether evidence provided to the OFT by the leniency applicant which in turn had been made available to another cartelist, for example, as part of access to the file, would have to be disclosed by the other cartelist, for example, as defendant in civil litigation, through the usual disclosure processes. Again it is untested whether a UK court would require such disclosure in full proceedings. However, there are statutory restrictions on disclosure of information obtained by the OFT which are set out in Part 9 of the Enterprise Act 2002 (sections 237 – 246 of the Act). Information obtained by the OFT can only in limited circumstances be passed on and in those instances there are restrictions on further disclosure. Moreover, in a recent judgment on an application for strike out or summary judgment, the court noted confidentiality obligations imposed on one of the parties by the OFT in relation to a statement of objections which, as a result, was not before the court (*Safeway Stores Ltd & Ors v Twigger & Ors* [210] EWCH 11, dated 15 January 2010).

The OFT has stated, in the context of its recommendations to the UK government for improving the effectiveness of private damages actions for breaches of competition law (OFT916resp, November 2007), that it is committed to protecting the effectiveness of the leniency programme. It therefore recommended to the government that it should be provided, by statutory instrument, that leniency documents be excluded from use in litigation without the consent of the leniency applicant. However, this has not been progressed further to date.

18. Are there any precedents in which evidence from a leniency application has been discovered in a private enforcement claim?

There has not been a case where it has been tested whether a UK court could require the OFT or a leniency applicant or co-defendant to produce evidence from a leniency application in the context of a private enforcement claim (see also response to question 17 above).

RELATIONSHIP WITH THE EUROPEAN COMMISSION'S LENIENCY NOTICE AND LENIENCY POLICY IN OTHER EU MEMBER STATES

19. Does the policy address the interaction with applications under the Commission Leniency Notice? If so, how?

The Leniency Guidance Note includes a five-page section on the interaction between the criminal cartel offence and the position of EC immunity applicants. This section attempts to allay concerns that an undertaking seeking immunity from the European Commission could inadvertently expose its employees and directors to prosecution under the UK criminal cartel offence if the cartel behaviour has an effect in the UK.

Firstly, the OFT points out that most applicants who qualify for immunity under the EC Leniency Notice will be able to benefit from blanket criminal immunity for all current and former employees and directors provided that undertaking separately applies for Type A or Type B immunity in the UK.

In addition, the OFT indicates that even if an undertaking is unable to obtain Type A or Type B immunity in the UK (and hence blanket criminal immunity for its employees and directors), the undertaking may still be able to obtain some comfort from the OFT. The OFT may be able to do this by reassuring the undertaking's adviser, on the basis of a set of hypothetical facts, that the case would not be of a type where the OFT would contemplate bringing a criminal prosecution. Further, in a case where an undertaking has obtained immunity from the European Commission (but has not qualified for Type A or Type B immunity in the UK), the OFT has indicated that it will normally be prepared to grant a no-action letter to any implicated current or former employee or director of that undertaking. A no-action letter is not however likely to be forthcoming in the following situations:

- there is already a pre-existing criminal investigation in the UK;
- the OFT suspects that the applicant may be attempting to 'game the system' (eg, the undertaking is too late for Type A immunity in the UK and an application has been made to the Commission largely as a device for trying to procure no-action letters);
- the cartel is not one which the Commission would be particularly well placed to investigate within the terms of the Network Notice (ie, the cartel does not have effects in more than three EU member states); or
- there has been an unreasonable delay between the approach to the Commission and the subsequent approach to the OFT.

In light of the uncertainty surrounding the grant of criminal immunity to the employees and directors of an undertaking that has qualified for EC (but not UK) immunity, undertakings which have obtained immunity from the EC are, if the cartel has an effect on the UK, recommended to make a prompt approach to the OFT to try to secure Type A immunity (and hence blanket criminal immunity for its employees or directors). This could be achieved via a no-names marker (available when an EC immunity application is to be filed) or via the standard marker approach.

When an undertaking has only qualified for a reduction in fines from the European Commission (partial leniency), the OFT will not normally issue a no-action letter. However, the OFT notes that potential Commission applicants will not increase the likelihood of prosecution under the UK criminal cartel offence of any of its current or former employees and directors by making an application for partial leniency from the European Commission.

This is due to the restrictions on information sharing set out in the EC Network Notice, which as emphasised in the Leniency Guidance Note, prevent the OFT from using, either as intelligence or evidence, any leniency-derived information obtained from the Commission to further its criminal cartel enforcement functions. Further, the OFT has indicated that it will employ an 'information barrier' between staff having access to information derived from the Commission leniency application and staff on a team investigating the same activity under the criminal cartel offence provisions. Staff having access to information derived from the Commission leniency application will not be permitted to pass on information directly or indirectly to the team investigating the activity under the criminal cartel offence provisions. However, whether a criminal court in which the OFT sought to bring a criminal prosecution were to respect such an 'information barrier' is a separate, currently untested question and may appear doubtful.

20. Does the policy address the interaction with applications for leniency in other EU member states? If so, how? Does the authority accept summary applications in line with the ECN Model Leniency Programme?

Neither the outline of the UK leniency policy set out in the Penalty Guidance nor the Leniency Guidance Note address the interaction with leniency applications made in other EU member states.

Steps have however been taken by the ECN to address the concern that has arisen as a result of the discrepancies between the leniency programmes of the EU member states, via the ECN Model Leniency Programme which sets out the treatment which an applicant can anticipate in any ECN jurisdiction once alignment of all programmes has taken place.

The OFT accepts summary applications in line with the ECN Model Leniency Programme, as discussed in response to question 2 above.

RELATIONSHIP WITH SETTLEMENT PROCEDURES

21. What is the relationship between leniency and applicable settlement procedures? Are they mutually exclusive?

Unlike the European Commission, the OFT does not currently have a formalised settlement procedure for cartels. However, the OFT is prepared to consider settlements in many cartel cases and has entered into some settlements. (In contrast to the European Commission's approach, the OFT has indicated that it may also be willing to accept settlements in cases concerning competition law infringements other than cartels and also that it has not set a fixed ceiling regarding the maximum settlement discount available.)

There would appear to be no reason for the OFT's leniency regime and the OFT's settlement procedures to be mutually exclusive. Leniency is usually at issue at an earlier stage in the investigation than a settlement, which is discussed at a later stage with a view to administrative resource savings. There have been no published decisions where both leniency and a settlement discount were granted but it has been mentioned that both types of reductions may have led to the £121.5 million penalty in the negotiated OFT settlement with British Airways (OFT press release published on 1 August 2007) but there has been no formal decision on this yet.

Directors of the OFT have stated that it considers that, to ensure equality of treatment, it is important to achieve consistency in penalties. To this end, the OFT undertakes penalty modelling in accordance with its Penalty Guidance. As part of this exercise, the OFT compares the initial fine arrived at with previous cases. Settlement prospects are taken into account at step 4 of the OFT's Penalty Guidance and once the settlement discount has been applied, the OFT again verifies the consistency of the reduced fine with previous cases.

The OFT has stated informally that it is also prepared to consider 'partial settlements' ie, settlement by some but not all of the parties to whom an SO is addressed. The OFT may also consider settlement by a party in respect of some but not all of the allegations contained in an SO. Again, this must be contrasted with the European Commission's approach which has excluded this possibility.

REFORM/LATEST DEVELOPMENTS
22. Is there a reform underway to revisit the leniency policy? What are the latest developments?
On 11 December 2008, the OFT, after lengthy consultation, published its current guidance on the handling of leniency and no-action letters (the Leniency Guidance Note), which supplements and elaborates on (and to some extent amends) the procedures set out in the OFT Penalty Guidance and the OFT Guidance on the Issue of No-action Letters, but does not replace them. The OFT emphasised at the time of publication that while the guidance was final, it does not rule out further amendment as a result of its future experiences when applying the leniency and no-action policies.

One of the key recent developments in the OFT's cartel enforcement practice relates to the criminal prosecution of cartels. The OFT brought a first successful prosecution of three individuals in the *Marine Hose* cartel in June 2008, in circumstances where the defendants pleaded guilty. (On appeal, the three individuals received prison sentences of 30 months, 24 months and 20 months respectively. In addition two of the individuals were disqualified from acting as company directors for seven years and the third was disqualified for five years. Further, two of the three individuals, who the court was satisfied had benefitted financially from the crime, had a combined total of just over £1 million worth of assets confiscated.) Moreover, the OFT is currently prosecuting four current and former employees of British Airways in the *Passenger Fuel Surcharges* cartel in circumstances where the other involved undertaking benefits from immunity.

In relation to follow-on damages actions, the OFT published recommendations to the UK government for improving the effectiveness of private damages actions for breaches of competition law in November 2007 (OFT916resp). In this context, the OFT noted its commitment to protecting the effectiveness of the leniency programme. Indeed, it recommended to the government that it should be provided, by statutory instrument, that immunity recipients are not jointly and severally liable with other wrongdoers, so that they would only be liable for the harm caused themselves. However, this has not been progressed further to date.

United States

Simpson Thacher & Bartlett LLP Kevin J. Arquit & Andrew M. Lacy

BACKGROUND

1. What is the relevant legislation containing the leniency policy and what is the enforcing body?

The Antitrust Division of the Department of Justice (the Division) enforces the leniency policy. It has published both a corporate leniency policy (also known as the 'amnesty programme') and a leniency policy for individuals. The Division first published the corporate leniency policy in 1978, and revised and adopted a new corporate leniency programme on 10 August 1993. The Division revised the amnesty programme in three major respects. First, the amnesty becomes automatic ('automatic amnesty') if the applicant comes forward before the Division initiates an investigation. In this case, the grant of amnesty is certain and is not subject to prosecutorial discretion. Second, when automatic amnesty is not available, the Division may grant amnesty even after it has initiated an investigation, subject to prosecutorial discretion. Third, all employees, directors and officers of a corporation that qualifies for automatic amnesty will also qualify for amnesty.

The Division issued its leniency policy for individuals on 10 August 1994.

2. What are the basic tenets of a leniency/immunity programme? Is leniency available also for other types of competition law violations other than cartels?

The amnesty programme is available only in connection with cartel behaviour and has three basic components.

2.1 Automatic amnesty

The Division will automatically grant amnesty if the corporation contacts the Division before it has started an investigation and if the corporation satisfies the following six conditions:
- the corporation must be 'first in the door'; that is, the Division must not have received information about the illegal activity from any other sources;
- the corporation must have taken prompt and effective action to terminate its part in the activity upon its discovery. Termination does not require announcement of withdrawal from the illegal activity to other participants in the activity. Termination can be effected by reporting the illegal activity to the Division and refraining from further participation unless the Division approves continued participation;

- the corporation must co-operate fully;
- the corporation must not have coerced another party to participate in, and must not have been the ringleader of, the activity (the Division distinguishes between the ringleader, and two or more founding corporations, of the cartel. While any one of the companies forming the conspiracy can seek amnesty because it is not the ringleader of the cartel, the ringleader or organiser cannot seek amnesty);
- where possible, the corporation must make restitution to injured parties; and
- the confession of wrongdoing must be a corporate act, as opposed to isolated confessions of individual executives.

2.2 Alternative amnesty

If a corporation comes forward after the Division has initiated an investigation or otherwise does not meet the conditions above, the Division has the discretion to grant amnesty ('alternative amnesty'). To qualify for alternative amnesty, the amnesty applicant must satisfy the following seven conditions:
- the corporation must be the first to co-operate;
- the corporation must co-operate fully;
- the corporation must have taken prompt and effective action to terminate its part in the activity upon its discovery;
- where possible, the corporation must make restitution to injured parties;
- the confession of wrongdoing must be a corporate act, as opposed to isolated confessions of individual executives;
- when the amnesty applicant comes forward, the Division must not yet have evidence against the applicant that is likely to result in a sustainable conviction; and
- a granting of amnesty must not be unfair to others, considering the nature of the illegal activity, the corporation's role in it, and the time the corporation comes forward.

2.3 Corporate employee amnesty

Corporate directors, officers and employees will receive automatic amnesty if the corporation qualifies for automatic amnesty. Amnesty, however, is not available to corporate 'ringleaders.'

The leniency policy for individuals applies to individuals who approach the Division on their own behalf, not as part of a corporate proffer. If the individual comes forward before the Division has received information about the activity, the Division will grant leniency to the individual, provided that the individual reports the activity completely, co-operates fully, and was not the ringleader of the illegal activity.

3. How many cartels have been unveiled and punished since the adoption of the leniency policy?

Because the Division does not disclose the identities of amnesty applicants without their consent, there are no exact statistics on the number of cartels unveiled and punished since the adoption of the amnesty programme. Recently some new information on the number of cartels has come to light in connection with a settlement between the Division and Stolt-Nielsen. As discussed further in the response to question 12 below, Stolt-Nielsen is the sole applicant from whom the Division has attempted to revoke amnesty. In protesting the revocation, Stolt-Nielsen made a Freedom of Information Act Request (FOIA) for all Division amnesty letters from 1993 to 2005. After protracted litigation, the Division settled with Stolt-Nielsen and produced the 100 amnesty letters it had issued from 1993 to 2005, redacted to protect the identities of the applicants.

Additional information comes directly from public statements by the Division. For example, Division officials have reported that while they had received only one amnesty application per year before the 1993 reform, this number has increased to two per month since the revised amnesty programme. (See Scott D Hammond *DOJ Cracks Down on Antitrust Penalties Electronic Business*, 1 May 2005.) The Division also has reported that, since the 1993 reform, the co-operation of amnesty applicants has led to the collection of over $4 billion in criminal fines by the Division and has resulted in scores of criminal convictions. In the past 10 years, the Division has reported fines exceeding $10 million in 56 cases, and fines exceeding $100 million in 11 cases, of which three were fines of $300 million and one was a fine of $500 million. Indeed, in the first half of fiscal 2009, the Division obtained nearly $1 billion in criminal fines against corporate defendants. In fiscal year 2008, the Division had 137 pending grand jury investigations and filed 54 cases against 59 individuals and 25 companies.

4. What is needed to be a successful leniency applicant? Is documentary evidence required or is testimonial evidence sufficient?

The conditions that an amnesty applicant must satisfy are identified in question 2 above. The applicant need not meet evidentiary standards when presenting its application. But the applicant must present enough substantial and direct evidence for the Division to evaluate the application. The Division does not require the applicant to present 'decisive' evidence of the existence of a cartel. On the contrary, the Division has made clear that an amnesty applicant who played only a peripheral role in the cartel is a more attractive applicant, as it is less culpable than other members of the cartel though it most likely has less information on the existence of the cartel. On the other hand, the Division will not grant amnesty to the ringleader of the cartel.

The Division accepts paperless submissions, allowing applicants to avoid creating documents that could be used against them in a civil case.

TIMING
5. What are the benefits of being 'first in' to co-operate?
As noted in question 2 above, being first in to co-operate is of paramount importance because amnesty is generally available only to a corporation or

an individual that is the first in. While the first amnesty applicant typically pays no criminal fines and its culpable executives are spared criminal exposure, no such accommodations are granted to subsequent applicants. The three most important benefits of being first in to co-operate are that: (i) the corporation will not be criminally prosecuted; (ii) the individuals within the corporation will not be criminally prosecuted; and (iii) the corporation will pay no fines.

Being first in to co-operate is particularly important for the individuals involved in the activity, as it may make the difference between not being prosecuted and being convicted and sentenced to jail. In some cases, the first applicant in the door may provide sufficient information to remove the possibility of a no-jail deal for the executives of a company that is second in the door. In other cases, where the evidence is not as developed, the Division tends to offer no-jail deals deeper into the investigation.

The Division's investigation and successful prosecution of the fine art auction case provides a recent example of the benefits of being the first in to co-operate. Christie's was the first to co-operate while Sotheby's was the second. The Division did not fine Christie's, and did not prosecute any of its current executives. In contrast, Sotheby's pleaded guilty to price fixing, the former CEO, Diana Brooks, pleaded guilty to price fixing, and Alfred Taubman, former chairman of the board, pleaded not guilty, was tried and convicted. Mr Taubman was sentenced to one year and one day in prison, and a $7.5 million fine.

6. What are the consequences of being 'second'? Is there an 'immunity plus' or 'amnesty plus' option?

One of the critical differences between the EU and the US leniency regimes is that US amnesty is available only to the first in to co-operate, while the EU leniency notice provides some forms of leniency to corporations that come forward later in the process. In the US, the second firm in the door – even if only by a few hours – and all of its culpable executives, will be subject to full prosecution. This is critical in cases of two-firm cartels when being second means being last to co-operate. For example, since Sotheby's was second in the door after Christie's in the fine art auction case, the Division granted amnesty to Christie's, while it fully prosecuted Sotheby's.

In other instances, corporations and individuals that come forward after the leniency applicant and offer to co-operate may enter into plea agreements, but this process falls outside of the amnesty programme. Nonetheless, the Division offers compelling incentives to being the second corporation to report. In exchange for prompt and genuine co-operation, the Division will seek minimum sentences or downward departures from the sentencing guidelines for both fines and jail time. Firms second to report have received fines of roughly 15 per cent of their respective volume of commerce, whereas firms that co-operate later pay average fines of 25 to 35 per cent of their respective volumes of commerce. In some international cases, where the size of the affected markets are large, the difference between reporting second and third can be tens or hundreds of millions of dollars in fines.

In addition, corporations can benefit from the US amnesty plus policy. In 1999, the Division announced that the corporate leniency policy had been extended to include an 'amnesty plus' provision, under which a corporation may bring evidence of illegal activity in a second market to the Division in exchange for amnesty with respect to that conduct and a reduction in the fine from the first investigation. (See Gary R Spratling, Deputy Assistant Attorney General, Antitrust Division *Making Companies an Offer they Shouldn't Refuse: The Antitrust Division's Corporate Leniency Policy – An Update*, address before The Bar Association of the District of Columbia's 35th Annual Symposium on Associations and Antitrust, 16 February 1999.) This policy has generated numerous investigations. The Division has noted that more than half of its investigations are initiated as a result of leads generated during an investigation of a completely separate market.

Conversely, the Division will punish corporations that are late to co-operate. Corporations that elect not to participate in amnesty plus may be subject to the harsh consequences of the 'penalty plus' policy. If a corporation participated in a second antitrust offence and does not report it and that conduct is later successfully prosecuted, the Division, in appropriate circumstances, will recommend that the sentencing court consider the corporation's and any culpable executive's failure to report the conduct voluntarily as an aggravating factor under the US sentencing guidelines. For a corporation, the failure to voluntarily report a violation under amnesty plus may result in a fine as high as 80 per cent or more of the volume of commerce affected by the second offence as compared with no fine at all for the amnesty plus product. For an individual, failing to report under amnesty plus may mean the difference between a lengthy prison sentence and avoiding prison altogether. While the Division will negotiate a corporate disposition which will require a larger fine, the culpable officers, directors, and employees will be carved out of the non-prosecution of the plea agreement. These individuals will then have to negotiate separate pleas or be subject to indictment.

In a recent example involving Hoechst AG, the Division asked the court to impose a sentence on the corporation that was roughly 30 per cent above the maximum guideline fine and 130 per cent above the minimum guideline fine, as the company was a recidivist antitrust offender. Hoechst ended up paying a fine of $12 million, or approximately 70 per cent of the volume of affected commerce. And three Hoechst executives were carved out of the plea agreement.

Finally, the Division's policy to ask the 'omnibus question' to all parties should force corporations to benefit from the amnesty plus option. The Division will ask executives who are subpoenaed and compelled to provide sworn testimony under penalty of perjury whether they have any information of any cartel activity in any other markets as well as the market under investigation. The Division will also ask this question to the amnesty applicant.

7. Are subsequent firms given any beneficial treatment if they make a useful contribution? How are 'useful contributions' defined?

As noted in question 6 above, there are material benefits to reporting early in an antitrust investigation. Although amnesty is offered only to the first in the door, the Division may offer reduced sentences and fines when it receives previously unknown and useful information, especially when this information comes early. Moreover, sanctions for those who report later in the process have grown significantly over the years.

For example, Showa Denko Carbon, Inc., the Japanese firm that was second to report in the graphite electrodes investigation, received fines of $32.5 million or roughly 10 per cent of its volume of affected commerce. In contrast, SGL Carbon AG (SGL), the German-based corporation that reported last, received fines of $135 million or close to 30 per cent of its volume of affected commerce. SGL was, in fact, eligible for higher penalties, but received a reduction under the sentencing guidelines because of its inability to pay the full fine.

While the Division has not defined what 'useful contributions' are, the corporations who report late in the process are unlikely to assist the Division in mounting a case, and are unlikely to convince the Division that it should recommend reduced sentences and fines.

SCOPE/FULL LENIENCY
8. Is it possible to receive full leniency? And, if so, what are the conditions required to receive full leniency?

Yes, as noted above in question 2, it is possible to receive full leniency. The main requirement for amnesty is to be 'first in' to co-operate.

8.1 Can ringleaders/coercers receive full leniency?
As discussed above, ringleaders/coercers cannot receive full leniency.

8.2 Is there a requirement to 'co-operate fully and on an ongoing basis'? What does it entail?

As discussed above, leniency applicants are required to fully co-operate with the Division. As described in the Division's model corporate leniency letter, this requires that the leniency applicant: (i) provide all known facts; (ii) provide documents, information, and any other relevant materials; (iii) use best efforts to secure the co-operation of its current and former directors, officers, and employees; (iv) facilitate the appearance of any current or former directors, officers and employees before the Division; (v) use best efforts to ensure that current and former directors, officers and employees who provide information to the Division do so completely, candidly and truthfully; (vi) use best efforts to ensure that current and former directors, officers and employees who provide information to the Division make no attempt to falsely protect or falsely implicate any person; and (vii) make all reasonable efforts to pay restitution.

8.3 Does the regulatory authority require the applicant to cease participation in the cartel conduct after its application?
As discussed above, the Division requires that leniency applicants cease participation in the cartel conduct.

9. How many companies have received full immunity from fines to date?
As noted above in question 3, the Division does not disclose who has applied for amnesty, unless the amnesty holder has granted consent. Thus, the Division has not published the number of successful leniency applicants. However, as a result of the Stolt-Nielsen FOIA request it is now known that more than 100 companies have received immunity since 1993 and the Division has noted that it had received approximately two amnesty applications per month since the 1993 reform of the amnesty programme.

PROCEDURE
10. What are the practical steps required to apply for leniency?
Once the corporation uncovers an illegal activity, and completes a preliminary investigation that convinces it that it wishes to apply for leniency, the process will usually progress in five phases. First, the corporation's counsel will informally contact the Division to enquire whether amnesty is available and to apply for a marker to save the corporation's place in line. Second, the corporation's senior management and outside counsel will meet with the Division's staff and present the corporation's proffer of evidence. Third, the Division will grant conditional amnesty to the corporation. Fourth, the Division will launch a thorough investigation to confirm the statements made by the corporation in its proffer of evidence. Fifth, once the matter is completed, the Division will grant the successful applicant a final amnesty letter.

10.1 The application for a marker
Because time is of the essence for amnesty applicants, the Division allows potential applicants to contact it to put down a marker before providing substantial evidence that they should qualify for leniency. The date of this 'marker' is the official date on which the cartel members contacted the Division. This allows amnesty applicants to secure their place in line and ensure that they can benefit from amnesty.

While it is critical to put down a marker quickly, corporations should conduct a quick internal investigation before deciding to contact the Division. Amnesty applicants should carefully consider the scope of the marker. Putting down a marker that is too narrow in scope will not shield the applicant from activities it has not reported and putting down too broad a marker may lead the Division to expect information that will not be forthcoming. The Division, however, often expands the scope of the protection if the applicant's investigation unearths additional offences that were not reported when the applicant put down its marker.

After the applicant puts down a marker, the Division will then give the amnesty applicant a period of time to complete its internal investigation and present a proffer of evidence. This period of time may vary from a few days to several weeks, depending on the scope, complexity and circumstances of the case. It will also vary depending on whether the Division has initiated an investigation. The period of time will be longer if the Division has not initiated an investigation. It will be shorter, or the marker may not be available at all, if the Division has initiated an investigation. If the company fails to present its proffer of evidence within the time allocated by the Division, it risks losing its place in line and other companies will be considered for amnesty in the order in which they placed their markers.

10.2 The proffer of evidence
To ensure that it meets the conditions necessary to obtain amnesty, the applicant must make a thorough and detailed proffer of the evidence that the corporation or individual seeking amnesty will provide. Counsel typically makes this proffer in person with the Division's staff. The proffer should contain the most important facts and refer to the documents and facts that emerged during the corporation's internal investigation. To avoid having to produce a written proffer document to plaintiffs in private litigation, the applicant can make the proffer orally before the Division's staff. An effective proffer can take several days to complete.

10.3 Conditional amnesty letter
After the proffer, if the Division decides to grant leniency, it will send a conditional leniency letter to the amnesty applicant. In 2008, the Division issued revised model conditional leniency letters for corporate and individual defendants and posted them on its website. As discussed above, these letters are conditional on the applicant's performance of certain obligations over time, such as co-operating with the Division and making restitution. These letters are also contingent on the Division's investigation of the facts presented in the proffer.

10.4 Division investigation
The next step will be for the Division to conduct a thorough investigation of the facts presented in the proffer. The amnesty applicant will respond to the Division's inquiries, provide witnesses, and provide full and general co-operation with the Division's investigations.

Amnesty applicants should understand that this process can place a significant burden on the corporation's senior management, who should make themselves available to respond to the Division's requests. In many instances, this process will cause a significant disruption in the corporation's activities. The senior management of the corporation must take this obligation to co-operate fully seriously, as it is a prerequisite to receiving amnesty, and failure to co-operate fully could cause withdrawal of amnesty.

The amnesty applicant, however, is not required to waive its attorney-client or work product privilege.

10.5 Final amnesty letter

After the Division concludes its investigation and closes the matter, it issues a final amnesty letter confirming that amnesty has been granted. This letter is binding on the Division.

11. Is there an optimal time to approach the regulatory authority?

The best time to approach the Division is as soon as practicable, and as soon as the corporation has preliminarily evaluated its exposure. Clearly, a corporation or individual is always in a better position to negotiate while the Division is mounting its case rather than when it is near the end of its investigation. However, before approaching the Antitrust Division, a corporation should already have completed an internal investigation, in which implicated corporate employees have fully co-operated, so that it has sufficient evidence to present to the Division to support its application. In addition, corporate management must support the decision to seek amnesty.

Amnesty applicants in the United States should evaluate whether they need to seek leniency in other countries as well, most notably in the European Union and Canada. If the activity discovered has worldwide effects, the US amnesty applicant should probably also seek amnesty in other jurisdictions.

12. What guarantees of leniency exist if a party co-operates?

As noted in question 10 above, a final accepted amnesty is binding on the Division. Since 1993, the Division revoked amnesty in only one case, that of *Stolt-Nielsen*. In March 2004, the Division revoked the conditional amnesty in the *Stolt-Nielsen* case after it learned that top Stolt-Nielsen executives, including its managing director, had continued to meet with competitors and participate in the conspiracy for months after the discovery of the conspiracy by Stolt-Nielsen's then general counsel. The Division also claimed that Stolt-Nielsen had both withheld and provided false and misleading information about the true extent of the conspiracy.

In February 2004, Stolt-Nielsen filed lawsuits seeking an injunction to prevent the Division from revoking the amnesty. The US District Court for the Eastern District of Pennsylvania granted the injunction in January 2005. In March 2006, the Court of Appeals for the Third Circuit reversed the District Court decision and, in June 2006, denied petitions for rehearing. Attempts by Stolt-Nielsen to recall and stay the mandate of the Third Circuit failed, and on 24 August 2006, the District Court dissolved the injunction against the Division. Assistant Attorney General for Antitrust Thomas Barnett commented that: '*Stolt-Nielsen is the first company to have its conditional leniency revoked since the current programme was announced in 1993, (…) [r]emoving a company from the corporate leniency programme is not something the Division takes lightly but regrettably was necessary in this case to maintain the integrity of the programme, which requires that those in the programme provide full and truthful co-operation.*'

Perhaps in response to the Stolt-Nielsen suits, the Division's conditional leniency letters now require the applicant to acknowledge that the applicant 'understands that the Antitrust Division's Leniency Programme is an exercise of the Division's prosecutorial discretion,' and an agreement by the applicant 'not [to] seek judicial review of any Division decision to revoke [the applicant's] conditional leniency unless and until [the applicant] has been charged by indictment or information.'

CONSEQUENCES
13. What effects does leniency granted to a corporate defendant have on the defendant's employees?

As noted in question 2 above, all directors, officers, and employees of the corporation who admit their involvement in the activity of a corporate defendant that is granted automatic amnesty are also granted leniency as long as those employees are not corporate 'ringleaders'. Provided that the employees admit their wrongdoing and fully co-operate, they will not be charged criminally and will not pay a fine for their involvement in the activity.

If a corporation does not qualify for automatic amnesty, the directors, officers and employees of the corporation who come forward with it will be considered for immunity from criminal prosecution on the same basis as if they had approached the Division individually.

Moreover, individuals can gain significant benefits from co-operating with the Division, even when the Division refuses to grant individual amnesty. As discussed in question 6 above, the Division will negotiate plea agreements and recommend no or reduced jail sentences if the individuals co-operate with the investigation. This can be particularly beneficial to co-operating foreign nationals. To ensure that a criminal conviction does not result in deportation and permanent exclusion from the United States of a co-operating foreign national, in 1996 the Division entered into a memorandum of understanding with the Immigration and Naturalisation Service (MOU), which provides the pre-adjudication of co-operating individuals' immigration status before they enter into plea agreements with the Division. Therefore, the MOU gives co-operating foreign nationals written assurance in their plea agreements that their convictions will not be used by the INS as a basis to deport or exclude them from the United States.

In contrast, as noted in question 6 above, not requesting amnesty or being late to co-operate with the Division can have devastating effects on the corporation's employees. When individuals are carved out of the non-prosecution of the corporate agreement, they face indictment and jail terms. If foreign national culpable individuals remain outside the United States, they run the risk of becoming international fugitives. In 2001, the Division adopted a policy of placing indicted fugitives on a 'red notice' watch-list maintained by INTERPOL. A red notice watch is essentially an international 'wanted' list that, in many INTERPOL-member nations, serves as a request that the subject be arrested, with a view towards extradition. As such, the individuals could be arrested, detained, and held for trial if they travel to or through the United States or one of its territories. Moreover, they could be arrested, detained, extradited to the United States, and held for trial if they travel to or through any one of the countries with which the United States has an extradition treaty covering antitrust crimes. This possibility has been the subject of the Division's ongoing attempts to extradite Ian Norris, a British citizen and former CEO of the Morgan Crucible Company plc, on price fixing charges. On 1 June 2005, UK district court judge Nicholas Evans found that price fixing was an extraditable offence and ruled in favour of the Division's request that Norris be extradited. On 29 September 2005, the UK Secretary of State ordered Norris extradited. However, on 12 March 2008, the House of Lords overturned the extradition decision, finding that at the time Norris engaged in the anti-competitive conduct, price fixing was not a criminal offence in the UK. In July 2008, Judge Evans again ruled that Norris should be extradited on the additional charge of obstructing the course of justice and in September 2008, the UK Secretary of State again ordered Norris extradited. At the time of writing, Norris was appealing to the UK Supreme Court arguing that the European Convention on Human Rights precluded his extradition because of his medical conditions. If the Division is successful in its action, it will be the first time that the Division has successfully extradited a foreign national on price fixing charges.

14. Does leniency bar further criminal or private enforcement?

The amnesty programme protects applicants from federal enforcement actions only. State attorneys general are in no way prohibited from enforcing state antitrust provisions. More importantly, the amnesty programme does not protect a company from exposure to private, civil treble damages actions under section 1 of the Sherman Act. An amnesty applicant should try to understand this exposure before applying for amnesty before the Division, or otherwise seeking leniency in other jurisdictions.

Private litigants will invariably sue following announcements of guilty pleas, and often sue following the mere announcement of investigations or dawn raids by the Division or foreign competition authorities. The major disincentive to seeking amnesty is the virtual certainty that private action will follow. While the amnesty holder is not prosecuted by the Division, plaintiffs will know the identity of all market participants and name all participants in damages actions. For example, while Rhone Poulenc SA received amnesty in the vitamin cartel, it paid $86.8 million to food and animal-feed companies to settle a follow-on class action lawsuit. Thus, the amnesty applicant will most likely have to defend class action lawsuits from direct purchasers in federal courts, class action lawsuits from indirect purchasers in state court, and opt-out actions in state and federal courts.

14.1 Class actions

The US statutory scheme strongly favours private enforcement. Section 4 of the Clayton Act provides that victims of antitrust violations can recover treble damages. Plaintiffs can also recover attorneys' fees, and bring a suit on behalf of the class of purchasers injured by the cartel. A class action is a procedural device available in federal and state courts that, if certain prerequisites are established, allows one or more persons or entities to sue on behalf of a large class of similar plaintiffs. Federal cases are governed by Federal Rule of Civil Procedure 23, which generally requires plaintiffs to establish that: (i) the class is so numerous that joinder of all members as plaintiffs is impracticable; (ii) there are questions of law or fact common to the class; (iii) the claims of the named plaintiffs are typical of the claims of the class; and (iv) the representative plaintiffs will fairly and adequately represent the interests of the class. In many cases, plaintiffs must also establish either that: (i) defendants have acted on grounds generally applicable to the class, making appropriate injunctive or declaratory relief with respect to the class as a whole; or (ii) questions of law or fact common to members of the class predominate over questions affecting only individual members, and a class action is superior to other methods for the fair and efficient adjudication of the controversy.

Class actions frequently are employed in cartel cases because the claims lend themselves to satisfying the prerequisites for class certification. The class (all purchasers) frequently is quite numerous, the same activity by defendants is at issue with respect to the claims of all members of the class, and all members of the class suffer the same kind of harm – higher prices. In addition, the plaintiffs bar favours prosecuting cases as class actions because named plaintiffs are often passive parties. More importantly, courts typically award attorneys' fees to plaintiffs' counsel where cases are won or settled, and the large number of plaintiffs in a class generally creates a large amount of potential damages, which results in the award of millions of dollars in attorneys' fees due to the fact that attorneys' fees are typically tied to the size of the recovery. For example, the settlement agreement in the vitamins cases awarded $122.4 million in attorneys' fees.

14.2 *Prima facie* effect to convicted co-conspirators
The criminal convictions that amnesty applicants have helped to secure will serve as *prima facie* evidence in the follow-on civil trials. If a defendant loses an antitrust case that was brought by the Division, the defendant cannot require the follow-on private plaintiffs to prove the case on the merits. Section 5(a) of the Clayton Act, 15 USC §16(a) (2000), provides that a judgment against a defendant in an action brought by the United States is admissible as *prima facie* evidence of the matters decided in subsequent private antitrust suits. While there will be no *prima facie* effect towards the amnesty holder, since it was not found guilty, this statutory scheme incentivises the plaintiff bar, and pushes convicted defendants towards quick settlements.

14.3 Direct/indirect purchasers' distinction
In addition to defending federal suits brought by direct purchasers, defendants will have to defend state suits brought on behalf of indirect purchasers. The US Supreme Court laid down a bright-line rule 25 years ago in *Illinois Brick Co. v Illinois,* 431 US 720 (1977): under federal law, only those who have purchased directly from a member of a price-fixing conspiracy or a monopolist can assert claims from overcharge damages caused by that

conduct. Indirect purchasers cannot assert damages claims under federal law. Indirect purchasers, however, can bring damages claims in state court under a growing number of state laws. A number of states have enacted local laws, commonly called 'Illinois Brick repealers,' which expressly provide that indirect purchasers may recover overcharge damages. In other states, local courts have interpreted existing statutes to encompass indirect purchaser claims. As a result, a large number of indirect purchaser lawsuits are now being litigated in diverse state courts, and a company considering entering the amnesty programme has to factor in the prospect of civil treble damages both at the federal level for direct purchasers, and at the state level for indirect purchasers.

14.4 Opt-out actions
Finally, defendants will also have to defend actions brought by individual victims of the conspiracy who decided to opt out of the class action.

14.5 The Antitrust Criminal Penalty Enhancement and Reform Act of 2004
The Bush administration recognised that the strength of private enforcement may create a disincentive for companies to apply for amnesty. On 22 June 2004 President Bush signed into law the National Cooperative Standard Development Act. Title II of the Act, the Antitrust Criminal Penalty Enhancement and Reform Act of 2004 (ACPERA) strengthens the amnesty programme by 'de-trebling' damages that the amnesty holders must pay in civil litigation. This de-trebling is meant to increase a corporation's incentives to enter into the amnesty programme. The 2004 Act reduces the amnesty holder's civil antitrust liability from treble to single, in both federal and state litigation, if the applicant also provides 'satisfactory co-operation' to the civil plaintiffs.

The 2004 Act provides the following list of what will constitute 'satisfactory co-operation' in civil cases:
(i) providing a full account to the claimant of all facts known to the applicant or co-operating individuals that are relevant to the civil action;
(ii) furnishing all documents or other items potentially relevant to the civil action that are in the possession, custody, or control of the applicant or the co-operating individual wherever they are located; and
(iii) in the case of a co-operating individual:
- making themselves available for such interviews, depositions, or testimony in connection with the civil action as the claimant may reasonably require; and
- responding completely and truthfully, without making any attempt either falsely to protect or falsely to implicate any person or entity, and without intentionally withholding any potentially relevant information, to all questions asked by the claimant in interviews, depositions, trials, or any other court proceedings in connection with the civil action; or
(iv) in the case of an antitrust leniency applicant, using its best efforts

to secure and facilitate from co-operating individuals covered by the agreement the co-operation described above.

Because it will be up to the courts to decide whether the amnesty holder has provided satisfactory co-operation, it is unclear whether this amendment will affect litigation strategies. Practically, such determination is made at the end of a trial, after the defendants have had to incur a significant burden and costs. While the 2004 Act does not relieve defendants of this burden, it may facilitate and accelerate settlement negotiations in civil litigations, and may lower the cost of these settlements. Indeed, and even before the 2004 Act, parties to price-fixing settlements typically negotiate and settle on the basis of single, and not treble, damages estimations.

PROTECTION AGAINST DISCLOSURE/CONFIDENTIALITY
15. Is confidentiality afforded to the leniency applicant and other co-operating parties? If so, to what extent?

The Division treats as confidential both the identity of the amnesty applicant and any information obtained from that applicant. The Division will not disclose an amnesty applicant's identity, without prior disclosure by or agreement with the applicant, unless authorised by court order. This gives the amnesty applicant some time to prepare its restitution strategy, and to try to limit the scope of the private lawsuits by individually negotiating with the victims of the illegal activity.

15.1 Is the identity of the leniency applicant/other co-operating parties disclosed during the investigation or in the final decision?

As discussed above, the Division does not disclose the identity of leniency applicants during the investigation or in the final decision. The identities of co-operating parties generally become public through public indictments and the resulting guilty pleas.

15.2 Is information provided by the leniency applicant/other co-operating parties passed on to other undertakings under investigation?

The Division generally does not pass on information provided by the leniency applicant or other co-operating parties to other undertakings under investigation. However, in the event that the other undertakings do not plead guilty, and instead elect to go to trial, certain evidence provided by the applicant/other co-operating parties may be passed on as part of pre-trial discovery.

15.3 Can a leniency applicant/other co-operating party request anonymity or confidentiality of information provided?

A leniency applicant can request that the information it provides be kept confidential under the FOIA. However, this will not protect the confidentiality of the information in all circumstances, including the pre-trial scenario described above.

16. Is the evidence submitted by the leniency applicant protected from transmission to other competition authorities with whom the authority in question co-operates? If so, how?

The Division will not disclose the amnesty applicant's identity or information obtained from an amnesty applicant to foreign authorities without prior agreement with that applicant. This is an important inducement for amnesty applicants because foreign enforcement authorities are increasingly scrutinising international cartels. This also gives the amnesty applicant some additional time to consider whether it wishes to apply for leniency in other jurisdictions.

Notwithstanding this policy, the Division has frequently obtained waivers on sharing information with a jurisdiction from which the applicant has also sought and obtained leniency.

17. To what extend can evidence submitted by the leniency applicant (transcript of oral statements or written evidence) become discoverable in subsequent private enforcement claims?

The ACPERA permits a leniency applicant to avoid the treble damages typically available to successful civil antitrust plaintiffs by providing 'sufficient co-operation' to the plaintiffs. Accordingly, in order to avoid treble damages, the leniency applicant will typically identify itself as such to the civil litigants. Civil litigants will then typically make discovery requests asking for the materials provided to the Division as part of a leniency application. If an amnesty applicant refuses, a domestic court may order production of the leniency application materials. In addition, civil litigants may request and be granted discovery of any materials produced as part of a leniency application even where the defendant does not seek the protection of the ACPERA.

17.1 Can leniency information be subjected to discovery orders in the domestic courts?

As discussed above, leniency information can be subjected to discovery orders in domestic courts.

17.2 Can leniency information be subjected to discovery orders in foreign courts?

Pursuant to 28 USC §1782(a), a federal district court 'may order' a person residing or found in the district to give testimony or produce documents 'for use in a proceeding in a foreign or international tribunal... upon the application of any interested person.' In deciding whether to order discovery a district court considers, among other factors, whether 'the person from whom discovery is sought is a participant in the foreign proceeding... the nature of the foreign tribunal, the character of the proceedings underway abroad, and the receptivity of the foreign government or the court or agency abroad to US federal-court judicial assistance.' In addition, courts consider 'whether the section 1782(a) request conceals an attempt to circumvent foreign proof-gathering restrictions or other policies of a foreign country or the United States... [and whether the request is] unduly intrusive or burdensome.' *Intel Corp. v Advanced Micro Devices, Inc.*, 542 US 241 (2004).

17.3 Can leniency information submitted in a foreign jurisdiction be subjected to discovery orders in the domestic courts?
Leniency information submitted in a foreign jurisdiction can be, but is not always, subject to discovery orders in the domestic courts. For example, in *In re Vitamins Antitrust Litigation*, the court balanced the international comity factors and concluded that the defendants were required to produce documents submitted to a number of foreign antitrust authorities. Misc. No. 99-197 (TFH), MDL No. 1285, 2002 U.S. Dist LEXIS 26490 (D.D.C. Jan. 23, 2002) and 25815 (Dec. 18, 2002). In doing so, the court rejected *amicus* briefs from the European Commission and the Canadian government arguing that production of the documents would undermine the EU and Canadian leniency regimes. *Emerson Electric Co v Le Carbone Lorraine*, S.A. No. 05-6042, 2008 WL 4126602 (D.N.J. Aug. 27, 2008); see also *In re Vitamins Antitrust Litigation*. In contrast, in *In re Methionine Antitrust Litigation*, the court, again looking to considerations of international comity, and giving significant weight to *amicus* briefs from a number of foreign enforcement agencies, denied the plaintiffs' motion to compel documents previously produced to the foreign enforcement agencies. MDL No. 00-1311 CRB (N.D. Cal. June 17, 2002); see also *In re Rubber Chemicals Antitrust Litigation*, 486 F. Supp. 2d 1078 (N.D. Cal. 2007);

18. Are there any precedents in which evidence from a leniency application has been discovered in a private enforcement claim?
Civil litigants have requested and been granted discovery of evidence from leniency applications. For example, in *Emerson Electric Co v Le Carbone Lorraine, S.A.*, plaintiffs brought suit on the basis of defendants' alleged participation in the electrical carbon products cartel. No. 05-6042, 2008 WL 4126602 (D.N.J. Aug. 27, 2008). Plaintiffs requested and were granted discovery of documents produced in connection with the defendants' US Department of Justice leniency application in the separate, but allegedly related, Isostatic Graphite investigation.

RELATIONSHIP WITH THE EUROPEAN COMMISSION'S LENIENCY NOTICE AND LENIENCY POLICY IN OTHER EU MEMBER STATES
19. Does the policy address the interaction with applications under the Commission Leniency Notice? If so, how?
Not applicable.

20. Does the policy address the interaction with applications for leniency in other EU member states? If so, how? Does the authority accept summary applications in line with the ECN Model Leniency Programme?
Not applicable.

RELATIONSHIP WITH SETTLEMENT PROCEDURES
21. What is the relationship between leniency and applicable settlement procedures? Are they mutually exclusive?
As discussed above, corporations and individuals that offer to co-operate, but come forward after the first leniency applicant, may enter into individually negotiated plea agreements with the Division, but this process falls outside of the amnesty programme. It is important to note, however, that plea agreements must be submitted to a federal district court and, under the most common form of plea agreement, a court maintains discretion to alter the terms of the sentence agreed to by the party and the Division.

REFORM/LATEST DEVELOPMENTS
22. Is there a reform underway to revisit the leniency policy? What are the latest developments?
There is no reform of the Amnesty Programme underway. The ACPERA, however, has further strengthened the amnesty programme by raising the maximum sanctions for antitrust offences. The ACPERA increased the maximum jail term under 15 USC §1 from three to 10 years, the maximum individual fine from $350,000 to $1 million, and the maximum corporate fine from $10 million to $100 million. This brings the penalties for antitrust offences more in line with those for other white collar offences.

Contact details

GENERAL EDITORS
Jacques Buhart,
Herbert Smith
66, avenue Marceau
75008 Paris
France
T: +33 1 53 57 70 70
F: +33 1 53 57 70 80
Brussels T: +33 251174 50
E: jacques.buhart@herbertsmith.com
www.herbertsmith.com

Kevin J. Arquit
Simpson Thacher & Bartlett LLP
425 Lexington Avenue
New York, NY 10017-3954
T: +1 212 455-7680
F: +1 212 455-2502
E: karquit@stblaw.com

AUSTRALIA
David Poddar, Lisa Huett,
Morag Bond
Mallesons Stephen Jaques
Level 50, Bourke Place, 600 Bourke
Street, Melbourne VIC 3000
T: +61 3 9643 4163
F: +61 3 9643 5999
www.mallesons.com

AUSTRIA
Franz Urlesberger, Stefanie Stegbauer
Schönherr Rechtsanwälte GmbH
Tuchlauben 17
A-1010 Vienna
T: +43 1 534 37 196
F: +43 1 534 37 6196
E: f.urlesberger@schoenherr.at
    s.stegbauer@schoenherr.at
www.schoenherr.eu

BELGIUM
Thomas De Meese
Crowell & Moring
Rue Royale 71
Brussels 1000
T: +32 2 2824082
F: +32 2 2306399
E: tdemeese@crowell.com
www.crowell.com

BRAZIL
Leonor Cordovil
Grinberg Cordovil e Barros Advogados
Alameda Jau, 1742, 6 floor
Jardins
São Paulo 01.420.002
T: +55 11 3371 5050
F: +55 11 3371 5059
E: lac@gcba.com.br
www.gcba.com.br

BULGARIA
Peter Petrov
Borislav Boyanov & Co
82, Patriarch Evtimii Blvd.
Sofia 1463
T: +359 2 8055 055
F: +359 2 8055 000
E: p.petrov@boyanov.com
www.boyanov.com

CANADA
Graham Reynolds QC, Janet Bolton
Osler Hoskin & Harcourt LLP
Box 50, 1 First Canadian Place
Toronto M5X 1B8
Ontario
T: +416 862 4868
F: +416 862 6666
E: greynolds@osler.com
www.osler.com

Contact details

CYPRUS
Eleana Spyris
Andreas Neocleous & Co LLC
Neocleous House
195 Makarios Avenue
P O Box 50613
Limassol CY 3608
T: +357 25 110000
F: +357 25 110001
E: info@neocleous.com
www.neocleous.com

DENMARK
Jens Munk Plum, Erik Bertelsen,
Morten Kofmann
Kromann Reumert
Sundkrogsgade 5
2100 København Ø
Rådhuspladsen 3
8000 Århus C
T: +45 70 12 12 11
F: +45 70 12 13 11/+45 70 12 14 11
E: JMP@Kromannreumert.com,
    MKO@Kromannreumert.com,
    ERB@Kromannreumert.com
www.Kromannreumert.com

ESTONIA
Tanel Kalaus, Heleri Tammiste
Raidla Lejins & Norcous
Roosikrantsi 2
Tallinn 10119
T: +372 640 7170
F: +372 640 7171
E: tanel.kalaus@rln.ee
    heleri.tammiste@rln.ee
www.rln.ee

EUROPEAN UNION
Adrian Brown, Hanna Anttilainen
Herbert Smith LLP
Central Plaza
25 rue de Loxum
Brussels BE-1000
T: +32 2 511 7450
F: +32 2 511 7772
E: adrian.brown@herbertsmith.com

hanna.anttilainen@herbertsmith.com
www.herbertsmith.com

FINLAND
Johan Åkermarck, Hanna Laurila
Dittmar & Indrenius
Pohjoisesplanadi 25 A
Helsinki 00100
T: +358 9 681 700
F: +358 9 652 406
E: johan.akermarck@dittmar.fi;
    hanna.laurila@dittmar.fi
www.dittmar.fi

FRANCE
Sergio Sorinas, Estelle Jégou
Herbert Smith LLP
66, avenue Marceau
Paris 75008
T: +33 1 53 57 70 70
F: +33 1 53 57 70 80
E: sergio.sorinas@herbertsmith.com;
    estelle.jegou@herbertsmith.com
www.herbertsmith.com

GERMANY
Dr Matthias Karl, Dr Martin Beutelmann
Gleiss Lutz
Maybachstrasse 6
Stuttgart 70469
T: +49 711 8997 112
F: +49 711 855 096
E: matthias.karl@gleisslutz.com;
    martin.beutelmann@gleisslutz.com
www.gleisslutz.com

HUNGARY
Dr Chrysta Bán
Bán S. Szabó & Partners in
cooperation with Gleiss Lutz
József Nádor Tér 5-6.
Budapest H-1051
T: +36-1 266 3522
F: +36-1 266 3523, 266 1010
E: cban@bansszabo.hu
www.bansszabo.hu

Contact details

INDIA
Farhad Sorabjee, Reeti Choudhary
J. Sagar Associates
Vakils House, 18 Sprott Road,
Ballard Estate
Mumbai 400 001
Maharashtra
T: +91 22 4341 8600
F: +91 22 4341 8617
E: farhad@jsalaw.com;
 reeti@jsalaw.com
www.jsalaw.com

ITALY
Massimo Merola
Bonelli Erede Pappalardo
Square de Meeûs, 40
1000 Brussels
T: +32 2 552 0070
F: +32 2 552 0071
E: massimo.merola@beplex.com

Luciano di Via
Bonelli Erede Pappalardo
Via Salaria, 25
00199 Rome
T: +39 06 84 55 11
F: +39 06 84 55 12 01
E: luciano.divia@beplex.com
www.beplex.com/

JAPAN
Hideto Ishida, Shigeyoshi Ezaki,
Yusuke Nakano, Koya Uemura
Anderson Mori & Tomotsune
Izumi Garden Tower, 6-1,
Roppongi 1-chome
Minato-ku
Tokyo 106-6036
T: +81 3 6888 1141
F: +81 3 6888 3141
E: hideto.ishida@amt-law.com
 shigeyoshi.ezaki@amt-law.com
 yusuke.nakano@amt-law.com
 koya.uemura@amt-law.com
www.amt-law.com/

LUXEMBOURG
Léon Gloden, Stéphanie Damien
Elvinger Hoss & Prussen
2, Place Winston Churchill,
L-1340 Luxembourg
T: +352 44 66 44 0
F: +352 44 22 55
E: leongloden@ehp.lu
 stephaniedamien@ehp.lu
www.ehp.lu

MEXICO
Ricardo Ríos Ferrer, Alejandro
González Muñoz
Ríos-Ferrer, Guillén-Llarena, Treviño Y
Rivera, SC
Avenida Insurgentes Sur 1605, pisos 11 y 12
Colonia San José Insurgentes
Delegación Benito Juárez
Mexico City 03900
T: +52 55 5980 0350
F: +52 55 5980 0385
E: rrios@riosferrer.com.mx
www.riosferrer.com.mx

THE NETHERLANDS
Maurice Essers, Gert Wim van de Meent,
Robin A. Struijlaart, Marc Wiggers
Loyens & Loeff N.V.
Fred. Roeskestraat 100
Amsterdam 1076 ED
T: +31 20 5785136/31 20 5785538
F: +31 20 5785862
E: maurice.essers@loyensloeff.com
 gw.vdmeent@loyensloeff.com
 robin.struijlaart@loyensloeff.com
 marc.wiggers@loyensloeff.com
www.loyensloeff.com

SOUTH KOREA
Kyung Taek Jung, Han Woo Park,
Michael H. Yu
Kim & Chang
Seyang Building,
223 Naeja-dong, Jongno-gu,
Seoul 110-720,
T: +822 3703 exts:1101, 1045, 1338

Contact details

F: +822 737 9091 3
E: ktjung@kimchang.com
hwpark@kimchang.com
mhyu@kimchang.com
www.kimchang.com

SPAIN
Pedro Suárez
Herbert Smith LLP
Paseo de la Castellana, 66, 4º
Madrid 28046
T: +34 91 423 4032
F: +34 91 423 4132
E: pedro.suarez@herbertsmith.com
www.herbertsmith.com

SWEDEN
Tommy Pettersson, Dr Johan Carle, Elin Gilmark
Mannheimer Swartling Advokatbyrå
Norrlandsgatan 21
Stockholm 111 87
T: +46 8 595 061 03
F: +46 8 595 060 01
E: tpe@msa.se
jca@msa.se
egk@msa.se
www.mannheimerswartling.se

SWITZERLAND
Dr Franz Hoffet, Dr Marcel Dietrich, Dr Gerald Brei
Homburger
Weinbergstrasse 56-58
PO Box 194
CH-8042 Zurich
T: +41 43 222 10 00
F: +41 43 222 15 00
E: franz.hoffet@homburger.ch
marcel.dietrich@homburger.ch
gerald.brei@homburger.ch
www.homburger.ch

TURKEY
Kayra Üçer, Derya Genç
Hergüner Bilgen Özeke Attorney Partnership
Süleyman Seba Caddesi, Sıraevler 55
Akaretler, Beşiktaş
İstanbul 34357
T: +90 212 310 1800
F: +90 212 310 1899
E: info@herguner.av.tr
www.herguner.av.tr

UK
Stephen Wisking, Kim Dietzel
Herbert Smith LLP
Exchange House
Primrose Street
London EC2A 2HS
T: +44 20 7466 2387
   +44 20 7466 2825
F: +44 20 7098 5387
   +44 20 7098 4825
E: stephen.wisking@herbertsmith.com
   kim.dietzel@herbertsmith.com
www.herbertsmith.com

USA
Kevin J. Arquit
Simpson Thacher & Bartlett LLP
425 Lexington Avenue
New York, NY 10017-3954
T: +1 212 455 7680
F: +1 212 455 2502
E: karquit@stblaw.com

Andrew M. Lacy
Simpson Thacher & Bartlett LLP
1155 F Street, N.W.
Washington, DC 20004
T: +1 202 636 5505
F: +1 202 636 5502
E: alacy@stblaw.com
www.simpsonthacher.com